THE
MAKING OF
ENGLAND

THE MAKING OF ENGLAND

FROM ROME TO REFORMATION

TOBY PURSER

AMBERLEY

To my sons, Elgan, Ralph and Laurie.

First published 2022

Amberley Publishing
The Hill, Stroud
Gloucestershire, GL5 4EP

www.amberley-books.com

British Library Cataloguing in Publication Data.
A catalogue record for this book is available from the British Library.

ISBN 978 1 3981 0506 5 (hardback)
ISBN 978 1 3981 0507 2 (ebook)

1 2 3 4 5 6 7 8 9 10

Typesetting by SJmagic DESIGN SERVICES, India.
Printed in the UK.

'And the Past, Kay,' he added, 'is a big book with many, many pages...'

John Masefield, *The Box of Delights* (1935)

We should have more bright breasts in the Army if each man was able without witnesses, to write his own despatch.

T. E. Lawrence, *Seven Pillars of Wisdom* (1940)

So. The Spear-Danes in days gone by
And the kings who ruled them had courage and greatness.
We have heard of those princes' heroic campaigns.

Beowulf (c.750), lines 1-3 (trans. Seamus Heaney, 2000)

Contents

Part Three: Conquered England, 1066–1300

Part Four: Imperial England, *c.* 1300–*c.* 1550

Preface

In the summer of 1939, local archaeologist Basil Browne continued excavating the man-made mounds on the grounds of Mrs Pretty's private estate at Sutton Hoo, Suffolk. He had already identified the robbed remains of an Early English ship burial the previous summer and now he dug the largest mound. Basil Browne identified the full shape of a new ship and an untouched burial chamber. This was excavated, with Cambridge archaeologist Charles Phillips taking charge under the authority of the Ministry of Works, and Basil Browne as his assistant. Silver dishes, spoons, gold buckles and ornaments, some decorated with garnets and glass, a gold purse-lid and shoulder-clasps, fragments of weapons and armour and a purse of gold coins were amongst the finds, dated to around 625 AD. The treasure was stored under Mrs Pretty's bed. At the Inquest in August, it was found that the grave goods were the property of Mrs Pretty, who gave them to the nation. War was looming, and the treasures were hidden in the London Underground.

The body of the person buried in the ship at Sutton Hoo was never recovered, but it is thought to be that of an Early English prince or king of the East Angles, possibly Rædwald. Whoever was buried in the ship probably belonged to the new elite of Germanic and Danish migrants who had arrived in the 5th and 6th centuries and established mastery over the native British following the collapse of the Roman administration. The grave goods at Sutton Hoo included artefacts from Sweden, France, Germany, Syria and Istanbul. They displayed both British and Early English craftsmanship and both pagan and Christian associations.

The dig at Sutton Hoo that summer of 1939 was a transcendent moment. It was typically English in that it was led by a self-taught local Suffolk man at the behest of a wealthy private landowner. Basil Browne opened up not only a tomb but overturned all the assumptions of the so-called 'Dark Ages', revealing a complex and cosmopolitan world of princes and warriors, a world of seafarers, migrants and settlers with wide horizons, a deep longing for their past and a strong sense of ownership over their new lands. It is still the greatest find in all English history.

It is the beginning of the making of England.

Medieval fantasists: yew trees at St Edward's Church door, Stow-on-the Wold, Gloucestershire; Tolkien's Doors of Durin? (Author's collection)

In Search of Medieval England

In Quentin Tarantino's cult movie *Pulp Fiction*, the character Marsellus Wallace vows revenge by pledging that his men will 'git Medieval on your ass'. There is no need to explain to his victim why 'medieval' is bad news, or indeed to the audience: we just know it's bad, because it's medieval and 'medieval' means barbaric, cruel, ignorant, and simplistic. It's *Game of Thrones* – it's heads on spikes, castles and kings, Horrible Histories, dungeons and dragons, plague, poverty, peasants, and monks, Monty Python and Blackadder.

In popular medievalism, there are two versions of the Middle Ages, the grotesque and also the romantic, chivalric deeds and courtly love.[1] The medieval past is seen as a period of ignorance (or innocence); it is the 'Dark Ages' awaiting the Renaissance, the Reformation, the Enlightenment, and progressive reforms of the nineteenth century. Popular belief in progress sprung from the humanists' need to distance themselves from the Middle Ages. Only in English of all European languages is there a phrase for 'the Dark Ages'.[2] This is a modern conceit that assumes that the pagan post-Roman world was a barbaric age, whereas in fact the level of destruction caused by Christians on the pagan world – such as burning books and smashing statues and artworks in late antiquity – was extensive.[3] Time was divided into Classical-Medieval-Modern from Petrarch in the fourteenth century onwards and Humanists were obsessed by periodization, 'light' and 'dark'. The Reformation attacked medieval superstition, Protestants were keen to highlight the 'magic' of Catholicism against the supposed rationalism of the new, Anglican Church. The Humanist programme was deliberately elitist and backward-looking; it was not about bringing literacy to the masses, since the Classical languages of Latin and Greek prevailed in the schooling of the upper classes from *c.* 1450 to the 1960s.[4]

By the time of the eighteenth century, it had become the 'Dark Ages' in Gibbon's *Decline and Fall*, which refers to 'the darkest ages of the Latin world' after the sack of Rome in 410. Late nineteenth-century historians used medieval history to explain the ultimate success of English unity and democracy, which influenced twentieth-century historians, even though there was a vibrant critique of the English narrative.[5] There is a long tradition in scholarly and popular literature of representing the Germanic peoples of early medieval Europe as gathered in clan-like tribes constantly nursing their wounds and their anger, until the French arrived with a superior system of law. This habit was rooted in nineteenth-century nationalistic scholarship which constructed the Saxon (simple, virile, egalitarian)/Norman (luxurious, privileged, cultured) divide.[6] Walter Scott's *Ivanhoe* (1820) and Charles Kingsley's *Hereward the Wake* (1866) influenced the serious histories in ways that would now be seen as racist. Late nineteenth-century popular histories of England emphasised the lack of British in favour of Germanic blood. Here is E. A. Freeman, Professor of History at Oxford University extolling the virtues of breeding: '...the Norman was a Dane who, in his sojourn in Gaul, had put on a slight French varnish, and who came to England to be washed clean again.'[7] Meanwhile, German philologist Leopold Von Ranke pioneered the objective approach to historical writing – to show 'how it essentially was' in his own words, not to judge the past by the present – and to examine critically the primary sources.[8] This ran counter to the Victorian historians who were quick to judge and condemn moral failings of medieval societies and individuals.

For much of the twentieth century, historical pageants were one of the most widespread and popular forms of public engagement with the past.[9] The Victorian cult of the 'Anglo-Saxons' culminated in the millennium celebrations of King Alfred in 1901 (although he died in 899). To the Victorians, the Anglo-Saxons were the founders of English law and government and the main source of English Christianity. The pre-First World War pageants paid considerable attention to the Danish aggression and Alfred's defence, particularly the navy (reflecting the escalating Edwardian arms race with Imperial Germany); they saw the Norman Conquest as a time of authoritarian government, violent and brutal – especially the pageants in northern England – something reflected in the school textbooks of the time.[10] King John was singled out as a tyrant, a threat to national unity; Magna Carta was used to represent the origins of parliament, the 'constitutional Middle Ages' assuming the authority of the English Church. Notable historians were involved with writing and performing pageants, including Charles Oman, G. M. Trevelyan, and writers Arthur Bryant and Lawrence du Garde Peach (author of several *Ladybird* books on English history).[11]

'The clever men at Oxford, know all that there is to be knowed,' sang Mr Toad, and what Norman Cantor called the 'Oxford fantasists' – including C. S. Lewis, J. R. R. Tolkien and F. M. Powicke – created a new branch of medievalism.[12] Fantasy fiction has its modern roots in Tolkien's *Lord of the Rings* and is used for escapist purposes from daily drudgery and the rational, appealing to an adult audience.[13] While there were no trolls or hobbits in Medieval England there were certainly shires, heroes and orcs aplenty in life and art – 'orcnéas' in *Beowulf*, a real-life Frodo in Domesday Book and a Middle Earth, or *Middangeard*.[14] The original 'Oxford fantasist', Geoffrey of Monmouth, writing in Osney Mead in the 1130s, gave us the updated and extended King Arthur, who never existed (at least not in the form he takes in the national myth) but the point is that generations believed he did and if it ought to be true, then it is true: King John owned a sword called 'Tristan', Edward III founded the Round Table and Henry VII named his first-born son and heir Arthur (who died a teenager) so there very nearly was a 'King Arthur'. Perhaps the greatest Oxford fantasist of all, medievalist, archaeologist and leader of the Arab Revolt, T. E. Lawrence (Lawrence of Arabia), took with him a copy of *Morte d'Arthur* to read during the desert war in 1917.[15]

Much though the famous *1066 And All That* (by Oxford graduates W. C. Sellar and R. J. Yeatman) parodied Edwardian and 1920s school history with its 'memorable' kings and 'Good Things', it was itself a product of the Oxford historians who praised personalities and progress above all else, combined with the influence of new tutoring that critiqued Whig history still written in romantic and literary style.[16]

A new generation of constitutional historians could not quite leave Victoriana behind. Two World Wars had sharpened the pens, if not the judgement, of some historians of the Norman Conquest. 1066 serves as a dividing line between the 'Anglo-Saxon' (with an emphasis perhaps on the old, in Old English) and the 'Medieval'; the Normans are up-to-date and above all else, efficient. With only the second successful invasion to cross the Channel in 900 years, nationalist sentiments were very much to the forefront but no longer the pan-Germanic 'good old cause' Freeman had written about. Professor Frank Stenton's magisterial *Anglo-Saxon England*, first published in 1943 (auspiciously) and reissued in 2001 (remarkably), created the narrative of a 'constitutional monarchy' complete with the anachronistic 'royal council'.[17] The danger that 1066 becomes a demarcation line rather than a subject of historical enquiry was also apparent. Professor D. C. Douglas's 1964 biography *William the Conqueror* (reprinted 1990) remained the standard text for generations, but buried deep (p.184) in an otherwise immensely scholarly volume is the claim that Harold's defeat at Hastings was 'to the *ultimate benefit* of England' (it was literally, a Good Thing).[18] Professor R. A. Brown was more openly partisan in 1969 (reprinted in 2000): 'Old English intellectual activity was essentially old-fashioned... Old English architecture was obsolete in style and inferior in concept...' He declared his side to be 'with duke William at Hastings'.[19] These views held sway for generations and only relatively recently have they been revised by Professor David Bates's masterly 2016 biography, which sets William the Conqueror firmly in his own time.[20]

If 1066 remained an unchallenged border for decades after it ought to have done, the framework within which Magna Carta is studied remains unchanged and unchallenged; it is one of the few grand narratives that survive substantially in place today, Professor Peter Coss argues.[21] Leading Magna Carta scholar Professor Nicholas Vincent doesn't mince his words:

> The myth of Magna Carta lies at the whole origin of our perception of who we are as an English-speaking people: freedom-loving people who've lived with a degree of liberty and under a rule of law for 800 years. It's a load of tripe, of course. But it's a very useful myth.[22]

Magna Carta gave rise to a new mythology in English history, but it is simplistic to view the Charter as freedom's 'foundation stone' or the 'first step' on the road to constitutional democracy; this assumes that the way we do things is best and that other systems have failed to arrive at the perfection of western democracy. It also distorts our understanding of the past. Britain obtained neither internal peace nor constitutional stability because of Magna Carta.[23] Magna Carta is strongly connected with a variety of national myths, including the relative stability of British political life, seen as a prime factor in promoting an unusual degree of liberty and security; English exceptionalism, a belief that institutions that evolved in England are of higher quality than elsewhere, echoed in two recent scholarly works that both follow the grand narrative of bringing the king within the law, liberties proclaimed and representation established.[24]

Modern historical writing reinforces the stereotypes: medieval women are invariably 'mothers,' giving birth to the nation or 'she-wolves,' 'jezebels'; the men are 'warriors,' or 'kingmakers' engaged in a 'struggle for mastery/supremacy' in 'turbulent' times, fighting over a 'bloody crown', language which reduces national history to the battlefield or the bedroom. A recent scholarly biography of Edward the Confessor is subtitled *The Last of the Royal Blood* (he was not) and is populated with 'ravening' or 'feeding' wolves where the Godwinsson 'cubs' fight for 'every scrap of meat'.[25] The development of Early English history is often portrayed in real time, like a journey, with 'dawns' and 'births' and 'roads' where medieval England is a precursor to an enlightened, modern society in an inevitable progression towards the sunlit uplands of a united nation-state.

The implication is that medieval England and its history is infantile by contrast to the 'adult' modern age, an approach that echoes Victorian teaching of medieval history which was used for the pedagogical, moral instruction of children in their reading books since the late nineteenth century. Textbooks for older children started with Elizabethan England since that was seen as intellectually more demanding; the early medieval English settlement provided plenty of lessons in seafaring, colonisation, settlement and fair rule, love of liberty and conversion to Christianity in a sort of 'enlightened patriotism'.[26] There was an explosion of interest in *Beowulf* at the end of the nineteenth century and the heroic and nationalistic ideology of the editions produced for children, with specific typefaces, bindings and book design – a bibliographic code matched a linguistic code of archaic language, all geared to teach Early English history in a very particular manner.[27] The hero Beowulf was placed alongside King Arthur and Robin Hood, whose legends played an important role in the construction of British national identity, promoting racial theories of 'Anglo-Saxon' superiority over foreign peoples with an emphasis on violence and gore that suited the late Victorian popular culture of duty, loyalty, sacrifice and honour.[28] In 1911, the first *Handbook for Boys* was published by the Boy Scouts of America, which included a chapter on the 'history of chivalry'; by 1914 the print run had climbed from 300,000 copies to three million and combined a US twist on the Victorian version of the Middle Ages.[29] The illustrations of these books, with horned and winged helmets (a nineteenth-century invention) created continuity between historical objects (swords, harps) and fictional elements, giving the impression that *Beowulf* was historical record rather than a myth, something explicitly set out by H. E. Marshall.[30]

Marshall's *Our Island Story* (1905, reprinted 2005) was used as a textbook in schools between the wars and essentially repackaged the Whig progressive narrative into a 'story' for a school-age audience.[31] The Britons are patiently described as rather gullible, lacking intellect and leadership and failing to learn their Latin from the Romans (not unlike errant schoolchildren). King Arthur is written in as factual history and crucially for the racial construct, the Saxons killed 'nearly all the Britons' except those who fled to Wales and Cornwall.[32] The famous story of the English slaves seen by Pope Gregory the Great ('Non Angli, sed angeli') with their 'fair complexions, handsome faces and lovely hair' described so eloquently by Bede is elaborated further into 'pretty children' with 'rosy cheeks', eyes 'merry and blue' and hair shining 'like gold' by Marshall, in language which reflects the early twentieth-century belief in racial supremacy over the dehumanised natives.[33] In 1905 the supremacy of white heredity was at its height with all its assertions of fixed, biological differences.[34]

It is important to note that in *Our Island Story* kings are condemned, the rule of law and overthrowing tyranny are all included in what is a deceptively progressive narrative; it was not called 'Our island *History*' but it has been taken to mean this. In 2010, *Our Island Story* was chosen by then Conservative Prime Minister David Cameron as his favourite childhood book and again referenced during his appearance on *Desert Island Discs*.[35]

Writers of history have long categorised and labelled the past for their own convenience. When William Caxton printed his *Book of the Order of Chivalry* in 1484, he laid out the essence of twentieth- and even twenty-first-century history curricula when he listed Richard the Lionheart, Edward I, Edward III, Henry V and the Arthurian heroes Galahad, Tristan and Lancelot. Before that, Henry of Huntingdon's influential *Historia Anglorum* (1140s) divided English history into five periods that wouldn't make an Ofsted inspector blush: the Romans (55BC), Picts and Scots, the Anglo-Saxons (fifth century), the Danes (ninth century) and the Normans (1066), almost exactly match the English primary curriculum.[36]

In the sixteenth century, classification by reign was common but not by *dynasty*. The knowledge of the reordering of religion was probably the most widespread indicator of change; there was no single perception of the medieval past in early modern England.[37] Periodisation by dynasty, the 'Tudors,' and 'Plantagenets' is a construct cemented into school curricula, textbooks and reference books, but it was not used by contemporaries. Henry VII referred to himself as Richmond, since Tydder was used by Richard III as a term of contempt for his lowly origins. If the term was not contemporary, it provides a false reality, so that a 'Tudor dynasty' ruled over a 'Tudor people' becomes misleading.[38] It also perpetuates the 'kings and queens' narrative of history. This means that when Henry 'Tudor' won the Battle of Bosworth he not only ended Richard's reign but he single-handedly ended the Middle Ages, an absurdity that conjures up images of everyone waking up on 23 August (the day after Bosworth) in a wholly different world. In reality, Henry VII and Henry VIII were 'medieval' kings and it was not until the Reformation and the destruction of the monasteries that the 'Middle Ages' ended, violently and abruptly.

The Wars of the Roses rather quaintly describes an internecine conflict within the ruling dynasty and is still in common usage by historians. We have Shakespeare's (entirely invented) scene in the Temple Garden where the nobles pick red or white roses (*Henry VI*, Part 1, II, iv), and Walter Scott's nineteenth-century usage to thank for this.[39] (The Yorkist house did use the white rose but there is no definite evidence that the Lancastrian house displayed the red rose, though it had been an emblem of the house of Lancaster in the later fourteenth century; and the red and white rose emblem was an invented tradition after 1485.)[40] The term 'Hundred Years' War' is another misnomer since it was neither a hundred years long (nearer 150) nor a discrete war since there were long periods of truce; the 'French Wars' would be a better phrase. Both invented phrases give the impression of endless conflict (and so perpetuate the primitivism of medieval England) when in fact only a minuscule proportion of the population were on the campaign at Agincourt. The 'Wars of the Roses' involved 18 months of actual campaigning over a 30-year period, again involving tiny proportions of the population. Even the Norman Conquest, which was undeniably a brutal invasion with permanent change for England (and obviously never called such by contemporaries), was arguably an act of atonement whereby the Duke of Normandy had to rule England because of the sins of the people.[41] The expansion of early medieval kings across England in the tenth century is better described as 'dominion' rather than 'conquest'.[42] There are no medieval words for 'patriotism' or 'nationalism' since the words *patrio* and *nation* – from the Latin *natus*, 'that which has been born' – mean something more personalised, so again, these are meanings projected onto the past.[43]

The term 'Dark Ages' has been eroded from popular and historical writing, but the anachronistic phrase 'Anglo-Saxons' is very much alive, apparently since it has been in use for so long it should continue.[44] There was no such thing as *the* Anglo-Saxons any more than the 'Tudors' or the 'Plantagenets', so the phrase needs reconsidering. There were Angles, Saxons, Jutes, Frisians but rarely a contemporary use of 'Anglo-Saxons'. Contemporaries instead used *angli, anglorum, saxonum, angelcynn, Engla lond* and *Englisc*. Continental contemporary use of the term 'Anglo-Saxon' was more common, such as in Paul the Deacon's *History of the Lombards* (before 796) where he talks of the 'AngliSaxones' with regard to their clothing, but rarer in the insular Anglo-Latin sources, with only a few dozen examples and almost all were charters using the term in royal titles specific to the union of Saxon Wessex and Anglian Mercia, almost half of those referring to Alfred or his son Edward.[45]

The earliest insular use of 'Anglo-Saxon' were the charters of King Alfred, which refer to him as *Anglorum Saxonnum rex*, though he is also referred to as *rex Anglorum et Saxonum*, and variously as king of the English, king of Wessex and king of the Saxons.[46] This usage of 'Anglo-Saxon' did not refer at all to 'England' and under Alfred's grandson Æthelstan the balance shifted from Wessex (*Saxonnum*) to Mercia (*Anglorum*) along with grandiose claims and titles to the 'whole of Britain'.[47] The use of 'Anglo-Saxon' was even rarer in Old English insular sources and absent until the mid-tenth century. More common up until this point was the usage of Saxon (*seax*) commonly in compounds of West/ East/South Saxon; there is no documented use of the term *Angli* in Britain before the eighth century.[48] Before 1066, therefore, the English people did not refer to themselves as Anglo-Saxons but most commonly as *Englisc* or the *Angelcynn*. After 1066, it almost vanishes entirely in Middle English apart from sporadic Anglo-Latin references.

It was not until 1589 that George Puttenham referred to 'Anglo-Saxon' in the first English-language use of the phrase and by the mid-seventeenth century, 'Anglo-Saxon' was in popular usage as a description of the people of pre-Conquest England. This increased in the eighteenth century and by the later nineteenth century had become part of a concerted effort to link white people with an imagined heritage based on indigeneity to Britain, associated with the British Empire, colonialism and in the twentieth century, white supremacy.[49] There is, however, a sharp divergence between US, Canadian and Australian usage of the phrase, which is dominated by ethnoracial associations, and British usage, which is mostly concerned with Pre-Conquest political and cultural associations.[50] The phrase 'Anglo-Saxon' perpetuates a rather infantile perspective of early medieval England that fits with the Victorian narrative.

'Anglo-Saxon' remains the phrase of choice in a recent Cambridge History of Britain, since it was a 'genuine but minority usage in the Earlier Middle Ages', but the author urges sensitivity to all sides.[51] Given that the phrase 'Anglo-Saxon' is overwhelmingly anachronistic and scarcely employed by contemporaries, this book will instead use the more appropriate phrases 'early England,' 'Old English' and 'early medieval'. 'Anglo-Norman' is another hyphenated anachronism but that is used in this book since it denotes the true nature of the colonialization of England after 1066, though historically speaking, 'Norman' England is better, followed by 'Angevin'; but all of these labels are constructed terms and need to be approached with caution.

The term 'Viking' too, is problematic (but will be used in this book) since contemporaries referred to them as '*pagani*' (to emphasise the struggle between good and evil, Christian and heathen) but did use *wicing* in Old English (*víkingr* in Old Icelandic) which strictly meant 'raiders' or 'pirates'. They also referred to them accurately as 'the Danes', since Denmark was the most populous part of Scandinavia and certainly after the 990s it is the Danes who finally conquered England in 1016.

Is the 'Middle Ages' itself a 'random invention, a confidence trick perpetrated on the future by a few scholars?[52] This classification, like 'Anglo-Saxon', also emerged in the post-Reformation era. Most historians would probably agree that all history is in essence presentist, given that we study and write in a particular time.[53] Contemporary medieval historians did not distinguish between legend and history – history was moral teaching, not facts, akin to the late nineteenth-century schoolbooks. John of Salisbury, the greatest intellectual of the twelfth century, wrote: 'All the chroniclers who have come before me have had but one purpose: that is, to relate noteworthy matters, so that the invisible things of God may be more clearly seen by the things that are done on earth.'[54]

The received history of early medieval England is Bede's *Ecclesiastical History*, written, in Professor David Dumville's words, 'in national mode', which had a profound effect on the developing English church and, in turn, political development.[55] Bede wrote of an English people well before an English kingdom existed; his models were the Chosen People from the scriptures, the children of Israel, and so the English people was a literary construct, a pious hope.[56] Views vary on Bede from his being the most brilliant historian, a fundamentalist, or simply a propagandist.[57] About a quarter of Bede's *Ecclesiastical History* is devoted to miracles performed by saints or by God directly, which were expected in an age of faith; the very conversion of the English people was a consequence of divine intervention. Bede's intention was not to write *the* truth of history but *a* true law using oral traditions that may have been factually suspect, but which recorded a truth which ought to have been true.[58] The only other insular narrative source for Early English history in the period *c.*380-890 is the monk Gildas, who wrote a short moralising sermon on the sins of the British in around 540; that's it until the late ninth-century *Anglo-Saxon Chronicles* begin (referred to as the *Chronicle* in this book), written at King Alfred's behest to narrate the rise of Wessex and the defeat of the Vikings by himself.

The problem for us all is that Medieval England as history was destroyed several times. Accidental damage, hoarding and natural wastage over a millennium is to be expected, documents which were commonplace were discarded, since they only had short-term value. A 'mere fragment' of Old English poetry survives, the fabulous treasures of Sutton Hoo and the Staffordshire Hoard were discovered 1,400 years after they were placed in the ground and new finds appear every year, the artefacts or remains sometimes confirming written histories (Richard III's hunchback, seemingly) or contradicting the histories (King Alfred's alliances at a time when he was supposed to be fighting 'alone').[59] More documents survive from the south and the west because the north and east suffered Viking invasion, but the losses may have been enormous.[60] The Norman Conquest demolished churches and cathedrals and cast out Early English literature; the devastation of Yorkshire in 1070-2 may partly explain the paucity of documents. The loss of fabrics and precious metal objects from the royal collections of medieval England is almost total; most of the items that were owned by Norman and 'Plantagenet' rulers are known only from records or chronicles. The jewel accounts of Henry III (1216-1272) are the earliest to survive and tell us that in 1234 there were more than 2,000 objects, including 173 rings, 103 gold brooches, and 219 cloths of gold.[61] The Henrician Reformation of the 1530s and ensuing iconoclasm damaged, smashed, and eradicated medieval art, artefacts, architecture, and manuscripts beyond compare in a wilful and calculated policy of cultural extermination.

These acts were of their time, heinous though they might have been. Most tragically for an age of burgeoning antiquarianism, in October 1731 a fire at Ashburnham House, containing the Cottonian library, destroyed 13 manuscripts and left many others as charred fragments or badly scorched, such as the unique *Beowulf* manuscript. Asser's *Life of Alfred* and the poem *The Battle of Maldon* were completely lost. The earliest texts of Gildas, the *Chronicle,* two of the earliest copies of Bede's *Ecclesiastical History* and the Burghal Hidage were lost or badly damaged, the bull conferring the title

'Defender of the Faith' on Henry VIII was reduced to shrunken and distorted fragments (ironically, one is tempted to add), in what was 'perhaps the greatest bibliographical disaster in modern times in Britain'.[62]

In 1753 the British Museum was established and many manuscripts thought to be lost were painstakingly restored over the next century, but some material was further damaged during restoration and another fire in 1865 completely destroyed the late ninth-century manuscript of King Alfred's Old English translation of Pope Gregory's *Pastoral Care*, among other early manuscripts, some of which had been restored after the 1731 fire. It is worth considering the impact of the loss of these manuscripts and the century-long absence from historical enquiry upon the emerging Victorian interpretation of the past.

Of the 2000 extant early medieval English charters, more than half are grants by kings.[63] None survive from Northumbria or East Anglia. The story is almost exclusively that of the West Saxons and Mercia. The chronicles were written by men: monks, secular clerks and laymen. No woman is known to have written a chronicle in medieval England.[64] The written evidence is restricted to the upper educated strata of society, surviving in 3 million words, favouring survival of religious texts over secular, heroic poetry over cradle songs and lamentations, privileged upper clergy or kingly authors over commoners, and English speakers over any other vernacular; it has been likened to a corpus of Oxbridge theological English being taken to stand for British English as a whole.[65]

This book will attempt to reconstruct the origins and formation of what became England through the lens not only of the written sources, but oral, literary, and archaeological sources. Coin-hoards, burial goods, execution cemeteries and rood-screens tell us of another, hidden history. Landscapes, climate, sea-crossings and mountains explain where people settled and prospered. History cannot simply rely upon written sources any longer; it must encompass all disciplines if we are to achieve a modicum of understanding about our distant past. The history of chronicle and text is linear, sequential, and teleological; they filter and forget the heroes and myths. Literacy is equated with education and the growth of literacy with the extension of civilisation and secularisation, but it is a false assumption that literacy is the only medium for communicating educative ideas.[66] The interplay between imagination, memory and the terrain shapes and forms any writing, but the centuries of oral tradition and its cultural impact should not be forgotten. Who is to say that *Beowulf* is a mere story when Bede himself used oral traditions and hearsay? Written histories can limit our knowledge as well as enhance it.

The making of England was a process as well as an event, constructed, amended, and remade over the medieval millennium; it has been interpreted, and re-written ever since. The traditional model of the emergence of the seven English kingdoms (the so-called heptarchy) reduced to four and finally to one, following the defeat and conquest of the Scandinavian regions, is no longer a sustainable historiography.[67] The history of early medieval England has to be viewed in the context of the British and the island of Britain which the migrants settled in. By a process of cultural assimilation and conquest, the minority of English settlers assumed authority over the former British kingdoms. The British largely remained where they were, initially set aside by apartheid and then either enslaved or with limited freedom and legal rights. By the mid-tenth century a single English kingdom emerged, partially hammered on the anvil of a war for survival with the Vikings, but in no way was its existence or its survival inevitable. The multiple British kingdoms in what is now Wales and Scotland flourished and the English state itself was conquered twice decisively in the eleventh century. The foreign elite used the insular English administration to impose extraordinary powers over the people, but the nature of the conquests accelerated a long tradition of collective government and it was that conflict between the king and the elite that created a rules-based government based upon consent and representation still with us today.

The influence of Rome, first the Empire and then the Papacy, of paramount significance in the origins and identity of England, only ended with the Henrician Reformation in the late 1530s. Also essential to the development of the English kingdoms were the relations and influences with Continental Europe and Scandinavia, a constant factor from Rome to Reformation. The Roman Empire itself did not transition from a single 'panorama' but consisted of continuing regional variations of urban centres and rural estates. The links with eastern England, Scandinavia and the Low Countries illustrate the regional diversity of the sophisticated built environment, and the problem with using regional sources applied to England as a whole.[68] Medieval England produced exceptional documents such as Bede's *Ecclesiastical History*, the *Chronicle*, Domesday Book and Magna Carta, but this does not necessarily make England exceptional when placed in the wider European context.

This work is primarily concerned with reassessing the creation and identity of the political entity of England, but ordinary men and women are there throughout, sometimes coming into view: Imma the thegn captured and sold into slavery; Helmstan the cattle-thief identified by a bramble-scratch on his cheek; Æthelric of Marsh Gibbon who told the Domesday Book commissioners that he held four hides freely in 1066 but now held them 'at farm' and 'in heaviness and misery'; and the unfortunate Desiderata who playfully wrestled a male friend and accidentally stabbed herself through the heart with a poisoned arrow he had under his belt. It draws upon key written works by men and about men, though the other 50% of the population, like Desiderata, are sometimes permitted fleeting glimpses – from the Frankish Bertha who arguably brought Christianity to

Kent, Abbess Hild at Whitby and fictional queen Wealhtheow in Beowulf, to King Alfred's daughter Æthelflæd of Mercia, and the redoubtable Emma of Normandy. Women were not only subordinate to men but were struck out of the historical records at the time.

We cannot put names to the thousands of slaves and then serfs who toiled for their lord or were slain on the battlefields of Hastings, Evesham, Towton and Bosworth in pursuit of their masters' grand designs. From the tenth century there was perhaps one kingdom of England but for most people, more important than the community of the realm were the communities of village, town and shire. Most people did not share the kings' priorities.[69] But if we're asking, 'whose history?' Ian Mortimer suggests that Edward III (1330-1376) is a common ancestor to over 95% of the living English-descended population of England – so the political history of England up to the reign of Edward III is perhaps the collective family history of the English people after all.[70]

PART ONE

After Rome: Bede or *Beowulf*?

c. 380–793

Frontispiece of Bede's Life of St Cuthbert, showing King Æthelstan
presenting a copy of the book to the saint himself. Originally
from MS 183, f.1v at Corpus Christi College, Cambridge.

ONE

Continuity and Collapse

For centuries Britain was part of the Roman Empire. It was not an outlier, added as an afterthought, rather it was integral to the Roman world. Outside Rome, London was the largest city in the West. Britain's natural resources were key to the economy of northern Europe and in turn Britain was dependent on supply-chains from across the Mediterranean. The withdrawal from Britain in the late fourth and early fifth century triggered rapid decline, but the built environment of Roman cities, temples, baths and walls did not disappear overnight, and the field systems proved long-lasting. Decline was not caused by barbarian invasions into Britain; quite the opposite, since the early settlers initially wished to become part of the Roman world.

To start with, there was no England, only 'Britain'. Britain has long been an interconnected, cosmopolitan region, before and after the Romans. The grave of the Amesbury Archer, who was buried in around 2300 BC, revealed over 100 objects, including pots, copper knives, stone wrist-guards, gold ornaments and 18 flint arrowheads; the metal in the knives came from France or Spain, the stone of the wrist-guard from Wales, the gold from Europe, a belt ring was made from Dorset shale, an antler pin was from Switzerland and the man himself had spent his early years in central Europe.[1]

We will not begin our narrative with the conventional view that the Roman legions departed Britain in a single ceremony, flags lowered and with the Last Post echoing across the valleys, for that is a fictional nonsense. Indeed, if we take the long-term, minimalist view that Britain was never conquered by Rome, only 'assimilated' as a satellite state, then there is the illusion of rapid collapse since 'sub-Roman' Britain developed out of the Later Iron age culture after three centuries of Roman 'influence'.[2] Archaeology and science have substantially revised the established literature. Towns were abandoned but the countryside flourished and land was cultivated; archaeology does not point to a change in land use or increased violence.[3]

We 'know' less now about fifth- and sixth-century Britain than we did fifty years ago; the certainties have gone, and no single narrative has, or can, replace them. There are no insular contemporary written sources for this period, but archaeology has ensured that the fire and slaughter interpretation has to be abandoned. Roman Britain was never an upward progression of prosperity. Towns declined in the third century, villas flourished. The archaeology of cities in third- and fourth-century Britain reveals them to have been dynamic places, changing in ways unrecognisable to early Imperial Rome; parts of the forum in London was abandoned in the late third century, the whole complex destroyed in the early fourth century, representing changes in elite-identity long before the withdrawal of the Roman state.[4] The transfer of power from the public spaces to the private residences pre-dates the cataclysmic fifth century. Fourth-century towns were different to the second -century towns: there were fewer public buildings, with space given over to manufacturing and processing. The fourth century was a prosperous period, but the prosperity shifted to the west in a territorial zone from Dorset to the Yorkshire Wolds and archaeology gives a picture of stability, although the Romano-British elite was not super-wealthy like many in Europe. British grain fed the Roman army on the Rhine and leather, meat and wool might have been equally important.

The key to understanding what happened in Britain in the early fifth century also lies in the political organisation of the early fourth century. There was no such thing as a single 'Roman Britain'. Emperor Diocletian broke up the single province of Britain into four units, two senior provinces, *Maxima Caesariensis* (in the south-east with London as its capital) and *Flavia Caesariensis* (East Midlands and East Anglia with Lincoln as its capital) and *Britannia Prima* (Wales, the West Country up to the Mersey with Cirencester as its likely capital) and *Britannia Secunda* (with York as its capital).[5] These provinces were administered by a *Vicarius* based in London, who answered to the Praetorian Prefect of the Gauls. There was one Diocese of Britain, clergymen based in London, Lincoln and York.

These provincial structures were still in place a century later when Britain left Roman control, a century of regional autonomy and administration on a local level. *Britannia Prima* was a thriving province, rich in natural resources, with towns Wroxeter, Cirencester, Gloucester, Caerwent, Dorchester and Exeter and a major military base at Chester. Villas flourished, the great baths and temple at Bath were refurbished. Smaller towns included Worcester, Droitwich, Kenchester, Shepton Mallet and to the far west, Carmarthen and the fort at Caernarfon. The Roman military interbred and recruited locally in the last decades of the third and fourth centuries.[6]

It is the interconnectedness with the Continent that explains what happened at the end of Roman Britain. Roman Britain may have been a far-off province, but it produced three usurper emperors who took power in Rome. The first was Constantine I, proclaimed emperor in York, 306, secondly Magnus Maximus, who reigned for five years 383-388, and thirdly, Constantine III, proclaimed emperor in 406.

It was Britain's close military and economic association with Roman Europe that triggered the most dramatic collapse – more so than other parts of western Europe – but these changes began decades before the traditional 'end' of Roman Britain. The British elites played their part. In 381 the Roman government withdrew from Trier to Italy. In-fighting and Goth rebellions ended the taxation regime with Britain in around 405 and the trade of grain and supply of coinage came to an end. The frontier of the Roman British province was perhaps withdrawn from Hadrian's Wall to the line stretching from the Severn Estuary to the East Yorkshire Wolds (Gloucester to York, roughly along the Fosse Way) by Maximus in the 380s to form a highland zone.[7] The recruitment of the barbarian *foederati* – auxiliary troops – first occurred under Emperor Theodosius I in 382 and crucially for the later settlement of Britain by the Germanic peoples, Maximus may have stationed Saxon *foederati* on Hadrian's Wall or well inland of the Romanized zone, which would mean Saxon settlement deep inside Britain long before the migrations of the fifth century. The so-called 'Saxon Shore' which derived from an incomplete imperial record, the *Notitia Dignitatum*, lists the forts from Portchester on Southampton Water to the Wash under the command of a Roman military 'count' and it was assumed that these forts were to keep the Saxons out, but were in fact lived *in* by the Saxons.[8]

South of that line the villa-zone and official metalwork is found. Those north of that line no longer had contact with the Empire but still considered themselves Roman. This area was governed by military rulers with quasi-Roman authority based in high status sites such as the forts along Hadrian's Wall and Wroxeter, large-scale sites not seen in the lowlands until the seventh century. The balance of power lay with rulers of what is now Cornwall and Wales, who traded as far afield as the Levant. When the local elites in western Britain transferred from villas to hillforts this indicates changing fashions as much as any 'decline' away from Romanization and it was in line with late Antiquity in the Mediterranean. Indeed, perhaps Britain was never fully 'romanized' at all, since at the end of Roman occupation, the old tribes re-emerged as it became a failed state. Roman administration units were based on pre-conquest British tribes, so Wroxeter was *Viriconium*, with the defeated Cornovii moved there from Wrekin hillfort.

Romano-British field boundaries, estate structures, animal husbandry, systems of assessment, tribute collection, building methods and designs and political units continued in use. In parts of East Anglia and Essex, trackways which defined pre-historic and Roman field systems survived in use to the mid-twentieth century; other examples of planned landscapes pre-dating the Roman period are to be found in eastern Kent, Sussex, East Anglia, Essex, the Peak District and Yorkshire Dales.[9] Landscape evidence suggests that the fields and pastures of late Roman Britain continued to be occupied and exploited through the Early and Middle English centuries.[10] The Early English settlers lived in hamlets or settlements scattered across a wide landscape. Villages and open fields did not come until the ninth century, in a marked difference between Early English and later Medieval England, since many Early English sites occupy marginal sites.[11]

Late Romano-British archaeology does show that a collapse occurred around 400. The sudden shock to the Romano-British economy was dramatic; within decades there was a collapse of the mass production of goods and a loss of distribution networks. British towns were abandoned at the end of the fourth century and in the period 400-425 villas also. The supply of coin from the Roman Empire dried up in around 410 and pottery production went into recession. The economic collapse of the early fifth century in lowland Britain also occurred in northern Gaul, but the further south towards the Mediterranean, the better the situation. Decline hit mid-century, with loss of currency and pottery production. Northern Gaul had strong links with the south, Aquitaine, Burgundy and Provence, where post-imperial survival was much greater, lasting longer in Aquitaine than anywhere else in western Europe.

Britain was hard hit. The towns of Wroxeter, Silchester, Bath and Verulamium (St Albans) all underwent rebuilding in parts and occupation into the fifth century and Wroxeter was occupied until the eighth century, but there is no trace of any production in the old Roman towns or evidence of trade or sign of coinage being used in the markets; villa abandonment was not a fashion this time; it was a result of severe economic constraints.[12] This led to an urban exodus. The cash flow had ended, communications and freedom of movement broke down, manpower and skills were lost. The loss of material goods and technical knowledge, plus the collapse of authority, resulted in a passive society unable even to make nails let alone defeat invading barbarians. The emotional impact of the journey from an urban, materialistic global lifestyle to a rural, subsistence economy in the space of one lifetime was devastating.

After the 370s, the amount of new iron produced was minuscule, as metal production had ceased; scavenging, stockpiling and reworking old iron and bronze became the new means of metal-working and by the 420s, two long-running metal-working sites at Southwark and

Ickham (Kent) had been abandoned.[13] The few locations which continued smelting into the fifth and sixth centuries produced tiny amounts, given the archaeological evidence of smelting slag, indicating the decline of metal working in Britain in contrast to parts of Europe.[14] The de-skilling of the British people after Rome cast a long shadow; wheel-thrown pottery disappeared for 300 years, and wood-working saws for even longer, 600 years, since all wood was axe-hewn up to the twelfth century.[15] The inability to make basic commodities such as pots, nails and boards made life harder and poorer.

By the second decade of the fifth century, the majority of Roman towns, manufacturing sites, forts, villas and temple complexes had been abandoned, but the materials were pillaged for reuse; large iron clamps, iron door and shutter handles, hinges, hooks, grills, grates, beams and nails, lead windows, gutters and pipes were all carted away for reuse, which why not a lot of metalwork is found by archaeologists.[16] Roman Bath is a good example of this; it was still in use in c400 but by c450 the walls and the temple and bathing complex were pulled down, all the iron clamps with lead settings hacked out of the walls. Bronze and brass objects were also being salvaged, villas stripped down and the materials reused repeatedly. John Leland's description of Bath in his Itinerary (1530s) includes Roman remains, inscriptions, engravings on the walls and gates 1,100 years after Rome departed Britain, although he doubted that they were set at the time of the Roman town, instead gathered up and reused.[17]

In the period 375 to 425, during one person's lifetime, busy town life with housing, heating, cash and trade reverted to thatch and timber, bartering and small-scale production. Let us imagine what it was like for a person born into a prosperous artisan family in around the 360s in the busy town of Cirencester (Roman *Corinium*), the capital of *Britannia prima*. Your family has lived here for as long as they can recall; you grow up in the town, which is laid out on a grid system of streets with a forum (open marketplace), basilica (town hall), courts of justice, inns, public baths and an amphitheatre (one of the largest in Britain).[18] The fortified walls over two miles in length enclosed the town, and an area of 240 acres, making *Corinium* the second largest town in Roman Britain. Your father was a glass maker and his father before him; you follow them into the trade, have a family and live your life out in the town, your sons taking over from you in due course. You are bilingual in Latin and British and you are literate in high Latin due to the cosmopolitan nature of the town and its military significance. You follow the new imperial religion, Christianity, and you grow up with absolute certainty that the world will never change. Even with the withdrawal of Roman troops and administration, Cirencester is maintained for a while (the walls restored) but as you enter your old age, by the 420s, town life has declined so much and the place you call home is disintegrating, soon to be abandoned; people are still living in the town, but town life has long since ceased.

Bewildered, you, your children and grandchildren evacuate the town which is now no longer safe to inhabit with its collapsing, pillaged buildings, blocked, infested sewers and seek refuge in a country dwelling to scratch out a living on the land, taking with you as much as you can carry – pots, pans, plates, tiles, nails and some treasured possessions. In your own lifetime, you have seen your world turned upside down, losing all the consumables and cultural artefacts taken for granted – from luxury goods, such as glass and wine, to the basics – and now you live your final years in rustic poverty with barely enough to eat and none of the home comforts you lived with all your life and expected never to lose. You still hope that one day, Rome will return and your children will flourish under the renewed prosperity, but this never happens; instead, they are condemned to live their lives out on the land, colonised and eventually ruled over by a small group of barbarian migrants from the Continent.

The politics followed, rather than caused, the end of Roman Britain. Constantine III, usurper-emperor and general, left Britain for Gaul with his army in the summer of 407 and in 408/9 came a Saxon incursion.[19] The system of provinces and administration was still flourishing in 407 and even then, there was no reason to suppose that Roman troops would not return to Britain to restore order (they had gone to deal with Roman rebels). Hopes and fears often overrule hard reality. For long afterwards, people regarded themselves as *Romani* and some Roman titles continued in use, but Britain did divide into many small kingdoms.[20] Gildas (writing in the later fifth century) records several pleas for help from Britain to Rome during the early fifth century and in the mid-sixth century there is a suggestion that the Romans still regarded Britain as under their sovereignty.[21] There is even some dispute over who left who; the 'British' – or some of them at least – seceded from the Roman Empire, expelling imperial officials and ceased living under Roman law. This was so dramatic that when the Emperor Honorius wrote to Britain in 410, he addressed the people, not a specific high official.[22] Or was the plea for help an attempt to rejoin the heart of Empire, not leave it? But 'the British' were not a single people, and it may have been a different faction that Honorius was responding to. There was no sense of 'nationalism', provincial allegiance or even Celtic self-awareness, and in any case Honorius was in no position to send support: Northern Italy and Rome were threatened, Africa was lost, Gaul devastated, and Spain ravaged.

Although official authority had gone, the writings of Patrick and Gildas demonstrate the survival of high-level Latin literacy and Roman education, learning and law among the elite well into the late fifth century. Their works are complemented by over 240 inscribed texts in stone in Latin or Latin and Irish found across the whole of western and northern Britain, dating mostly to the 5th and 6th centuries.[23] Areas in the western zone, *Britannia prima*, survived and flourished into the seventh century, archaeology again confounding the established view. Britain's first mid-fifth-century mosaic was recently discovered at Chedworth Roman villa (eight miles from Cirencester, Gloucestershire).[24] In 428 St Germanus of Auxerre came to *Britannia* to resolve a religious dispute, so Rome's authority remained (according to this Continental source). But none of this means the survival of sub-Roman Britain as a 'province'. Other Continental sources, *The Narrative of the Valentinianic and Theodosian Houses*, written in the 440s, says Britain was lost during Honorius's reign (395-423).[25] By the 430s, many in Britain had no memory of effective imperial governance. Most importantly, Romano-British authority had collapsed before Britain was permanently settled by the Germanic settlers, not because of those migrations, and it is to those settlers we now turn.

TWO

Natives and Migrants: What Happened to the British?

The settlement of sub-Roman Britain by Germanic migrants was a process, not an event, which took place over two centuries. The first settlers integrated into Roman Britain and it was only after the collapse of the administration that second and third generation settlers began to celebrate their cultural identity. They were relatively few in number and the bulk of the native British assimilated with the new arrivals, acquiring the new language and continuing to farm the Roman estates. Other Britons migrated to western Britain (to what is now Wales and Cornwall), France (Brittany) or were killed in battle. Many were enslaved. The British were at war with one another, and the western, less Romanised regions were less settled, if at all, by the migrants who did not move from east to west in any designed pattern. The wealthy Roman villa-zone in the central regions shaped the emerging kingdoms as much as the coastal settlements in Kent and Essex. There is only one, rather enigmatic, contemporary written source, and the narrative is dominated by much later English histories. Archaeology reveals a much more complex story.

Just as there was no grand departure from Roman Britain by the legions, there was no co-ordinated 'invasion' by the barbarians, wading ashore with winged helmets wielding Thor hammers to settle, populate and create 'England' as part of their manifest destiny. Early English society was lacking in clear hierarchy and the settlement of late Roman Britain took over two centuries. The settlers did not invade or conquer post-Roman Britain, or patiently await the return of Rome in the form of missionaries, not legionaries (Roman Britain was significantly Christianized, spreading through society under imperial patronage and extending into the Highlands by the time of Gildas). By *c.*600 they had established a network of kingdoms across Britain with both pagan and Christian beliefs in place. The Prittlewell princely burial pre-dates

31

Augustine's mission in 597 and the finds indicate that he was a Christian.[1] Christian cult sites in the east of Britain were maintained right up to the conversion, in London, Canterbury, St Albans and other sites in the south and east.[2]

The continuation of rural landscapes implies the survival of low-status peasant farmers across East Anglia, Essex, Kent and Sussex who may have been seen by the settlers in the same light as the Roman state had seen them. Most people were involved in agricultural subsistence farming and were profoundly poor in comparison with the prosperity of late Roman Britain; the written texts give the false impression that society was all about aristocratic warbands and their kings, owing to the nature of their audience.[3] The legacy of Rome cast a very long shadow: Early English cemeteries dated 425-450 have been found across eastern Britain (cremations) while inhumations in late Roman style, with some belongings, continued in the south and west.[4] The early medieval settlement at West Stow harboured Roman metalwork artefacts which included bronze spoons, bracelets, finger rings, ear scoops and 300 Roman coins.[5] Scavenging and reworking Roman metalwork continued into the seventh century, as seen in the settlement at Bloodmoor Hill (Suffolk) and the grave goods of a smithy from Tattershall Thorpe (Lincolnshire), which included a set of metalworking tools, a box of scrap iron, belt buckles, metal studs and Roman coins and glass.[6] Roman lead was also collected and reworked, found at sites across eastern England, especially at Mucking (Essex), which was near a Roman villa.[7] The Romano-British workshops that produced ornamental objects such as brooches and long-dress pins in the later fourth century survived into the fifth, if not the sixth centuries.[8] This continuation influenced pagan Saxon England, contributing to the so-called 'Celtic' art that came to fruition in the later masterpieces such as the Lindisfarne Gospels; by the turn of the seventh century, Germanic metalworking techniques had begun to transform Celtic skills.[9]

The North Sea coast of the Saxon homelands was closely bound to the *imperium*. Information, trade and culture was two-way; we have already seen that *foederati* were based in British Roman military camps in the later fourth century. The North Sea was an interconnected 'cultural province', not an opposing world, but this, too, ended abruptly in the fifth century. Manufacture and trade ceased *c*.400 causing a political crisis and the fracture of the Saxon 'confederacy' into tribal groups. It may be that these groups who hitherto sought protection and prestige in the Roman Empire now went to *Britannia*. The settlers were made up of a variety of ethnic groups; Bede lists the Angles, Saxons, Jutes, Frisians, Rugii, Huns, Old Saxons and Bructeri.[10] Archaeologists would add Franks, and Scandinavians from southern Norway to the list. These migrants would have settled in interspersed settlements, not ethnic blocks, mixing and fusing the groups over time. The rituals and cremations of burial customs appearing in Britain are entirely analogous with northern Germany, as are the jewellery and objects from northern Germany and Scandinavia from *c.*430.

Furnished inhumation graves are essentially found in the same lowland part of Britain as the villas, suggesting that the social hierarchy represented by the villas (which collapsed in the early 5th century) was in contention. Migration is indisputable, but since the first archaeological evidence dates from the 430s this does not mean they arrived at that time. Settlers and migrants saw themselves as part of the Roman Empire, wanting to fit in; only later generations expressed their cultural differences. This was perhaps not unlike the first generation of *Windrush* immigrants to Britain in the 1950s, which took at least two generations to evolve into a multicultural society.[11]

The major shortage of written sources in the period *c.*400-*c.*600 and the abundance of archaeology leading to opposing interpretations means that the period is difficult to comprehend.[12] The written sources are limited in their information but consistently portray the Saxon invasions as calamities; their subject was warfare though, not settlement, and conquest by *c.*441 was followed by a war of resistance to *c.*520.[13] With the exception of Gildas and the Continental source, *The Life of St Germanus*, there is no reliable written source for the fifth century. There are no independent 'witnesses' and no lost sources for this time that the later narrative sources, namely Bede's *Ecclesiastical History* (731) and the *Chronicle* (890s) were based upon, although there may have been many written sources in the period.[14] Professor Guy Halsall proposes that this be called a kind of 'interhistoric' period, rather than 'pre-historic' or 'historic'.

Gildas was possibly writing in western Britain (probably outside the Saxon zone of control) in the late fifth and early sixth century (even his name is not recognisably British and is quite unique) but his is the sole insular surviving written account of the Saxon settlement from which Bede and the *Chronicle* derive. Gildas was a conservative with respect to the established Christian authority, with an aristocratic, Roman view.[15] He was not writing an objective, historical account of British history but a sermon, a dialectic, in which Britain is like the Garden of Eden, which fell from grace through sin, a theme that resonates through Bede's concerns for Christianity in the early eighth century and into the eleventh century with the Viking and Norman conquests when England is overwhelmed in 1066 due to the 'sins of the people'.[16] The title of his work *De Excidio et Conquestu Britanniae* ('On the Ruin and Conquest of Britain') says it all. The Saxons are heathen savages, not fully human, employed by the British as mercenaries (the *foederati*, which we have already mentioned), but it was a stupid thing to do with hindsight; they rebelled, having not been paid. As far as Gildas was concerned, a Roman type of kingship survived up to the war with the Saxons, which began *c.*430 and ended *c.*441. 'Vortigern' and the councillors invited the fierce and impious Saxons to repel the invasions of the northern nations, who first landed on the eastern side of the island and were followed by successive companies of invaders who destroyed and plundered the British, putting them to the slaughter and enslaving them, and causing famine. They were responsible for destroying the Roman towns, way of life and civilisation. The invasions were hindered by the Romano-British 'Ambrosius Aurelianus' and the battle of 'Bath-hill' (Badon) 44 years after the landing of the Saxons. This British victory set back the Saxon advances for fifty years. It was not a decisive encounter but was the last British victory.

Gildas's account is corroborated by a contemporary Continental source, the anonymous *Gallic Chronicle* of 452, which tells us how the British provinces were laid waste by Saxon invasion and subjected to the authority of the Saxons by 441/2. The trouble with this is that it was written in southern Gaul and the earliest surviving manuscript is late ninth century, over four hundred years later and its chronology is jumbled to suit its stylistic purposes, listing the calamities across the Empire from north to south.[17]

At the time Gildas was writing, the cities are indeed no longer inhabited; they were forsaken, overthrown, and lying desolate. Gildas took for granted the endemic civil war and British emigration, the empty cities and the barbarian presence. While we know that urban life had ceased by the mid-fifth century given the cessation of market activity, a climatic downturn, the collapse of state funding and the impact of barbarian raiding and warfare, Gildas is deliberately disingenuous in his desire to communicate his warning. Although much rent and taxation was probably paid in kind, Gildas only assumed Roman law was passing at the time he was writing (early sixth century) and Gildas talks of *provincia*; the works of Gildas and St Patrick indicate a high level of literacy in the highland zone (Gildas mentions military manuals and books) and the British Church was involved in mainland ecclesiastical disputes and writings (in the 420s, the Pelagian missionary Agricola came to Britain and in 431 the first bishop was sent to the Irish Christians.) It is probable that those in the lowland zone moved to the highlands taking with them their learning. *Britannia Prima* shows little evidence for Christianity compared with the other provinces in the Roman era, it being the only province not sending a cleric to the Council of Arles in 314, but the exodus of Christian elites fleeing the incoming Early English in the mid-fifth century changed that.

What Gildas was actually describing was not the Early English invasions of Britain but instead the renewed migration westwards into *Britannia Prima*, coupled with British civil wars. It was when the new settlers turned invaders arrived on the new frontier of the province that Gildas cites the appeal for aid to the Roman consul Aëtius who was based in northern Gaul, dated to *c.*446-454. There is no demonstrable Early English settlement of much of the province until well into the seventh century, so the defence of *Britannia Prima* was maintained for 100-150 years.[18] The towns survived, most clearly at Wroxeter, where the bath complex was reconstructed as a private space, evidence for trade from the Mediterranean via south-west France and northern Spain can be seen at Dinas Powys and Tintagel, luxury goods such as olive oil, wine, maybe silk and books.[19]

Gildas's account of the Saxon arrival became the standard historical version. His theme of post-Roman collapse was taken up by Bede, whose writings were defined by the relationship with Rome, and he understood that the complex history of his island had been shaped by decisions made in Rome.[20] Furthermore, at the time he was writing, in *c.*730, the clergy still pursued unorthodox doctrine so that Bede, like Gildas was writing at a time of what he saw as declining standards and wanted to ensure correction and punishment of sin, which says more about 730 than it does about 500.[21] Vortigern was tricked into granting the Saxons Essex, Sussex and Middlesex and Bede elaborates, giving us the Hengist and Horsa ('Gelding' and 'Horse', lesser heroes or gods) origin myth (not unlike the founders of Rome, Romulus and Remus), who are descended from Woden.[22] Bede is the first insular source since Gildas, but Bede knew as little as we do (or less in fact) about the period 410-597. Bede, who specifically references Gildas, made an educated guess as to the exact arrival of the Saxons, used several Continental sources, telescoped events and tidied up the narrative to define the single event, the 'coming of the English' in 449.[23]

The third surviving insular narrative source of Saxon migration in the fifth century is the *Chronicle*, which appears to be reliable because it lists a series of facts and dates but is extremely dubious, based partly on Bede, who was himself unreliable for this period. As a source written for the royal house of Wessex it makes adaptations to fit its own origin mythology, begun at a time of Alfredian ideological and cultural dominance following the Viking conquests and West Saxon survival. It should not be seen as a coherent work of history but instead as an amalgam of traditions and inventions that tells us more about the 880s than the 450s.[24] The *Chronicle* sets the date 449 in stone and moves east to west in the account of the settlement, suggestive of a concerted campaign. The natives could not hold off the Early English advance forever, so at the battle of Dyrham in 577, Gloucestershire, the British kings of Coinmail, Condidan and Farinmail were killed and Gloucester, Cirencester and Bath captured.[25]

We can discern some possible reality in the midst of the 'group-think' narrative of Gildas, Bede and the *Chronicle*; could it be that the Emperor Maximus who originally deployed Saxon *foederati* in Britain in the 380s was in fact Gildas's Vortigern?[26] This would set the *adventus Saxonum* back seventy years and align with the archaeological evidence of Saxons in late Roman Britain. The *Chronicle* has Hengest and Horsa land at Ebba's Creek, near the Roman fort of Richborough, Kent, one of the 'Saxon shore forts,' and the location of one of the largest collections of Roman coins in Britain.[27] We cannot place 'Hengest' and 'Horsa' as Saxon *foederati* based at Richborough in the late 380s – they did not exist – but we can suggest that the site was well-known enough for later sources to conflate their own origin myths with hard evidence of late Roman military and political networks.

Whatever a reading of the tea leaves might or might not tell us, the simplistic and wrong narrative of the Saxon arrival was astonishingly powerful and held sway throughout the Middle Ages and into the early twentieth century. It linked with the Israelites' exodus from Egypt and was a cultural myth that endured in memory and spoke powerfully to the collective imagination. The triumphalist Old English tenth-century poem the *Battle of Brunanburh* boasted of how the English came from over the sea and 'won a kingdom by the sword's edge' (the sole direct reference to migration):

Since Angles and Saxons
Came here from the east
sought out Britain over the broad ocean,
Warriors eager for fame, proud war-smiths
overcame the Welsh, seized the country.[28]

In the late fourteenth century, Chaucer's Man at Law repeats the tale:

A pagan army and a pagan fleet
Had made their conquest of this northern shore,
To Wales had therefore fled a Christian core
Of ancient Britons dwelling in our isle,
That was the refuge of the faith meanwhile.[29]

Due to the paucity and inaccuracy of the written sources, archaeology has to be the main driver in our knowledge of the fifth and sixth centuries, but it should not made to fit the later texts, even though there may be overlapping agreement. Archaeological and literary evidence implies that an immigrant, barbarian population established itself in eastern Britain relatively early in the fifth century.[30] We should turn to the four provinces of Roman Britain once again for some answers as to what happened in the century. Each province invited a separate group of peoples to protect it, turning to the nearest part of the Continent for recruits. The silver plate and bullion coin hoards of Mildenhall, Hoxne and Thetford evidences the disposable income to pay for them.[31] The Angles wore small-long or cruciform brooches, had wrist clasps on women's dresses and predominantly cremated their dead, Saxons had circular brooches of differing designs and buried their dead. The Saxon-style brooches are clustered in the province of *Maxima Caesariensis* (in the south-east) but the Angle-type brooches are found in the province of *Flavia Caesarensis* (east Midlands, Norfolk).[32] The 'Quoit Brooch Style' objects are exclusively found in the province of *Maxima Caesarensis* and these are decorated in Germanic style but strongly based on Roman forms of military belt and other fittings, high-status items that continue a late Roman fashion of issuing gold and silver military fittings to senior military or civil service officials. This might suggest controlled settlement, in line with Bede and Gildas, who tell us of the invited Early English migrants.

The migrations to Britain were part of a wider, Mediterranean phenomenon. Migration is of course a constant of human experience. People migrated from *barbicum* east of the Rhine into the Roman Empire for centuries before 400 and people moved within the empire on a large scale. Migrations of comparable peoples in the fifth century include the Vandals and Alans crossing from Spain to Africa in 429 (around 80,000 joining the native population of Roman North Africa of 2.5-3 million); and Ostrogoths moving from the Balkans into Italy in the late fifth century (more than 100,000).[33] Immigrants from northern Europe to Britain arrived in smaller numbers than previously thought, possibly as low as 6% net immigration in the period 430-730, that is 175,000 people in a population 2.6 million; this is in stark contrast to the 90% replacement of the gene pool by the Beaker people 4,000 years ago.[34] A large rowing boat found in the Jutish bog deposit of Nydam dated to *c*.400 suggests how they travelled. Up to 200,000 migrations over 100 years represents only around 2000 a year, between 100 and 200 boats of the Nydam type.[35] Calculations suggest this would take 38 years, during May-August, using 20 boats in continuous transport. The marked increase in finds and cemeteries in the second half of the fifth century indicates that the migrations were a process, rather than the single event we see in Gildas and Bede's narrative.

The proportion of DNA in modern central/southern England inherited from the Saxons suggests a range of 10-40%, 'clearly excluding the possibility of long-term Saxon replacement'; 35% of them originated from north-west Germany, with Denmark another key place of origin.[36] A study of the whole-genome sequences from individuals excavated close to Cambridge proposes that on average the contemporary East English population derives 38% of its ancestry from Early English migrations, with close ancestry to modern-day Dutch and Danish populations (and samples from a Kent a similar percentage), overall 20-40% of the ancestry of modern Britons, with a higher percentage in the east of England.[37]

The earliest English finds in Sussex were outside the large Roman town of Chichester, perhaps signifying native control of the minority incomers before later conquest across Wessex.[38] In East Anglia there was large-scale immigration and settlement of family groups, but the Romano-British population was very considerable in East Anglia and the East Midlands, which would mean that the incoming Germanic settlers were very still much in the minority.[39]

Male incomers were an average of 1¾ inches taller than Romano-British indigenous populations, a differential which ceased in the seventh century, the very time when social status differences increase. Weapon burial was a barbarian, Germanic rite across Europe, not associated with Romano-British society, and the early cemeteries suggest male Britons made up as much as half of the male population of communities identified as 'Anglo-Saxon'; the proportions of weapon burials range from 30%-82% corresponding to the proportions of Early English and native Britons across England.[40] Many bladed objects of the early medieval period were not very serviceable; knives and spearheads excavated from Early English cemeteries are of poor quality because of the limited access to freshly smelted iron and steel. Perhaps they were tokens made for burial since there was plenty of recycled Roman material available.[41]

The cemetery of Berinsfield (Dorchester, Oxfordshire) in use from the late fifth to the early seventh centuries suggests that Germanic immigrants and their descendants lived together with native Britons in the same social unit but did not intermarry, implying status differences, even prohibition of intermarriage, something we see in the Early English law codes of the late seventh century.[42] A very different situation occurred in Warwickshire at Stretton-on-Fosse (near the Fosse Way, a Roman road) where cemeteries demonstrate Romano-British and Early English concurrent use and thereby interaction, which is absent in the contemporary literature.[43] The proportion of males with weapons is 82% buried alongside two Romano-British cemeteries. The Germanic males were taller than the Romano-British males and it seems that here the incoming males took control of the local community and married native women, given continuity of textile techniques and epigenetic traits.[44] But this type of settlement was much less frequent than the kin group model seen at Berinsfield.

At this point, we should move away from the debate about when and where the migrants came, to ask a more pertinent question: what happened to the British? If the burial evidence points towards a model of elite dominance compatible with Gildas's account of the first Germanic settlers arriving as 'federates,' such groups of powerful immigrants may have formed hierarchical but non-kingly systems of power after Rome and before the English kingdoms emerged.[45] In this way, the incoming Germanic settlers formed an elite who farmed the large estates worked by the native British who became culturally indistinguishable from them over time.[46] This 'elite emulation model' may disguise something altogether more brutal. Bede created the written narrative of the repopulation of post-Roman Britain – for example King Æthelfrith of Northumbria was celebrated by Bede as 'having first exterminated or conquered the natives'. Bede wrote of genocide (*exterminum gentis*) of the Britons by the English who he believed were God's new chosen people.[47] Bede sugars the pill by inventing the origin myth of the Britons themselves as incomers from 'Amorica' (modern-day Brittany) suggesting that since the Britons were immigrants, their replacement by the English was therefore a natural racial progression but with an evangelical purpose (although he adds, with classic Bede-like caution 'so it is said.')[48] Across the Channel, there were Continental parallels in this growing myth of racial supremacy since in 735 the *Book of the History of the Franks* came to a similar conclusion, in that the Franks must have slaughtered the Gauls and the Romans (though they learnt Latin from them before killing them, unlike the English who now all spoke English).[49]

Are we looking at mass migration and enslavement of the British natives by the English masters, or, more extreme, are we looking at the genocide of the British? By a process of actual slaughter alongside or followed by an apartheid system that restricted the native British as to resources and status, this was, in effect, Professor David Dumville argues, genocide. Assimilation, flight or slavery were the only methods of survival when faced with invasion and colonisation.[50] Bede may not have meant literal 'extermination' since the word used could also translate as 'to drive off'.[51] There was southward emigration to western Gaul which may have continued for centuries: to Brittany, or 'Little Britain' – two peaks of emigration to Brittany, 450-550 and the second after 577, exacerbated by the world-wide climatic downturn 535-545; and to northern Iberia (Britoña in Galicia, Spain) and widespread individual settlements in post-Roman Gaul along the Atlantic coast.[52] Eastern England shows the lexical evidence that incomers moved into a landscape from which there had been a 'major withdrawal'.[53] There were certainly great battles, but migration and enslavement were the key factors of the 'conquest'. Migration to the west, to Cornwall, Wales and to Brittany could have involved hundreds of thousands of people on the move, akin to the Great Trek in South Africa in the 1830s, the Partition in India in 1947/8, or more recently, the Great Migration in the US from 1910-1970. For those who remained – perhaps the women with young children who could not travel while they waited for the able-bodied men to win victory in battle and return for them – enslavement was the means of ensuring cultural domination, developing a steep hierarchy over the de-skilled peasant British who had lost civic and military structures after *c*.407. This is cultural annihilation as well as literal slaughter of the British. The new masters make no effort to communicate in the slaves' languages and so the imperative is there to learn the new language, and meanwhile nothing is recorded of the vanishing native customs and terminology.[54] The conquered British learnt the new language in order to survive and their children grew up speaking 'Old English'; such a complete submission could explain how a minority ethnic group acquired domination over this period.

Slavery was one of the more durable legacies of the Roman Empire and it can provide evidence as to the nature of the Germanic settlement. When the last legions left Britain in *c*.407, enslaving captives was common practice among the Germanic peoples who came to be the Early English.[55] Gildas's graphic depiction of wholesale slaughter (taken up by Bede) cannot be taken as wholly accurate, but it is likely that many of the indigenous British peoples were enslaved by the incoming Early English, many quite possibly continuing as slaves under new Germanic, rather than Roman, masters.[56] The story of St Patrick, seized from the south-west and transported to Ireland, is probably a typical experience. The earliest Frankish law code, the *Compact of Salic Law* (*c*.511), references the power to recover freemen sold into slavery 'across the sea'.[57] The employment of Celtic women as slaves was very common in the southern core areas in the early times, given the textual evidence for *wīln* (female) and *wealh* (male) and if the lower classes were those who remained in the Roman towns and villas as house slaves, it was in their interest to learn their new masters' language; but it was not all one way.[58] In later Wessex, the term *wīln* meant more generally 'female slave' rather than a woman of Celtic origin, and West Saxon itself had become Celticized to a considerable extent.[59]

Concomitant with physical and cultural annihilation is apartheid. Intermarriage between dominant immigrants and subject natives was banned in Visigothic Francia and Spain in the late fifth or early sixth century and it may be that a similar scenario occurred in post-Roman Britain.[60] Apartheid would explain the discrepancy between modern Y-chromosome DNA and archaeological-historical expectations. A gradual process of acculturation started early, but there is no evidence in the fifth century; it was well under way at Wallingford in the sixth century though.[61] Acculturation was a one-way process, not a mixed or hybrid Anglo-British common culture, which mirrors the linguistic process; the exception was Northumbria (Bernicia especially) with a noticeable Celtic contribution to art and culture. In Bernicia, a small group of immigrants may have replaced the native British elite, since the native population survived to a greater extent than in the south.

The extermination, enslavement and mass migration south and westwards explains why the cultural domination in Britain was almost entirely one-way, absorbing only 30 or so British words into the new vocabulary, although perhaps there was a greater influence of Celtic vocabulary on the English language than that.[62] The disappearance of any Brittonic communities that might sustain the ancestral language cannot be squared with 'genetic' Britons forming a massive element of the population of England.[63] It was assumed that the majority of Celts fled or died since Old and Modern English contain very few Celtic loan words (the percentage of the Celtic share of Modern Standard English is 0.34).[64] If the model of a small incoming elite replacing a native elite but not the native population is accepted, the paucity of lexical borrowing must be explained; the Britons left no literary imprint of their own, even though they remained an ethnic and legally distinctive group (the laws of Ine in the later seventh century imply they were still Brittonic-speaking).[65] But if they were a majority, how come our present language is not a heavily Brittonicized variety of Germanic?

This is not straightforward, since it does not take into account the immigration before and after the Early English period, or that eastern Britons spoke a Germanic language before the Roman occupation, and the immigrants themselves were not genetically homogeneous.[66] And there is no evidence of a general 'Celtic' population in the non-Saxon parts of the UK, rather many distinct genetic clusters.[67] Furthermore, Britain represented the same type of habitat as the old home of the Early English, familiar fauna and flora, neighbours and opponents that Germanic invaders had been in contact with on the Continent for centuries; rather than loan words, the influences can be seen in the syntax.[68] It is also argued that there is phonetic continuity between pre-Roman British Celtic and Old English, suggesting the presence of a pre-English population shifting to Old English; the original language was ancestral to Old Irish, too.[69]

To find an answer we need to return to late Roman Britain again. Just as the migrants did not form a single linguistic or ethnic group, neither did the native Britons – there was no such as thing as 'Britain' just as there was no such thing as 'England' until the tenth century. We have talked of the provinces and how those influenced the settlement. To the west, *Britannia Prima* retained its identity, in that it generated the Welsh and the Cornish, both of whom speak a language derived from the Brittonic Celtic spoken by the people of *Britannia Prima*.

Was 'sub-Roman' Britain divided into 'highland' and 'lowland' zones? Inscribed stones in the western, 'highland' zone in Latin and Primitive Irish, coincide with the pagan, Early English burials occurring in the east, the 'lowland zone', civil government and stratified society, though there was no sharp division. One feature of the lowland zone was the re-occupation of the Iron Age hillforts, including South Cadbury, where there is evidence of re-fortification and domestic occupation, including Mediterranean pottery.[70] British Celtic was spoken in the 'Highland' zone and in the Romanised, eastern 'Lowland zone', Latin was spoken, and Latin-Celtic bilingualism was widespread.[71] We know that the local Celtic language in northern Gaul was replaced by low Latin and the same is probably true of part of Britain and if so, there are hundreds of Latin loan words in Old English.[72]

If we do not accept that Latin was widely spoken (just written), the Brittonic language was nevertheless deeply Latinized and south-eastern Britain at least was Latin-speaking.[73] This would mean that the Early English settlers encountered late-spoken Latin when they arrived in the British Lowland Zone, with more Celtic-speaking people the further north and west they went.[74] Celtic influence on Old English occurred via the medium of late-spoken Latin, which was identical with the Romance variety underlying Old French. This British Celtic/British Latin divide was geographic and so the most important border of modern Britain was not the English Channel but the boundary running from northeast to southwest.[75]

This leads us back to questioning the extent of annihilation, contrary to Gildas and later on, Bede, and suggests assimilation as well as undoubted enslavement and killings. When we look again at the archaeological evidence from the perspective of ethnicity, further questions are raised over the picture of total annihilation, since we lack a sound basis for the assumption that Early English burial costume expresses ethnicity.[76] 'Furnished inhumation' grave goods does not necessarily mean a Saxon burial, but rather the desire to express wealth and status at the very point of economic collapse. Such burials are found nearest the villa-zone and may not always include 'Early English' but Roman Britons who adopted a Saxon identity. The Quoit Brooch Style objects are a classic example of the changing interpretations of settlement, ethnicity and cultural identity. Mentioned above as possible evidence of controlled immigration into the south-eastern Roman province of *Maxima Caesariensis* either as mercenary equipment, or Germanic settlement in line with Gildas and Bede's narrative of invited peoples turned invader, the Quoit Brooch Style objects have been proposed as variously Gallo-Roman, Romano-British, Frankish, Early English – or just 'Germanic'.[77]To focus on the genetic origin is to miss the ethnic point, since these belt fittings were used alongside other late-Roman belt fittings for reuse, repair and modification, part of the culture of recycling in sub-Roman Britain (given the collapse we have seen in smelting facilities in Britain by the 420s). The mercenary connection is unlikely since most of them were worn by women. The form and style of bracelets and belt fittings point towards northern Gaul and demonstrate a littoral cultural zone of cross-Channel communications, especially via the western Channel route, which corresponds to the migrations of Britons to Brittany.[78]

The bulk of sixth-century swords, high-status objects and often beautifully crafted, have been found in Kent and the south-eastern coast or Thames Valley; the high quality of these pattern-welded weapons suggests access to freshly smelted iron-alloy bars which were probably imported from the Continent, where large-scale smelting was still in progress.[79] The successful accumulation of such treasured objects depended upon trade networks and traders as much as pedigree and we should see the Early English migrations as a series of cultural zones where information and influence went in both directions. This would include the North Sea and the western Channel route. The Binham Hoard (Norfolk), discovered and recovered by metal-detectorists between 2004 and 2013, is the largest collection of gold from sixth-century Britain, consisting of two bracelets, a silver brooch and six gold bracteates (neck pendants derived from the practice of wearing pierced Roman coins as jewellery, developed in Scandinavia and northern Germany in the fifth century). Three bracteates from the Binham hoard used a central design of an armed male figure holding a sword and fighting a beak-nosed creature with a short runic inscription (only about 20 objects with runic inscriptions made before *c.*650 are known from England.) This discovery shows that the practice of hoarding bracteates in eastern England was the same as north Germany and southern Scandinavia, sharing similar or identical designs, suggesting ongoing communication between the elites of the North Sea and a network of sites.[80]

Ethnicity then, is not a given but a flexible and situational concept, in the heart, not in the blood, so 'Early English' burials and 'Celtic' artefacts would represent a cultural statement of perceived group affiliation.[81] Modern Y-chromosome DNA points to Early English origins in Dutch Frisia, northern Germany and Denmark, which agrees with the archaeological, textual and linguistic evidence, but genetic similarities can spread without any mass movement and European DNA has been intertwined since prehistoric times. Ethnic identity is multi-layered, a matter of belief; it can be changed, and it cannot give a sense of all the layers of that person's ethnicity. Icenic tribes became 'Roman', British people became East Anglian, or English, adopting a Saxon identity to improve their standing in a world now dominated by Early English warrior elites; similar processes were at work in mainland Europe from the fifth to the seventh century, so material cultures cannot be linked to ethnic identities with certainty: cultural appropriation is not new. DNA data can be misused and can view a person's identity as entirely derived from their biological and geographical origins. There is also a danger that it reduces identity to the nineteenth-century nationalist ideas of race. Ethnic identity is therefore a construct that fashions communities through real and fictive stories and memories; it cannot be identified through purely archaeological means.

It is also time to abandon the belief that the diverse peoples migrating to Britain from the fourth to the sixth centuries shared a coherent, 'Germanic' cultural ethos.[82] This leads us back to the migrations themselves. The traditional model of a Saxon 'invasion' starting in 449 should be set back to the initial Saxon settlements in the late fourth century (in Roman Britain) followed by later migrations in the mid-fifth century. Once we have acknowledged that this was not a singular event and acknowledge that many different tribes arrived at different times over many decades, we must also accept that this is not a 'British' or 'English' event either. There were many different British 'kingdoms', (for want of a better word) such as Tintagel, South Cadbury, Dinas Powys, Dumbarton (kingdom of Strathclyde). The wars Gildas discusses are not between British and 'Saxons' but between British tribes. Gildas does not mention barbarians or Saxons, that is a later assumption, since his concern is with citizens and enemies and religious malpractices. The newly arrived Saxons in Britain became embroiled in local political in-fighting, in alliance with the Romano-British aristocracy, as well as competing for dominance with the established Saxons of late Roman Britain. Continental events for the early fifth century are much better documented and suggest that late Roman Empire priorities were dealing with internal disputes and wars, with alliances made with the 'barbarians' when it suited, or ignoring them altogether in pursuit of shoring up the Empire first and foremost. It is worth remembering that the alleged founder of the House of Wessex was Cerdic, a British name. His son, Cynric, has an English name but similar to the British or Irish Cunorix.[83]

The idea that the migrations progressed from east to west like a military campaign needs challenging. Migration follows particular routes, with established communities the initial destination rather than flooding a wide area. Inland military bases (the *foederati*) could have been an early point of settlement, as well as coastal approaches. In England, the River Thames plays a crucial part in the tribal, kingly and finally, political settlement of 'England' from the fifth to the tenth century, as we shall see. The Quoit Brooches, insular or not, have almost all been found south of the Thames, mainly in Kent, but the 'Saxon Relief style' material is to be found north of the Thames, in East Anglia, Lincolnshire and Yorkshire. Rather than an east/west migration, a north/south divide seems more likely, with pockets of established immigrants since the late fourth century. The later Early English kingdoms of England emerged inland, in the Upper Thames valley. The cores of Wessex, Mercia and Northumberland all lie on the border between the lowland/highland prosperous zone of Roman Britain; Mercia means 'border dwellers' and Deira, the southern half of Northumbria, derives from the British Deur. They may have been based originally on Romano-Barbarian alliances in the fifth century and expanded from the interior to the 'Saxon shore'.

After Gildas, there is nothing on the record but deafening silence in Britain. Merovingian Gaul shows a similar archaeology of Roman collapse and responses in terms of settlement forms and burial rites, but the written sources for fifth- and sixth-century Gaul are far better than for Britain and reveal that by 535 northern Gaul was the heartland of the Merovingian Frankish realm, and by 561 the realm encompassed all of France except for Brittany, Narbonne and the Rhineland and included modern Belgium and the Netherlands. This large overkingdom taxed, used a literate bureaucracy, had registers of a military bureaucracy but remained archaeologically invisible, similar to post-Roman Britain.[84] Professor Guy Halsall proposes that it could be that there was a similarly large overkingdom in Britain that simply has no written contemporary record or any archaeology. By c.700 the Merovingian kingdom had divided into two, and perhaps what we see in seventh-century Britain is not the emerging Early English kingdoms but actually the splintering of one vast kingdom; Bede tells us that Ælle (c.500), king of the South Saxons, was the first to hold sovereignty over all territory south of the Humber, followed by Cealwin (victor at the battle of Dyrham in 577).[85]

The gradual decline of such a large overkingdom may have been triggered by events outside Britain, but this time of an epidemiological nature. The bubonic plague of the mid-sixth century began in Egypt and spread from Constantinople in 541 to Italy, Gaul, Carthage, Spain and the British Isles. The plague reached Britain in 544 according to genomic evidence recovered from a burial site at Edix Hill (Cambridge), near Roman Ermine Street (the same *Yersinia pestis* strain re-emerged in the late medieval pandemics that included the fourteenth century 'Black Death').[86] The possible origins of the Early English kingdoms after c.550 such as Bernicia, Deira, Essex and Kent, could indicate a new start.[87] The plague may have caused tens of millions of deaths, reducing the population of the Mediterranean and Europe by a third. This transformed Late Antiquity. This model of catastrophe, or 'collapsology' has been rejected with an emphasis on continuity rather than change, but the debate continues as to the severity of the plague and its impact.[88]

On the earliest available evidence, major overkingships had come into existence not later than the end of the sixth century.[89] 'Britain' was a theatre of inter-kingdoms and international politics. Early English kingship was an intensely local institution, probably with hundreds of petty kings across England with rising layers of sub-regional, regional and quasi-national overkingship. Whether they had existed from English origins in Britain or had grown is uncertain since there may have been small groups of free peasants crossing to Britain or groups with leaders, or both. We have seen how the scant written record should be reassessed in the analysis of the migrations to Britain in the fifth and sixth centuries. DNA and archaeology are not immune to revision, even if they reveal new finds where the literary sources cannot. The migrants acted within constructed cultural zones over long periods of time, sharing memories and common identities that varied from the point of origin; settled migrants were initially invisible and even burial evidence is subject to ethnic appropriation. The Roman provinces influenced the pattern of settlement, which was more north/south than east/west and there may have been a large British overkingdom like the Merovingian kingdom in Gaul. However, all these are models of sub-Roman Britain. Like the inhabitants of Plato's cave, we are staring at the fleeting shadows, believing them to be a reality, so we would do well to remember the words of Professor James Campbell: 'The natural vice of historians is to claim to know about the past. Nowhere is this claim more dangerous than when it is staked in Britain between AD400 and 600.'[90]

THREE

Rome Returns – Conversion and Coercion

By 600 AD Britain was a patchwork of dozens of petty kingdoms, British and English, composed of the various tribal groups who had migrated since the early fourth century. Western Britain retained much Christian religion, but the new settlers were staunchly pagan, probably a minority amongst their own peoples, the native British who were now subjugated to them. After two centuries, Rome returned, in the guise of missionaries rather than legionnaires, using the strong links between Merovingian Francia and Kent as a bridgehead. Conversion was rapid enough, and what emerged was a new sacral kingship founded as much upon the pen as the sword. Laws, customs and property agreements previously based upon oaths or other oral agreements appeared on the page for the first time. The new political landscape was dotted with monasteries filled with libraries and learning closely allied to the network of kings. This was very much a Roman triumph over Celtic Christianity. It was also part of the ongoing conquest of the 'English' over the native British.

The unpalatable truth of the conversions of the pagan English is that they are steeped in slavery from start to finish. When Pope Gregory the Great saw the Early English slave boys at the market in Rome the fact that the boys were slaves – with their 'fair complexions, handsome faces and lovely hair' – was not a problem for Gregory; the problem that weighed heavy on Gregory was that they were heathen. Sighing deeply, he proclaims: 'Alas that the author of darkness should have men so bright of face in his grip, and that minds devoid of inward grace should bear so graceful an outward form.'[1] Presumably this was not an issue for Bede, either. The most famous of Early English slaves was Bathild, wife of the Merovingian king Clovis II (639-57), bought for a small sum as a household slave for a mayor of the palace.[2] Marseilles was a major centre for the trade. Roman law included a special form of manumission but at no time did the Church condemn the institution of slavery in the Middle Ages.[3] Slavery is a constant, though shadowy, feature of Early English history from Gregory's market trip to the post-Conquest era five centuries later; when looking at the conversions to Roman Christianity it is bound up not only in the origins of the 'English' but with the fate of the 'British'.

The story of the slave children was already well-known when Bede retold it in his *Ecclesiastical History* since it is included in the anonymous Monk of Whitby's *Life of St Gregory c.*704-714 and Bede says how it came down as a 'tradition of our forefathers'.[4] We have already seen how the story has become part of the national mythology of the birth of England and England's racial superiority, but to what extent Bede was concerned with the notion of 'England' rather than the 'English' is questionable. Significantly, but often overlooked in the teleological search for a united England, is the connection with *Rome* above all else. Gregory's missionaries of 597 were not interested in surviving British Christianity, evidenced by the cult of saints which had spread to almost every part of the island under British control by the sixth century (and so might account for the 'miraculous' conversions of the masses).[5] Their aim was establish the Church of St Peter in Rome (597 was also the year that Columba of Iona, the first to bring Christianity to the northern Picts, died and so the year coincidentally pivots Celtic Christianity with Roman Christianity).

The inconvenient truth of the treatment of the British Christians for Bede was explained away by following Gildas's lead as just punishment from God, exemplified by the slaughter of the monks of Bangor, who had refused to submit to or accept Augustine. In Bede's words, Augustine warned the monks that they would suffer the 'vengeance of death', and this came to pass 'through the workings of divine judgement' in the form of their slaughter by the pagan King Æthelfrith of Northumbria, already noted by Bede as a ravager, exterminator and conqueror of the Britons.[6] In Bede's eyes at least, it was better to be an 'English' pagan than a 'British' Christian, since it was subjection to Rome that mattered and by the time Bede was writing, the conversions had taken place and he could look back on Æthelfrith as a kind of Saul, king of Israel, pagan or not.

Northumbria, Bede's own region, not 'England', was Bede's key point of reference (the *Ecclesiastical History* is dedicated to King Ceolwulf of Northumbria).[7] The boys Gregory saw at the market were from the kingdom of Deira (Northumbria combined the two British kingdoms of Deira and Bernicia). Not only do the *angli* boys have 'angelic' faces but Bede has Gregory pun on Deira which becomes '*De ira*! Good! Snatched from the wrath of Christ and called to his mercy.' The third pun is on the name of the already notorious King Ælle, whom we know from Bede to have been the first king of all those south of the Humber, but in this instance Gregory proclaims 'Alleluia! The praise of God must be sung in these parts.'[8] It does not matter that Ælle was a pagan because he was English and it was his son Edwin, who became king of a united Northumbria and was baptised in 627.[9] Ælle's descendants were not only kings of Northumbria but saints and abbesses and his reputation flourished throughout the Middle Ages; William of Malmesbury, writing in the early twelfth century, thought he was one of the main foundation stones of Christianity among the English, a measure of Bede's enormous impact.[10]

It was Gregory's mission that specifically addressed the notion of the English. He sent Augustine firstly to Arles where he was consecrated 'archbishop of the English race', and Gregory's letters initiated a papal diplomatic usage of *rex Anglorum*, which would make Gregory the father of Englishness itself.[11] Gregory consistently referred to *Angli* in his letters, seemingly regarded the name as referring to the inhabitants of England as a whole since he described Æthelberht of Kent as *rex Anglorum*, 'King of the English' in a letter copied by Bede.[12] Perhaps Gregory was either poorly informed as to the different tribes of Jutes, Angles and Saxons, or he understood *gens Anglorum* to mean the collective 'Germanic peoples of the island of Britain' a century before Bede and this terminology was followed by Pope Boniface V, who addressed Edwin as 'king of the English' in a letter coped by Bede in 626.[13] Augustine's mission in 597 marks a change in Bede's own terminology since before 597 he refers to the pagan Germanic people as 'Saxon' but afterwards the 'Saxons' are more specifically the East, West and South Saxons.[14]

Bede's conception of the 'Angles' was that of the Canterbury church and of its papal founder, but his vision of England was that of God's dealings with a Chosen People – the *gens Anglorum* were a people of the Covenant as much as the Israelites of the Old Testament.[15] Bede, like Gildas, warned that if the English went down the same sinful path as the British, they would suffer the same fate. Bede did not invent the term *gens Anglorum* and he wrote in Latin, not English, and did not think necessarily think of himself as English.[16] *Gens* is ambiguous: it is a people, not a nation or tribe. *Anglorum* could refer to the Continental Angles, or those in Northumbria, or the Mercians or to the tribes who eventually become the 'English', or to those who spoke English.

It is not necessarily the case that Bede or the Early English thought themselves God's elect as writers from later periods believed, or that Bede's writing were another step in the inevitable rise of Christian kingship.[17] The impact of the rise of Islam was known by Bede and sharpened his convictions in his writings; it may have shaken his conviction of the dominance of Christianity and with that perspective in mind, Bede's writings are not so much 'nationalist' but an advocacy for Christendom more generally, foreshadowing the great existentialist crisis the English kingdoms would face when almost vanquished by the Viking 'heathens' in the later ninth century.[18] Bede would have been familiar with the ten books of the *Histories of the Franks* by Gregory of Tours, the late sixth-century bishop who created the narrative of God's reward for the conversion of their first great king, Clovis, and he understood that one way in which new ethnicities were developed was by manufacturing a common history; according to Bede, Augustine landed at Thanet and the late ninth-century *Chronicles* place the arrival of the mythical Hengest and Horsa in east Kent, too, thus combining the origins of nationalism with Christianity.[19]

Since we are not looking at 'England' at this point – or indeed for another three centuries – but instead at the wider notion of the Christian world, we need to look beyond Britain, for the origins of the Roman conversions lie more with the rather prosaic but complex political and economic links with the Continent, specifically with Francia, rather than with the blond English slave boys of legend. There were bigger things at stake. In 589, King Reccared of the Goths formally abandoned Arianism and adopted Catholicism, but crucially, Augustine was not cold-calling when he arrived in Britain eight years later in 597 on his mission from Rome. King Æthelbert of Kent's wife, a Frankish lady named Bertha, was already a Christian. Bertha arrived with the Frankish bishop Liudhard and was herself the daughter of a discarded wife of a dead king; Æthelberht's marriage to Bertha might suggest subordination to the mighty Merovingian kingdom across the Channel, especially since he 'received her on condition that she should be allowed to practise her faith and religion unhindered'.[20]

A letter from the Frankish king Theudebert I to Emperor Justinian I (525-565) lists the people over whom he has authority, including the *Eucii* – the Jutes of Kent and the south coast. Kent was peripheral to both central Britain and the Merovingian realm across the Channel. The Merovingians exercised influence over the Saxons, Thuringians, Alamans and Bavarians over the Rhine. The death of Childebert II of Austrasia in 596 left the Frankish kingdoms partitioned into three and it was at this point that Æthelberht asked Rome for a bishop. The continuing influence of the Merovingian kingdom is seen when the Frankish realms were reunited by 614 under Chlothar II and at a council of bishops, the bishops of Dorchester and Canterbury attended.

The presence of Frankish objects in Kentish grave goods now takes on a new political meaning, associating materials with culture rather than the genetic origin of the buried people as part of a show of power-alliances across the Channel. A Frankish alliance would also support Æthelberht in the internal wars between the various Early English 'kingdoms' of the late fifth century if we are to accept the model of a large kingdom in Britain beginning to lose its authority to the smaller kingdoms of Kent, Sussex, Essex and the West Saxons. In this light, England's experience becomes different to that of the European states and there is the need to create an origin myth; the Angles, one of the various groups of Saxons and Jutes, was the named group that caught the attention of Gregory the Great, which led to a common Christian identity combined with ethnic origin: a single English kingdom was anticipated by a single English Church.[21]

Conversion was rapid but far from conclusive. Bede described Æthelberht as 'the third English king who ruled over the southern kingdoms, which are divided from the north by the river Humber and the surrounding territory, but he was the first to enter the kingdom of heaven.'[22] This was the new model of rulership unknown to the Early English, one based on biblical teachings. However, in Bede's own words, there was a 'severe setback' after the death of Æthelberht in 616.[23] Æthelberht's successor and son Eadbald was not Christian when he became ruler and it was not until his son, Eorcenberht, became king in 640 that the royal command was given to destroy idols in the kingdom, according to Bede.[24] It is uncertain how many people in Kent were Christian, but it is likely that communities had not converted or had indeed reverted to non-Christian beliefs. Rædwald was initially converted in Kent but 'on his return home, he was seduced by his wife (a piece of Biblical licence from Bede, perhaps, or testimony to the influence of a king's wife) and by certain evil teachers and perverted from the sincerity of his faith.'[25] The West Saxon king Cynegisl was baptised around 635 but his successor Cenwealh was not a Christian when he became ruler, like Eadbald in Kent; as late as 688 Wessex had a non-Christian ruler when Cædwalla abdicated and went to Rome to be baptised.[26] When Theodore arrived in England in 669, there was no bishop in Rochester, or in East Anglia, Mercia and Wessex.

In Bede's view, the pagan sons of the new Christian kings suffered for their apostasy. Eadbald, Æthelberht's son, was punished by fits of madness and the pagan sons of Sæberht of the East Saxons were defeated by the *Gewisse*, the people of Wessex. When the kings of Deira and Bernicia abandoned their Christian faith they were killed by Cædwalla of the Britons, and it was then that Oswald, a man beloved of God, succeeded.[27] Bede also tells us that King Sigeberht of the East Angles was a good and religious man who resigned the office of kingship to his kinsman Ecgric and went to a monastery, but when Penda (a heathen) attacked East Anglia he was asked to fight alongside Ecgric in order to inspire the army with confidence. He refused, 'so they dragged him to the fight from the monastery.' He was killed in the battle carrying only a staff.[28]

Oswald was the ideal of kingship, 'the saintly and victorious king'.[29] Bede's account of the battle of Heavenfield (634) refers to the erection of a cross at the site of the battle when Oswald himself held the shaft of the standing cross while it was fixed in position and then the army knelt and prayed to God to defend them from their enemy, 'for He knows, that we are fighting in a just cause for the preservation of our whole race.'[30]

Bede saw kingship as a morally neutral thing, between the sacred and the diabolic; the essential goal of kingship in Bede's thinking was the furthering of religion and the extension of Christianity and it should be remembered that the *Ecclesiastical History* was intended to be heard as well as read, and was for an audience that included the laity.[31]

Archaeology can illuminate the written accounts. The remarkable 3,500 silver and gold pieces from the Staffordshire Hoard, uncovered in 2009 by a metal-detectorist, was the largest hoard of Early English gold ever found. Since most of the objects are pieces of warrior equipment, the one complete cross and various cross fragments may suggest the presence of monks on or near the battlefield, invoking God in battle. A small strip of gold alloy bears an inscription taken from a verse from the Old Testament book of Numbers: 'When he had lifted up the ark, Moses said "Rise up, Lord, and may your enemies be dispersed and those who hate you flee from your face."'[32] At Winfarthing (Norfolk), a trove of artefacts uncovered in 2014 from a high-status female furnished burial include a circular gold pendant, two pendants made from Merovingian coins and a gold cross-shaped pendant, which suggests the woman was a Christian convert.[33] Most famous of all, of course, are the finds at Sutton Hoo, which in 1939 revealed both Christening spoons and pagan-style grave goods. They also demonstrated the cosmopolitan nature of early seventh-century England; finds include a shield and helmet from Sweden, silver bowls and spoons from Byzantium (the eastern Mediterranean), a sword with gold and garnet pommel from France, cloaks from Syria, combs from northern Germany and a gold buckle from closer to home, in East Anglia.[34] If Sutton Hoo was indeed the grave of King Rædwald, the finds reflect his personal ambiguity towards the two faiths, something Bede explicitly describes: 'he seemed to be serving both Christ and the gods whom he had previously served; in the same temple he had one altar for the Christian sacrifice and another small altar on which to offer victims to devils.'[35]

The conversions and Christianisation of Britain did not occur in the heat of battle. In one of Bede's most famous passages he describes the conversion of King Edwin of Northumbria, but only after 'hours' of deliberation with Bishop Paulinus, a vision, a narrow escape from death in battle with the Rædwald, king of the East Angles and consultation with his 'loyal chief men and counsellors' (a theme of kingship throughout the Middle Ages).[36] With an eye on his secular audience (and written a century later of course), Bede has one of the king's chief men (not Paulinus) describe in evocative language the warrior community they would appreciate, but infused Christian symbolism:

You are sitting feasting with your ealdormen and thegns in wintertime: the fire is burning on the hearth in the middle of the hall and all inside is warm, while outside the wintry storms of rain and snow are raging; and a sparrow flies swiftly through the hall. It enters in at one door and quickly flies out through the other. For the few moments it is inside, the storm and wintry tempest cannot touch it, but after the briefest moment of calm, it flits from your sight, out of the wintry storm and into it again. So this life of man appears but for a moment; what follows or indeed what went before we know not at all. If this new doctrine brings us more certain information, it seems right that we should accept it.[37]

It is Coifi, the high priest of the pagan faith, who rides off on a stallion with a spear (both forbidden) to destroy the shrine at Goodmanham (Yorkshire) with the lance (an inversion of the account of the piercing of Christ's side at the Crucifixion) so that the water flows out to baptise the Northumbrian people.[38] Once King Edwin had made this considered and collaborative decision, he 'with all his nobles of his race and a vast number of the common people' received the faith. Thus persuasion, miraculous intervention and collective agreement form the process of the conversion of Edwin and his peoples, followed by the desecration of pagan shrines and the building of churches.

The issue of pagan shrines had already been thought through by Pope Gregory since they were not to be destroyed but adapted instead, altars and relics incorporated within them and sprinkled with holy water, for 'when this people see that their shrines are not destroyed they will be able to banish error from their hearts and be more ready to come to the places they are familiar with, but now recognising and worshipping the true God.'[39] Fountains and wells could be dedicated to the Virgin, grave goods encouraged to continue as a form of alms-giving or rationalised within the framework of Christian belief, as in the kind of relics placed in the tomb of St Cuthbert (d.687) – a comb, scissors, a golden chalice and a gold pectoral cross.[40]

The network of alliances and common shared practices of the culture of kingship lay behind the early conversions. One of the reasons Edwin converted was because when he sent ambassadors to King Eadbald of Kent (Æthelberht's son) for the hand in marriage of his sister, he was told that it would not be a lawful union since her Christian faith might be 'profaned' by such a union.[41] Edward agreed to safeguard her faith and consider converting himself (perhaps the sort of arrangement Æthelberht had when he married the Frankish Bertha). Following his conversion, Edwin then persuaded Eorpwald, son of Rædwald, to convert. But conversion did not protect these kings since death in battle was something of an occupational hazard. Eorpwald was killed by a heathen called Ricberht. Edwin died with one of his sons, Osfrith, at the battle of Hatfield against Penda in 633, and the other son, Eadfrith, was later murdered by Penda.[42] The saintly Oswald was later killed in battle by Penda at *Maserfelth* (Maserfield) in *c*.640.[43] Edwin's widow, Æthelburh, fled to safety in Kent and sent Edwin's children and a grandson to Gaul under the protection of King Dagobert, which underlines not only the connection with Kent but with Merovingian Gaul.

Pope Gregory's letters with instructions to his missionaries, to Augustine to Æthelberht of Kent and Pope Boniface's letter to King Edwin of Northumbria illustrate the concerted intellectual campaign of conversion. To coin a phrase, the pen is mightier than the sword. The event of conversion might include persuasion and mass coercion of the people under orders of their king, but it would only be made permanent with churches and literacy in a two-way channel of communication and information from Britain to Rome, Gaul and the wider Mediterranean world.

When Augustine arrived in 597 there were no schools and no trace of the educational system of the Roman Empire.[44] Roman monks came with the Gregorian mission. Aidan established the school at Lindisfarne probably in the 630s; the Early English had to learn Latin as a foreign language for Christianity to flourish. Older monks tutored the young boys: rote memorization, repeating aloud, dictation onto wax tablets. Latin was the language of the church, indispensable for understanding the scriptures, formal poetry, letters, treatises, legislation and the language of instruction. The earliest schools in Britain followed the pattern of those in Gaul with the functional aim of teaching future clergy how to read and understand the Bible and perform the liturgy. By *c*.630 schools in Kent could supply teachers for a new school founded in East Anglia by King Sigeberht (who had been baptised during his exile in Gaul) and these schools provided the first native bishops, Ithamar of Rochester, 644, and Deusdedit of Canterbury, 655.[45] Bede's *Life of Benedict Biscop*, a royal thegn turned monk and creator of Wearmouth and Jarrow, tells us of his six journeys to Gaul and Rome in the 660s, and the purchase of the holy relics, gifts, and 'a large number of books' that formed the basis of Bede's own learning.[46] But the 1,400 or so Early English manuscripts that have survived whole or in fragments represent a small proportion of the books that once existed.

The early Christian missionaries would have brought manuscripts from the Mediterranean. These included the St Augustine Gospels, made in Italy in the late sixth century. Archbishop Theodore of Tarsus (668-690) was born in the Greek-speaking part of the eastern Mediterranean. Abbot Hadrian of Canterbury (d.710), 'a man of African birth' according to Bede, possibly from what is now Libya, accompanied Theodore and together they established an internationally renowned school at Canterbury and may have introduced the study of Greek to the Early English.[47] A student of that school was Aldhelm, later bishop of Sherborne, who wrote a book of riddles inspired by the North African writer Symphosius, whose enigmas may have been brought to England by Hadrian. Hadrian may also have brought with him one of the earliest books known in post-Roman Britain, containing fourth-century letters by Cyprian, another North African, works known to Bede, who quoted them. Hadrian spent 41 years in Britain and is credited with introducing the Early English to astronomical theories inherited from Plato and Aristotle.

It was a two-way process; in 716 Abbot Ceolfrith left Wearmouth-Jarrow to take a great bible to Rome, the *Codex Amiatinus* and its style was so closely modelled on Continental design that it was thought to have been made in Italy until the nineteenth century. Bede's own work was copied and widely disseminated. The earliest extant copy of Bede's *History* is the Moore Bede, and it may well have been copied at Wearmouth or Jarrow within a few years of his death, perhaps as early as 735.[48] The single scribe used insular minuscule to write economically and at speed, in long lines and without breaks, decorations or illustrations, in order to service demand for copies of Bede's works. The manuscript was in France possibly by the reign of Charlemagne (r.768-814) where it remained until the seventeenth century.

Monastic schools were the principal seats of learning throughout the Early English period and the concern of monasteries was not with learning as end in itself but as a means of serving God. Women had the same opportunities as men since there were 'double houses' which were under the rule of an abbess. Hild is famously prominent in Bede's *Ecclesiastical History*, typically of noble birth, abbess of Hartlepool and then Whitby. Her sister, Heresith, was also a nun (and mother of King Eadwulf of East Anglia).[49] Women followed the same curriculum as men and they composed letters and verse in Latin, no different from the rest of Europe. The church was a major channel for re-importing Roman ideas including new concepts of royal obligations and moral responsibility between kings and subjects.

Christianity, royal power and social networks were indivisible by the mid-seventh century. The dynastic structures of the royal houses incorporated highest-ranking churchmen and women from the same families in a 'religio-colonial' force.[50] By c.670 the majority of significant churches were run by men and women from royal and noble families and formed an integral part of the networks of power, and by the eighth and ninth centuries it is difficult to distinguish a lay estate from a religious house.[51] It would be a mistake for us today to separate the 'ecclesiastical' from the 'secular' in the early medieval period since most foundations were part of a network of minsters and monastic culture, integral to the royal and noble families who controlled power in the Early English kingdoms. There was, however, a clear distinction between the monasteries and the minster churches, that is, the monks and clergy, in Bede's work as well as other works. There is also evidence for clerical marriage, much to Bede's disquiet, as he thought sexual activity was incompatible with service at the altar, although chastity was a matter of choice at this time.[52]

Seventh-century laws are some of the earliest texts which provide evidence about the presence of Christianity in the English kingdoms; they consist of three Kentish law codes, one West Saxon law code and penitential and canonical material associated with Archbishop Theodore of Canterbury (668-690).[53] Ecclesiasts were primarily responsible for recording and keeping decrees, which explains why the surviving laws were issued only by Christian kings; the conversion to Christianity and the acceptance of Christianity is reflected in the use of written law. 'Conversion' is understood as a personal religious experience in contrast to Christianization, which may include an attempt to enforce Christian rules or values across a society, or the ongoing evangelization in a society during the process of conversion. Early English royal laws are focused on regulating society and do not provide information about individual beliefs.[54]

The law codes of King Æthelbert of Kent, *c*.602, were mentioned by Bede, who states specifically that they were 'written in English'. They are the earliest extant codes of English law and it is no coincidence that they appear five years after Augustine's arrival.[55] They include regulations about churches and their property which may pre-date Augustine's mission, since Æthelbert's wife Bertha was a Christian Frankish princess; or they were produced during Augustine's time in Kent between 597 and 609.[56] The practice of writing in English seems to have originated from the conversions and the use of English implies the existence of a common national language.[57] England was exceptional in developing a written Early English vernacular that functioned alongside Latin. The extensive codes did not come from nowhere; traditional laws were transmitted orally based on Germanic roots, but the arrival of Augustine, who came bearing the Bible packed with Mosaic laws, set them in writing and indeed, Augustine may have drafted the codes.[58]

The Early English had two types of alphabet, the Roman alphabet, learned from the earliest missionaries, and the runic 'futhark' alphabet, brought to England at the time of the migrations and based on the same principles as the Latin alphabet, so literacy survived; we have seen that Gildas wrote within a culture of learning in the early sixth century, probably in the highland zone. Runic letters were designed to be inscribed on stone, wood, metal or bone, but runes were copied into manuscripts out of curiosity; the Franks Casket (in the British Museum) an eighth-century rectangular whale's bone box of Northumbrian origin, is engraved with runes and Roman script.

We should be wary of presenting Augustine's arrival as switching on the lights of 'Dark Age' Britain with Roman Christianity, but also of the Romanised view of 'literacy'. It is assumed that the Early English kingdoms did not tax and were illiterate until St Augustine's mission, but there is no secure basis for this assumption since the silence of the record is uniform on every topic and almost no written sources survive from the highly literate administration of contemporary Merovingian Gaul either.[59] Æthelbert of Kent presumably communicated with Rome by letter and when negotiating with the Franks for his bride, Bertha. The law code was issued only a few years after Augustine's arrival, something the visiting monks surely would not have done in such a short time. All of this reaches back into the late sixth century at least.

It seems a paradox that the laws followed the example of Rome but were written in English but in using the vernacular to speak to his people, Æthelberht was communicating directly with them. Language is power. Old English words contain all the key modern English concepts: life, death, heaven, forgiveness. That said, seventh-century Britain was multi-lingual: British, English, Pictish and Irish, to which we can add Latin; the 'vernacular' in this instance was English and very much based in southern England, in this case Kent.[60] Æthelberht's law code was probably based on an oral tradition whatever the literacy possibilities. It reveals intimate details of social status and a cash compensation culture that reflects the wealth of Kent. It also demonstrates that a change had already taken place rather than showing the process of change. Most of Æthelberht's laws are concerned with theft, murder and compensation for injury and do not explicitly mention Christianity, although the entire code is shot through with the Christian faith. The priority was restitution, not reprisal or retribution and the victim and his family were the enforcers, not the king, so that any feuding was regulated by compensation.[61]

It is remarkable how far the 'state' imposed, or attempted to impose, on all areas of life, with emphasis on breaching the peace, killing and sexual misconduct. Every man had his price and everything was paid for; church property, any injuries at a gathering summoned by the king, theft from the king, killing on the king's estate, killing a freeman, the king's smith or messenger, killing a ceorl, killing a freed slave (or native British person), breaching the king's protection. There was a price for sexual relations with a maiden belonging to the king, sex with a nobleman's serving woman, with a freeman's wife, with a ceorl's serving woman, with a slave woman, abduction, providing weapons in a dispute, highway robbery, breaking enclosures. Even hair-pulling incurred a fine of 50 *sceattas* (probably because long hair denoted free status and therefore this indicates an assault on a free woman). There are *thirty-nine* chapters dealing with compensations for wounds and injuries of all kinds, from toes to testicles.

The injuries are listed from the crown of the head to the toes of the feet, making them easier to remember, suggesting an oral tradition.[62]

Each of these crimes and misdemeanours was costed according to social status. Clearly, for a law to lay down prohibition of such behaviour, we can assume that murder, abduction, fornication, property damage and even hair-pulling was occurring. Marriage was a financial transaction; women were bought and sold. A bride payment is to be paid and if a woman is abducted, her 'owner' is to be paid compensation, unless he returns the woman or compensates her betrothed; if a free woman (marked out by her 'long hair') committed any 'misconduct' then she had to pay compensation. Women could 'go away with the children' though, and she would have 'half the goods'.

It is clear in this law code that the Church was attempting to regulate behaviour, norms, and values in secular society as part of the conversion process. We can see the thinking behind the law codes in Augustine's communication with Gregory that Bede inserts into his *Ecclesiastical History*; with all the authority of two celibate holy men steeped in biblical texts, they decide the issues that will affect women for over the next millennium and a half regarding marriage, pregnancy and baptism, childbirth and church-going, sexual relations after birth, Holy Communion and menstruation, adultery and fornication.[63]

This then, represents the 'official' view of what the Church (including Bede) and Æthelberht of Kent desired in the early decades of the seventh century. But how far these intentions were ever a reality is the question; these laws were an expression of Biblical kingship in alliance with the Roman Church but essentially served as guidance for the people. Avoiding and mitigating violence was a key intention since the 'state' did not exist in such a form as to execute or imprison felons in *c*.602; even the huge financial penalties are problematic, since no coins were minted in Kent until Eadbald in *c*.625 (Æthelberht's successor), so we have to assume that the imported coins were Merovingian in origin, all part of the strong connections with Gaul and the Continent.[64] Coins were used still as bullion and jewellery (such as at Winfarthing), and it is not until the later seventh century that a currency economy was fully functioning, so it is possible that the financial penalties listed in Æthelberht's laws were intended to be symbolic or a code for the future. The only coins in the Sutton Hoo purse (*c*.625) are thirty-seven Merovingian gold coins minted between *c*.575 and *c*.620, but the slightly later Crondall Hoard, *c*.640 (found in Hampshire, now at the Ashmolean Museum) contained mostly English struck coins from London and Kent.[65]

The written and archaeological evidence suggests that these societies underwent a period of religious transition that lasted quite some time; Archbishop Theodore's materials reveal problems arising in such transitional societies over matters such as marriage between Christians and non-Christians, baptism and divorce. One example of the effects of theology in a society acculturating to Christianity are judicial oaths. Oaths probably existed as part of legal process in the English kingdoms before conversion, but in the decrees of Hlothhere, Eadric and Wihtrid, kings of Kent from the 670s to the 690s, there is reference to swearing innocence at the altar; kings and bishops did not need an oath but priests, deacons, clerics, kings thegns and freemen swear at the altar in different ways and according to Ine's laws the oath was equal in value to their *wergild* (the value set upon human life according to status).[66] The decrees about oath-swearing reveal that trustworthiness was connected with Christian belief and standing within the Church and oaths fitted in with consecrated or sacred objects such as crosses or relics. They were part of the process of dealing with new meanings for old concepts. Swearing at the altar is only mentioned once in Hlothhere and Eadric's laws, but by the time of Wihtrid there were a large number of regulations about it.[67]

The laws of King Ine of Wessex in the later seventh century (688-94) take the presence of Christianity as an accepted norm. They were drawn up with the advice of bishops and produced at assemblies attended by religious and secular leaders.[68] Ine's laws demand that children should be baptised within 30 days and include regulations on working on Sundays (a freeman could forfeit his freedom for working on a Sunday without his lord's permission), calculate time according to church feasts, and prohibit fighting in minsters.[69] Wihtrid's laws (690s) forbid working on Sundays, prohibit irregular marriages and prescribe fines for eating meat in a period of fasting, perhaps using Theodore's material as a model but giving the impression that Christianity was well embedded at this stage. Virtually no mention is made in Early English legal material of religious belief or practice other than Christianity with the exception of vague references to 'offerings to devils' and 'heathen worship'.[70] Punishments were not all financial, and included flogging, forfeiture of freedom, the ordeal, maiming (losing a foot or hand) and the death penalty. Responsibility lay upon the accused to pay, his household or community to enforce the penalty. Ine's laws also take a great interest in territory, 'the boundaries of our kingdom', and breaches of the peace: 'foreigners' could be killed as thieves (with financial gain to be had here, two-thirds of the *wergild* going to the king, half if there is no kinsman). Widowed women were to have maintenance and a ten-year-old child was considered of criminal age, still the case in England and Wales in 2022.[71]

In addition to telling us about the Christianisation of society following the event of conversion, the early law codes tell us a great deal about social structures, in particular slaves and the ongoing concern as to what happened to the 'British', which could either be subjugation through slavery or apartheid *en route* to assimilation. The native British survived far longer and were more widespread than hitherto accepted; placenames in Latin and Celtic origin are also seventh- and eighth-century and the 'native' Y-chromosome DNA varies regionally from 27% to 76%.[72]

Slavery features heavily in the law codes of King Æthelbert and Ine, and not just with regard to the 'British'. An enslaved Englishman caught escaping is to be hanged, or if he is killed, no compensation is to be paid. A freeman working on a Sunday without his lord's permission could be enslaved and stealing with the knowledge of the household meant that the whole family went into slavery. There were fines for selling a 'countryman', slave or not. Having sex with a slave woman meant a lower fine. Slaves paid twice as much compensation for stealing. Bede's story of Imma, a Mercian thegn captured on the battlefield by a Northumbrian (in 679) reveals details of social status contemporary to the law codes of Ine. Imma claimed he was a peasant – and so was enslaved – but was found out to be a thegn and later bought back his freedom.[73] Imma was detected by his 'appearance, his bearing and his speech', but the Northumbrian thegn did not kill him as he ought, to avenge his brother in battle, but instead sold him to a Frisian in London. This exposes the honour code of war, where the warrior class, if captured, might be killed and indicates a peasant class who were enslaved.

The laws of King Æthelbert reference the *laeti*, a distinct social group (half-free, possibly manumitted), whose *wergild* was lower than that payable to a free man; similar *wergild* differences between immigrants and natives were found elsewhere in the Frankish kingdom, but this racial distinction had gone by the time of Alfred's laws in the 890s.[74] The racial apartheid between English and British was to some extent exemplified in the law code of Ine of Wessex where the *wyliscmen* (that is, native Britons) are identified differently to his own people with lower levels of *wergilds* (set at 120 shillings) than the Saxons of comparable status, who were called *Englisc* (*wergilds* commonly 600 or 1200 shillings).[75] This effectively granted the British legal status. The archaeological evidence suggests that seventh- and eighth-century average height of males in Early English cemeteries dropped by 15mm, most marked in Wessex with a fall of 1 inch, explained by increasing intermarriage and gradual assimilation of native populations into Early English communities as the social elite became ethnically mixed.[76]

The meaning of 'slave' is not uniform (women were 'bought' and 'sold' into marriage, after all); slave status was one form of a more general legal inequality between Saxons and British that we see in early Wessex, at least.[77] The fact that they were included in Ine's laws suggests that there were enough of them to require protection under law and that the British were an important ethnic group in Wessex. Complete integration between Saxons and Britons had not yet occurred in Wessex, but Ine's code was one stage in the process of assimilation during this time of co-existence under the same authority and was perhaps a mechanism to encourage assimilation. It shows that even by the late seventh century, almost three hundred years after the first Saxons arrived in Britain, there were legal differences between those who had not chosen to adopt the dominant culture of the migrants. Since the Early English were uniquely pagan in the post-Imperial world, conversion now removed a key difference, if we accept that the native British population was Christianised before 597. In this sense, the pagan-warrior kings of the later sixth century were out of step not only with Europe, but their people, too, and these law codes create new delineations of status.

The ecclesiastical organisation set up by Augustine was based primarily on the monastery and to support this lifestyle of prayer, land which produced a surplus was needed, land that was permanently alienated by charter. The warrior class were quick to see the advantages of this. The connection and mutual reliance between the Early English church and the secular elite is clearly reflected in the documentary evidence but also in landscape archaeology. The Church was fundamental in shifting authority from tribute-orientated regimes to ones rooted in agricultural exploitation; power was materialised through agricultural production and the lived experience of rural communities as a social hierarchy, which considered the place of kings as divinely appointed.[78]

From around AD 600 there was a growing interest in altering the landscape, which coincided with intensified agriculture across north-west Europe; cemeteries were planned in orderly rows and buildings aligned on ritual axes; placename evidence – such as Shipton, rendering sheep to its estate centre and Butterley, take a guess – supports the notion of more coherent agricultural units, but the most important evidence is from the written records of the ecclesiastical houses.[79] Minsters were a crucial means of sustaining royal authority and were overwhelmingly populated by royal personnel. From *c.*675, charters demonstrate the dramatic increase of endowments to churches, a 'step-change in the motors of royal power', since warfare and gift exchanges were ultimately an unstable way of organising power relationships; more permanent power required more sophisticated economic and ideological frameworks.[80] Romano-British remains reconnected with Rome, such as the monasteries of Reculver and Bradwell, and since the Early English took no interest in fortifications in the seventh century, the Roman towns were transferred to ecclesiastical control to found cathedrals and ministers.[81]

Christianity equipped kings with a hierarchical belief system and a legacy through the written record. Granting land to the church strengthened horizontal ties between elites in a way similar to gift-exchange. Patronage over appointments, many of which went to royalty, maintained their status and ensured stability within the elite. The Christian faith legitimised kings as divinely appointed leaders, adding further to social cohesion. For the murder of two Kentish princes by King Egbert, their sister Mildrith chose land as compensation to found a monastery, rationalising forgiveness and eschewing blood revenge.[82]

The power of the church in stabilising the economy and society was significant. Churches were focal points in the landscape since the great minsters owned large tracts of land which they could monitor and control through the use of texts. They were the centres of mass-consumption and craft-production. Monasteries were central to the most extensive system or regional and local distribution of commodities since the Roman period. The Church was associated with new kinds of infrastructure such as the watermill, and even different attitudes to labour that were associated with Christianity.

Early medieval law codes show that royal entourages maintained an itinerant lifestyle at least until the middle of the ninth century and indeed the 'farm of one night' survived until the time of Domesday Book. In contrast, most members of ecclesiastical institutions were more static and their practices of prayer, worship and reflection meant that they drew upon a servile community to provide year-round foodstuffs for consumption; this led to more direct forms of agricultural exploitation throughout the seventh and eighth centuries, resulting in core areas or zones of surplus-producing agricultural land called 'inland' or 'home farms'.[83] The main beneficiaries of this were the royal patrons and the vast majority of inland sites seemed to be in the western half of England, examples include land endowed by King Cenwealh of Wessex at Glastonbury (a bounded inner precinct exempt from geld at the time of Domesday Book).[84]

There were economic units typical of home farms in eastern England, such as Fordham in Cambridgeshire, recorded in Domesday Book as part of the demesne of the royal manor at Soham, site of a minster founded by Felix of Burgundy in the 630s but it did not survive the Viking raids of the ninth century. Archaeological evidence shows that Fordham was a dependent home farm for the minster at Soham.[85] Formal grid plans were used in the construction of churches and laying out of settlements from the seventh century, based ultimately on Roman principles, thus realising a type of imperial form and artistic display. West Fen Road, Ely, is the most detailed example of a home farm anywhere in England, dating to the early eighth century and again, a product of gridding. A community living in relative poverty operated a mixed farming economy geared to large-scale food production here.

Malmesbury, in western England, originated as an Iron-Age hillfort and had a minster of great significance by the late seventh century, which was situated within an extensive estate; included in this estate was the home farm at Foxley, laid out in grids.[86] These home farms were not solely concerned with feeding mouths but were a means of materialising new perceptions of social order. Tenement plots represent a shift in concepts of social space, enforcing the ideological position of the servile peasants in the Early English landscape.

The very success of trade, commerce and the monasteries of the later seventh century was to prove fatal when the Justinianic plague returned in 664, arriving in the south coast in the summer but reaching Northumbria by October; this did not occur by overland routes but by multiple entry points from the sea provided by the monasteries in the north, which served as trading centres and engendered a 'maritime epidemic'.[87]

Whitby, Hartlepool, Lindisfarne, Coldingham and Tynemouth were all seaboard monasteries. The close-quarter living conditions of the monks made them especially vulnerable and Bede recounts the 'cruel devastation ... laying low a vast number of people'.[88] By 716, when Abbot Ceolfrith departed for Rome, he left behind around six hundred brethren at Wearmouth and Jarrow, – maybe not all monks – but in the 680s these religious houses had been overwhelmed by the plague.

At the turn of the seventh century Christianity had arrived at a glorious literary and artistic stage. The standard of written books in England was as accomplished as anywhere in Europe, including the works and treasures of Bede, the lives of Cuthbert, Wilfrid, the Lindisfarne Gospels, the *Codex Amiatinus*, Cuthbert's coffin and its precious relics. This recovery may have been the result of the concentration of the smaller houses into the larger ones as well as population renewal, or we must accept that the death toll was not anywhere near as high across the general population, a possibility discussed earlier.[89]

The kings of the seventh century utilised the Church as a primary means with which they created more stable and lasting power.[90] The language of Christianity matched temporal power, the 'heavenly kingdom' of Caedmon's lost verse – the earliest in Old English - which we only know from Bede.[91] Roman Christianity was an empire of the mind, a unifying factor; the supremacy of Canterbury was recognised by all the bishops of the Early English provinces in 669. The Early English kings and bishops, in contrast to the British, associated with major Roman towns such as Canterbury, London and York.

The gradual Christianisation of the English kingdoms during the seventh and eighth centuries had a massive impact on relationships between the populations. It also played an important role in the dual process of state formation and ethnogenesis – but this was not an inevitable process. English paganism may have gone – or at least vanished from view – but paganism in England was reintroduced by the Viking settlers after Bede's death and continued into the eleventh century, when Cnut had to condemn such practices as worshipping heathen gods, the sun, the moon, fire, flood, wells, stones and any kind of forest trees, in his law code of 1020.[92]

Bede wrote that he had sought to put on record 'those events which *I believe* to be worthy of remembrance,' echoing Isidore of Seville's words:

'History is a branch of grammar because whatever is worthy of memory is committed to writing.'[93] Bede's work of reconstructing and remembering the notable events can be taken as a work of suppressing, eliding, not mentioning, and forgetting. What did not make it into Bede's history was, in effect, no longer a part of English history. Even Cædmon's hymn found in Bede is only there by chance, not by historical diligence.[94] But what of those events not thought to be worthy of remembrance? It is to that other, parallel world we now turn, a world of heroes and monsters that complements, not contradicts, Bede's vision of the past and enables us a far deeper understanding of the making of England.

FOUR

Heroes and Monsters

There is another story of the English, a tale told word-of-mouth from generation to generation for perhaps three centuries. It was a story of heroes and kings from the old country in the days before the migration. The hero, Beowulf, might even be part-human, part animal – a wolf, or bear – his name whispered in dark corners of the halls in awe and fear; so mighty were his powers that he ripped a monster limb from limb before vanquishing its mother under the water. He reigned for fifty years before fighting a dragon to the death and was buried in a ship under a mound with all his treasure. Nowhere else is the name 'Beowulf' found in Old English documents or literature. The poem is no mere fantasy; it tells us of the customs and codes of warriors, kings, and of honour, and is in a sense as much a record of the settlement and conversions of the English as the chronicles and charters.

If what is not written down is not worth remembering, then it is consigned to oblivion. This is almost true of the greatest poem in Early English history. The poem *Beowulf* was composed between the mid-seventh and the end of the tenth century – and possibly within a generation of Bede's death – in Old English, the spoken language of the new Early English settlers, as opposed to Bede's Latin, the language of the clerical elite.[1] Only one manuscript of *Beowulf* survives, and only by chance survived the Ashburnham House fire of 1731. It is dated to *c.* 1000 and written in West Saxon hand.[2] Only 30,000 lines of vernacular poetry from the Early English period survive, a mere fraction of what once existed.[3] Until its publication in 1815, it was virtually unknown. *Beowulf* is the longest epic poem in Old English, more than 3,000 lines long, and survives as a single manuscript (undated) alongside several other medieval texts including 'The Marvels of the East', which was itself based on the *Liber Monstrorum*, a Latin text originally composed in the late seventh/early eighth century, which provides an account of 32 creatures. One of them is a 150-foot long dragon, which is of particular relevance given the content of *Beowulf*.

The fact that *Beowulf* is largely taught as a work of literature is testament to the power of the official 'history'. *Beowulf* is literature, Bede is history. Can such a work of fiction, based on centuries of oral tradition, be used as historical evidence? Patrick Wormald argued that the poem constitutes 'vital evidence' for the conversion of the Early English aristocracy.[4] It is a poem, Wormald argued, that represents cultural memory: a new God had been accepted but the memories of the old ways were not (quite) forgotten and in that sense, *Beowulf* is evidence for the totality of the Early English conversions to Christianity (it is a Christian poem throughout).[5] Taken with archaeological finds and DNA research, *Beowulf* as an historical source provides a balance to the conventional account of the period by Bede and offers an alternative vision of England's history and creation, that of memory and landscape intertwined, told and retold to reassure, warn and educate.[6]

Beowulf is a fantasy of hot-blooded heroes and monsters in stark contrast to Bede, but in its own way it informs us of historical facts. The poem is the living, breathing world that was excavated at Sutton Hoo in 1939 and illustrated in even greater detail in the recent discoveries of the Staffordshire Hoard and the princely burial at Prittlewell. It is documentary evidence as to how early kingship actually worked, littered with references to warriors, armour, helmets, halls, swords (in 30 different words), cups, golden neck-rings, objects and gifts. The poem reminds us that the medium is not the message; primarily it is language itself which forms mentalities, not literacy.[7] *Beowulf* is a multi-layered depiction of the heroic life contained in a living tradition of sung poetry. History in this way resides in stories and songs, not textual records and annual chronicles, where the sung past is contiguous to the present; the repeated phrase in the poem 'on that day of this life' suggests the relevance of the vanished age to the living one.

It is an historical narrative, but it is not linear and there are no 'dates': there are memories of the glorious warrior past, fame and glory made ironic by the knowledge of the destruction to come. Meaning and value are transferred through time and the exchange of stories. Beowulf himself is a new kind of hero, a hero of thought, word, and deed; he retells his exploits, revealing his creativity. *Beowulf* is in the epic tradition, from Virgil's Aeneid to the Chansons de Roland and the *Morte d'Arthur* of the later Middle Ages.

Beowulf displays a deeply absorbed sense of the myth of the ancestral migration from the Continent as the founding and defining event that gave the Germanic tribes a shared identity.[8] Just as Bede in his *Ecclesiastical History* was not forming a vision of 'England' (rather the 'English' and

Rome), *Beowulf* does not mention 'England' or the Early English once. In this sense, it can also be taken as an anti-nationalist source, concerned with preserving Continental, pan-Germanic ethnicity rather than the hegemonic, political formations of insular origin Bede was describing, in order to emphasise the racial differences between the Germanic settlers of England and the native Celtic inhabitants.[9]

Biblical and Early English cultural origin myths were superimposed on the past and their point of contact is migration. Kings promoted the songs about their predecessors (Alfred the Great had a lifelong interest in vernacular poetry) and the figures in *Beowulf* were thought to be real people in a real lineage. The mythical Hengest and Horsa, (descended from the god Woden) mentioned by Bede and by the *Chronicle* could have come from the world of *Beowulf* and remind us that 'fact' and 'fiction' were not seen as they are today.[10] The royal House of Wessex blended the fictitious founders of the royal house with 'real' ancestors and the god Woden, too, but went further all the way back to the Biblical patriarch Noah and thence to Adam 'the first man, and our father who is Christ.'[11] Alfred's biographer Asser also traces the descent of the Wessex royal house from the biblical patriarchs.[12] The son of Noah is Seth, born in the Ark and right at the beginning, *Beowulf* associates the sea-borne foundling with Scyld Scefing (Seth), a reference that would not be lost on the audience.[13] Germanic legend is thus integrated within Christian universal history.

The division of the secular and the biblical is artificial since *Beowulf* incorporates Biblical allusions. Whilst the societies in *Beowulf* are pagan, neither Hrothgar nor Beowulf are explicitly identified with pagan belief. Beowulf is, however, favoured by a singular 'Lord.' Beowulf (the name is unique in Early English literature and records generally) is the 'barley wolf' who arrives like a nameless force at the coastal periphery of the kingdom, and like the last sheaf at harvest time he is brought to the heart of the community. He becomes the champion of Hrothgar against the predator who targets not grain but men – Grendel as 'grinder' – who is the descendant of Cain exiled into the moors and marshes away from the productive landscape. Beowulf, the 'bee-wolf' or bear, is the defender of the community and the fields.[14] He is part-enchanter, part-monster, his name so unique to society that it was perhaps only whispered for fear of conjuring him up from the shadows. In a time of already established traditions and growing bureaucracy in kingship and government, Beowulf is the outsider; dangerous and romantic, an essential counterfoil to the rather mundane rules-based society that was becoming the norm.

We might discern real events behind *Beowulf* in the Swedish Wars, which provide a meaningful backdrop to the main action of the dragon fight and Hygelac's Frisian raid can be dated to *c*.530.[15] The night-time raids of Grendel could also be said to represent the real-life lightning raids such as the one on Sandby Borg, on the shore of the Oland Island, off the south-coast of Sweden, during the Migration Period in the mid-fifth century, the dramatic time of *Beowulf*. Inhabitants of the village were massacred in a devastating raid and their bodies left to rot, including old men, teenagers and babies. The raid was so catastrophic that time stopped; nobody buried the dead, leaving their possessions untouched (including jewellery and Roman coins) and the livestock to starve to death.[16]

Beowulf describes three pagan kingly ship burials, two of which could be the Sutton Hoo burial down to the finest detail; the first is Scyld Scefing, laid to rest in his ship, arrayed with 'weapons of war and harness of battle' with 'many precious things and treasures brought from far away' and how the 'massed treasure was loaded on top of him.'[17] The third burial is Beowulf's, closing the narrative arc of the poem, but this time rather than setting the ship afloat into the sea, the corpse was burnt on a funeral pyre and thereafter a memorial tomb was built on the 'seaward slope' or 'headland' and in the mound was laid 'armlets and jewels, 'abandoning the treasure of mighty men to earth to keep' – at least until the summer of 1939, in the case of Sutton Hoo, at the headland overlooking the Debden.[18]

Beowulf's funeral scene was based on Roman funerary rituals drawn from the close relations between the late Roman Empire and Germania and connections have been made between Attila the Hun and the Sutton Hoo ship burial, a reminder of the prevailing pan-Germanic culture.[19] However, the account of Attila's funeral also included reference to a human sacrifice, so the author of *Beowulf* has probably toned it down to integrate heroic values into the Christian world view.[20]

In *Beowulf* we see how the (male) bonds of society operated, the norms and values that charters and law codes don't fully express. Service to the lord was everything: sharing the hall in times of peace and being prepared to die for their lord in war. Lordship was even greater than kinship and this was no mere literary convention. Warriors followed their lords into exile and died for them; in 685 King Ecgfrith fell in battle along with all his bodyguard. In 625, Lilla, a thegn of Edwin of Northumbria, took the assassin's sword; Bede tells us that Cwichelm, king of the West Saxons, was sent with a poisoned sword under the pretence of delivering a message: 'He suddenly leapt up, drew the sword from beneath his cloak and made a rush at the king.'[21] The greatest treachery was a lord or household troop turning against its king; in 757 Æthelbald king of the Mercians was 'treacherously killed at night by his bodyguard in shocking fashion' and in 759 Oswulf of Northumbria was 'treacherously' killed by his household.[22]

The king grants land and gifts, his men give him their plunder and treasure from the battlefield. The giving of arms and gifts had a symbolic significance and went much further than material benefits. In *Beowulf*, friends and kinsmen flocked to Hrothgar's ranks and he built a mead-hall, a throne-room where he would dispense his 'God-given goods to young and old'. This 'hall of halls' was named Heorot with gables 'wide and high'.[23] After Beowulf kills Grendel, the hall was rebuilt in even greater splendour with gold threaded hangings and the scene is set for feastings, drinking and gift-giving. Beowulf is given a gold standard, breast-mail and helmet and after the minister performed the heroic saga of Finn (a saga within the saga as it were) the queen, Wealhtheow, gives a long speech and passes Beowulf the drinking cup, which serves as a baptism of the new hall, since it has been 'cleansed'. Beowulf is then given gold arm-bangles, mail shirt and rings - which in turn Beowulf will give to his king Hygeleac who dies in battle wearing them.[24] (One of the other six women featured in the poem – queens, warriors, hostesses, peace-makers, mothers and mourners – is Onela's queen, who was apparently 'a balm in bed for the battle-scarred Swede'.)[25]

This bling is exactly the sort of treasure found at Sutton Hoo, the Staffordshire hoard and at Benty Grange (Derbyshire) a boar-crested helmet was excavated in 1848, just as described in *Beowulf*, when Grendel's mother attacked the hall and her sword razed 'the sturdy boar-ridge' off a helmet. Beowulf goes into battle with Grendel's mother with a helmet of beaten gold, 'princely headgear hooped and hasped' and embellished with boar-shapes.[26] The Benty Grange helmet was the first Early English helmet to be discovered and was probably ceremonial; the boar is a pagan symbol but there is a Christian cross added to the nasal, both symbols illustrating the ambiguity towards pagan and Christian faiths of the early to middle seventh century.[27]

Swords too, were vital symbols of power and strength not only in *Beowulf* but in the warrior society the poem illustrates. (The origin of the word 'Saxon' derives from 'seax' a short, stabbing sword). When he sets off to fight Grendel's mother, Beowulf takes with him a rare and ancient sword named 'Hrunting' which had never failed man before (it does this time though, since only a magical blade can kill her). Geoffrey of Monmouth's early twelfth-century re-invention of King Arthur has a sword named 'Caliburn', forged in the Isle of Avalon; King John had a sword named 'Tristan' and by the time of Thomas Mallory's fifteenth-century *Morte d'Arthur* this has become the fabled 'Excalibur'.[28] The named sword and its magical powers are a further example of how the warrior-culture we see in *Beowulf* echoes through time, fact and fiction overlapping to become reality.

Beowulf references more than a dozen feuds, no mere literary trope but central to Early English culture; the one with Grendel is central to the poem and Beowulf is the outsider who joins someone else's feud to establish his reputation.[29] *Beowulf* gives a powerful account of the disasters that can accompany acts of unprovoked or retaliatory violence. Violence and bloodshed permeate *Beowulf* – not randomly but as breaches of the peace followed by restitution in money or in blood, vengeance in the form of peace-making, something the early law codes were attempting to assert.[30] The feud was a process and violence did not always ensue. Killing for the sake of vengeance was not felt to be incompatible with Christian ethics, either, since one of the functions of the law codes was to distinguish illicit acts of revenge from lawful ones, sanctioning vengeance as a recourse after injury.[31] When King Ethelred of Northumbria was murdered in 796, his murder was avenged by one Torhtmund, who was described approvingly by Alcuin in a letter to Charlemagne in 801 as a 'faithful servant ... a man proved in loyalty, strenuous in arms, who has boldly avenged the blood of his lord.'[32]

Beowulf tells us something about the nature of kingly succession during the transition period from older 'Germanic' assumptions with many heirs, to the newer Christian ideals with an emphasis on specific sons.[33] The shift to a direct male line – a three-generation group – also parallels the movement away from smaller, multiple kingdoms contested by many individuals. The rules may not have been written down but were deeply felt. Shared rule was the norm in early Kent and in early Wessex, wherein the chief king nominated his successor in his lifetime and enabled security to develop. The church's concern with legitimate heirs, limiting the candidates to favoured sons following their fathers to the throne was most apparent at the time of the conversions; while Germanic and Christian practice overlap in their emphasis on sons and genealogies (including gods and God as we have seen), the sons must be born of lawful union. A report of legates to Pope Hadrian from 786 records that

> Kings are to be lawfully chosen by the priests and elders of the people and are not to be those begotten in adultery or incest ... neither can he who was not born of a legitimate marriage be the Lord's anointed and king of the whole kingdom and inheritor of the land.[34]

Beowulf was himself an 'ætheling', a member of the royal family and becomes joint ruler of the Geats with Hygelac, who gives him 'the best example of a gem-studded sword in the Geat treasury':

> This he laid on Beowulf's lap
> and then rewarded him with land as well,
> seven thousand hides and a hall and a throne.
> Both owned land by birth in that country,
> ancestral grounds; but the greater right
> and sway were inherited by the higher born.[35]

Incidentally, Hygelac's gift of seven thousand hides was exactly the assessment of the South Saxon kingdom in the 'Tribal Hidage', a document listing hides across the populations of 'southumbria', dated to the seventh/eighth century.[36] This grant of land cemented Beowulf's power and authority and when Hygelac is killed in battle, the 'wide kingdom reverted to Beowulf'.

Beowulf rules for fifty years until he must fight his final monster, a dragon. This is the third monster in the poem; the first was Grendel, half-man, half-beast, killed easily by Beowulf; the second, Grendel's mother, killed in a much harder fight and with a sword from the days of giants, so huge and heavy only Beowulf could wield it; finally, the dragon, which is not of this world and which will kill Beowulf. *Beowulf* is devoted to the freeing of human habitations from the ravages of supernatural creatures that inhabit the fens and from a dragon residing in a prehistoric burial-mound.

The audience would not have felt these themes fantastic or trivial. Monsters were there to advise, warn and teach the audience and Old English literature abounds with dragons, serpents, giants, demons, dwarfs and elves. Significantly, Grendel lives on the margins; he is a 'border-walker', condemned among the kin of Cain, and who bears 'God's ire'. He is a cannibal, haunting the margins, among the 'giants and elves and orcs'.[37] And he was real to the people of the time of *Beowulf*. In the boundaries of a charter dated 739, where Æthelheard, king of the West Saxons, grants Bishop Forthhere of Sherborne 20 hides at Crediton, there is a references to 'grendeles pyt' and in half a dozen other charters, too, Grendel is mentioned.[38] In Derbyshire and Worcestershire there is a Drakelow ('dragon's hill' from the Old English *draca,* a loan word from Latin *draco*); Wormhill near Cambridge derives from *wyrm,* the Old English for serpent or dragon.

Grendel was the outsider and his place on the borders of civilised life reflects the understanding of how landscape functioned in post-Roman Britain. The thirty or so Early English execution sites were located on the boundaries of hundreds and kingdoms from the later seventh century onwards.[39] *Beowulf* refers to the gallows ('...like the misery endured by an old man/who has lived to see his son's body/swing on the gallows.')[40] The later excavations at Sutton Hoo revealed that there were actually three cemeteries at Sutton Hoo; a family burial ground of the sixth century, the elite barrows of the early seventh, and two groups of executions from the eighth through to the eleventh centuries. The first two sites were linked, those earlier burials progressing towards elite status and international prominence. The executions were mainly of young men who were denied burial in the churchyard and interred alongside the road, there to be seen by passers-by.[41]

Kinship, religion, and geographical identity could all construct a 'tribe', but was this enough to support the construction and the riches at Sutton Hoo? The past itself was a source of social power that kings drew upon to control their people and their labour. Some Early English lineages buried their dead within ancient monuments, such as round barrows from the Bronze Age, which were regarded as the dwellings of ancient or ancestral peoples and re-using them created a connection between the deceased's lineage and the world of the ancestors, but in late sixth century monument reuse changed to a focus on single, very rich burials. In the very late sixth and early seventh centuries stratification in society can be more confidently discerned in the archaeological record, alongside the written evidence which records 'kingship' in the 590s as an institution already well established.

Cemetery evidence shows that differences in wealth became clear in the later sixth century with status differences stabilising at the beginning of the seventh.[42] It is no coincidence that the princely burials at Prittlewell and Sutton Hoo were first constructed at this time, as well as other richly furnished graves belonging to powerful ruling elites, such as Taplow in Buckinghamshire. At this stage, these individuals' power-bases were founded upon tribute rather than transferable farming surpluses, similar to Iron-Age tribal leaders. Early English brooches and funerary urns are adorned with symbols expressing that connection to the past, to ancestral origins, in order to construct a new group-identity. If status and position derived as much from real or fictitious ethnic origins as from land, control over the manufacture and distribution of these objects was the source of power.[43]

Beowulf's final battle with the dragon is deeply associated with the power of the landscape, for the dragon guards a hoard in a 'stone-roofed barrow' which is disturbed and this rouses the dragon to a fury. This warning to tomb-raiders illustrates how past peoples were ever present in the minds of Beowulf's time and reminds us how the landscape was littered with Roman temples, Neolithic long barrows, Bronze Age barrows and Iron Age trackways. The Germanic immigrants reused barrows and pre-historical monuments from the sixth to the eighth centuries as physical expressions of land claims and links to ancestors, giving sense to a landscape that the newcomers did not find empty. There was a cultural remoteness of the pre-conversion Early English from the Roman remains in the English landscape, unlike on the Continent where the Franks thought themselves the heirs to Roman civilisation; the immigrants to Britain encountered an entirely different built environment and 'brought with them a different tradition of architecture, in wood rather than stone, small enclosures rather than villas and cities, without the roads, bridges, walls and aqueducts of Roman civil engineering, choosing to live outside those Roman sites in their own settlements.'[44]

This was still in a landscape dotted with the remains of the Roman stone world, reused in later centuries, but in the migration period they would have been derelict places of awe and wonder, referred to directly by Bede and more obliquely in vernacular poetry, most famously in *The Ruin*, which describes the wondrous wall-stones, halls and baths (it could be Roman Bath) with that phrase *enta geweorc* (the works of giants) which also appears in *Beowulf* and *The Wanderer*.[45] The layout of the seventh-century royal palace at Yeavering was based on the pattern of prehistoric monuments where kings grounded their present in the prehistoric past to legitimize their control over land, resources and social groups.[46]

The increased use of ancient monuments in the seventh and eighth centuries was widespread – perhaps a pagan reaction to the Christian conversions – but more likely the ethnic process of assimilation, creating continuity and redefining legitimation and inventing an indigenous tradition for the descendants of immigrants.[47] In this light, the early law codes of Æthelberht and Ine and Bede's *Ecclesiastical History* present a more certain rhetoric of conquest, but in themselves suggest that the new elites had to reinstate ethnic and religious distinctions in writing. The loss of connection to the vernacular tribal past in gaining written laws, chronicles, and a sweep of history from creation to salvation means that people no longer participate in the remembered past or its transmission, which makes *Beowulf* such a vital link to that tribal past.

There is a sense of futility and loss in *Beowulf*. The world will end, men will die despite their glories and there is a profound exploration of death; *Beowulf* is about an ending, not a foundation. *The Wanderer*, one of the best-known Old English poems, like *Beowulf*, has been seen variously as a Christian and a pagan poem, and like *Beowulf*, cannot be dated, since it was created as a performance.[48] *The Wanderer* (and *Beowulf*) represent the cultural shift from a world of oral discourse to a world of textual authority, from communal song to chronicle. Their very survival demonstrates how we are part of that shift, enshrining those texts while lamenting the loss of *Beowulfs* that were never transcribed – the poetry becomes the ruins of the past, rebuilt and reorganised. *The Wanderer* speaks of the past, of loss and mourning, and shines a light onto cultural mores; the mead-hall, gift-giving, lordship, the mail-clad warriors, and exile. The poem lingers on the scenes of ruin and destruction of the crumbling banqueting halls; the ruins represent the obliteration of memory and a nostalgia seen in *Beowulf*, and another poem, *The Seafarer*'s lament for lost kings, emperors and treasure-givers.[49]

These poems have none of the certainty of Bede's *Ecclesiastical History*, rather a grief for those who have gone before, the ghosts of the vanished heroes in the ruins of the past. They consider not only the transient nature of life on earth but the memory of migration and pilgrimage from across the sea (*Beowulf*'s 'whale-road'), a reminder of the cultural identity of the Early English as immigrants. Bede saw the ruins all around him as reminders not of judgement (like Gildas) but of past success and how the Christian church could restore and regenerate.

In the words of Professor Michael Clanchy, 'Literacy may liberate or it may confine.' The poem *Beowulf*, though infused with Christianity, is mourning for a lost world that is entirely non-Roman in outlook. There are no dates, or linear format, and no salvation at the end; but what is seemingly literary fantasy is evidenced by the archaeological discoveries of the nineteenth and twentieth centuries. The more we find, the more it becomes a reality. *Beowulf* is no diversion into literature; it does not conflict with those other, 'official,' written sources, it is a part of the very fabric of the early medieval world. It is one area where historical accuracy and fantasy collide. It is the privilege of the poet to invent or to exaggerate for dramatic purposes just as historians did, as we have seen. *Beowulf* adds colour and heat, light and darkness onto the historical canvas of honour and loyalty. It shows us, uniquely, what it was to be a good lord or king in the land that the migrants now inhabited, which they would one day come to know as 'England'.

FIVE

Saints and Kingdoms

By 700 AD the English were a dominant force in parts of Britain but there was in no way a sense of an emerging, unified 'England'. The English kings were pre-eminent at various times and places south of the Humber, from Northumbria to Mercia and to Wessex, but their identity and survival was strongly linked to Rome. A cult of saints replaced the pagan warriors and the written word advanced the authority of the rulers. A functioning monetary economy entrenched the wealth and power of the kings and London, as in Roman Britain, was the richest trading port. Ethnic supremacy over the native British was clear and those outside the laws and fiscal codes of the English kingdoms were marked off by a vast dyke stretching 150 miles along what is now the border with modern-day Wales.

We have the heroic death and dramatic funeral of Beowulf, but we also have a detailed description of Bede's own death to set against the imagined retro-pagan scene in *Beowulf*, only this time with all the faith and hope of Christian redemption. The scholar's death is as heroic as the warrior's. Beowulf was buried with his weapons, but Bede dies with his pen in his hand. Cuthbert the deacon, disciple of Bede and later Abbot of Wearmouth and Jarrow, writes to Abbot Cuthwin with news of Bede's passing in 735.[1] It is fitting to have such extraordinary information (even the date of Bede's death, 25 May) about the individual who gives us so much about his own time and recent history.

Taken ill before Easter, Bede continued his prayers and teaching until the end, weeks later, even though breathless and in pain. Finally, and most famously, Bede urges his pupil, a boy named Wilberht, to keep writing, saying (as any good schoolmaster does): 'It is not hard. Take your pen and mend it, and then write fast.' Even into the evening, when he had shared out his few treasures – spices, incense and cloths – and bade a tearful farewell to the fellow monks, he tells the boy Wilberht to finish the last sentence, which he does, whereupon Bede sits on the floor of his cell, singing, before breathing his last.

Bede's influence was immediate and enormous. Archbishop Egbert of York was Bede's friend and former pupil at Jarrow – he and his successor Æthelbert built up a school of York on the model of Jarrow. Their pupil was Alcuin who became director of the Palace School of Charlemagne. Though Bede's popularity declined after the twelfth century, Bede's textbooks were fundamental to education in the Middle Ages and were copied up to the age of printing with a degree of accuracy usually reserved for the Bible.[2] Over ninety manuscripts written in Old English that contain works by Bede survive, 10% of all manuscripts from this period. Five copies of the *Ecclesiastical History* survive from the eighth century, there are no insular copies from the ninth or tenth century – but eleven copies survive from ninth-century France and Germany.[3] William of Malmesbury, one of the key post-Conquest historians, drew extensively on Bede's *Ecclesiastical History* in the early twelfth century.

It would wrong to deny Bede's writings some of the charismatic properties of *Beowulf*. His *Ecclesiastical History* is packed with kings, priests, thegns and nameless warriors acting rashly, bravely, and mindfully, in fits of violence, considered diplomacy and moments of peace. There are acts of savage brutality, kindness and love, visions and miracles. Bede was familiar with English poetry and he seemed to write in English, too, according to Cuthbert's deathbed account. As we have seen, he was partial to repeating gossip and comfortable with merging 'fact' with 'fiction'. Indeed, Bede has more in common with *Beowulf* than we might think, since much of Bede's material in the *Ecclesiastical History* seems to have been hitherto unrecorded traditions, transmitted orally or by letter.[4] Bede's purpose in writing history was to participate in the dynamic process of the unfolding of God's purposes for mankind as the world moved towards final judgement and the end of time. This links to hagiography – the lives of the saints and their miracles – which to Bede were wholly appropriate to historical narrative.

The Early English saints became a shared heritage; celebrations of the festivals of Saints Gregory and Augustine, apostles of the English, had been prescribed since 747 and the list of saints of God resting in Britain was modelled on similar guides to the shrines of Rome.[5] An eleventh-century manuscript (the *Secgan*) lists the resting places of 89 saints from the seventh to the tenth century. The first half of the list is of mainly the Early English saints with predominantly Northumbrian and Mercian resting places, reflecting the supremacy of those kingdoms in the pre-Viking period, whereas the second half of the list includes mostly saints located in Wessex and western areas from the tenth century, reflecting the shift towards the dominance of Wessex.[6] The saints were above all prized for their links to Rome, particularly Gregory the Great, a reminder yet again of the long reach of Rome, which came first over the later, teleological concepts of English nationalism.

Early eighth-century saints' lives had championed a Christian form of warrior kingship and we have already noted how Bede portrayed St Oswald setting up the banner of the Holy Cross before his great victory at Heavenfield. The tradition of murdered saints in the seventh to ninth centuries created cults which were a means of expressing and focussing opposition to the killers.[7] Christian burial rites transformed pagan grave goods into the practice of relics, which included body parts. Bizarrely, Oswald's right arm found its way to the south transept at Peterborough. Since Oswald had died in battle fighting the Mercian ruler Penda in 642, as well as having no particular historical or geographical relevance, he had a rather awkward relationship to the abbey's founding family (Peada, son of Penda, founded the original monastery).

Originally in the possession of St Peter's Church at Bamburgh in Oswald's native Northumbria, the arm was brought to Peterborough by a monk named Winegot some time before the Norman Conquest – a high-profile case of the relatively widespread phenomenon of relic theft. Oswald's body finally rested at Gloucester and his dismemberment was an exception to the norm of keeping the earthly remains of a saint in one piece. Bede describes in graphic detail how Penda ordered his hands and head to be severed from his body, but the arm and hand remained uncorrupt in a silver shrine at Bamburgh, his head went to Lindisfarne while his bones were eventually taken by Oswald's niece Queen Osthryth of Mercia to the monastery in Lindsey.[8]

Bede wrote about kings, the conversions and saints primarily through the perspective of the English people returning to Rome. In doing so, his ethnic terminology of the *gens anglorum* (the English people) was influential and created a new narrative after his death. Alcuin of York's surviving letters date from the 780s to 804 and follow this terminology as well as referring to the whole island of Britain as 'English'.[9] Alcuin writes as if the English church was the church of Britain and the English bishops the bishops of Britain. A small group of charters preserved at Worcester, probably written there, seem influenced by Bede's ethnic terminology. In one, in 736 King Æthelbald of the Mercians is styled king of the 'Suth angli' – south of the Humber – which mirrors Bede in what is a charter of undoubted authenticity.[10] Bede sought to persuade his readers that as a Christian people they were all 'English', but this was in sharp contrast to most writers who thought of themselves as 'Saxons'. This was in part a Northumbrian agenda to extend English control over the whole of Britain though, not an idea necessarily entirely welcome in the churches and royal courts of the southern kingdoms.

It was rare for texts and documents to refer to the English. Later draftsmen styled Offa as 'king of the Mercians' but the only charters in which Offa appears as *rex Anglorum* (King of the English) are texts written or rewritten in the tenth century – by that time, an English kingdom had been established.[11] Forgeries of the twelfth and thirteenth centuries produced at Evesham, Crowland, Peterborough, Westminster and Canterbury all refer to Anglia, *angli* or the English language – but the originals did not mention the English or England.

Bede wrote of the seven kingdoms, which has been interpreted to mean an inevitable transformation to a single state. Until the ninth century, no clear mechanism for royal succession existed; from 685-802, for example, no king of Wessex was succeeded by his close kin.[12] The Northumbrian overkingdom was constructed from the kingdoms of the Bernicians and Deirans in the late sixth century to 679. The Mercian overkingdom was constructed by Penda (d.655), conqueror of England from the Thames-Severn line and the Northumbrian frontier – 'Greater Mercia' – which grew after his death into south-eastern England. In Wessex, the reign of Ceadwalla (685-9) marked the moment of transition, followed by Ine's long reign (689-725/6). The rule of the sub-kings of Surrey, the South Saxons, Kent and the East Saxons was not finally ended until 825-8 when Ecgberht, king of the West Saxons, relieved the Mercian overkings of their south-eastern kingdoms.[13]

The Northumbrian 'supremacy' gave way to the Mercian 'supremacy' in the mid-eighth century, but English 'unification' was treated as if there was an English identity waiting from the outset to be realized, promoted by the 'Bretwalda'.[14] Britain's post-Roman history was much more traumatic than that of most parts of the western Empire, as we have seen. New political entities came into existence and the subsequent refusal of the Northumbrian, Mercian, East Anglian and West Saxon kingdoms to submit to each other rebuts the view that 'England' was proceeding towards unification. There was actually less in Early English history to suggest its future emergence than in comparable European states and no Early English king claimed to be 'king of the English'.[15]

Twelfth-century historians interpreted Early English history through the concept of the seven kingdoms (the so-called 'Heptarchy'), a concept that prevailed until the 1970s.[16] The idea of empire (*imperium*) meant simply the power exercised by one kingdom over another, or others, and these included 'international relations' at a variety of levels within the Early English polity as well as between the English, Britons, Gaels, Picts and Scandinavians.

Behind the kingdoms of the Early English age lay a significant complexity whose dynamic has seldom been understood. The knowledge that the constitutional fact of English monarchy dated to the tenth century has had an all-pervasive impact on the writing of Early English history;

scholars have not bothered with lesser grades of kingship, other than to note the 'tribal' in a pejorative manner; the inevitability of the English, later British, union has derailed scholarly interaction with the evidence for pre-union, pre-monarchical political organisation among the English.[17] Offa, overking of the Mercians 757-96, had forged diplomas in his name with the title *rex Anglorum,* and his actions have been judged in the light of his failing to maintain or develop his predecessor Æthelbald's achievements and therefore paving the way for the terminal decline of the Mercian hegemony.[18] Lesser grades of kingship have been assimilated into aristocratic status, writing out the royal dimension of sub-national government. We should not assume, therefore, that the larger kingdoms emerging in the 700s were either inevitable or that the single 'kingdom of England' that emerged in the 900s was bound to happen, either.

The view that there was a complete and rapid systems collapse in fifth-century Britain leading to a peasant-mode, tribal society reduced to subsistence farming would mean that the first Early English kingdoms that emerged were based on warfare and tribute rather than taxation and exploiting landed resources. This may be true to some extent in the age of Sutton Hoo, but by the eighth century, economic changes were occurring that underpinned political events. Smelting was re-established and by the ninth century large-scale production on farms and estates provided their own high-quality agricultural tools to use and to trade.[19] This production contributed to the re-emergence of a steeply hierarchical society in Britain, spurring on social change in the seventh to ninth centuries. The period 750-950 also saw a tremendous change in the hierarchy landholding practices within Early English society.[20]

The model that any advance towards sophisticated statehood must have been a leap forward, perhaps achieved at royal behest stemming from Viking raids and the Carolingian Renaissance with the reigns of Offa and Alfred as major staging posts, has to take into account the underlying economic developments.[21] Taking the even longer view, and recalling the sub-Roman model of highland/lowland zones where the highland zone retained its prosperity after the collapse of imperial authority in the east, with the early Saxon *foederati* settled in the villa-zone on the new frontiers from where the Mercian/Wessex/Northumbrian kingdoms begin to emerge, the 'Mediterranean system' gave way to the Continental system that shifted trade and power to the south-east to the English, just at the point when the documentation becomes visible *c.*600. By the later sixth century the dominance of the lowland zone was assured.[22] By the latter part of the seventh century kings had centralised control of many essential resources and were taking a cut in profits of manufacture and commerce and by 700, specialised emporia, or *wics*, at London, York and Ipswich were increasingly under royal control and provided markets for agricultural surpluses, which suggests that rural communities were living beyond subsistence.[23] Rapid and standardised dissemination of coins from the late seventh century demonstrates royal control; and the delegation of rights of minting and toll concessions to religious communities reflects how these were adjuncts of royal and noble family power rather than separate areas of ecclesiastical authority.[24]

A monetary economy certainly existed in the early Middle Ages; gold and silver coins changed hands frequently in the countryside as well as the towns. Monetization was deeply embedded in existing social relations.[25] This was not just an era of primitive gifts, barter and exactions of tribute, since coinage became a regular feature at all levels of society, but this need not negate the social underpinnings of human exchange. The considerable wealth of the chief English kingdoms derived from foreign trade conducted through ports of the south and east, Ipswich, London, Hamwic. Silver was imported and minted at Canterbury; Kent was at the centre of this trade, charters from the 730s to 760s relating to the ports of Fordwich, Sarre and Minster-in-Thanet, as well as London. The axis of trade extended from London to Frisia and Dorestad at the mouth of the Rhone. From *c.*700 the West Saxon port of Hamwic traded across to Quentovic, near Etaples, Rouen and the Seine basin. Offa's currency, upwards of six million coins, suggests large quantities of foreign silver entering in exchange for slaves, woollen cloth and hides.[26] Control of Kent underpinned Offa's hegemony in the late eighth century and that of Wessex in the early ninth.

Early English kingdoms were also part of overlordship systems of authority that included Celtic rulers and some members of the Early English elites were of British or other Celtic origin, particularly Northumbria. The Early English kingdoms of southern England were more closely influenced by their connections with the Franks, who may have exercised direct overlordship over some areas of southern England, in addition to having important influence over the formation of the earliest kingdoms and the conversion of the royal houses and aristocracy.[27] This pattern of borrowing from Francia had a major impact in the late eighth/early ninth centuries that lasted well into the tenth century.

There was the common experience of overlordship which put all kingdoms under the command of a temporary dominant authority, the *bretwaldas*: Bede believed that these overlords exercised significant power. Kingdoms did not exist in isolation from one another but were enmeshed in overlordship with larger kingdoms. When the early independent kingdoms were incorporated into larger kingdoms, they preserved their identity as shires since they were set up to function as units to provide payments and services.[28] There was a shared common court culture within the early kingdoms, furthered by intermarriage and alliances, and codes of behaviour such as gift-giving. Movement between courts was a part of the conversions; imitating the Frankish practice of royal nunneries controlled by female relatives in Kent and East Anglia. The *sceatta* coinage minted in Kent had been widely imitated in other kingdoms by the 670s.[29]

In the seventh century the regional overkings – perhaps the heirs of the leaders of the barbarian forces in the fifth century – were in frequent conflict with one another, but we also have glimpses of the dependent royalty operating on a more local level, less interesting and all too often invisible.[30] The model is that the emergent kingdoms of *c*.700 had swallowed up those little kingdoms. The post-imperial 'kingdoms' were tiny, perhaps only a valley or two. Archaeology does not identify an established elite as such, rather groups of kinship than of wealth or class. The number and size of overkings is clear, but what were they before then is evidenced from charters, the Tribal Hidage, and placenames.

Bede mentions the 'provincia' of the Meonware, the 'regio' of Ely linked strongly to the inhabitants and the kindred and these could have been quite extensive lordships but were not a uniform administrative network. Bede also tells us how Mercia was divided between southern and northern Mercia.[31] The Tribal Hidage dates from *c*.700 and lists kingdoms of Wessex, Sussex, Kent and smaller units that may have been lost kingdoms – the *Gyrwe* of the Fens or the *Arosaetna* near Redditch, Worcestershire, the Hwicce in Worcestershire and Gloucestershire, with titles like *sub-regulus* and *regalis*. One illustration of this is a grant to Chertsey Abbey, which talks of Frithuwold, local king (*subreguli*) of *Suthrige* (Surrey) and acknowledges the overlord, King Wulfhere of Mercia.[32] There are four *sub-reguli* on the witness list who may represent other local kings in Surrey and a network of local units or *provincial* or *regio*, as Bede called them.[33] A grant by Uhtred, sub-king of the Hwicce, to Æthelmund, ealdorman and 'prefect' of King Æthelbald of the Mercians, dates to 770 and is the first to mention the three public dues, the *Trinoda necessitas,* the 'three-knotted obligation'.[34] The grant includes Ealdred, also 'sub-king' of the Hwicce, in the witness list. Uhtred also appears as sub-king in a charter of 767, possibly a model for the 770 grant.[35]

Christianity may even have survived in the Hwicce region after the Romans and the British Christian may have converted the incoming Early English; the earliest church in Worcester, St Helen's, may have served as the seat of a British bishop. The continuity of salt production and of Christian practices and possible existence of ecclesiastical authority suggest that the Hwicce region was ordered and stable before the coming of the Mercians, so they assumed control of British authority as well as British territory, rather like Mercian Yeavering.[36] A grant of King Edgar to his thegn Æthwold at Kineton, Warwickshire, in 969, shows the boundary distinctions between Mercia and the Hwicce still existed.[37]

We should not then use later medieval assumption of 'kingship'. Were these small kingdoms even 'states'? They were small regions compared with the Frankish kingdoms, had shifting borders and their fortunes could change in a generation; they are best described as *gentes* recognising a particular royal house. Even though Bede encourages us to see kingship practices tending towards a norm, charters and law codes reveal variations between kingdoms.[38] Professor Barbara Yorke proposed that Early English kingdoms were probably at best 'proto-states' rather than states.[39]

The earliest Eritten Old English records, apart from the Kentish law codes, date from *c.675*; these documents and the earliest narrative sources mention the assessment of land in 'hides', meaning 'land of one family', a unit that fits with Roman to post-Roman systems of the exploitation of the profits of land by elites, yet more evidence of continuity from sub-Roman Britain to early England, even to field systems and minor roads which antedate the Roman conquest, possibly to the Iron Age.[40] The hide was the unit of reckoning on which obligations were levied and was used as such by the time of Ine's law codes, where the *wergild* was based on how many hides of land the victim had.[41]

The Tribal Hidage lists numbers of 'hyda' pertaining to population groups across Southumbria and Bede uses the Latin *familia* in the *Ecclesiastical History* (translated into *hid* in the Old English Bede). Bede lists the hidage of the Isle of Man and Anglesey under the lordship of King Edwin of Northumbria.[42] Southern Mercia consisted of 5,000 hides, Northern Mercia 7,000.[43] The hide was not a standardised measure of surface area, rather a productive capacity, and it was families of certain status who had hides. 'Hide' was not universal across England – 'sulung' was used in in Kent and 'ploughland' in the north-east under Scandinavian settlement.

Regarding the *Trinodo necessitas,* demands and payments varied from one region to another but a 'common burden' or public service, such as bridge-work and fortress-work implies a concept of the state by the mid-eighth century which could also provoke complaints when too much was imposed, as a letter to King Æthelbald of Mercia (716-757) shows, accusing him of 'violating many privileges of churches and monasteries' and stealing from them 'certain revenues'.[44] Kings could call upon a variety of means to get major works completed including personal lordship and wealth, greater lords and their allegiance, the hide system and the *'provincia'*. The English kings were not exceptional in having units of land upon which obligations could be levied. In the early ninth century Francia used the *mansi* (dwelling) as a reckoning of service owed.

The shifting sands of these growing overkingdoms moved dominance away from Northumbria to Mercia in the early eighth century. Bede notes that 'all these kingdoms and the other southern kingdoms which reach right up to the Humber, together with their various kings' were subject to Æthelbald of Mercia in 731. A charter of 736 (a Worcestershire scribe, admittedly) styled him 'king not only of the Mercians but also of all the peoples which are known by the general name South Angles.'[45]

The rise of Mercia owed as much to the profits of peace as to the spoils of war. The English economy experienced rising prosperity in the period 675-725 more generally, with enormous expansion of the silver coinage from *c.*700. Ipswich expanded, York was probably founded around this time, but London dominated with a population of 5,000 to 10,000. The River Thames gave London the advantage, reaching into Oxfordshire, the west Midlands, Chilterns and Cotswolds. Gold coins bearing the legend *Londenus* were struck for Ealdbald, king of Kent 616-640, and by the time of Egbert of Wessex who ruled the city in 829, they were inscribed with *Londonia Civit[as]*, recalling London's Roman past, which gave added authority to the ruler of the city.[46]

Control of London, England's greatest trading port, and the Droitwich brine-pits, chief source of salt, provided the Mercian kings with wealth to bolster their kingship.[47] The brine springs at Droitwich ('Wic') in Worcestershire had been worked for salt since the Iron Age, were exploited in the second century in Roman Britain and were famous in Bede's time. Monopoly control of Droitwich salt was as calculated as the Mercian appropriation of the territory around London in south-west Middlesex.

London, or 'Lundenwic,' began to develop economically from around 650, expanding from the 670s to the 730s and reaching its zenith from 730 to the 770s with population increase, textile production, and the production of luxury goods and artisan goods. London had trading connections to the north European seaboard, from Normandy to the Rhine mouth and from the Seine valley to the Meuse. Bede calls it an 'emporium for many nations who come to it by land and sea'.[48] It may also have been a slaving capital like Viking Dublin, fuelled by Mercian wars, and we have already heard of Bede's story of the captured Northumbrian nobleman Imma, given to a Mercian lord after the battle of the Trent in 679 and sold on to a Frisian slaver in London.[49]

Toll stations could be established where any river crossing or upland pass served as a funnel for commercial traffic, such as at Lechlade, or at the wics themselves, London, Droitwich and Hamwic. The toll remission for the Bishop of Worcester and the Worcester community *c.*745 by Æthelbald points to the trading links between Droitwich and London.[50] Granting salt-rights, lands and remitting tolls stimulated the growth of monasteries as well as trade. Exemptions and remissions demonstrate that commerce was already subject to tax.

Aethelbald of Mercia called himself 'king, not only of the Mercians but also of the neighbouring peoples over whom Divine dispensation wished me to rule without judgement on my merits.' But Mercia reached the summit of its fortunes under Offa (757-796).[51] Offa extended the borders of Mercia outwards to Lindsey and East Anglia, west to the Hwicce and the southern kingdoms of Kent, Surrey, Sussex, Essex, minting coins in Canterbury, London and Ipswich and in 794 executing the king of East

Anglia; his daughters married kings of Wessex and Northumbria. The sub-kings may have been reduced to ealdormen, but there was no drive towards conquering the major kingdoms.

Offa's rule was strongly affected by the Carolingian Renaissance, he founding new churches at Westminster and Bedford and receiving the first papal legates since Augustine's mission in 786. He used the Church to bolster his dynasty and kingship. Offa was in correspondence with Charlemagne and his Northumbrian advisor Alcuin and received gifts from the Avar hoard in 795; like Charlemagne, he crowned his son Egfrith as king in 787 and suggested a Carolingian princess in marriage, but Charlemagne also played the diplomatic game that lasted a millennium between the Continent and England, harbouring exiles at his court, including Egbert and Eadbert who became kings. Offa was a pan-Germanic ruler who saw himself on the same podium as Charlemagne. The 149-mile Dyke between England and Wales was as much a statement as a practical border; the primary function of Offa's Dyke was perhaps ideological, not military, part of the 'pan-Englishness' of Offa's domination south of the Humber, similar to other European large-scale works such as the *Danevirke*, an earthen wall across the southern end of Jutland, separating Germany and Denmark, Charlemagne's planned canal connecting the North Sea and the Rhineland with the Danube River, and the Kanhave Canal on the Danish island of Samsø (*c.*726) 1, 640 feet long.[52]

Offa was no mere collector of tribute. There were Continental alliances – nothing new since we have seen the influence of the Frankish kings on English internal affairs since the late sixth century; there was an appreciation of the cultural glue that held together kingship, of show and grand statements. He was styled *rex anglorum* (in later documents) but more commonly *rex Merciorum*. He was clear about his dynastic priorities, 'purging' his collateral heirs, something referred to in a letter from Alcuin to a Mercian ealdorman, in order to guarantee his son Ecgfirth's succession: 'For you know very well how much blood his father shed to secure the kingdom on his son.'[53] This backfired though, since in 796, at Ecgfrith's death, a distant relative succeeded.

None of this need point towards Mercia being a necessary but flawed precursor to the Wessex-focussed kingdom of the English.[54] The Mercian kingdom was seen as more fragile and decentralised than Wessex, but Mercia had systems of fortification and military obligations a century before Alfred of Wessex. The rulers of Wessex would adopt and extend Mercian systems so effectively that they would be assimilated into the Wessex achievement.[55]

It was not in Offa's power to end the petty kingship in England among the West Saxons and Northumbrians; the kingship of the East Saxons outlived Offa by thirty years. In the mid-ninth century there were at least fourteen kingdoms in the island of Britain (Asser tells us that there were at least five in Wales in 893); five of these lay partially in what would become the post-Conquest kingdom recorded in Domesday Book in 1086: Cornwall, Northumbria, East Anglia, Mercia, West Saxons.[56] In 825 the balance of power was overturned by Egbert, king of Wessex at the battle of Ellendon (Wroughton, Wiltshire) and by 829 Kent, Surrey, Sussex, Essex, East Anglia and Mercia submitted to him. In 830 he gained the submission of the Northumbrians.

The building of the Dyke effectively created the modern border with Wales and cemented not only England's western boundary but settled the permanent exclusion of the 'Welsh' from the *Englisc*. Ecgberht of Wessex led an army into Wales in 830 and reduced them into submission, according to the *Chronicle*.[57]

It is no coincidence that at precisely this time of English expansion the earliest evidence for a British hero appears, that is, King Arthur. Nennius, writing in Wales in the early ninth century (although the earliest manuscript dates to *c.* 1100) refers to the so-called Battle-list of Arthur, in his *History of the Britons,* a list of twelve battles dated to the fifth/sixth centuries.[58] Nennius knew about Badon from Gildas (or from Bede who cites Gildas). The poem known as *Y Gododdin* was written by Aneirin, a poet mentioned in the *History of the Britons*, around the same time, which describes the feats of a warrior but says 'he was not Arthur' (he does not tell us who Arthur was) although it does suggest that he had heard of Arthur, real or not. The Welsh Annals were compiled in the tenth century and two entries refer to Arthur with precise dates: in 516 Arthur won the battle of Badon and in 537 at the battle of Camlann 'Arthur and Medraut [later known as Mordred] perished.' This is the sum of all evidence for Arthur between 500 and 1000 AD. Rather like the English hero Beowulf, he did not exist, and is located in a fictitious earlier time, in this case not the migration period, rather the crisis of the British kingdoms following the departure of Rome. Arthur's arrival on the literary scene tells us more about the events of the early ninth century than the fifth century where he is placed. Arthur was to become the emblem of the later medieval English warrior elites.

The events of 829/30 point to a change in direction, certainly, but not to the inevitable 'rise of Wessex' and consequently, 'England'. This was happening for another reason altogether. The Early English kingdoms were about to discover a force more monstrous than Grendel, his mother and the dragon put together, something that neither God nor any of the compensatory attributes of the vendetta could deal with: the Vikings.

A modern sculpture of monks carrying the coffin of St Cuthbert; Viking raids on Northumbria would force them to carry his remains around in search of a safe resting place. This sculpture now rests at St Mary's Church on Lindisfarne.

PART TWO

The Fury of the Northmen

793–1066

SIX

Alfred or Guthrum?

The English kingdoms were all but wiped out by the Viking raids that became full-scale invasion and settlement in the later ninth century. The English who had settled, assimilated and enslaved the native British population were themselves engulfed. There is little doubt that they faced extermination since their ferocious enemy was pagan, so it was to be a cultural as well as a military conquest. But one king in the western region survived, with good luck more than anything else, and fought back just enough to hold the line. This king, Alfred of Wessex, knew that military successes were not enough. He needed all the force he could get from Rome, and this came through the written word as much as prayer. New histories of the English were written, and a renewed identity was shaped by the greatest existential crisis the English had ever faced. Even so, there was no 'England' yet.

On 8 June 793, 'heathen man came and miserably destroyed God's church on Lindisfarne, with plunder and slaughter.'[1] It had been a strange time of portents in Northumbria, with immense flashes of lightning and fiery dragons seen flying in the air, and famine followed. The Viking raid destroyed the great library of Bede and all but extinguished Christian learning in Northumbria, sending shockwaves through Europe. In Charlemagne's court, Alcuin of York wrote that the 'church of St Cuthbert is spattered with the blood of the priests of God, stripped of all its furnishings, exposed to the plundering of the pagans.'[2] The ransacking was perhaps a sign of some 'great guilt', a theme that runs through the Viking raids and eventual conquest of England to 1016. The murderer of King Ælfwald of Northumbria, Sicga, killed himself and was buried on Lindisfarne weeks before the Vikings attacked and this was seen as a cause of the pagan assaults.

Other sources shed light on the early Viking activity as well as the letters of Alcuin, including a letter to the clergy and nobles of Kent in 797. The Annals of Ulster record extensive raids from 794 onwards on the Gaelic churches of Ireland and the Royal Frankish Annals, which record Viking raids on Francia, suggest communication between Pope Leo III, Charlemagne, King Coenwulf of Mercia and the Vikings over hostage-taking. Charter evidence as early as 792 from Kent reveals how preparations were made for building bridges and fortifications 'against the pagans'. This was a privilege granted by Offa, king of the Mercians, who ruled over Kent at that time and the Viking raids may have been an opportunity to introduce the three-fold obligations of army, bridge and fortress service into Kent.[3]

The Viking raids on England, from Lindisfarne to Kent, were no isolated event but part of a wider movement that also attacked Francia (Aquitaine and Frisia), which increased after Charlemagne's death in 814. From the Western, Christian perspective, these assaults come down to us as a bolt from the blue, but Scandinavians were no strangers to the British Isles or the Continent, since they had formed cultural contacts for centuries, including the very migrations that made up the English peoples, as we have seen from the physical evidence at Sutton Hoo and the literary memory in *Beowulf*. They were a part of the trading network between Britain, Frisia and Francia, a European commercial diaspora that looked towards the west since Dublin was one of the great commercial entrepots of the western world, trade based on maritime enterprise and slavery. The assault on Lindisfarne may even have been a mistaken or opportunistic landfall (the monastic community survived) and many of the furnished graves in Britain and Ireland were of Frankish origin, so we are not necessarily looking for a 'colonial' Scandinavian imprint.[4] The recent discovery of the Galloway Hoard, unearthed in 2014, reveals how the 100 or so objects that include silver jewellery, ingots, amulets and jewelled æstels were distinctly Early English in many ways, but associated with Viking discoveries around the Irish Sea coastlands.[5] To what extent the written record has created a binary narrative of Christian/Viking as much as the original English/British narrative we explored in chapter two is pertinent here.

The impact of Viking activity from Scandinavia to northern Francia and the British Isles, including Ireland and the Northern Isles, explains what happened to the English kingdoms. It was the early Viking raids in Kent that allowed Wessex to wrest control of Kent from Mercia. Following the death of Coenwulf in 822, King Ecgberht won his famous victory at Ellendon over King Beornwulf of Mercia and sent an army to bring Kent under West Saxon control. Wessex was thus the inheritor of Mercian authority, annexing Kent in 825, placing the monasteries under his lordship. Kent was hard hit by the Viking raids; Sheppey devastated in 835 and 841, with 'great slaughter' in the attacks on Canterbury, Rochester and London in 842.[6] It grew far worse in the 850s when the Vikings wintered in Thanet and Sheppey, returning in 865 to devastate eastern Kent. The trading ports of Reculver, Minster-in-Thanet and Sarre failed to survive in the later ninth century, shrinking to villages. The religious communities of Lyminge, Folkestone and Dover also failed and even the religious community at Canterbury came close to extinction.[7] London was captured in 877 but had ceased to produce coins in the mid-850s to 860s. The coinage was heavily debased as a result of these raids: only 16% of Alfred's coins contained silver in the mid-870s and this downward trend reflects the increasing severity of the raids from the 830s onwards. The great port of Hamwic declined and collapsed, virtually abandoned by 880, to be replaced by its neighbour, Hamtun (Southampton). Canterbury ceased to be the predominant mint.

There is no doubt that this was the greatest existentialist threat to the English peoples since the conversions. The established balance of power between the emergent kingdoms of the eighth century, the common culture of kingship and the spiritual empire that placed those kingdoms on the periphery of Rome, was facing oblivion and the Early English knew it. One common formula in charters in Canterbury, Worcester, Winchester and Rochester from 790s-868 is the phrase 'as long as the Christian faith shall endure among the English in the island of Britain', reflecting the insecurity of English Christian writers after the sack of Lindisfarne in 793 and during the century of pagan Viking activity that followed.[8] The Viking army had established themselves at York 868-9 and Thetford 869-70 and this time captured Edmund, king of East Anglia and brutally killed him. In 870 they were in Reading and in 871 fought battles against the West Saxons, a second Viking army also arriving at Reading. Thus from 865-871 the Vikings had overthrown the ancient kingdoms of Northumbria, East Anglia and Mercia.

Enter Alfred, 'the Great,' who became king of the West Saxons in 871 at this 'darkest hour'. He was never supposed to be king, he only became so after the death of his brother Æthelred in the midst of these campaigns; Alfred was ill and his two nephews also claimed the throne. After more battles, Alfred 'made peace' with the Vikings, in that he bought them off. The unfolding destruction of the Early English kingdoms is simply told: in 872-6 the Vikings settled at Repton, secured and settled Northumbria around York, and Cambridge.[9] In 875-6 they returned to Wessex and Alfred again made peace, as they went to Exeter and then Gloucester. There were more treaties in 876-7 and payments of tribute and the Vikings settled the area of the 'Five Boroughs' (Lincoln, Leicester, Nottingham, Stamford and Derby) and land around Northampton, Bedford and London. In 878 the winter raid on the royal estate of Chippenham almost captured Alfred; it was Christmas, they were under a truce, and another

Viking army landed at Devon, possibly with the intention to take Alfred, but they failed. Alfred was taken, if not by the Vikings, but certainly by surprise and fled into the Somerset marshes, with only a 'small troop' not unlike a scene from *Beowulf* itself, where he fortified Athelney.[10]

Asser's *Life of King Alfred* describes the ignominy of the escape from Chippenham in graphic detail:

> King Alfred with his small band of nobles and also with certain soldiers and thegns, was leading a restless life in great distress amid the woody and marshy places of Somerset. He had nothing to live on except what he could forage by frequent raids, either secretly or even openly, from the Vikings as well as from the Christians who had submitted to the Vikings' authority.[11]

This came after 'many men of that race [the West Saxons] were 'forced to sail overseas' and 'very nearly all the inhabitants of that region submitted to their authority.' The brutal reality was that this final invasion of Wessex was aimed at no less than the complete conquest of Wessex and there was no inevitability about Alfred's survival either, after the escape from Chippenham in 878. But in an astonishing turn-around in May 878, Alfred met his army at Egbert's Stone east of Selwood, defeating the Vikings in battle at his royal manor at Edington in Wiltshire. Alfred besieged Chippenham and forced their surrender; they gave hostages to Alfred, but this time he gave none in return; three weeks later Guthrum came to Aller (near Athelney) and Alfred, like a true son of Rome, baptised rather than executed him.[12]

At this point we must pause the narrative, dramatic though it is. The problem with Alfred's reign is that almost all of the written sources may have originated with Alfred himself or his immediate entourage, including the preface to his laws, the laws themselves, autobiographical comments, translations of Pope Gregory and others, the *Chronicle* and Asser's *Life*.[13] The *Chronicle* was produced at Alfred's court in the early 890s so for Alfred's reign it is a contemporary record; it was widely distributed across the expanded kingdom.[14]

Just as Bede's *Ecclesiastical History* dominates the first half of the Early English period, the *Chronicle* dominates the second half and specifically creates a narrative of Wessex supremacy that held into the late twentieth century. We have already seen how the *Chronicle* invented the chronology of the arrival of the English in the fifth century and the royal house of Wessex descended from Woden and the biblical patriarchs, but now that it is recording near contemporary events, we should read it considering Alfred's survival after 878. If that desperate winter and spring of 878 was a '1940' moment, then Alfred anticipates by over 1,000 years the other great 'saviour' of England, Winston Churchill, who was fond of saying: 'I shall leave it to history, but remember that I shall be one of the historians.'[15] Churchill as historian had access to official secrets and confidential cabinet papers no other historian had, putting him, like Alfred, at the centre of not only the politics, but the historical record of the politics, too.[16]

The (re)writing of history starts long before the raid on Chippenham, since the earliest *Chronicle*, the 'A' text, was written a century after the events at Lindisfarne. The Lindisfarne raid apparently followed the initial Viking incursion in 789 when a group of 'north men' had landed on the coast near a royal residence and killed the reeve at the harbour (not named as Portland in Dorset until late eleventh-century sources).[17] The Wessex compilers of the *Chronicle* may have wanted to show that the first Viking raid was in Wessex; there is then a gap until 835 concerning Viking activity since that was the reign of Ecgberht, Alfred's grandfather.[18] At the time of writing, the 890s, Wessex was the sole surviving Early English kingdom and so the official history was creating an inevitability around this fact, spurred on by the return of the Vikings in 893. The A text was written at the end of the ninth century to 891 at the Old Minster, Winchester (moved to Canterbury in 1011) and thereafter at intervals by various scribes and it ends in 1070; the B text was written from *c.*977, C in the mid-eleventh century (Abingdon), D also in the mid-eleventh (Worcester) and E (Peterborough) in the early twelfth century. F was an early twelfth-century copy.[19] The Chronicles drew upon a range of sources including annals, regnal lists and genealogies, a list of bishops, encyclopaedic books in circulation, the now lost Annals of St Neots and oral tradition.

The Viking voice has no contemporary or near contemporary written record; the sagas date from the twelfth century leaving us only with English sources.[20] In addition to the *Chronicle*, we have Asser's *Life of Alfred*, which is the earliest known biography of an Early English king, written in Alfred's forty-fifth year (893) partly to strengthen the English resistance. The story of the manuscript is itself instructive of how history is made as well as written. The original manuscript was dated to *c.* 1000, salvaged by John Leland from the destruction of the Reformation and was destroyed in the fire of 1731 at Ashburnham House (which nearly destroyed the *Beowulf* manuscript) but a facsimile was made in 1722; the source has been subject to suspicions of it being a mid-eleventh century forgery, but this is no longer accepted and it is now seen as a rare example of Insular Latin prose from the late ninth century.[21]

Asser was a Welsh priest from St David's, who didn't meet Alfred until 885; his *Life* was also written with Welsh readership in mind, since by that time all the rulers of the Welsh had submitted to Alfred and he uses the *Life* to call for the Welsh to unite with the English. Asser was therefore writing under the influence of Alfred himself. He styles Alfred as 'king of the Angul Saxons' throughout, the Vikings are pagans and the English are Christians, thereby perhaps setting out the Holy War. It is at the point of Alfred's desperate days in the Somerset marches that the legend of Alfred and the cakes (from the late tenth-century *Life of St Neot*) was interpolated by Archbishop Parker, who got hold of the manuscript of Asser's *Life* sometime after Leland's death and obviously thought that if Alfred hadn't burnt the cakes then he should have.[22] It is probably not true but it indicates how desperate the situation for Alfred was and how this was becoming legend only a century later; the story snowballed in the twelfth and thirteenth centuries, the legend gradually becoming fact.

Was the situation in 878 as desperate as Asser makes out? Other evidence throws some light on what was going on. The Viking raids on Kent at the end of the eighth century enabled the kingdom of Wessex to move in and assume control, but Egbert did not enforce his supremacy since coinage and marriages shows evidence of Wessex-Mercian alliances in the mid-ninth century, an ongoing policy. The great heathen army pushed Wessex and Mercia into closer alliance, and in 868 Alfred married Ælhwith, of Mercian royal descent, and coinage again evidenced the alliance. A charter of 875 given by King Ceolwulf II Mercia, demonstrates how he was accepted as king of Mercia (*rex Merciorum*) by his subjects since it was witnessed by his bishops and ealdormen, but the *Chronicle* dismisses Ceolwulf as a 'foolish thegn' who had been granted Mercia by the invaders (he was the last Mercian king, though).[23] Archaeology, as usual, illuminates the missing or retrospective written sources: the Watlington Hoard (in the Ashmolean Museum Oxford), discovered in 2015, includes thirteen examples of the rare 'Two Emperors' penny, which shows Alfred and Ceolwulf seated side by side below a winged figure of Victory or an angel, suggestive of another alliance between Wessex and Mercia and dated between 878 and 879, the very moment Alfred and his band apparently stood 'alone'.[24]

During the 870s, when Alfred was buying off the Vikings, the terms were probably not as favourable to Alfred as the *Chronicle* makes out. A lease by the bishop of Worcester in 872 reveals the far-reaching taxation to pay tribute to the Danes, the 'very pressing affliction and immense tribute of the barbarians'.[25] It is clear from Asser and the *Chronicle* that Alfred had few people with him during the spring of 878, which might serve to emphasise his miraculous reversal of fortune, but it also reveals how little support he had. The battle of Edington was a local affair, according to Asser, involving 'all the inhabitants' of Somerset, Wiltshire and Hampshire – apart from those who had fled overseas – though the *Chronicle* says only part of Hampshire.[26]

Battles were a huge risk and often indecisive (Alfred had fought eight in one year, losing several) but perhaps Alfred had no money to buy them off this time, so battle was the last resort; maybe on this occasion Alfred outnumbered the Viking army.

Alfred's kingdom was small (250 miles east-west and 50 miles north-south) and his knowledge of Somerset was intimate; Alfred travelled extensively from Cornwall to Kent but it was at Athelney that he took refuge in 878, where he built a fort and monastery and it may here where the *Chronicle* was written. It was near Athelney that the famous 'Alfred jewel' was found, and at Aller near Athelney, where Guthrum was baptised. The peace with Guthrum was completed at Wedmore, in the heart of the kingdom and not far from Wedmore was the royal manor of Cheddar. Five of the burh-fortresses of the Burghal Hidage were in Somerset, more than any other county; most of the royal estates were bequeathed to Alfred's eldest son, Edward. The kingdom of Wessex was not even a single entity or designed to be ruled as one. Alfred's father Æthelwulf was king of Kent in Egbert's lifetime and he divided Wessex into two between Æthelbald and Æthelberht with the agreement that the brothers, not the sons, would succeed. It was the events of 871-8 that forced the latter brother into uniting his resources in a final throw of the dice.

After Edington, everything changed. In 879 the Vikings shared out the land in East Anglia, the last stage of settlement following Northumbria in 876 and eastern Mercia 877, but Alfred's victory discouraged a third Viking army from invading Wessex, which sailed for the Continent where it remained until 892. The debasement of the coinage ceased in both Wessex and Mercia soon after the battle of Edington; the tribute paid by Guthrum after his defeat may have restored the currency, which remained at a pure standard. The capture of London by Alfred in 886 was vital to economic recovery, giving him access to new silver. Alfred's authority in Kent in the 880s saw the resurgence of trade; tolls and grants all reflect prosperity and sources of income for the king. The Viking wars were economic as well as military turning points.

The treaty with Guthrum, made between 886 and 890 (Guthrum's death), includes London on the English side and was agreed and confirmed with oaths by King Alfred, King Guthrum, the 'councillors' of the English race and all the people in East Anglia; the borders were up from the Thames to the Lea, to Bedford, then up the Ouse to Watling Street.[27] Englishmen and Danes were worth the same *wergild* (eight half-marks of refined gold), ceorls and Danish freedmen at 200 shillings, revealing clear ethnic and social stratification. This was the limit of Alfred's success; he had reconquered and restored the Wessex-Mercian hegemony (including Kent) of the mid-ninth century. He had overcome the monsters that stalked the *Heorots* of Wessex, even entering Grendel's marshes to summon up his deepest reserves of strength.

Alfred did not rest on his laurels, following Vegetius's maxim, 'Let him who desires peace, prepare for war.'[28] Alfred's military reforms in the years of peace between 878 and 992 created a network of fortresses, a standing field army and a navy. The 'Burghal Hidage' evidenced the network of defences built by Alfred, none more than 20 miles away from one another.[29] This list of 31 fortified towns (30 in Wessex, Buckingham outside) developed under Alfred, incorporated Iron Age, Roman, and new-builds from scratch, towns with internal grids of streets. Winchester had five miles of streets surfaced with some 7,900 tons of cobblestones. Towns were designed for defence and for trade, such as at Worcester.[30] Each assigned one man per hide, 27,071 hides in total: Winchester and Wallingford, 2,400 hides, Southwark, 1,800 hides, down to Lyng (Athelney) 100 hides, the smallest, extending west-east from Exeter to Southwark, south-north from Chichester to Buckingham (1,600) and Oxford (1,500), demonstrating the core of Alfred's restored kingdom.

The administrative structure of the Early English kingdoms, such as shires, shire fyrd, ealdorman, land assessment by hides, reeves and local courts, all existed by 870. Royal income derived from tribute, taxes, tolls and rents, and levies were taken in cash.[31] Charters of the late eighth/ early ninth centuries refer to army service and labour on bridges and forts (the *trinoda necessitas*) but in the Burghal Hidage, the burdens of labour were not evenly distributed, falling mainly in the south, where the royal estates were. The measurements – one person per hide, four people per 16 feet – was not a standard measurement and varied from burh to burh; it matched at Winchester but that was where the formula may have been developed and was not necessarily how it applied to all burhs.[32] The Burghal Hidage does not tell how the service was actually extracted and performed, whether were they all garrisoned the walls or whether the service was far more general, such as repair work (unskilled mass levies) or trained warriors (the king's thegns) or for how long – a couple of weeks in a year would not be a heavy burden. The *Chronicle* tells us in 893 that the king had separated his army into two, with half in the field and half at home 'except for those who had to hold the fortresses.'[33] Asser fills in a few more gaps when he tells how Alfred's household was organised, in three shifts serving a month in rotation.[34]

The question of who served remains unanswered and perhaps the clues lie in the private wealth of Alfred rather than a prototype 'national service' or conscription, which summons unrealistic images of a fully functioning, all-powerful state. This recalls a much more personal style of kingship and brings us back to *Beowulf* where the world of tribute, gift-giving and treasure was not mutually exclusive to hides, shires and public service. Alfred was regarded by Bishop Wulfsige as 'his ring-giver... the greatest treasure-giver of all the kings'.[35] Asser tells us that Alfred handed out one-sixth of his revenue to his warriors (and how he despised wealth, like Solomon) but it is Alfred's will that indicates the extent to which he relied on his own retinues to form the bulk of a royal army, using his own personal wealth, which was considerable.[36]

The will of King Alfred is the earliest surviving will of an English king (made *c*.888, albeit preserved in early eleventh-century hand), though Asser has an account of his father King Æthelwulf's will, which is referred to in Alfred's will as being read to an assembly of West Saxon councillors.[37] Alfred's will left £1,800 of silver and 1,500 mancuses of gold, including 100 to his ealdormen in every shire. Land, too, was of course a source of wealth; Alfred was the probably most substantial landowner south of the Thames, which would mean that he (and his successors) could call upon the greatest resources in Britain at the time without the need to coerce or conscript the masses of untrained levies, which they did from time to time. This wealth remained in the royal house until 1066 (Alfred's will stipulates that his land should pass through the male line, as his grandfather had bequeathed his land 'on the spear side and not on the spindle side'.)[38] The personal wealth of Alfred and his successors had meant that they had greater resources than any other rulers in Britain in the ninth and tenth centuries, a significant fact when it comes to the emergence of one English kingdom under one dynasty.

This wealth had increased exponentially after 878, starting with the tribute paid by Guthrum, the annexation of London in 886 and the increase is a reminder of that dark side to society: slavery (bound up to the fate of the British). The subjugation of Cornwall ('West Wales') in the ninth century led to the enslavement of many of its inhabitants and by 1086, the time of Domesday Book, slaves formed a higher proportion of the population of Cornwall and parts of Devon than in almost any other county (21%).[39] Alfred's lands in Cornwall were more extensive than those of Edward the Confessor and Cornwall is referred to in Alfred's will as 'among the Welsh'.[40]

There was a source of wealth closer to home for Alfred: the Mendips were a heartland of Roman silver mining and two great manors covering most of the Mendips were in Alfred's hands – Chewton Mendip, one of the largest and wealthiest manors in Somerset, close to the Roman mining sites of Green Ore and Priddy; and Cheddar, close to the largest Roman mine at Charterhouse, where silver was still being extracted in the nineteenth century.[41] There were eight mints within twenty miles of Charterhouse by the end of the tenth century and a further three within thirty miles. There was no similar concentration of mints anywhere in Early England, although the output was sporadic and small-scale.

Alfred's will illustrates his West Saxon localism, but like Bede, whose home was Northumbria, Alfred was no little Englander, for all the desperate retreat into the Somerset marshes, since his horizons reached to Rome and it was Rome, not any idea of 'England' that underpinned his survival and recovery in the great war of 871-8 between Christian English and pagan Vikings. Alfred had twice been to Rome before he was eight years old, a unique experience, blessed ('hallowed') by the pope on the first visit in 853 and he thought in later life that he was favoured by this. He stayed for many months in Rome on the second visit with his father King Æthelwulf in 855, when gifts were exchanged. On the return journey they stayed for months at the court of the Frankish King Charles the Bald, grandson of Charlemagne; Æthelwulf married his twelve-year old daughter Judith, whose education had influence on Alfred's own learning and later, his court of scholars. As king in the 880s he sent embassies to Rome, the capital of 'Christendom' and the pope sent him a piece of the True Cross, the most precious of relics. In the tradition of two centuries of Early English kingship, Alfred's family had maintained the Continental connections of previous Early English dynasties, this time intermarrying with the descendants of Charlemagne, and Alfred's retinue was internationalist, composed of Franks, Frisians, Scandinavians, Irish and Bretons.

This was Alfred's world and he had grown up steeped in the mentality of this great war, fighting, winning and losing battles with the heathen all of his life. His contact with Rome gave him not only the strength to survive 878 but to rebuild a new Wessex afterwards, including his kingship and that of the English. Alfred was styled as *rex Saxonum* in the 870s and 880s, *Angulsaxonum rex* 'king of the 'Anglo Saxons' in the latter part of his reign and *Westseaxna cyning* 'king of the West Saxons' in his will, retaining elements of the Saxon.

Alfred's court scholars may have deliberately adopted a new identity, as *Angelcynn*; the translations of Gregory, Boethius and St Augustine were, so they all tell us, translations into the 'English' language, never into 'Saxon'.[42] The early *Chronicle* makes no mention of *Englaland* or *Englisc* but *Angelcynn* and *Angelcynneslond* are used, both convey the sense of 'England' and the *Chronicle* is focused most thoroughly on 'Greater Wessex'. The key phrase *Angelcynn*, was first attested in a Worcester charter of 855 but in the 880s came to signify the amalgamation of the Anglian kingdom of 'Mercia' and the 'Saxon' kingdom of Wessex.[43] *Angelcynn* is defined primarily as 'the English race, English people' – but not necessarily 'England' – and there are some 225 occurrences, mainly in the *Chronicle* and the *Old English Bede*.[44] The major significant instance of *Angelcynn* is in the 886 *Chronicle*, recording the occupation of 'London fort' and the submission to King Alfred of 'all the English'.[45] This reflected the new hegemony of Wessex over Mercia and Kent, seen in Alfred's title in the charters, which became *rex Angul Saxonum* now, rather than the previous *rex Saxonum*. London was entrusted to the control of Ealdorman Æthelred, ruler of the Mercians following Ceolwulf, and later husband to Alfred's daughter, Æthelflæd.

The term *Angelcynn* has explicit Mercian or Anglian connotations; Bede's generic use of *gens Anglorum* and the influence of the Mercians in Alfred's court account for this. It is found in *The Laws of Alfred*, preface to the *Pastoral Care*, and the Treaty of Wedmore. If *Angelcynn* disseminated the new political order, then *here* was used to describe the Danish forces with equally powerful linguistic connotations, in contrast to the English army, the *fyrd*.[46] In the Laws of Ine (appended to the Laws of Alfred) a *here* was a band of more than 35 thieves, so using that term was deliberately associating the Danish with criminality, to be repeated in the Chronicles into the eleventh century.

The origins of the royal chancery are traced to Winchester and the court of Alfred, its Carolingian precursor based on Merovingian kings and Roman emperors, becoming increasingly centralised in the first half of the tenth century; this was a professional bureaucratic community employed by the West Saxon kings, which may also have been responsible for the *Chronicle,* possibly written at Winchester.[47] It has also been suggested that Asser not only wrote Alfred's biography but also had a prominent role in the writing of the charters, too, thereby strengthening a core 'message'.[48] Mercian influence was very strong, but Alfred's decisive social role in the network gives him the central position, as evidenced best by the inscription on the Alfred Jewel (*aelfred mec heht gewyrcan*, 'Alfred had me made') – without his direct order, it would not be made. Alfredian norms were the norms selected, enforced and promoted by the Winchester elite network.[49]

The threat of the Vikings triggered historical and legal writing on an unprecedented scale; this was an act of political and cultural identity, defining common loyalties and enemies. The 'Alfredian network' included scholars from Mercia, Wales, Flanders, Saxony, Alfred himself being the sole West Saxon. Alfred was an educationalist, for whom education was a road to salvation as well as practical advancement.[50] The main purpose was Christian instruction (Asser portrayed Alfred as the *rector* of all the Christians of the isle of Britain) rather than to invent an English destiny. Alfred did not necessarily seek to model the English as a chosen people, but as one of many Christian peoples.[51] It is not conclusive that Alfred saw himself as 'king of all England', but rather the king of an extended Wessex to include Mercia. In the literature there was no programme to promote an English kingdom; the emphasis was on Christendom in the great struggle between Christianity and paganism.[52]

Learning had been in decay since the 'Golden Age' of the late seventh/ early eighth century, which was seen as a divine punishment. The scholars Werferth, bishop of Worcester, and Plegmund (later archbishop of Canterbury) were from Mercia, but Alfred sent messengers to Gaul for support, and John the Old Saxon, and Grimbald, a monk from St Bertin's in Flanders came to join him – the latter released somewhat reluctantly by Fulco, archbishop of Rheims. Asser, too, joined Alfred's court, all of them around 886. They probably brought with them manuscripts to restock the libraries ransacked and destroyed by the Vikings. Alfred himself learnt Latin and was primarily responsible for four translations into English: Gregory's *Pastoral Care*, Boethius's *Consolation of Philosophy*, St Augustine's *Soliloquies* and the first fifty psalms of the Psalter. Bede's *Ecclesiastical History* was another translation prepared at this time, in Anglian (Mercian) dialect. The *Pastoral Care* was immensely popular throughout the Middle Ages, providing spiritual guidance for secular clergy but also for temporal rulers and leaders.

Seven Books of History against the Pagans by the early fifth-century writer Orosius was also translated at Alfred's court, concerning the continuity of the Roman Empire and how paganism in the Empire had been defeated with God's favour. The word *cristendom* first appears in Old English in Alfred's translation of *Seven Books of History against the Pagans*. Alfred was attempting to use history in order to educate the English (in their own language) to survive the Viking pagan assaults.[53] The word *cristendom* did not mean a geographical area inhabited by Christians, rather being in a Christian state of mind; and being Christian meant an awareness of divine protection and guaranteed victory over enemies. Orosius looked to history to defend Christian faith against the pagans, Old Testament history as well as Roman history. The significance of Orosius's work is represented by the large number of manuscripts that survive, more than 250 copies in Latin were made the later Middle Ages.[54]

The earliest extant reference to 'Engla londe' is in the *Old English Bede*.[55] The greatest cluster of occurrences of *Angelcynn* is also in the *Old English Bede*, but whether Alfred's court was consciously forming a nationalist programme or simply using Bede for educational purposes is unclear.[56] It is not a full translation of Bede's *Ecclesiastical History*, there are omissions and abridgements that reduce the length by a third. Many of Bede's documents are excluded to form a streamlined account of the arrival and conversion of the peoples who became the English, leaving out papal correspondence and instead placing Bede and the English church at the fore.[57] It appears to have been quite widely copied (five manuscripts survive, housed all across England in Durham, Canterbury, Exeter, Burton-on-Trent and Cerne Abbey). It was designed to be read aloud, with the aim of providing basic instruction in good Christian living, primarily a store of examples to inculcate Christian behaviour, not as an account of a single *gens Anglorum* with a special relationship with God.[58] There is no link either, within the text of the *Old English Bede* to Alfred and it is not mentioned by Asser, but the abbreviations and translation into English gave it a national focus that goes beyond an ecclesiastical history, whatever Alfred's intentions.[59]

Alfred's translation of Gregory's *Pastoral Care* had instructions on circulation and copies, and famously tells us that all free men of means should learn to read English and those destined for the church will study

The Making of England

Latin.[60] The Old English translation of Pope Gregory the Great's *Pastoral Care* was sent out to the bishops, ealdormen and earls in the shires; several of these manuscripts survive and one has a note on the first page saying 'This book shall go to Worcester.'[61]

Giving priority to English as the language of wider literacy was a revolutionary idea and Alfred's example was followed in the tenth and eleventh centuries.[62] Alfred recalls the destruction wrought by the Vikings and that few people could read those (Latin) books before he became king, but now there are 'any provision of teachers'. However, ignorance of Latin was a common phenomenon in Early England from the eighth to the eleventh centuries and it is clear that Alfred was seeking to highlight the literary achievements of the Wessex court.[63])

That said, 'many could read things written in English.' He orders that one will be sent to every see in the kingdom and each will have a book-marker, the æstel, worth 50 mancuses (the price of 300 sheep or 50 oxen, that is, of great value) which shall not be taken from the book in the church unless it is with the bishop, or on loan, or 'someone is copying it.'[64]

The æstels bring us closer to the political virtue of wisdom that Alfred promoted through literacy but in a new twist on the Germanic gift-giving we see in *Beowulf*.[65] The most elaborate at 6cm long is the 'Alfred Jewel', found in a field at North Petherton, Somerset, in 1693, a few miles from Athelney (which certainly supports the narrative of his retreat there) and now in the Ashmolean Museum, Oxford.[66] It consists of a piece of rock-crystal, a gold frame, gold engraved plate sitting in a sheet-gold dragon-like head that clasps a short golden tube in its mouth. It probably formed part of a group of precious objects, seven in total so far, which were possibly book-pointers (derived from the Latin *hastula*, little spear), since Alfred's English translation of *Pastoral Care* mentioned an æstel on or in each copy he sent out to his bishops (they each have a flat back to sit between pages). Each æstel was to be kept with the book and each book kept in the church.

Of these seven æstels found so far, four were found in the kingdom of Wessex, the others in south Yorkshire, but the furthest æstel to be found was in the far north of Norway, at Borg in the Lofoton Islands, where it is known that a wealthy trader named Ohthere brought to Alfred's court walrus-teeth and walrus-bone.[67] The Borg æstel might have been given to Ohthere and taken back to Norway by him as part of a wider network of honoured associates – or it could have been Viking loot taken during the raids of the ninth century.

Alfred's translation of the phrase 'power and jurisdiction' from Boethius's *Consolation of Philosophy* redefines it as 'laying down of laws and exaction of taxes', but these were not new features of his reign, rather a part of his inheritance from Early English kingdoms which were

100

assimilated into his political thought, along with Carolingian thought.[68] It is questionable whether Alfred's law codes contained anything new, since many clauses treated compensation in the same manner as the laws of Ine had.[69] Alfred deliberately linked his laws to his forefathers, his kinsman (King Ine), King Offa and Ethelbert and there is a sense of personal authority where it reads 'I, Alfred'.

Furthermore, surviving law codes from the seventh to the early eighth centuries are from Kent and Wessex, from the post-Viking period, Wessex alone, contributing further to the distortion towards the kingdom of Wessex as the core of 'England' (though Offa may well have issued a law code which Alfred's code refers to, but it does not survive).

There was a death penalty for theft in Ine's code but not for homicide until the late 1180s; murder was an offence against the person and his family, not the king.[70] Murder was still a matter for the kindred, not kingship, and compensation had become Christian salvation.[71] If a man plotted against the king, however, or his lord, he 'is to be liable for his life' (but could clear himself by oath).

There is a conscious echo of the Bible (Exodus, xxii, xxiii) in the introductory clauses of Alfred's Laws, telling us how this had been modified by the Christian Church and transmitted throughout the whole world, also to the *Angelcynn*; Early English law was like the law given by God, a kingdom of souls as well as bodies.[72]

Here, Alfred's code differs from earlier codes. In the first main clause, oath- and pledge-breakers are to be excommunicated as well as outlawed, the first time in England where secular and ecclesiastical sanctions are used to reinforce each other.[73] The oath and pledge in Alfred's law code marked a change in royal justice (and had Carolingian precedents from 802); all men over the age of 12 swore an oath of fidelity which committed them to hunt down suspects or turn them into the public courts, but settlement, not judgement, was the preferred option, and by violence if necessary. The king was one of many players in the scenario.[74] Even the courts and their justice were viewed as an extension of a feud-based system of private redress for personal wrongs.[75]

No consideration is given to the British/Welsh ethnic issue in Alfred's law codes and it is assumed that the 'British' had been integrated into Early English society since the time of Ine.[76] Slaves still very much exist and suffer the worst physical punishments since they cannot pay compensation – castration if a slave rapes a slave. The Christmas and Easter holidays and other holy days were not permitted to slaves and unfree labourers either.

The 'Fonthill' letter written by or on behalf of Ealdorman Ordlaf to King Edward the Elder (899-924) illustrates the lived experience of Alfred's legal system.[77] A certain Helmstan was accused of stealing a belt, which led to a legal dispute over five hides at Fonthill (Wiltshire). In a letter, Ordlaf, Helmstan's godfather, tells King Edward that he interceded on Helmstan's behalf to King Alfred, who ordered that the various parties should be brought to agreement. Helmstan possessed the title-deeds to the property and at Wardour, where King Alfred was 'washing his hands' in the chamber, he judged that Helmstan could give the oath which proved his rights. This tells us how the law functioned, with reference to a suit, mediation, oath, written documents and the personal involvement of the king (Asser also says Alfred used to sit on judicial hearings for both noble and common people); it is a glimpse of humanity beyond the manuscripts.[78] It didn't go well for Helmstan though, for a couple of years later he stole untended oxen from Fonthill and in a touch of human drama that echoes across the millennia, he scratched his face with a bramble on the run, something which was used in evidence against him. Due to Alfred's code, Helmstan was both outlawed *and* excommunicated. Helmstan visited King Alfred's tomb where he either swore an oath or gained some sort of warranty in a penitential act in an attempt to correct his previous wrongs, brought a seal to Ordlaf who was staying with King Edward, and gained a royal pardon.[79]

Whilst we have an overwhelmingly idealized portrayal of the saintly, Christian king from Asser, the *Chronicle* and the court writers, it is not wholly impossible to glimpse the warrior-king who must have existed alongside this ideal. Alfred survived the Chippenham raid seemingly by the skin of his teeth when Guthrum, like Grendel, burst into the hall and it is Alfred the soldier who led his war-band into the Somerset marshes to fight another day. Desperate times like those were surely inspired as much by a heroic culture as much as by religious devotion. *Beowulf* was very likely known by Alfred, since leading characters in the poem are listed in the *Chronicle* for 855 under Æthelwulf's genealogy (Alfred's father), where 'Beow' appears.[80] As we have seen, *Beowulf* was certainly a part of a wider canon of myths and legends which have not survived, hinted at in scenes on the ninth-century Franks Casket that include the story of the Germanic warhero 'Weland', or Wayland, the legendary Germanic smith, a tale of violence and rape. This legend is alluded to in the Old English translation of Boethius's *Consolation of Philosophy* putatively commissioned by Alfred's court, linking Wayland's 'wisdom' with Alfred.[81] The Neolithic long barrow, 'Wayland's Smithy,' is close to the victory of Ashdown in 871 and is specifically mentioned in the bounds of a charter of 955 (recalling 'Grendel's Pit' of seventh-century charter-bounds).[82]

During the long winter months of 878, Alfred came to know every landmark of his much-reduced kingdom, calling upon his ancestral heritage for strength against a relentless and merciless foe. The time for prayers, baptism and forgiveness would come only after dreadful violence on the field of battle had secured those indulgences. Heroes were needed to fight these Northmen-monsters.

In 890, Guthrum died. He had been baptised 'Æthelstan' at Wedmore, and he issued coins under that name and was perhaps buried at the royal estate at Hadleigh in Suffolk.[83] In 892/3 the Vikings returned from the Continent, but Alfred was ready this time. Campaigns raged across England and Wales, from Chester to Exeter, Essex, Kent and the Isle of Wight, making full use of the burhs and new ships commissioned by Alfred, but it is clear that the struggle remained hard, if not as desperate as 878. In late 899, Alfred died during a cessation of these wars, 'king over all the English race except that part which was under Danish control', so the *Chronicle* tells us. His son Edward succeeded but immediately his nephew, a disgruntled Æethelwold, rebelled, occupying Wimborne manor before carrying off a nun to Northumbria; he later joined with the Viking force in East Anglia to attack Wessex.[84] It was business as usual in early medieval England.

In 1935 Henri Pirenne completed his masterpiece *Mohammed and Charlemagne*, finally published in 1954; Pirenne's much criticised thesis was that the advance of Islam caused the break with antiquity.[85] The pagan Viking invasions of England after 793 had a similar impact on the creation of an identity of 'England' in English historiography.[86] In Germany, too, in the tenth century the Ottonian dynasty found in the pagan Magyars a useful enemy.[87] The existentialist threat of the Viking invasions destroyed the Early English kingdoms – except Wessex – and ended the centuries-old balance of power. In short, no Guthrum, no Alfred. That does not necessarily lead to no Alfred, no England, though. The undoubted surge in literature transformed Bede's *Angli* into the *Angelcynn* but this is not England as we know it, and far from it in 899 at Alfred's death. If anything, it was the fantastical notion of 'Britain' that mattered more.

Bede had portrayed Edwin and Oswald as rulers of Britain and gave Augustine the title of 'Archbishop of Britain'; Æthelbald and Offa of Mercia had been styled 'king of Britain' and Asser flatters Alfred by calling him 'ruler of all the Christians of the island of the British'.[88] There is no evidence for a sudden change in the evolution towards the late Saxon state in the eighth and ninth centuries; there were significant borrowings from contemporary Francia in the reigns of Offa, Æthelwulf and his son Alfred, such as coinage reforms, the anointing of kings in the reign of Offa and the oath of loyalty in the law code of Alfred. But these were modifications to existing systems rather than major innovations.[89]

Alfred's kingship was deeply personal. The heroic wars, the Somerset marshes and burhs, the conversion of Guthrum, the spread of literature has the personal stamp of Alfred all over it. Even Alfred's extreme piety and Carolingian-style religious devotion may have been driven by his chronic illnesses (possibly Crohn's Disease) that symbolised his heroic efforts to overcome bodily sickness as well as pagan adversity, described in detail by Asser.[90] He is the first king we can rightly say changed – and indeed wrote – history, but his limits are quite well defined. Survival and restoration were his watchwords. He was, first and last, king of Wessex. His wealth, his family and his loyalty looked to Wessex and to Rome. In that sense, he is better seen as the last king of the Early English rather than the first king of England, or even the founding father of England.

SEVEN

Unification?

The destruction of the Early English kingdoms left a power vacuum which the Viking settlement did not successfully fill. Alfred's son and daughter extended the kingdoms of Wessex and Mercia into the Danelaw territories. This was not a 'reconquest' since it had never been under those kingdoms before. Alfred's grandson Æthelstan proclaimed himself 'king of all England', the first to do so. A crushing victory over the British kingdoms at Brunanburh did not quite consolidate power over all of the Early English kingdoms and after Æthelstan's death the fragility of this new kingdom was exposed, threatening to reprise the dual monarchy of Wessex and Mercia. During the reign of Edgar (959-975) the power of the royal House of Wessex was consolidated and the imperial claims over all of England become a reality.

In 927, Æthelstan, grandson of Alfred of Wessex, conquered the Scandinavian kingdom of the Northumbrians centred on York. At a meeting on 12th July at Eamontbridge, by Penrith on the Cumberland-Westmorland border (the frontier between the kingdoms of Strathclyde and England), he confirmed peace with pledges and oaths with the chief non-English kings ruling Britain, having previously received the submission of the English king of northern Northumbria, based at Bamburgh.[1] These kings were Hywel, king of the West Welsh, Constantine, king of the Scots and Owain, king of Gwent.[2] At, or soon after Eamontbridge, Æthelstan's court poet Peter wrote to the Queen Mother and the prince and announced Æthelstan's creation of England: '...he now rules with this/England made whole' (*perfecta Saxonia*).[3]

Athelstan called himself *rex totius Britanniae* and the kings of the Scots, Cumbrians, North and South Welsh, the Archbishop of York, and Northumbrian bishops witnessed his charters. His coins 927x939 bruited grand titles such as *rex Anglorum* ('king of the English'), and *rex totius*

Britanniae/Albionis ('king of the whole of Britain.').[4] Bede had written about the seven overkings who intermittently dominated the Midlands and south of England and in 827 the *Chronicle* listed Egbert of Wessex, Alfred's grandfather, as the eighth 'bretwalda', but it is from 927 that there is explicit evidence of the deployment in Latin of royal styles of entitlement to rule Britain.[5]

The origins of how he came to make such a proclamation in 927 lie in the Viking conquests of the English kingdoms during the 860s and the Viking raids on Kent in the decades from the 790s, which prompted the Wessex-Mercian hegemony. The succession disputes following Alfred do not indicate that Wessex was any more 'special' than Northumbria or Mercia in previous centuries, perhaps luckier instead; Alfred excluded his nephews from a share in the succession in favour of his son Edward, but Alfred's nephew Æthelwold died in battle in 904 along with a Mercian ally (not mentioned in the *Chronicle*) and possibly Viking troops, too.[6] Æthelstan had been raised in Mercia by his aunt and godmother Æthelfæd, who ruled Mercia independently of Wessex until 918. The Winchester manuscript of the *Chronicle* (A) deliberately omitted Æthelfæd's role. As wife of Ealdorman Æthelred, she ruled with him as 'Lady of the Mercians', but after his death in 911 she ruled independently, rebuilding and fortifying a dozen towns across middle England, leading campaigns against Danish army bases and presiding over the Mercian assemblies. One Irish source referred to her as 'queen of the Saxons'. At her death in 918 she was succeeded by her daughter, Ælfwynn – the only case where a daughter followed her mother – formally recognised by the Mercian nobles.[7]

Early English queens generally do not have a good press: Asser describes the lurid tale of Queen Eadburh, daughter of Offa of Mercia who poisoned her enemies, including her husband King Beorhtric in 802 and who died in exile in Pavia after being caught in adultery as a nun.[8] Eadburh's eventful life was a warning to the elders of Wessex, who refused to allow the queen to sit beside the king or indeed be called queen, rather the 'king's wife', but Alfred's father, Æthelwulf, insisted that Judith, daughter of the Carolingian Charles the Bald, should sit beside him. Charter evidence supports the view that the 'king's wife' was kept in the background in Wessex, though in the late seventh and eighth centuries there are references to the 'queen' (*cuen* or *regina*) in charters and the *Chronicle* (written of course, after 892) for Mercia, and a gold finger-ring found in Yorkshire is inscribed 'Queen Æthelswith'.[9] Alfred's wife is not referenced in the charters, so Asser's information is accurate; but the status of queens improved in the tenth century, with their consecration service included with the king's.

Ælfwynn was deposed by her uncle Edward of Wessex and the two regions were re-united under one ruler. This not new; the assimilation of

Mercian London by Alfred indicated that Wessex was expansionist, as it had been since the 820s, and his daughter Æthelfæd's rule over Mercia continued this. The conquest of the 'Danelaw' by Edward was not a 'reconquest' but in fact a new conquest of formerly Mercian regions, bringing them into the overlordship of the kingdom of Wessex; this was achieved not only by military force, since two charters of 926 show that Æthelstan was encouraging his thegns to buy estates in Danish territory before he began the conquest of the Danelaw.[10] The Danelaw Treaty of 886-890 had disintegrated by 911; the Treaty does not mention the Mercians, only King Alfred, King Guthrum and the councillors of all the English (*Angelcynnes*) and the people of East Anglia.

If Alfred's public fortifications and military boroughs built upon earlier Mercian concepts, then the absorption of the Mercian kingdom itself by Wessex and then of London in 886 was arguably not a conquest but rather a political renegotiation process.[11] Indeed, the term 'Danelaw' or *Dena lage* first appears in the eleventh century and is misleading since it did not form any coherent unit, evidenced by the ease with which Edward the Elder and Æthelflæd captured Derby, Leicester, Stamford and Nottingham in 918.[12] Given the relatively limited input of Danish DNA (at its highest in Orkney, 25%) the frontiers of the 'Danelaw' sketch a settlement that may never have been a political reality.[13]

By the time of his death in 924, Edward had built or acquired fortifications and territory far beyond Mercia, in north Wales, Chester, and most parts of Southumbria, gaining widespread recognition as the most powerful man in Britain. His power extended into Wales, York and Bamburgh and over the Scottish and Cumbrian kings. This was not a 'reconquest' of the Danelaw in some sort of manifest destiny – it was conquest, assuming the authority created by the destruction of the old kingdoms by the Vikings in the 860s. It was a fragile authority since Edward had several sons by three women, and it was Ælfward who was initially backed by Winchester on Edward's death in what might have been another dual-kingdom. Æthelstan was 'chosen as king by the Mercians', where his earliest extant charter is witnessed solely by Mercian witnesses (he is styled *rex Anglorum,* king of Anglia). Only after Ælfward's death do the charters style him *Angulsaxonum rex*, witnessed by men north and south of the Thames.[14] Æthelstan was crowned at Kingston-on-Thames, the boundary between the two old kingdoms, using a revised coronation *ordo* that specifically referred to the two peoples, and Archbishop Æthelhelm of Canterbury used new regalia: a crown, a ring, sword and rod of office in what was probably the first coronation of an English king; Æthelstan is the first king to appear crowned on coins, too.[15]

Like his grandfather Alfred, Æthelstan was perhaps never supposed to be king but there is something even more of the outsider about him. Despite his success as the first 'King of all England', was always seen as a

Mercian and never quite incorporated into the Wessex 'narrative'. He was mentioned in just six of the annals of the *Chronicle* and he was buried at Malmesbury, a Wiltshire abbey with few previous royal associations. He never had children, never married, and was succeeded by his half-brother, Edmund, so was something of a caretaker king.[16] Perhaps, like all outsiders, he was in a hurry to make his name.

After Eamontbridge, Archbishops of York attested his charters, as did the church of St Cuthbert, the most powerful landowner between the Tees and the Tyne; in 934 he campaigned as far north as Caithness and Dunottar, the first to do since Agricola (*c.*80 AD).[17] However, the wide-ranging alliance brought to bear against Athelstan in 937 indicated the fragility of this imperium, this new 'England'. The kings of the Scots, Strathclyde Welsh, the Picts, the King of Dublin, Viking leaders from Ireland and the Western Isles, and Northumbrians all came together, their intention to restore the kingdom of Northumbria in York, as a buffer zone between the Scots and south English.[18] The kingdom of Strathclyde had since 871 been a satellite of the Viking kingdom of Dublin; the kingdom of Alba (Southern Picts) entered into alliances with the Dubliners and Dublin remained a significant factor in this relationship until *c.*980.

There is no doubt that the battle of Brunanburh was a great battle, perhaps the greatest since the English first came to Britain, remembered decades later as the 'Great War'. Among the dead were two of Æthelstan's cousins. It was recalled in the alliterative poem, the *Battle of Brunanburh*, which we have noted referred to the English migrations, and it speaks to us not in the language of the clerics but of *Beowulf*:

> Here King Æthelstan, leader of warriors
> Ring-giver of men, and also his brother,
> The ætheling Edmund, struck life-long glory
> In strife round Brunanburh, clove the shield-wall
> Hacked the war-lime, with hammers' leavings...
> The field darkened
> With soldiers' blood, after in the morning-time
> The sun, that glorious star
> Bright candle of God, the Lord Eternal,
> Glided over the depths, until the noble creature
> Sank to rest. There lay many a soldier
> of the men of the North, shot over shield.
> Taken by spears, likewise Scottish also...
> They left behind to divide the corpses,
> To enjoy the carrion, the dusky-coated,
> Horny-beaked black raven,
> And the grey-coated eagle, white-rumped,

Greedy war-hawk, and the wolf,
Grey beast in the forest. Never yet in this island
was there a greater slaughter...[19]

The *Chronicle* makes it clear that it is Æthelstan and his brother, Edmund, who are leading the Wessex-Mercian alliance into this great victory, since it is Edmund who succeeded Æthelstan as the next king, in 940. It is typical of so many things Early English that we do not even know the exact location of this battle that secured Æthelstan's proclamation in 927. The location of the battle was possibly Wendun, or 'Went Hill'; the River Went was an important boundary stream, the frontier of Northumbria/Mercia which crossed the vital Roman road to York between Doncaster and Castleford. This was a military zone that included an Iron Age fort and a Roman fort at Burghwallis and was a base for Edward I in the 1290s. It was also a long-established customary assembly place for greeting and submission where Edward IV met the chief citizens of York in 1478, where Henry VII met the Earl of Northumberland and in 1536 the Pilgrimage of Grace gathered to face the army of Henry VIII, submitting to the king in 1541 on that spot. The zone is a reminder of the intensely regional character of 'England' from the Early English to Reformation eras.[20]

Æthelstan made his theoretical claims become a reality. His grand designs reached beyond England; he was an imperialist who looked to Europe for inspiration to model his kingship on and has been called an English Charlemagne.[21] Æthelstan's half-sisters bound him in a web of Continental marriage alliances that attached him to almost every ruling house in Europe: his nephew was the Carolingian king Louis IV and his brother-in-law Otto I. Gifts and holy relics formed part of the diplomatic exchange.[22] Opposition to the claims of the Scandinavian kings of Dublin to rule at York and military intervention in Scotland and France were policy.[23] There were close connections with the German Ottonian kings in Æthelstan's use of relics and formal crown-wearings introduced in the eleventh century.[24] Æthelstan was steeped in relic culture; he gifted a Byzantine silk embroidery to be wrapped around St Cuthbert's body at Durham, leaving a personal written testimony; this was no doubt evidence of Æthelstan's piety but also helped to anchor his political identity.[25]

Æthelstan was also a law maker, as we might expect and his codes reflect the growing severity of punishments. The age of twelve was decided as the age of adult criminality; thieves would suffer death and public display of their corpses, as would those who harboured thieves; there was stoning for males, burning for females, free women were pushed off a cliff or drowned. The age of twelve was relented upon for first offences, and execution set at fifteen years of age in a later code of Æthelstan's when the number of boys being hanged was queried, in consultation with the councillors.[26] Æthelstan's second code is the first to explicitly mention penance as a punishment, since anyone guilty of swearing false oaths could not be buried on consecrated ground, thereby strengthening Alfred's code on oath-breaking. Edmund's law codes a few years later required homicides to perform penance before entering the king's presence.[27] Prohibition and protection, not punishment, remained the priority, achieved by local policing: local inhabitants were quite capable of holding meetings without orders from outside to deal with local matters, including crime. Æthelstan's law codes encouraged this, organising guild members into 100 people, subdivided into tens, reeves exacting pledges.[28] A further clause of Æthelstan's proclaimed that if a thegn chose an amicable agreement over legal proceedings, this should be just as binding.

Despite the victory at Brunanburh, West Saxon power in the east Midlands collapsed in 940 following Athelstan's death, indicating that the individual, not the 'state', maintained the most effective authority. The invasion of Anlaf Guthfrithson from Ireland had the support of the Northumbrian witan and the 'whole region' submitted to him.[29] Cumbria was ceded to the Scots in 945. From 939 to 954, seven different kings ruled in York in nine separate reigns and there were seven military expeditions in the zone between York and the Five Boroughs. There was no inevitability about the unification of England in the tenth century. York, still very much a Roman city, was a multicultural melting-pot of the English and Scandinavian worlds, a rich and international trade-centre, the moneyers of York minted coins for Anlac and Eric 'Bloodaxe', entwining Norse gods and Christianity.[30]

The Chronicles portray the Mercian/Northumbrian border as a war-zone in these years; Tamworth was raided with great slaughter (943), Leicester besieged (943), King Eadred's army was slaughtered at Castleford (948) and Thetford put to the sword in 952 in revenge for the murder of Abbot Eadhelm of St Augustine's Canterbury. It didn't help that King Edmund was stabbed to death at Pucklechurch, Gloucestershire, in 946 by the robber Liofa, which doesn't say much for royal security or respect for royalty.[31] The Church was divided, too: in the North it was led by Archbishop Wulfstan who rode south on the 940 campaign which sacked Tamworth and secured the Five Boroughs against King Edmund; King Eadred destroyed the seventh-century Ripon Cathedral in 948 on a scorched-earth campaign, accompanied by the Archbishop of Canterbury. The bones of St Wilfrid were taken to Kent in a deliberate policy of cultural and political appropriation and in 952 Archbishop Wulfstan was placed under house arrest in Essex, never to return north (he was buried at Oundle, the site of St Wilfrid's death – all the later archbishops of York came from south of the Humber).

It was a reminder not only of the illusion of English unity but of the wider British polity. Edmund and his brother Eadred had to co-operate with the non-Scandinavian rulers in Britain such as the Bamburgh lords, Welsh kings, Cumbria and the Scots, to prevent any coalition centred around York and a repeat of the Brunanburh campaign. 'Imperial' pretensions were maintained by violence. Hostages, gifts and grants were the peaceable side of the coin but blinding, burning and slaughter the other. Æthelstan ravaged Northumbria in 934, Edmund attacked Cumbria in 945 and blinded the sons of its king.

English assertion of royal power depended upon Hiberno-Scandinavian politics, which impacted upon rule in Northumbria. 'England' at its fullest extent in the mid-ninth century was bounded by the English Channel to the south, the Cornish and Welsh borders to the west and in the north-west by the kingdom of Dumbarton and the north by the boundary with the Picts; in effect, this was the same dimension as the Roman province, later the diocese of Britain. 'Britain' could therefore mean either the Roman imperial diocese or the island of Britain. The Britons held it to be their own sphere, a place of ethnic and political diversity to include Britoña, Brittany, Cornwall, Wales, or British-speaking northern Britain as *Britannia* without qualification.[32] As we shall see, the British-speaking Britons were not wholly conquered by England until the thirteenth century.

When Eadred died in 955, both the sons of Edmund succeeded in what became a dual monarchy. Edgar was first king of Mercia and Northumbria and only king of Wessex and thus of the whole kingdom when his brother Eadwig of Wessex died in 959.[33] There was a long period of peace in England from 954 into the 980s along with an improving climate, the start of the 'warm middle ages,' rising agricultural extraction, more towns and trade, all of which would have benefited the kings of Wessex as the wealthiest and greatest landowners and now the sole kings in England, if not always *of* England. George Molyneaux argues convincingly that it is Edgar's reign, not Æthelstan's or Alfred's, that advanced the state with hundred and wapentakes, new shires and shire meetings, reeves, currency and legal reforms all familiar in Domesday Book in 1086; but we should be wary of projecting that system onto the earlier period. We know shires and hides existed since the seventh century, but we do not know precisely how they operated and we should not assume from the silence in the records before the 960s that the machinery of government was already there.[34]

Edgar's coronation at the Roman city of Bath served to articulate Romano--British pretensions, and the *ordo* was amended to include the prayer that the king be honoured 'above all the kings of Britain' (but there is no evidence that Welsh, Scottish or Cumbrian magnates were present).[35] A meeting followed Edgar's coronation in 973 with six kings – possibly eight, including the king of the Scots – in Chester, who pledged him co-operation. (Edgar had a significant naval force with him at Chester, which probably helped.)[36] The assembly at the Roman town of Chester consciously aped the Continental gathering at Quedlinburg in eastern Saxony, where Otto I (Holy Roman Emperor since 962) celebrated Easter in the company of the dukes of Poland and Bohemia, along with legates from the Greeks, Beneventans, Hungarians, Bulgars, Danes and Slavs. Edgar had sent an embassy to Otto shortly before and would have known about the Quedlinburg gathering and attempted to copy it at Chester.[37]

The ceremony at Chester was used by nineteenth-century historians as part of the glorification of the 'English' over the British peoples, the story elaborated to link Edgar's status to the Empire, but it was actually a part of the pan-Germanic rather than the 'English' narrative that we have seen from Sutton Hoo and *Beowulf* to Offa and Æthelstan.[38] Chester was not Bath, either, it was border country between the older Mercian-Wessex kingdoms and the North.

Edgar was described as 'ruler of the Angles, friend of the West Saxons and protector of the Mercians'. The coronation liturgy presented the monarch as king of three peoples (up from two in Athelstan's *ordo* when it was first used), the Saxons, Mercians and Northumbrians, but the literature does not point to the suppression of 'Saxons' in preference to 'Angles' or indeed a royal programme of nation-building.[39] English overlordship of Scotland and Wales was not continuous; it was a loose and intermittent hegemony, enforcing temporary personal domination of one ruler over another and declining after Edgar's death to 966.[40] How far Edgar's authority or dominion (*anwealh*) extended beyond the River Tees and Ribble (although north of the Humber) or in Wales, since there were no hundreds or wapentakes, is questionable and far from the *Anglia* that appears in Domesday Book in 1086.

The legislation Edgar issued 966-975 at an unidentified place called *Wihtbordesstan* was the first known legislation explicitly covering Scandinavian settlement 'common to all the nation, whether Englishmen, Danes or Britons, in every province of my dominion [*anwealh*]', with the earl of Northumbria (Oslac) and the *here*, meaning the Danish settlers (no longer a raiding party) giving their support. The code was to be copied and sent to the ealdormen of Mercia and East Anglia.[41] It was issued because of a devastating plague which clearly was God's response to sin and the withholding of tribute; the remedy was to impose and reinforce rents and dues at all levels in order not to anger God (the code was probably drafted by archbishop Dunstan). Twelve sworn witnesses for each borough, hundred or wapentake were to stop the sale of stolen goods. The word 'wapentake' is first attested in this legislation and is of Old Norse derivation (*vápnatak* meaning 'to take weapons' or brandish them in assent at an assembly).[42] The previous ordinance of the bishops and reeves of the London district describes the 100-person groups to organise policing but the hundred was sometimes identified by 100 hides.

(Tribal Hidage assessments are all multiples of 100 hides.)[43] It may even be of Merovingian origin – the *centena* appears in Merovingian legal texts as a term for a district and a policing group. By the end of Edgar's reign these units could be taken for granted and used to standardise procedure, with a shift from ports and burhs under Æthelstan to hundreds and wapentakes under Edgar.[44]

Edgar's Andover decrees declare that the *scirgemot* (shire meeting) be held twice yearly and the *burhgemot* three times in the presence of an ealdorman or bishop. Cnut repeated these provisions. No accounts of shire meetings survive before the 960s. While there were assembly meetings held in the shire as far back as Ine in the 690s, it is not certain they were regular. Some shires were much older than others – those in the south-east correspond to ancient territorial units which take their names from early the Early English kingdoms of Essex, Kent, Middlesex, Surrey, and Sussex, all subsumed into the Wessex-Mercian hegemony by the mid-ninth century; Cornwall had been a Brittonic kingdom. Mercia was probably not divided into shires until at least the middle of the tenth century; Eadred's will (951-55) lists every Domesday shire south of the Thames except Cornwall but references only 'Mercia'.[45] Norfolk, Suffolk and Yorkshire do not emerge until the mid-eleventh century.

Edgar's code states that 'every man, whether rich or poor, is to be entitled to the benefit of the common law and just judgements are to be judged for him,' which may be a grand gesture (and anticipates the reforms of Henry II by two centuries) but it may also indicate the intention that these laws be made a reality.[46] The issue as to what extent Early English law codes were 'guidelines' rather than rules is one that follows us from the very first law codes of Æthelberht in *c*.600 with its huge financial penalties (before minting in Kent) and drastic physical punishments for every sort of offence. We know that Æthelberht's laws were passed down orally before Augustine's arrival in royal proclamation, but were the codes formal records of them, or little more than points for discussion? By the later Early English period, written law circulated perhaps quite widely and was respected, but the surviving law codes were not intended to be comprehensive and customary law continued alongside them, often not written down at all; royal law codes are not framed as complete statement of the law, but rather as additions to it, mingling with existing traditions.[47] Written norms were respected but were the starting point for discussion and adaptation.

Edgar's currency reforms were another certain change and were linked to local administration.[48] All moneyers (there were 120 at the time of the reforms) from the Channel to the Tees began striking the same design of coins sometime in the later years of Edgar's reign, probably 973, the increase in the volume of English currency perhaps due to the flow of silver discovered in mines in Germany in the 960s. The striking of a single type at any one time remained the norm until Stephen's reign. They almost always had a stylized royal portrait, the reigning king's name, the title *Rex Anglorum*, the moneyer's name and when the design was changed every few years, most coins in circulation were converted. Edgar could have used hundreds and wapentakes as a means of calling in old coins. These sort of coinage reforms were not exceptional to England; indeed, they occurred a century earlier in Frankia, under Charles the Bald after the Edict of Pîtres (864), which recalled all coinage and issued uniform design, metal and weight and was implemented with considerable success (except in Aquitaine).

One aspect of coinage, legal reforms and increasing central power of the late English state is Peter's Pence. This was a distinctly Early English phenomenon, illustrating the strong bond between church and kingship, England and Rome, which originated in the tradition of taking of gifts and donations to Rome in the seventh century by prominent ecclesiasts such as Benedict Biscop, Ceolfrith and Wilfrid, formalised into the 'hearth-penny' from every household in Edgar's Andover code.[49]

Edgar died in 975, only two years after his triumphant coronation in Bath and the imperial summit at Chester. He had become king of Wessex and Mercia aged only sixteen, so to what extent he personally was responsible for the reforms is open to question. There was a moral imperative for reform which we have already seen in the penances included in the law codes and from the 950s charters included 'dei Gratia' or words similar with marked frequency, manuscripts liken the kings to an abbot from Edgar onwards, with the king as model and corrector of his people ('vicar of Christ', 'shepherd of shepherds'). The *Chronicle* accounts of Edgar's coronation at Chester in 973 both point out his age – almost 30 (the same age as Christ at his baptism) and the new coronation *ordo* moved the three commands at the end of the ceremony into three promises at the beginning – peace, justice, and forbidding wrongdoing. Divine exhortation was becoming a common theme of enforcing laws, fines and punishments we see in the *Wihtbordesstan* decrees. There was a proliferation of Benedictine monasteries under Edgar, with close ties to the house of Wessex, which were extremely wealthy, based mainly in the south, and boosted royal power in the localities.

The driving force behind Edgar's administrative reforms, which should be seen as bound closely to the moral and religious reforms, was Æthelwold, Edgar's tutor, monk at Glastonbury, abbot of Abingdon and then Bishop of Winchester. Æthelwold started off in Æthelstan's household, served Eadwig, Edgar, Edward and finally Æthelred. His influence was significant, attesting almost all of Edgar's charters and forming a powerful influence on Æthelred, who became king at the age of twelve in 978.[50] Since Edgar became king in his late teens what we might determine as 'his' reforms in 'his' reign should be viewed in the light of Æthelwold's influence and in the reign of Æthelred, it is Wulfstan, archbishop of York, who is the key person who ensures continuity into the reign of Cnut.

Kingship was no longer a solitary business – if it ever was. Kings had always taken advice (as Bede tells us over Edwin's considered conversion) but regularity and wider, national, scope is another thing altogether. There is clear evidence for regular, well-attended royal assemblies – the *witan* (literally 'wise men') in the late ninth and early tenth centuries, handling much of the administration of the realm. When the *witan* was unable to meet or only met irregularly, much of the business of kingship was put on hold, hence in the early years of Æthelstan's reign few charters were issued and no law codes. The brief reign of Edward the Martyr produced few diplomas and no known legislation.[51] These assemblies were scattered from Eamont (927), to Chester (973), Nottingham, Stamford, Buckingham, Colchester and Aller in Somerset, but the vast majority were in southern England, the new heartland of the English kingdom (Wessex, London, Kent – 31 dated meetings) organised into what Levi Roach calls 'diplomatic' meetings, peace-making or submission (such as Guthrum's baptism in 878), 'legislative meetings' when law codes were issued (mostly south of the Thames) and the 'dispositive' meetings that produced royal charters.[52] Witnesses in attendance on Æthelstan's charters suggest at least 100, since other unnamed men were present, a marked change from earlier reigns, the average in attendance at Alfred's was fewer than 19, the longest witness list.[53] Those present always included the Archbishop of Canterbury, sometimes York, many bishops, a few abbots, 6-12 ealdormen and a large number of thegns. Æthelstan's charters show Scandinavian names and Edgar's include the greatest men from Mercia and Northumbria. Rulers from Wales and the far north, Strathclyde, appear.

Few kings from Æthelstan onwards travelled much north of the Thames; instead, the king's great men came to him. From Æthelstan's time onwards the assemblies had a place in the calendar: Easter and Christmas in Mercia and Wessex from the early ninth century, with origins in the Carolingian government. By Æthelstan's time, Whitsun was added, and this triadic calendar continued into the twelfth century.[54] Festival crown-wearing played a part in promoting the charismatic qualities of the king. The first evidence in England is from Eadred and notoriously, Eadwig, who in 956 had gone missing from the feast with two women, his crown (apparently bound with wondrous metal, gold and silver gems) on the floor; St Dunstan, at that time abbot of Glastonbury, put the crown back on his head and marched him back to the feast.[55] Perhaps, who knows, this reprimand had something to do with Eadwig's expulsion of Dunstan, who was recalled by Edgar and eventually became Archbishop of Canterbury.[56] The origins of crown-wearing were Carolingian but the more immediate precedents were German, an ongoing influence on the English monarchy throughout the ninth century.

Edgar's death aged thirty-two in 975 did not lead to the sort of collapse we saw in 940 after Æthelstan. The succession was again not clear since although it was Edgar's son Edward 'the Martyr' who became king, he was murdered in 978 and succeeded by Edgar's other son Æthelred by his consecrated queen Ælfthryth. The claims and pretensions of Æthelstan and Edgar to have realised the vision of Bede must be tempered with the reality of administrative reform, which may be said to have been a revolution in government from the 960s, consolidated by decades of peace. The dual monarchy of Wessex and Mercia had become cemented into one dominion by 978, reaching north of the Humber. This 'unification' – or more accurately, expansion by the Wessex royal house – would be completed not by further reform but by invasion and this time, conquest, of the Northmen.

EIGHT

Nemesis

In the late tenth century the existential threat of the Danes returned to England, initially for plunder and – as the wars became a matter of ethnic hatred – for conquest. Æthelred returned to power only on condition of good governance, a clear break from past traditions. His son Edmund was defeated at Ashingdon but even so, agreed with Cnut to divide the kingdom back to the old Danelaw of Alfred's time. At his death, Cnut took over the entire kingdom in 1016, exiling the Early English monarchy. This conquest was only possible due to the wealth and strength of the English polity. Cnut made few changes and reigned over three kingdoms, bringing England firmly into the Scandinavian orbit. After Cnut, the royal House of Wessex returned in the guise of Edward 'the Confessor', more by chance than design, again very much on condition of good governance.

One of the most successful pre-Conquest kings of all England was ironically – or perhaps fittingly – Danish. The *Chronicle* records the conquest of the kingdom of England in 1017:

> In this year King Cnut obtained all the kingdom of the English [*eallon Angelcynnes ryce*] and divided it into four, the West Saxons for himself, the East Angles for Thorkel, the Mercians for Eadric and the Northumbrians for Erik.[1]

Prominent ealdormen and their sons were executed, including ætheling Eadwig, one of Æthelred's sons, and in August Cnut ordered that Æthelred's widow, the daughter of the duke of Normandy, Queen Emma, be fetched to him as wife.

England was conquered not once but twice in the eleventh century. In 1066, Duke William of Normandy, Emma's great-nephew, defeated King Harold at the battle of Hastings, and at Berkhamsted received submission from the archbishop, royal prince, and earls after a campaign straight out of the military manual; he was crowned on Christmas Day in Westminster Abbey.[2] The totality and speed of William's conquest was testament to the coherence and centralization of the eleventh-century English kingdom, since it was a definite entity that one leader could seize from another.[3]

Six kings reigned in this period. Three centuries of Early English kingship came to an end in 1016. There was no certainty that it would resume. The break in the royal succession had been made, and the consequences of the Danish conquest meant that the future governance of England would be open successively to a Danish succession, to the surviving members of the Early English royal house, to a native, non-royal magnate and finally, to a double foreign invasion – Norwegian and Norman; none of these were inevitable and several alternative scenarios might have played out, including an earlier Norwegian invasion scare and an exiled prince from Hungary. The sacral monarchy of Old England was transformed. The corpse of one king was exhumed and flung in a ditch; another had his tomb smashed to pieces and a third had his bones ground to dust under an abbey church built to mark his defeat. Cross-channel winds, sibling rivalry, murder, hostage-taking and decades-old dynastic alliances played a part. The rules of succession were extemporised depending on the ascendant faction and ultimately it was the sword that was the most decisive instrument.

The conquest of 1016 was violent and traumatic. Thirty years of intermittent warfare is recorded in the *Chronicle*, from the 980s harrying, burning and slaughter is repeatedly mentioned, followed by huge payments. London, Southampton, Ipswich, Norwich, Thetford, Oxford, Cambridge, Bedford were all burned or ravaged. Raiding parties attacked the south coast, Essex, the Humber region, Northumbria, Cheshire, Devon. The English lost innumerable battles, entire regions were pillaged, manors and churches destroyed, leading thegns and earls either killed in battle or blinded by their own king and the Archbishop of Canterbury taken hostage and murdered. The level of destruction must have had an impact for decades.

Eleventh-century England was a highly monetised economy; peasants routinely paid rent in coin, land tax was collected regularly and efficiently, and manorial surpluses supported lavish lifestyles for kings and lords. An agricultural revolution in farming led to food surpluses and urban growth, and long-distance trade was a feature of the time. But this wealth attracted invaders. It was the wealth, and the capacity to exploit that wealth, that made England attractive to invasion. The personal wealth of Alfred has been noted, and the landed estates passed through the royal House to 1066 when Edward the Confessor could draw in around £8,000 per annum, late Early English earls up to £3,000 and annual incomes of church institutions and lay aristocrats varied greatly but could be up to

£1,000.[4] The Early English charters reflect a multitude of transactions – gifts, sales, bequests – with gold and precious-metal objects prominent at the expense of silver coin.[5] The use of money was the norm at lower levels of society, too, a money economy of considerable breadth and depth developing long before the thirteenth century.[6] Æthelred's peace treaty with the Viking army in 991 was paid for with 22,000 pounds in gold and silver and in 1018, the year he assumed the throne, Cnut levied a 72,000-pound tax over all England.[7] The repeated Danish invasions reflect the wealth and efficiency of the English state; military service and taxation came under great strain but continued to function to the very end.

It wasn't just about wealth since Alfred bought off the Danes in the 870s. Since then, as we have seen, a highly sophisticated state had emerged in the later tenth century. By 978 a kingdom encompassing much of modern-day England had emerged and was stable enough to support the accession of a boy-king and a period of 'regency'. The conquests of England in 1016 and 1066 perversely demonstrate the strength of the Early English polity; a wealthy, well-administered entity divided by treachery and regional diversity. There must be, after all, something intact and identifiable to conquer: the better defined a state with borders and laws, the more complete the conquest. Successful invasion does not necessarily equate to a failed state, as the rapid and total conquest of modern France in June 1940 attests.[8] It is a paradox of the later Early English state that its strengths made it vulnerable.[9]

These conquests did not cause the kingdom to fragment, since Cnut retained control over the whole entity; in 1066 the kingdom was conquered again but remained a coherent unit. The invasions of the eleventh century could be said to have affirmed the state, just as the Viking invasions of the ninth century created the vacuum into which stepped the royal house of Wessex. We should not be asking therefore, was the Old English state a failed state, but rather, how the monarchy itself was unable to retain control of the state. Æthelred II was temporarily ejected 1013-14; his son King Edmund partitioned the kingdom with Cnut in 1016 and Æthelred's other son, Edward the Confessor, swore to uphold the laws of Cnut to assembled nobility before taking the crown in 1042.

The grand designs of 'England' under first Æthelstan and then Edgar were realised to some extent in theory and in practice but although Latin writers increasingly called the kingdom *Anglia*, Ealdorman Æthelweard's chronicle, written *c*.980s for a Continental Saxon reader, draws from the *Chronicle* but its use of 'Saxon' vocabulary at key points highlights that there may not have been such a coherent scheme to promote a vision of a united *Angelcynn*.[10] Kings were dependent on aristocratic support; successful kingship was based on the achievement of consensus, which made collective action possible. Coinage was a product of cooperation between moneyers and kings – many offices were hereditary by the 1000s and taxation arose out of the urgent need to raise heregeld later in Æthelred's reign, a communal rather than royal interest.[11] It is in Æthelred's reign that shires and shire-reeves are first regularly recorded, magnates executed, exiled, and blinded. Since Æthelred's reign experienced one of the most sustained foreign threats in English history, we should ask how much of the state – and its national identity – was a product of these crisis years rather than an earlier period, although this time, it was no great war of faith like Alfred's since Swegn Forkbeard and Cnut were Christian and invaded the kingdom of England from their own kingdom of Denmark.

In the early eleventh century, Ælfric of Eynsham (a student of Æthelwold) noted the concept of society as being in three orders, his thinking quite possibly stimulated by the Viking raids wreaking destruction in and bringing uncertainty to England, wherein all the people were being mobilised in the fight:

> You should know, however, that there are three orders in this world, set in unity. These are *laboratores*, *oratores*, and *bellatores*. *Laboratores* are those who toil for our food, *oratores* are those who interceded with God for us, *bellatores* are those who guard our towns, and defend our land against an attacking army. Now, the farmer toils for our food, and the worldly warrior must fight against our enemies, and the servant of God must constantly pray for us and fight spiritually against invisible enemies.[12]

The 'Sermon of the Wolf to the English', preached by Archbishop Wulfstan of York in 1014, recalls Gildas, writing about how the sins of the Britons so angered God that he allowed the army of the English to conquer their land.[13] Wulfstan echoed Alcuin's letter, shocked by the sack of Holy Island, Lindisfarne, in 793 and Alcuin knew men who knew Bede, so the message that the English must obey God's law or suffer destruction remained the same.[14] Wulfstan also wrote of the social orders and he believed that kings had a duty to protect the people; both Ælfric and Wulfstan shared the belief that society was not in the proper order and that the people were being punished for their sins.[15]

Famous in secular literature was the classic English defeat at Maldon (Essex) in 991 when Ealdorman Byrhtnoth and all his men went down to defeat after inviting the Danish raiding party across the causeway to join battle.[16] The beginning and the end of the late tenth-century poem The *Battle of Maldon* are missing and similar to Asser's *Life of Alfred*, the manuscript survived the Reformation only to perish in the Ashburnham House 1731 fire; fortunately, a facsimile had been made in 1724 and is 325 lines long. The battle at Maldon was real enough, recorded in the *Chronicle*, but the heroics are from the world of *Beowulf*.[17] The Danes suggested that the English troops pay them tribute rather than risk battle but Byrhtnoth refuses:

'Hear you, sea rover, what this folk says? For tribute they will give you spears, poisoned point and ancient sword, such war gear as will profit you little in the battle. Messenger of the seamen, take back a message say to your people a far less pleasing tale, that there stands here with his troop an earl of unstained renown, who is ready to guard this realm, the home of Æthelred my lord, people, and land; it is the heathen that shall fall in the battle...'

Here then, is the allegiance to the king, people, and the land (*folc and foldan*), perhaps an identity forged ever closer after the ten years of raiding and plundering by the north men. It didn't go well for Byrhtnoth, who died in the thick of the fighting, but his faithful warriors fought on to die with their lord or to avenge him (although the few who fled were carefully noted) and at the last, the old retainer Brihtwold exhorts those still on the field to fight on:

'Thoughts must be the braver, heart more valiant, courage the greater as our strength grows less. Here lies our lord, all cut down, the hero in the dust... I will not leave the field, but think to lie by lord's side, by the man I held so dear.'

These were the values of the battlefield that resonate from *Beowulf* to Maldon, Hastings (where Harold fell with his brothers, surrounded by the housecarls) and across time to the noble fellowship of death at Crécy, Agincourt and Bosworth.

After Maldon and the peace treaty of 991, the raiding continued and so did the tributes, growing increasingly larger, but in 1002 any semblance of honour was lost when Æthelred ordered 'all the Danish men who were among the English race to be killed on Brice's Day [13 November] because it was made known to the king that they wanted to ensnare his life – and later his councillors – and have his kingdom afterwards.'[18] This was nothing short of genocide, the extreme 'othering' provoked by decades of intermittent and deadly war without end. We have no record of similar orders in England and the silence does not mean it didn't happen, but the numerous references to Danes in law codes and treaties from Alfred to Æthelred regarding *wergild* and trade suggest attempts at a working relationship with the unwelcome neighbours, but this changed now. Was Æthelred's order obeyed? In a pit near Weymouth, archaeologists found a mass grave of decapitated men thrown into a heap, their heads piled to one side; this was dated to around 1000 and they were Vikings, not local people.[19] In Oxford, a mass burial of mostly young adult Viking males was excavated in 2008; they had been hacked to death and unceremoniously dumped. A charter of 1004 granted to St Frideswide's Church describes Æthelred's decree and the slaughter of the Oxford Danes:

> For it is fully agreed that to all dwelling in this country it was well known that, since a decree was sent out by me with the counsel of my leading men and magnates to the effect that all the Danes who sprung up in this island, sprouting like cockle amongst the wheat were to be destroyed by a most just extermination, and thus this decree was to be put in to effect even as far as death, those Danes who dwelt in the afore-mentioned town [Oxford], striving to escape death, entered this sanctuary of Christ [St Frideswide's], having broken by force the doors and bolts, and resolved to make refuge and defence for themselves therein against the people of the town and the suburbs, but when all the people in pursuit strove, forced by necessity, to drive them out, and could not, they set fire to the planks and burnt, as it seems, this church with its ornaments and its books.[20]

It may not be that the Weymouth and Oxford mass graves were those slaughtered on St Brice's Day, perhaps the execution of a raiding party (nevertheless still horrible) but this charter does reveal the chilling language of ethnic cleansing.[21] The Biblical 'sprouting like cockle' (Matthew xiii, 25) suggests some sort of impurity compared with the 'wheat' of the English (and recalls Grendel, the 'grinder' who comes in from the outside marshes to the community and has to be slain by Beowulf, the bee-wolf and defender of the productive fields). The graphic depiction of the Danes seeking refuge in the church and burnt to death or hacked apart while escaping suggest no mercy either. The church was a sanctuary, but the (Christian) Danes were not *given* sanctuary, something specified in law codes since Alfred.[22]

The order to kill all the Danes was perhaps what Ælfric had in mind when he distinguished a king who guides his people with restraint from a tyrant (*tyrannus*) who oppresses his people with power. The consequences of unrighteous kingship included ravaging, hunger, pestilence, bad weather and attacks by wild animals. Ælfric's homilies also allude negatively to various taxes and all new laws. Wulfstan (who drafted much of Æthelred's legislation) intensified concerns with the obligations of Christian rulership, earthly prosperity, and the consequences of breaching promises in that the sins of the king would be visited on the people.[23]

The attention thus switches to the king, and contemporaries and historians have condemned Æthelred *Unraed* alike as unfit to govern, despite wearing the crown for decades (although the Chronicles were written after his reign). Æthelred's personal kingship was judged to be unworthy; in 1013-14 he was exiled to Normandy and for the first time since the records began in the late ninth century, with their retrospective view to the fifth century, no English king, let alone any member of the royal house of Wessex, ruled England. It was Swegn Forkbeard who briefly ruled. Æthelred returned in 1014 but this return was conditional on governing justly, which reflects a shift towards a different type of kingship, more dependent upon the support of his people:

> Then all the wise people [witan], ecclesiastical and lay, advised that King Æthelred should be sent for, and they said that no lord was dearer to them than their natural lord if he would rule them more justly than he did before... And full friendship was established with word and pledge on either side, and they pronounced every Danish king an outlaw from *Engla lande* for ever.[24]

Note the use of 'natural lord' (rather than Swegn) and the condition that 'he would rule them more justly' the first recorded pact between king and people.[25] Swegn's son Cnut was still in England and war resumed; Æethelred died in 1016, ending a 38-year reign, the longest since Alfred's 28-year reign but with a rather different obit since he goes down in history as *unræd* ('bad counsel') to Alfred's 'Great'. According to the *Chronicle,* the witan chose Æthelred's son Edmund as king, but later sources cast some doubt on the unity behind Edmund's election.[26] Edmund fought a series of battles, winning some, losing some, but the turning point came at the Battle of Ashingdon (Essex) when Edmund suffered a crushing defeat, not helped by Ealdorman Eadric's treachery.[27] Eadric 'betrayed his royal lord and the whole nation' in a distinctly un-Beowulfian deed by starting the flight.[28] 'All the chief men' of the kingdom died at Ashingdon except Edmund, who eschewed the warrior's death and managed, remarkably, to bring Cnut to a peace treaty.

Edmund and Cnut met after Ashingdon on neutral ground at Olney Island (near Deerhurst by the River Severn in Gloucestershire), the site of an important Benedictine monastery and where St Alphege, former monk and archbishop of Canterbury murdered by the Vikings had once been a monk. The significance of the location would not have been lost on the two war-leaders. Two Early English churches survive intact today at Deerhurst a quarter of a mile apart. The partition of England between Edmund and Cnut showed the unity of all England to be illusory once again; Edmund succeeded to Wessex, Cnut to 'the north part' and 'Mercia', reverting to the Alfredian era of the 880s, although a twelfth-century source suggested that the *regnum* remained with Edmund since Cnut's authority north of the Thames was that of a sub-king.[29] The two men became 'partners and pledge-brothers', affirmed with oaths (London made a separate peace treaty, importantly). Not only was Æthelred's kingship dependent on his more just rule but his son Edmund now ruled the rump of the kingdom, what had been the Wessex heartland. It would be interesting to know if this lasted (probably not) but on Edmund's death in November, Cnut became king of all England. Perhaps Edmund died of wounds, perhaps the peace agreement at Deerhurst recognised that he had not got long to live – it is worth considering if Alfred had died soon after Edington and Wedmore, what then?

Cnut left no room for speculation, asserting his authority immediately, executing the treacherous Eadric alongside the ætheling Eadwig. The deal at Deerhurst was perhaps something of an embarrassment since he obviously saw Ashingdon as his great victory, building a new minster there for consecration in 1020, directly anticipating William the Conqueror's new abbey on the site of his victory near Hastings.[30] War stimulated change: the *heregeld* (army tax) was first levied in 1012 but under Cnut it was imposed across the whole of *Englalond* and so the administrative innovations of the late tenth century were being used within a few decades to impose burdens on the population and they increased royal power.

The English state survived but its rulers from 1016 onwards would be of non-'English' or part-English origin – Danish, Norman, French – for the following three centuries. In 1018 Cnut became king of Denmark and in 1028 king of Norway, bringing England into his Scandinavian 'empire', completing the cultural influence of the region in England's formation and identity since the first raids of the late eighth century and suggesting that a very different narrative was possible to that of the Early English destiny. Indeed, it might be argued that the brief flowering of English unity and reform in the tenth century was something of an aberration between two periods of Viking invasions and ultimate conquest.

The witan met at Oxford in 1018 and agreed the peace between the English and the Danes. Cnut's law code of 1020 was the longest of the Early English law codes and embodied much of the earlier legislation; the preface states that the witan would 'zealously' observe Edgar's laws.[31] There was no legislation under Edward the Confessor but he confirmed Cnut's laws, which became part of the transmission to the post-Norman period, passed down to Henry I as the 'Laws of Edward'.[32] During the northern rebellion of 1065 Edward the Confessor renewed the law of King Cnut after the rebels met Earl Harold at Northampton, suggesting pre-Conquest respect for Cnut's laws.[33] Many of Cnut's laws were drafted by the English Archbishop Wulfstan. We can infer that Cnut was also made to accept the conditions laid down to Æthelred in 1014 in his second law code of 1021/2, where clauses 69-83 promise his people relief from oppressions and particularly royal oppressions such as illicit purveyance, excessive heriots (taxes) and royal control of widows, issues we shall see re-emerging in Magna Carta in 1215. The oath of loyalty, first mentioned in Alfred's laws, is made explicit (every man over twelve years of age is to give an oath that he will not be a thief or accessory) and crucially Cnut made law as *ealles engla landes cyning* for *eall Englaland*.[34] From Cnut's reign onwards we find all versions of the *Chronicle* use *Englalond* frequently, whereas Æthelred was king of the *Angelcynn*; Cnut referred to his subjects as 'Danes or English' and so *Englalond* was now a territory regardless of ethnicity. *Engla lond* and *Englisc* were as much in use in the eleventh century as they are today.[35]

The two letters of Cnut (written in English) addressed to the English people in 1019/1020 and 1027 are unparalleled in any other country: these are widely addressed, perhaps intended for proclamation in the shire courts; the first promises good government and the second mentions 'the whole race of the English, whether nobles or ceorls'.[36] The letter of 1019 repeats that it is Cnut's will to observe Edgar's laws. The letter of 1027, following Cnut's pilgrimage to Rome, tells us how Cnut was honoured by Pope John and the German Emperor Conrad and many princes at a great assembly at Easter and how he negotiated safe passage for Englishmen and Danes alike undertaking the pilgrimage. Cnut was also greatly concerned that the sheriffs and reeves used no unjust force and that 'all men' shall have the right 'to enjoy just law,' which echoes Edgar's code regarding rich and poor alike having access to the 'common law'.

Cnut's Scandinavian followers were granted land in every shire in England but there was no replacement of native landowners on the scale of the Norman Conquest, although powerful earls appointed by Cnut like Godwin and Siward were to influence the successions of 1035 and 1041 and Harold Godwinsson was to take the throne in 1066.[37] The Viking conquest of Cnut left no trace of DNA except in Orkney, the British genes remaining in the majority, as with the pre-Saxon immigrations of the sixth century.[38]

Cnut went to Scotland in 1031 and received the submission of three kings, very much assuming the imperial, British, assertions of his Early English predecessors.[39] The North remained a distinctly separate entity under the Anglo-Danish rule of Cnut. Siward was the earl of Northumbria who came to power under Cnut, and who first appears on the record in 1033; he was of Danish origin and commemorated in legend in the thirteenth century Crowland Abbey chronicle as Siward Diagra, 'the Strong', since his son, Waltheof, was executed by William I in 1076 and venerated as a saint and martyr.[40]

Slavery remained in England. The 'British/Welsh' group defined in Ine's late seventh-century laws seemingly assimilated into one society by the time of Alfred, but slavery continued to flourish and we should ask whether the slaves were predominantly 'British' by ethnicity. The 'Exeter Book' dated to *c.* 1000 portrays the only drunken woman in Old English poetry, and she is a 'Welsh' slave. She is portrayed as sexually aggressive and dark-haired, and this hair colour is associated with slavery or lower social status in other riddles, whereas upper-class women are fair-haired. The tropes of 'evil' or 'ugly' outward appearance – dark-skinned, dark-hair – representing status and moral behaviour are present in the Early English values (and stereotypes like this continue well into twentieth-century literature and media). Slavery was largely, though not exclusively, agrarian, many slaves being employed as ploughmen in the late tenth and early eleventh centuries, and Domesday Book (1086) regularly associates the slave with the plough.[41] Slavery could also be imposed as a judicial penalty. There was nothing benign about Early English slavery, as Ælfric's ploughman cries out: 'Oh! Oh! The work is hard. Yes, the work is hard, because I am not free.'[42]

Æthelred's law code of 1009 prohibits the sale of men out of the country, as does Cnut's law code, which also prohibits selling them to heathen lands – so ownership of Christians by heathens was more distasteful than slavery itself.[43] Bristol was the centre of the slave trade (as it was in the eighteenth century) and connected to Dublin's slave market, an economy that had been flourishing since the seventh century and is largely invisible to the archaeological record and under-represented in the written sources, which are more concerned with the elites.

Cnut's death in late 1035 and the sudden, early deaths of his two sons without heirs within six years led to the chance return of the Early English monarchy under Edward the Confessor, who very soon faced threats from Magnus, King of Norway, and Denmark. It was by no means certain that the House of Wessex would return. Edward's brother Alfred was murdered in an abortive attempt to return home in 1036 (an event that would resonate to 1066) and at an assembly at Oxford, Earl Leofric of Mercia and all the thegns north of the Thames elected King Harold 'Harefoot', but Godwin, the chief men of Wessex and Queen Emma opposed this, remaining in Winchester to hold Wessex for Harthacnut, yet again dividing England into the old kingdoms of Mercia and Wessex, something we saw in 924, 955 and 1016.[44] Harold was the son of Ælfgifu of Northampton (daughter of a powerful Mercian lord) by Cnut and the pro-Godwin annal states slanderously that 'some men said' that Harold was the son of Cnut and Ælfgifu and that it seemed 'quite unbelievable' that Harold was full king over all of England.[45]

There was no attempt to salvage the hopes of the royal house of Wessex in 1036 by the ruling elites or by Queen Emma, whose priority was for her son by Cnut, Harthacnut. His absence in Denmark meant that he was eventually 'forsaken' in favour of Harold, suggesting that perhaps another dual monarchy would have been the solution if Harthacnut had arrived in England in 1036 – or at least, if this the Mercian 'coup' had succeeded. On Harold Harefoot's death in 1040, Harthacnut made no mistake; arriving with 60 ships, he was received as king and immediately ordered the body of Harold to be disinterred and flung into a ditch.[46] Harthacnut started as he went on, ruling like a tyrant (according to the C version of the *Chronicle*). In his brief, two-year reign, he levied a huge heregeld, raised a tribute to pay for his homecoming fleet, sent housecarls to ravage the town and shire of Worcester after the townspeople killed his tax-collectors, and organized the murder of Earl Eadwulf of Bernicia while the earl was under safe-conduct at the royal court, which made him a pledge-breaker.[47] It must have been some relief then, when he dropped dead 'at his drink', falling to the floor in an awful convulsion at Lambeth.[48]

Prior to Harthacnut's death, another ætheling of the royal house of Wessex, Edward, brother to the murdered Alfred and a son of Æthelred by Emma of Normandy, was recalled from Normandy in 1041. This was done through the intervention of Bishop Ælfwine of Winchester and Earl Godwin, and at Harthacnut's behest; as a reward, Godwin's sons Swegn and Harold were made earls in 1043 and 1045 and his daughter Edith married the king late in 1045.[49] Godwin, earl of Wessex, was the most powerful of Cnut's earls, and was adept as a kingmaker, having switched from Harthacnut to Harold and back to Harthacnut (and probably had a hand in Alfred's murder).[50] Godwin's power reflects the transient nature of English kingship, which was now not only potentially claimable by several heirs of the royal house (as it always had been) but by heirs produced by Cnut's new dynasty after the conquest in 1016. Edward the Confessor's accession in 1042 was not simply on the whim of Godwin though, since Edward had to swear an oath to uphold Cnut's Laws in 1041 at Hurst Head (a long shingle spit of land between Hampshire and the Isle of Wight) as a precondition to his kingship and election.[51] This was a pre-arranged gathering with the 'thegns of all England' (though in reality a delegation of nobles and gentry) and it fits the pattern of peacemaking and treaty negotiation in medieval Europe, which often happened on islands, boats or boundaries. We saw this at the meeting between Cnut and Edmund in 1016 on Olney Island (Deerhurst). The rowing of Edgar on the River Dee by eight kings in 973 may have been a treaty made between equals, in neutral space on a boat and at a border point. In 921, Charles the Simple had concluded a peace treaty with Henry I on a boat anchored in the middle of the Rhine.[52]

Edward swore an oath to observe Cnut's laws, making his return conditional and echoing the return of his father Æthelred from exile in 1014.[53] The *Chronicle* states that Edward was sworn in as king and the *Encomium Emmae*, written during 1040-42 at the behest of Queen Emma, says that Harthacnut asked Edward to come and hold the kingdom with him.[54] Queen Emma, wife to both Æthelred and Cnut, sought exile during Harold's reign and her support for Harthacnut was very clear; in 1043, after his coronation, he took troops to his mother's house in Winchester and confiscated all her treasure, a moment of emotional trauma, of rejection and bitterness in this family war between the generations. (There was a reconciliation in around 1052 judging by the grant of an estate to her in Norfolk).[55]

Following agreement to these conditions, Edward was crowned at Winchester by Archbishop Eadsige. Under Edward, festivals and assemblies continued without any innovatory change, but Edward's style and image were more regal, even imperial, than any king since Æthelstan.[56] The near-contemporary *Life of King Edward* tells us that his throne was covered in a cloth of gold. Spearhavoc, abbot of Abingdon and a famous craftsman, was commissioned in 1050 to make him a new crown, fashioned from gold and gems; his pendant seal, the first of its kind in England, shows him enthroned with sceptre and orb, an image repeated on Edward's sovereign coins. His crown, sceptre and royal ring were found in his tomb in 1102 when it was opened.

Edward's pedigree as reigning monarch of the royal house of Wessex and the projection of his power as king not only of the English but of Britain is continuous with the tenth-century assertions of Æthelstan and Edgar. In his royal charters, he appears as 'king of the English' and 'king of the whole of Britain'.[57] Wales was invaded and subdued in 1063, its princes swearing oaths of loyalty and surrendering hostages; Malcolm had been put on the throne of Scotland with Edward's support in 1057 but beyond that, he was merely 'within Edward's sphere of influence'.[58] Ireland remained completely independent; early in Edward's reign, Swegn of Denmark was his vassal, but Edward's actual power sat somewhere between wishful thinking and *realpolitik*: as a charter of 1050 says, Edward was 'king of the whole Anglo Saxon race and, by the grace of God, governor and ruler of all the other surrounding peoples.'[59]

By the end of Edward the Confessor's 23-year reign, Professor James Campbell concludes emphatically that 'late Anglo-Saxon England was a nation-state. It was an entity with effective central authority, uniformly organised institutions, a national language, a national church, defined borders ... and, above all, a strong sense of national identity.'[60] From Domesday Book we know that in 1066 there was only one national, kingdom-wide estate, the royal demesne; King Edward possessed manors in every shire and was the wealthiest in eighteen of them. The greatest concentration lay south of a line between Gloucester, Oxford, Westminster and Canterbury but there were estates in Mercia, East Anglia and Yorkshire. Royal assemblies were held in London, Westminster, Winchester, Gloucester, and possession of property within and *en route* to the zone of assembly politics was much prized by members of England's landed elite.[61] Physical proximity to power mattered as much as real estate; alongside the witness lists of royal diplomas, royal assemblies exercised a strong gravitational pull on the elite in the late Old English period. This ensured that the landed elite were more committed to the kingdom's political centre of gravity than to local power and were collectively aligned with the kingdom as a whole, which suggests that the English kingdom was held together as much by land tenure and lordship as by institutional structures.

The developments in England in the late tenth and mid-eleventh centuries were not peculiar to England. There were many borrowings first from Carolingian France and then Ottonian Germany (which had the most advanced chancery in Europe). They were three times larger than England, and their borders were relatively natural. The Northern Iberian kingdom known as Léon (910-1037) and Léon-Castile (1037-1157) expanded to the detriment of non-Christian rivals – problematically referred to as a 're-conquest' – and Hungary in the eleventh century used oaths concerning theft, groupings of ten similar to the frankpledge system in England, the ordeal, earls, lordships and offices, assemblies and a kingdom-wide system of taxation, all concepts again borrowed from the Carolingian models of government.[62]

The experience of fighting against a common enemy under Æthelred surely contributed to a collective feeling of Englishness. Contemporary writers certainly believed in the importance of one kingdom, including Æthelwold, Ælfric, Wulfstan II of York, the *Encomium Emmae*, the *Chronicle* and the *Life of Edward the Confessor*. The Benedictine reform movement asserted the principle of one rule and one country.[63] If external threat served to sharpen identity, then internal peace enabled consolidation and reform. Between 954 and 1066 no English king ever had to put down by force a rising of his own people.[64] The relatively low fertility rate of English kings, childless deaths and the killings of æthelings reduced the competition. Arguably, the kings of England 927-1042 – West Saxon and Danish – never succeeded in depriving the English north of its separate identity and incorporating it fully into their England, an issue which proved significant in 1066. It is to that crucial event in the making of England which we now turn.[65]

NINE

William or Harold?

England was at peace for decades under Edward the Confessor, but the legacy of Cnut's conquest cast a long shadow. The precedent of regime change had been established and the politics of Scandinavia closely linked to those of England. Furthermore, Edward had spent his exile in Normandy since his mother, Emma, was the daughter of the duke of Normandy. Cnut's administration enabled the rise of powerful earls, one of whom, Godwin, married his daughter to Edward. The failure to produce a male heir triggered a power struggle that ignored the collateral heirs of the royal House and brought the forces of the Anglo-Scandinavian and Norman worlds onto a collision course that destroyed Old England once and for all.

In early medieval England there was no regular institution of the 'heir presumptive'.[1] Royal succession practices in later Early England included the following: designating a successor; making a will and implanting the late king's will; the 'election' of those in power, the act of submission and oath of loyalty; the ritual of the king's consecration and the coronation oath.[2] We have seen how brothers, uncles and nephews succeeded to the throne, from Alfred to Edward the Confessor, but they were all from the royal house of Wessex. What changed this was succession by conquest, which Cnut had exercised in 1016 and duke William would also do in 1066. However, the clash between England and Normandy in 1066 was by no means inevitable, since Edward the Confessor did have an heir of his royal house, but Edward's inability to ensure a decisive succession in his final years, even with an obvious royal prince in his court left the kingdom at the mercy of his distant relation and an overmighty earl, both at the height of their powers and both believing that Edward had offered them the throne at different times. Since the conquest of England in 1066 was so catastrophically different to Cnut's conquest of 1016, the details of the succession dispute are of great importance and hinge around two key individuals: Earl Harold Godwinsson and duke William of Normandy.

It is hard not to see Edward the Confessor's reign as a prelude to the Norman Conquest, since the last fifteen of the twenty-four years of his reign were clouded with doubts and controversies over the succession. The problem with Edward's succession crises is that it is ostensibly teleological: all points lead towards the inexorable and inevitable conquest of England in 1066. It need not have been so, right up until the end of the day at Hastings in October 1066. But it was, and so the debates pick over the finite details of each chronicle, event, and motive of the key players to piece together a narrative that holds water. None entirely do. William of Malmesbury in his *History of England* (1120s) pointed out that the facts were uncertain and ever since then historians have failed to agree.[3]

Most of the details of the succession and the events of 1066 come from post-Conquest Norman sources justifying the conquest, but the English sources, sparse though they are, are just as politicised. The English annals for 1035-1066 are drawn from three manuscripts, known as C, D and E of the *Chronicle*. C was composed somewhere in Mercia and was near-contemporary from about 1043-1066 and it was hostile to the House of Godwin; E was composed in St Augustine's, Canterbury and was more favourable to Godwin.[4] Annalistic writing and factional politics were closely connected during this period and it is assumed that they were written during or soon after what they record. Version D was compiled by people close to Ealdred, archbishop of York (d.1069), probably composed during Ealdred's lifetime, perhaps contemporary from 1052 onwards, compiled at various places wherever Ealdred was; D was a conflation of versions C and E but with additional and unique material of its own.[5]

The rivalry between Godwin and the earls of Mercia (the 'ancient hatred' according to the *Life of King Edward*) was a significant factor in English politics from 1035 to 1066. Factional rivalry was a central fact of court politics of later Early England to the extent that the stability of the kingdom was to a large extent dependent on the king's ability to balance rival factions; power was dependent on negotiation and compromise.[6]

The balance of power began to tip in favour of Godwin from 1043 to 1045 with the marriage of his daughter Edith to Edward and his sons' appointments to earldoms. Edward married Edith, Godwin's daughter, in January 1045. Since Godwin had been instrumental in helping Edward ascend the throne in 1042 this seemed a just reward, even though Godwin was involved closely with the murder of Alfred, Edward's brother, in 1036; Edward also promoted two of Godwin's sons and a nephew to earldoms in the period, completing Godwin's pre-eminence in the kingdom. As time went by, it became clear that Edward and Edith were going to be childless, a cause of much speculation. It seems unlikely that he would remain deliberately celibate; the reputation of Edward as a saintly king who lived chastely and who treated Edith like a daughter started with the *Life of King Edward*, a biography commissioned by Queen Edith herself. This was perhaps an attempt to deflect attention away from the infertility of the queen and her perceived 'failure' to bear the king an heir; the twelfth-century historians further trumpeted Edward's saintliness as the case was made for Edward's canonisation, William of Malmesbury suggesting that Edith had committed adultery.[7]

Edward was understandably seeking to establish his own base, appointing Robert of Jumièges archbishop of Canterbury in 1051, overruling the choice of the monks of Canterbury, one of Godwin's kinsmen (Æthelric) and creating an earldom for his half-French nephew Ralph in the east Midlands, close to the Godwin heartlands (land which belonged to the murdered Beorn). He also appointed another kinsman, Rudolph, to the abbacy of Abingdon.[8] At around this time Osbern fitzOsbern, a cousin of both King Edward and duke William, brother of William fitzOsbern, one of duke William's closest companions from childhood and a major player in the 1066 invasion, joined Edward's chaplaincy before the early 1060s, serving Harold and then William, who made him bishop of Exeter in 1072.[9] Two Norman-Bretons, another Ralph and Robert fitzWimarch, were at court, the latter present at the king's deathbed and holder of Clavering castle; another Robert, from a Norman family, apparently grew up in Edward's court where he served as a squire, returned to Normandy as a young adult and came over with the Conqueror in 1066. He died fighting the Welsh in 1093.[10] Edward may not have 'packed' his court with kinsmen, but he certainly made efforts to side-step the suffocating embrace of the Godwins.

The spark that lit the fuse of open conflict between the king and Godwin was another Frenchman and relative of the king, Edward's brother-in-law, Count Eustace of Boulogne. Some sort of argument over lodgings at Dover spiralled into an armed skirmish in the streets, leaving dozens dead on either side.[11] Eustace appealed to the king at Gloucester, who ordered Godwin to 'go to into Kent with hostility', but Godwin refused to punish people in his own earldom and this was the nub of it: the so-called 'fracas' at Dover tells us more about the rival factions at court than it does a street-fight. Eustace arrived at Dover fully armed in order to provoke violence as part of a design to assert authority over the town, which lay in Godwin's earldom of Wessex; after the bloodshed he raced back to Edward to get his version of the events in first.[12] Eustace had married Gode, King Edward's sister and mother to Ralph, recently made an earl in the Midlands, now his stepson; Gode, who died in 1049, had substantial estates across southern England and Eustace was patron of the restored minster at Dover, a key strategic port and military town since Roman times, and his intervention posed a direct threat to Godwin.[13] The clash at Dover therefore, was not about English and 'foreigners' but about Edward's attempt to place his own men in key positions in the local communities, something Godwin objected to more generally, regardless of the specific events in Dover.

The showdown was at Beverstone, Gloucestershire, at the Longtree Hundred meeting-place. Earl Godwin and his sons arrived with a 'great and countless army ready for war' and the earls Siward and Leofric were also present with 'many men from the north' ready to attack Godwin if the king gave the word.[14] This was potentially the most dangerous moment the English state faced between 1016 and 1066.[15] Conflict was avoided though, because 'There was in those two companies most of the finest in *Ængla landa*, and considered they would be leaving the land open to our enemies, and great ruin among ourselves (it was hateful to almost all to fight against men of their own *cynnes*, because there was little else that was worth anything apart from *Englisce* on either side).'[16] The language certainly demonstrates acceptance of the 'English' national security and the need for unity in the face of foreign threats from other races, but a more prosaic reason for no conflict might lie at the heart of this; the thegns of England had been bought off. In early spring of 1051, the infamous 'heregeld' had been lifted by Edward, after thirty-nine years; this merited a rare entry in the Chronicles, and could have been a concession for the unpopular appointment of Robert of Jumièges as well as compensation for the thegns – the men in the middle – who were hardest hit by the heregeld.[17] It also signalled the end of the 'housecarls' stranglehold on the royal palace and possibly a move towards a kingship based on consent, which was more apparent at the autumn council meeting.[18]

The king guaranteed his peace at Beverstone and a council meeting in London in the autumn was set and hostages exchanged, but this time the Godwins were outmanoeuvred; Swegn was outlawed, Earl Godwin refused to present his counter-plea and his men melted away. This council issued summons to people in the earldoms of Northumbria and Mercia in what was perhaps of representative significance as well as, or instead of, military force, the force being the will or common assembly of people.[19] In the face of these overwhelming numbers, and far from 'being ready to do battle' Godwin's force had dwindled until all the thegns of the earls transferred to the king, perhaps because they were relieved of the heavy burden of the heregeld. The thegns rarely appear in the Chronicles but were the people who led the local communities and who appeared at the biannual shire-courts and witnessed the charters and diplomas at a local level.[20]

Refused safe-conduct and knowing the game was up, Godwin and his sons fled London by night, Harold to Ireland, Godwin, Swegn and Tostig to Bruges (Tostig had married Judith, half-sister of the Count of Flanders who gave Godwin his protection that winter); Queen Edith was stripped of her lands and possessions and despatched to Wherwell Abbey in Hampshire.[21]

It was an extraordinary fall from grace for a faction dominant in England for almost thirty years and would directly influence the succession. The *Chronicle* even said: 'It would have seemed remarkable to everyone who was in England, if anyone earlier had told them it would turn out thus, because he was formerly so very much raised up, *as if he ruled the king and all England*.'[22]

The moment the Godwins exit the kingdom, duke William of Normandy enters the stage. Edward was now free to consider duke William as a possible heir since he was William's kinsman (first cousin once removed) and already indebted to the ducal house for his exiled years; charters from the 1030s were issued in the name of Edward 'rex Anglorum' by Duke Robert of Normandy, which suggest that Edward was very much the 'king across the water' and treated so by the Norman dukes.[23] There was by then clearly no chance of a child with Queen Edith for whatever reason, and it was natural therefore to return to his Norman roots now that the Godwin faction had been removed.

In the trenchant words of Professor Sir James Holt, William's succession to the throne of England was based on a 'concocted, trumped-up claim' advanced so successfully by Norman propaganda that it has confused historians ever since.[24] William himself had succeeded to the duchy of Normandy (as a bastard minor) just as the rules of succession were hardening. Two generations or so later, he would not have stood a chance. The chief Norman source, duke William's chaplain, former soldier and eyewitness William of Poitiers, was writing in the 1070s for a wide audience (both English and Norman) and used classical allusions to highlight the legitimacy of duke William's claim; he was familiar with English geography and succession practices and his work was used by twelfth-century historians of the Conquest.[25]

William of Poitiers tells us that duke William was responsible for putting Edward on the throne in 1042 – unlikely since duke William was around 15 years old and facing multiple threats in the duchy at that time, although the close relations between duke Robert and Edward would lend it credibility – more likely, Edward designated William his heir, an offer conveyed by the Norman archbishop Robert of Jumièges in 1051 and sworn on oath by the leading English magnates with a son and grandson of Godwin handed over as hostages.[26] At a later date, Edward sent Earl Harold to confirm this grant with an oath, and Harold became William's man on this visit and swore to uphold the claim when Edward died, which means that he perjured himself when he took the throne after Edward's death in 1066. Furthermore, Harold was consecrated by Archbishop Stigand illegally, as seen in the Bayeux Tapestry, but William was crowned by Ealdred after an election with English nobles and bishops, completing his rightful claim that started with a papal blessing for the campaign. This post-Conquest Norman triumphalist narrative is riddled with anomalies. It is unlikely that Godwin would swear such an oath on his return to England in 1052 and Harold, at that time earl of East Anglia and leading nobleman, is not mentioned; Harold's oath on the infamous crossing to Normandy is placed variously at Bayeux, Bonneville, and Rouen.

To complicate things further, an English source, the *Chronicle* D manuscript, records a visit to England by duke William in 1051 after the Godwin family fall from grace, timing which would suit both William and Edward; this source was written under the auspices of Ealdred, bishop of Worcester (1042-1062) and archbishop of York (1061-69) who was involved in the succession issue, helping to arrange the return of Edward the Exile to England in 1057, crowning both Harold and William in 1066 while supporting Edgar Ætheling in between coronations.[27] It was Ealdred who was dispatched by Edward to pursue Harold and his brother Leofwine from London in 1051 and so Ealdred would have been an eye-witness to duke William's visit after the Godwins had fled.[28]

None of the Norman sources record such a visit, perhaps not wanting William to appear a supplicant; rather, his acceptance of Edward's offer from Archbishop Robert put him on equal terms with Edward, with the English magnates swearing an oath to support this placing them firmly in obeisance to the future king. Both the offer and the visit are possible. An offer conveyed earlier in 1051 and sealed by William's visit to England in the autumn, by which time the Godwins had departed, when there was no chance of an heir with Edith (the marriage about to be annulled) and when William was secure enough in Normandy to accept such an offer. A private agreement between Edward and William would not only overturn the balance of power established under Cnut but would exclude the English elite from their customary involvement, a huge risk for Edward and something the Norman sources did not like to draw attention to, since they were creating a narrative of William's inheritance based on consent as well as ties of kinship.[29]

In the spring of 1052, Edward's mother, the redoubtable dowager queen Emma, wife firstly to Æthelred and then to Cnut, mother of two kings of England, died; in death she preferred her second, Danish husband, to her English one, choosing to be buried alongside Cnut in the Old Minster at Winchester, where her son Harthacnut and nephew Earl Beorn were buried, rather than at St Paul's in London with Æthelred.[30] Duke William may have paid his great-aunt a visit – stripped of the Godwin clan protection, she perhaps advised Edward to offer the throne to William – but her death left Edward truly alone for the first time, all his in-laws banished from the kingdom and his Norman-French kinsmen and allies in the ascendant at court.

It was a brief episode of independence (perhaps the first 'Anglo-Norman kingship') because Godwin returned to England later in 1052, backed by the Count of Flanders and combining popular support from the south coast with violence – burning Milton Regis to the ground – with Harold approaching from Ireland, raiding and killing thegns in Somerset and Devon, before confronting the king in London. Once again, instead of armed conflict, they negotiated; the king granted Godwin and his sons their earldoms, restored Queen Edith and expelled all the 'French men', including Robert Champart, archbishop of Canterbury, whose replacement Stigand never gained approval from Rome, something the Norman cause would exploit later on.[31] It was a short-lived triumph as Godwin died in 1053. Edward then granted Wessex to Harold (Swegn had died abroad, on his way back from pilgrimage to Jerusalem in 1052.)[32]

With Queen Edith restored, Edward would not now be able to have a child by another wife. And whatever had been offered to duke William, it became clear that in England the succession had not been decisively settled in William's favour when a new plan emerged, involving some of the long-lost æthelings and a journey into eastern Europe to find them and bring them back. An 'ætheling' was not always an heir to the throne, but more generally a prince of the royal house, in theory eligible for the succession.[33] Edward's nephew Edward 'the Exile', the son of King Edmund, had been despatched abroad by Cnut in 1017 (presumably in the hope of his premature demise) but after passing through Sweden and Russia and eventually to Hungary, he married and had three children: Edgar, Margaret and Christina. Once again, it was Bishop Ealdred who was at the centre of the plan; he went to Germany 'on the king's business' and stayed almost a year, and in 1057 Edward 'the Exile' finally arrived in England.[34] Earl Harold may also have been involved in this diplomacy, since he was in Flanders in 1056.[35]

In another twist of fate for the royal House, the newly returned prince died before he had even seen the king, and this was a crucial fact because a meeting with the king would be the occasion to publicly declare him the official heir before the assembled court, just as King Edward had been, at Harthacnut's court in 1041.[36] Foul play should not be ruled out since the royal House was no stranger to assassination: King Edward 'the Martyr', Æthelred II's half-brother, was murdered in 978; Cnut banished and eventually murdered Edmund Ironside's brother Eadwig Ætheling in 1017; Edward the Exile was himself the survivor of Cnut's banishment; and most notoriously, Alfred Ætheling, Edward the Confessor's brother, died as a result of blinding in 1036. Edward the Exile's sudden death in 1057 could be seen as a tragic echo of that, but it remains speculation since there is no further evidence.[37]

The last ætheling remaining after Edward the Exile was his son, Edgar, aged around five in 1057. Significantly, Edgar's name is entered alongside

King Edward and Queen Edith in the *Liber Vitae* (Book of Life) of the New Minster, Winchester, all three entered at the same time and in the same hand, at some point between 1057 and 1066, placing Edgar very close to the royal family and in a book used for solemn liturgical purposes in the spiritual heart of the West Saxon regime at Winchester.[38] Tom Licence argues that Edward adopted Edgar by calling him 'ætheling' just as Edward himself had been sworn in by Harthacnut, and was clearly lining up Edgar for the succession. However, Edgar is not recorded in the Domesday survey as having any significant property, and it cannot be certain that he was promoted properly as Edward the Confessor's designated heir.[39]

The reason for this was the Godwinsson siblings. The balance of power Edward had judiciously struggled to maintain during the 1040s had collapsed by the late 1050s when he appointed three of Harold's brothers to earldoms. With Harold as earl of Wessex, the brothers now controlled four out of the five earldoms and their sister was of course still the queen; the boy Edgar was not appointed to any such position, even as a royal prince.

In 1057 Ælfgar succeeded to the earldom of Mercia but was again outlawed and returned in force in 1058 with the aid not only of Gruffudd but a Viking fleet drawn from Norway, Orkney, Hebrides and Dublin, led by Magnus, son of King Harald Hardrada, who would return in 1066 (although the *Chronicle* gives us no further details, 'since it is tedious to tell how it all happened' – maybe for him but not for us!).[40] It may only have been a raiding party but is a reminder of the web of connections outside England with the Celtic-Scandinavian world and that England was by no means isolated – it also foreshadows the multiple invasions of 1066. Ælfgar succeeded to his father's earldom of Mercia in 1057, but he was surrounded by the Godwin earldoms; his eldest son was passed over, but he bolstered his power-base by marrying his daughter Ealdgyth to King Gruffudd ap Llewelyn.[41]

In 1063 Harold and Tostig invaded Wales, bringing about the killing of King Gruffudd in a devastating campaign which not only had far-reaching consequences for Anglo-Welsh relations but further tipped the balance in favour of the Godwins in England since it destroyed the Mercian alliance; Ælfgar had died in 1062 and was succeeded by his young son Edwin, who presented no threat to the Godwin supremacy.[42] In what was something of a tradition now, Gruffudd's head was delivered by Harold to Edward at Westminster (Rhys ap Rhydderch, brother of Gruffudd, king of southern Wales, was assassinated by order of Edward in 1052 and his head brought to the king).[43]

It appears that in this period of the middle 1060s, Edward gradually retired from political life, spending his time in prayer, hunting and in charitable works, a saintly life memorably described in the *Life of*

Edward. But if Edward were so withdrawn from governing, and so seemingly powerless under the Godwin fraternity, why would he order Harold to travel to Normandy, probably in the summer of 1064, to confirm his offer of the throne in 1051 to duke William? There is nothing in the English sources – any version of the Chronicles or the *Life of King Edward* – about this visit, but the Norman sources explain it as an official mission sanctioned by Edward for Harold to confirm the promises of 1051-2; because that is what they wanted everyone to believe.[44] Indeed, 22 of the 76 remaining plates of the Bayeux Tapestry – made in England under Norman direction and suitably ambiguous throughout – are devoted to the Normandy 'mission'.[45]

The solution to these differences could lie in the hostages sent to Normandy by Edward to guarantee the peace between Edward and Godwin back in 1051-2.[46] Taken together, most of the contemporary English and Norman sources, and the later, twelfth-century sources agree that some sort of promise was made to William and that hostages from Godwin's family were sent to him as a guarantee for Godwin's good behaviour after his return to England later in 1052.[47] These hostages included Earl Harold's brother and nephew and he asked the king to go to Normandy to bring them home; the king agreed, but Harold walked into a Norman trap, forced by duke William to swear on holy relics that he would help to ensure the Norman succession on Edward's death. This information comes from Eadmer, an English monk at Canterbury, writing in around 1115 and his narrative fits nicely with the scenes in the Bayeux Tapestry.[48] Harold returned with only one hostage, leaving his younger brother Wulfnoth behind, who remained under house arrest until 1087, when King William released him.[49]

The offer of the throne and the hostages could be concealing something far more nuanced. Reading between the lines of contemporary and twelfth-century histories, an intriguing third suggestion has recently been suggested as the reason for Harold's ill-fated sea-crossing: that it was his intention was to gain a warranty of non-interference or at least gauge how Flemish and Norman rulers would respond to his kingship, rather than to confirm any offer of the throne or fetch hostages.[50] The Godwin connection with Flanders went back a long way. Swegn had been given protection there twice during his banishments in 1046 and 1049 and the entire family sought refuge there during the 1051-2 exile when Baldwin's half-sister Judith had married Tostig. The Flanders connection had further implications since Edward had ordered a blockade of the Flemish coast in 1049 in support of the German emperor Henry III.[51] By the time of Harold's mission in 1064, duke William was married to Baldwin's daughter Matilda and Harold needed to know what degree of support he might get when he launched his bid for the throne. The trip to Normandy in 1064 was more to do with Harold's desire to isolate Tostig, neutralise

Flanders and prepare to take the throne himself, rather than confirm Edward's offer of the throne to William.

What started as a cross-channel breeze turns into a storm, both literally and metaphorically; the Bayeux Tapestry famously depicts Harold's journey in a strong tailwind but does not tell us exactly what Harold promised. By the time the early twelfth-century historian Orderic Vitalis was writing, Harold is caught up in a storm and shipwrecked in Ponthieu.[52] The storm motif continues in the later twelfth-century histories but the journey could be interpreted as a fishing-trip blown off course and a cover for diplomacy with Flanders, Harold declaring himself on a secret mission, a 'commentum' (or pretext) to the Norman court, in order to obtain release from Guy of Ponthieu when it went wrong.[53] Harold was duly handed over to William where he variously discussed the freeing of hostages, a possible marriage to the duke's daughter and a friendship treaty, making promises he could not keep and had no intention of keeping at Bayeux, Rouen and Bonneville during the journey through Normandy and Brittany. In short, he was in a hole and he kept digging. The post-Conquest Norman writers did not want to highlight any dishonour shown to William, in that his daughter was spurned by Harold, and so were forced to tread the official line that Harold was confirming the offer of the throne to William made in 1051-2. The other near-contemporary sources – the *Life of Edward* commissioned by Edith, whose favourite brother Tostig had been expelled and killed in battle, and the Bayeux Tapestry – hint at oaths, hostages and the king's disfavour, the mixed messages perhaps telling us more about circumstances *after* 1066 than the actual events *before*.

William of Jumièges (1070) tell us that Edward sent Archbishop Robert to the duke with a message, appointing the duke as heir to the kingdom, later sending Harold to guarantee the crown to the duke by his fealty and confirm it with an oath.[54] William of Poitiers (*c.* 1071) echoes this, the initial pledge and Harold's mission to Normandy, blown off course and captured by Guy of Ponthieu.[55] According to William of Poitiers, Harold swore fealty to the duke and took an oath of his own free will to represent duke William at King Edward's court and to use all his wealth and influence to ensure William's succession.

Harold's intention to out-manoeuvre his brother Tostig (and perhaps his sister, the queen) during the botched mission in 1064 becomes apparent in October 1065 when Northumbrian rebels marched south to Northampton demanding Earl Tostig's outlawry for his oppressive government, which included despoiling churches and murder, while they themselves torched houses, murdering and enslaving hundreds en route. Among the rebels were Edwin of Mercia (who had succeeded his father Ælfgar in 1062) and his brother Morcar.[56] Harold was sent to negotiate and seemingly failed to find a peace, but Tostig accused him of treachery and fled the realm to Count Baldwin in Flanders again.[57] Morcar was appointed to the earldom of Northumbria and so the balance of power shifted dramatically in the north on the eve of 1066.

These events illustrate further what Harold's intentions towards the crown were since Harold had married Ealdgyth, sister of earls Edwin and Morcar (and widow of King Gruffudd, whose head Harold had sent to Edward in 1063); this marriage alliance resolved the decades-old dispute between the Godwin and Mercian houses and it could be the reason why Tostig accused Harold of treachery in 1065. The downfall of Tostig seems almost too convenient for Harold, and a clue lies in Wales, where Harold had built a new hunting lodge, at Portskewett (south Wales). In August 1065, this was raided by Caradog ap Rhydderch, an attack possibly instigated by Tostig or Edith.[58] Did Harold incite the revolt in Northumbria while Tostig was in Wiltshire with the king as revenge for this raid but also as part of his grand plan to take the throne, or did he exploit events to his advantage?[59] Certainly, Tostig's rule in Northumbria had been oppressive; twelfth-century sources tell us that he had two members of the Northumbrian aristocracy murdered under safe-conduct in his chambers in York and that Queen Edith had a third, Gospatric, killed in the royal court in December.[60] Both Edwin and Morcar were part of the revolt; Harold could appear to mediate at the talks in Northampton, having done a deal with Edwin and Morcar and either married or promised to marry their sister, which would also invalidate any promise of marriage he had made to duke William's daughter.[61]

Edward was powerless throughout this, unable to raise an army or reinstate Tostig by personal will; shortly after Tostig fled he fell ill with a series of strokes and died on 4 or 5 January 1066. One the day of his burial before the high altar in his newly consecrated abbey at Westminster, 6 January 1066, Harold was crowned king in a ceremony that would usually take place some months afterwards.[62]

The E version of the *Chronicle* (the most pro-Godwin) says that: 'Earl Harold succeeded to the kingdom of England just as the king had granted it to him, and also men chose him for it.'[63] However, the C version, generally hostile to the Godwins, says something rather different: 'The wise man committed the kingdom to a distinguished man, Harold himself…'[64]

Committing or entrusting the kingdom was not the same as granting the kingdom; the D version does not mention Archbishop Ealdred in Harold's coronation either, a telling omission given Ealdred's links to this version. Version C does uncharacteristically praise Harold as a 'distinguished man … a princely earl, who at all times loyally obeyed his lord', the first time this (Mercian) version has anything positive to say about the Godwins, possibly because by this time Harold had married Ealdgyth, sister of Edwin and Morcar.[65]

Another English source close to the events was the *Life of King Edward*, which paints the detailed portrait of Edward's deathbed scene used in the Bayeux Tapestry and has Edward say in similar terms to C and D of the *Chronicle*: 'I commend this woman [Queen Edith] and all the kingdom to your protection.' This could mean he was leaving the kingdom *to* Harold or it could mean he was appointing Harold protector *of* the kingdom; it is not explicit and written after the trauma of Hastings, it had the best interests of the dowager queen, not the slain Harold, at heart.

The deathbed scene in the Bayeux Tapestry is telling in what it does not tell: three men gather round the dying Edward in bed, a woman at his feet (Edith?). Edward reaches out to touch the hand of the man kneeling on his left (Harold?) and all the inscription says is: 'Here King Edward in bed talks to his faithful followers.'[66] It could mean that Edward offers the throne to Harold or tells him to hold the throne for another (Edgar?) or that he is telling Harold to support the succession of duke William. All of these are possible, but the weight of the English evidence (the Bayeux Tapestry, the *Life*, versions C and D of the Chronicles) all point towards some sort of protectorship rather than designation of Harold as king. He had already been designated 'underking' (*subregulus*) as a kind of regent.[67] And if he was protector most likely to Edgar, King Edward's great-nephew and royal prince, this poses an intriguing counter-factual scenario, since with Edgar on the throne, duke William's invasion would never have gained traction and the Early English state would have continued as it had under Edward.

None of these sources mention Harold's election. According to Herman of Bury, who was writing before 1070 and for Abbot Baldwin, King Edward's physician and therefore likely to have been at the deathbed, Harold won the crown by 'cunning force', favour and by 'extortion'. The Northumbrians only swore allegiance when he travelled north with Bishop Wulfstan and at the Battle of Hastings itself; version D of the *Chronicle* tells us that Harold fought hard '...with those men who wanted to support him', which clearly suggests that there were those who did *not* want to support him.[68]

William of Jumièges (writing *c.* 1070) tells us that Harold 'immediately seized the kingdom'. William of Poitiers is more agitated: 'This insensate Englishman did not wait for public choice, but breaking his oath, and with the support of a few ill-disposed partisans, he seized the throne.' He specifically says Harold was 'ordained king by the unhallowed consecration of Stigand'.[69]

If the post-Conquest, near-contemporary English sources equivocate, interestingly William of Poitiers also states that King Edward gifted Harold the throne on his deathbed and that the earlier promise made by Edward (during duke William's visit to England in 1051) and confirmed by Harold (during his visit to Normandy in 1064) gave William the better claim and it is the judgement of God at the battle of Hastings that decides the matter. In Norman eyes, a promise of succession could not be legally revoked; the offer made by Edward to William in 1051 was therefore a gift of property in testamentary law, considered binding and irrevocable; but in Early English law, a deathbed bequest superseded previous offers and by doing this (if he did) Edward the Confessor knowingly created the situation that could only be solved by war, since both Harold and William believed they had the right.[70] Having spent half his adult life in Normandy, Edward would have been aware of these legal differences and by building up the Godwin siblings and deliberately leaving aside Edgar Ætheling, he parted company with centuries of English custom and invited catastrophe on the kingdom. With the bones of the sources picked clean by historians, we are left with the thought that this was not a conspiracy but instead looks suspiciously like a cock-up.

Harold Godwinsson, conqueror of Wales, cousin to King Swegn II of Denmark, brother to the queen and brother-in-law to the earls of Mercia and Northumbria and with vast resources at his disposal, could make a strong case for starting a new dynasty, rather like the Capetians had done in France in 987 with the election and coronation of Hugh Capet, duke of the Franks, chosen for his vigour and nobility at a time of crisis.[71] If Harold had won the battle of Hastings, this ambition for a new dynasty could have been realised, re-orientating England in an Anglo-Danish sphere once again. But of course, he did not. Equally, if Harold's kingdom had survived the battles of 1066, the strength of the monarchy may have become as marginal as the Capetians in France, those competitive rivalries moving from influencing the throne to occupying it and leading to progressive collapse.[72]

If we follow the thinking that Harold was planning to take the throne sometime before Edward's death, evidenced by his alliance with the house of Mercia and overtures in Flanders (which went disastrously wrong), then it is Harold who triggered the Norman Conquest since Edward had an heir-designate – Edgar Ætheling. It is unlikely that William would have invaded if Harold had supported Edgar's election or stood in as a guardian, but Cnut's reign had set a precedent for regime change and Æthelred and Edward's kingship was conditional on 'good government', agreed with the *witan* in 1014 and 1041. The temporary rejection of Æthelred and the long exile of Edward had certainly damaged the reputation of the Old English monarchy, but Edward's long and peaceful reign had gone some way to restore it and there is no reason to think that Edgar Ætheling, who was in his late teens in 1066, could not have succeeded to the throne (King Edgar and Æthelred had been very young at the start of their reign), especially bolstered by a powerful church and mighty lords at his side.

The greatest lord in England did not stand by Edgar's side though, instead taking the throne for himself. Harold's coup had created the opportunity for others to muscle in. Post-Conquest Norman historiography presents duke William's invasion as blessed by the Pope, taking a papal banner into what was in effect a prototype holy war (a model refined and used with great success in 1095 in what became the First Crusade) and with an inevitable victory.[73] Harold's usurpation would be avenged by God. The reality was that in 1066 there were several possible outcomes. The invasions of Cnut had reinforced a pattern of invasion and conquest dating from the near destruction of the English kingdoms in the 870s. The invasion of Magnus's uncle, Harald Hardrada, in September 1066 was formidable, initially successful and a reminder of northern separatism; the northern English *fyrd* was wiped out outside York at the battle of Fulford Gate. Earl Tostig, Harold Godwinsson's brother, had defected, but Hardrada was defeated at Stamford Bridge in pitched battle weeks later.

The Battle of Hastings on 14 October 1066 was by no means guaranteed to be a Norman victory and does not necessarily suggest a feeble state lacking strong leadership and in need of modernisation. It was a monumental achievement of Harold's leadership and the Early English state to field armies to fight not one but three major battles in the space of one month; having waited all summer, the timing was critical and both invasion fleets arrived in late September. In William of Poitiers' own words, Harold guarded the coast 'with an innumerable army and was possessed of a 'great fleet and highly skilled sailors who had long experience of the dangers and hazards of sea-warfare,' whereas the Normans were apparently building a fleet from scratch.[74]

The Norman invasion planning and logistics were on a massive scale. The detail is in the Bayeux Tapestry for all to see; felling trees, creating planks, armour – hauberks, helmets, spears, swords – cartloads of food, bread ovens, forges, barrels and skins of wine, horses and the many ships needed to make the crossing; such an expedition far outweighed anything William and his companions had ever done in a lifetime of campaigning on horseback in the forests and borderlands of Normandy, Maine and Brittany and so the planning was all the more extraordinary.[75]

William's military experience was vast: during his lifetime he had resisted two domestic rebellions, repelled two major invasions, and led two major cross-border expeditions. He had mastered attritional warfare, avoided pitched battles, sieging, plundering, and competing for supplies and supply chains. In England, by contrast, there were three cross-border expeditions but no battles, no large-scale invasions, and no outbreaks of civil war, although it came close in 1051 but all stood back since 'they would be opening a way for our enemies to enter the county cause great ruin' and again in 1065, 'there was horror at what seemed like civil war.'[76] These sentiments suggest a sense of national unity in England before the

Conquest but they are also symptomatic of eventual ruin; peace and prosperity had made the state vulnerable.

In a lifetime of military campaigning, William had perhaps only fought two set-piece battles (Val es Dune 1047 and Varaville, 1057) before Hastings. They were rare and risky. Harold's stunning victory over Hardrada would in normal times be celebrated along the lines of another Brunanburh and secured him a legacy of invincibility, but these were not normal times. On hearing of William's late landfall at Pevensey (itself a remarkable success given the dangers of Channel crossings for one ship let alone an entire fleet), he turned his tired and depleted troops south to London, not pausing to rest and gather reinforcements, hoping to repeat the surprise victory at Stamford Bridge; in any case, it was in the interests of both parties to force an engagement with winter coming and William's back to the sea. Furthermore, William had already started burning, looting, kidnapping, and raping in Harold's personal patrimony to draw him into battle in a trial by combat.[77] William was ready and formed up on the road to London, so perhaps Harold was the one ambushed since 'William came upon him by surprise before all his people were marshalled ... before all his raiding-army had come.'[78] William of Jumièges tells us that Harold came south 'riding all night' to find William prepared and ready.[79]

According to Poitiers, Harold had gathered a 'vast host' from 'all the provinces of the English' who were, he adds rather begrudgingly, 'inspired by their love of their country which they desired, however unjustly, to defend against foreigners'.[80] As mentioned, the D *Chronicle* (the only contemporary English written description of the battle), says Harold fought 'with those men who wanted to support him'. Once again we could be seeing the old separatism of Wessex and Mercia, since neither Edwin or Morcar were at the battle but had fought at Fulford Gate. There were of course many thousands already dead and wounded at Fulford Gate and Stamford Bridge but many more perhaps were coming up from London, which may account for the battle continuing for so long.

The battle lasted all day (beginning at the 'third hour', perhaps around 0900) rare in medieval warfare, and only ended with Harold's death in the early evening. It is likely that the forces at Hastings were more evenly matched than the traditional view of the Norman 'David' against the English 'Goliath', with perhaps 10,000 troops on either side.[81] The English fought on foot and 'in very close order', on the high ground adjacent to a forest, not daring to fight on equal terms as they had done with Harald Hardrada, William of Poitiers tells us.[82] The Norman army advanced 'with the papal banner ... borne aloft at the head of his troops' in three ranks, archers and crossbowmen in the van; heavily armed infantry and then the squadrons of knights on horseback.[83] The use of cavalry, feigned retreats and archery is much debated and has served to illustrate the ultimate military superiority of Norman tactics; however, the set-piece battle at Tinchebrai in Normandy in 1106 was fought on foot and had always been the English style of fighting (Asser tells us that the English fought on foot in a 'compact shield-wall' formation at the battle of Edington in 878) but the rare set-pieces battles of the twelfth and thirteenth centuries always involved cavalry (such as Lincoln, Lewes, Evesham).[84]

Regardless of tactics and weaponry, the leader's survival was paramount. Harold had men joining the battle, William had finite reserves. It all depended on this throw of the dice. At one point, William was believed to be killed and his army faltered, some fleeing headlong (Breton knights, specifically, of course) but William raised his helmet and personally took command of the retreating Norman-Breton troops, halting the flight and cutting down the pursuing English, his actions recorded in the Bayeux Tapestry and by William of Poitiers, though the moment appears to come later on in the battle in the Tapestry.[85] Just as William's survival rallied the Norman cavalry, Harold's death lost the English the battle, possibly killed by an arrow and cut to pieces as depicted in the heavily restored Bayeux Tapestry, although William of Poitiers tells us nothing of how the English king died.[86] William of Jumièges tells us that Harold fell fighting in the front rank, 'covered with deadly wounds', at which point the English turned and fled into the night (no mention of the arrow.)[87] Harold's brothers Gyrth and Leofwine also died in the fighting, and as the evening light faded over the battlefield, perhaps we can hear Byrhtnoth's words at Maldon once again: 'Here lies our lord, all cut down, the hero in the dust... I will not leave the field, but think to lie by lord's side, by the man I held so dear...'

Bishop Ermenfrid of Sitten issued penances on the Normans who took part in the invasion and conquest of England on a visit in 1070 and they reveal the nature of warfare in its ugly glory: one year penance for each man killed, forty days for wounding in the 'great battle'; one year for killing in search of food and three years for killing for plunder during the campaign before the coronation of William; more lenient were the penances for rapes and fornication, to be punished as if committed in their own country and goods stolen from churches were to be returned and were not permitted to be sold.[88]

Harold was dead, but the English had other options: Stigand, Edwin and Morcar set up Edgar the Ætheling as king, but after the duke had skirted around London, Stigand surrendered to him at Wallingford. This was not a rerun of 1016 though, and not simply because Edgar was younger than Edmund; the enormous powers vested in the earls since Cnut coupled with one of their own taking the crown, left the English nobility utterly exposed; the extinction of the House of Godwin at Stamford Bridge and Hastings left a massive power vacuum and English opposition after 1066 was scattered. William of Poitiers tells the tale of how the Norman warlords persuaded the duke to take the crown, since the duke apparently preferred the 'peace of the kingdom to its crown'.[89] Before dismissing this as false modesty loosely disguised with a smattering of classical allusion, it is worth noting the role of the knights in giving their opinion in the matter since they had much to gain by duke William's accession (and did) whereas handing the crown to Edgar, having removed the usurper Harold, would ensure peace and continuity but no reward for the duke's followers.

William of Poitiers is at pains to state that the archbishop of York crowned the duke (not Stigand, who he claims crowned Harold) and that the English confirmed the coronation with oaths, 'the consent of the English or at least the desire of their magnates'. His hereditary title was due to the kinship between William's great-aunt Emma and Edward the Confessor, but the key departure was that William 'took possession of his inheritance by battle' (thereby getting round the inconvenient fact of Edgar Ætheling's existence).[90] This created the new style of English kingship that was to last five centuries; right by victory in battle, hereditary kinship and acclamation. To celebrate this victory, an abbey was built on the site of the battle, just as Cnut had built a minster at Ashingdon fifty years before.

William the Conqueror was no Cnut. In 1066 the destiny of the English, Gregory's 'angels' – the *Angelcynn* – had reached a traumatic conclusion, enabled by a Roman papacy which aided and abetted the destruction of the Early English Church in favour of a new world order. The worst fears of Bede and Alfred were realised at Hastings. It was, after all, the final conquest by the Northmen when Alfred's palace and cathedral at Winchester were destroyed and his bones scattered.[91] Fittingly, the sole contemporary English description, *Chronicle* D (commissioned by Archbishop Ealdred who crowned both Harold and William) sees William as an agent of divine punishment: 'And the French had possession of the place of slaughter just as God granted them because of the people's sins.'[92] This echoes the lament of Gildas, where the civil wars of the fifth century are a consequence of sin, and this thinking is repeated in the 'sermon of the Wolf' by Archbishop Wulfstan in 1002 who linked the Danish raids to English sins.

It was the end of Early England. No other conquest in European history has had such disastrous consequences for the defeated. The Early English kingdom had gone forever. It was to be replaced by a new polity, an Anglo-Norman empire that bound England to the Continent, specifically territories within France, for the following five centuries. It was this relationship with those French regions that determined the making of England for the remainder of the Middle Ages.

PART THREE

Conquered England

1066–1300

Recording the Conquest: Domesday Book folio, 1086, Bedfordshire [Leighton Buzzard]. (Courtesy of Professor John Palmer, George Slater and opendomesday.org under Creative Commons 2.0)

TEN

Domesday

At first, it looked as if the Norman invasion would repeat Cnut's invasion fifty years earlier – regime change with continuity among the elites – but when rebellions broke out all across England the new king reacted with a ferocity that stunned England into submission. The entire ruling elite was replaced, most of the landholding class removed, swathes of territory scorched and left to famine, churches and cathedrals demolished wholesale. A military regime governed from castles, armed to the teeth, commanded by a small group of men with lands in both Normandy and England, tied to the king by blood and marriage. The greatest triumph of their conquest was the written record of England's misery, Domesday Book, itself a testament to the conquered genius of the Early English state.

Considering England after 1066 is like looking into a cracked mirror: it is the familiar old face but distorted and permanently altered. Initially, it looked like William intended to rule rather like Cnut did, a foreign ruler devolving power to the native administration. William was crowned by Ealdred of York, who had probably crowned Harold using the same coronation *ordo*, and the earliest writs issued by William were in English and addressed to English officials, such as Eadnoth the Staller and Tofi the sheriff of Somerset in 1067.[1] Crucially, Early English administration continued for a while, William confirming rights and lands of Regenbald, Edward the Confessor's priest and 'chancellor' in a writ (in English) of 1067, which also refers to 'King Harold' and another writ which refers to Edward, 'my kinsman'.[2] The witness lists of two diplomas issued in May 1068 suggest that William might have governed like Cnut, through a joint elite, since they contain vernacular and Latin text and equal numbers of *Franci* and *Angli*.[3]

The monetary system survived intact (as we would except from such a sophisticated, wealthy kingdom); the moneyer Anderboba of Winchester

148

struck coins for kings Edward, Harold, and William in 1066, each with the same fundamental characteristics. The quality of these coins was far and away better than contemporary Norman coins, so no attempt was made to import Norman coinage. William I's coinage was produced to a single, standardised design, with high silver content and struck in large quantities in a royal monopoly across a wide network of mints, never a day's ride away in England south of York.[4] Many moneyers remained in office, most of them English, many of them working under Harold II, William I and William II. Mints were established at Durham, Rhuddlan and south Wales in the 1080s.

Early English legal traditions and customs continued: the detailed trial held on Pinnenden Heath, near Maidstone, in the 1070s, between Archbishop Lanfranc and Odo earl of Kent (William's half-brother), repeatedly appeals to the 'customary rights' of the archbishopric of Canterbury, and deliberately included 'those English who were well acquainted with the traditional laws and customs of the land.' The trial found conclusively in favour of archbishop Lanfranc.[5] There were no new law codes under the Anglo-Norman regime; the so-called 'Laws of William the Conqueror' was a compilation of legal enactments made at various times by King William and survives in an early twelfth-century form, noteworthy for the introduction of trial by battle in addition to the ordeal and the oath and prohibiting the sale of any man outside the country.[6] These ''laws' confirm the laws of King Edward, which did not exist in written form either, since they were based upon the laws of Cnut dating to 1020, as we have seen themselves based on the law codes of Edgar (960s), testimony to the strong continuity of English legal customs across the Danish and Norman occupations and conquests.

William used the custom of crown-wearing to emphasise his links to Edward the Confessor and made it more prominent, wearing the *cyne-helm* three times a year when he was in England, at Winchester (Easter), Westminster (Pentecost) and Gloucester (mid-winter).[7] William's key assembly meetings 1085 were consensual, such as the Whitsun assembly of 1072 when the primacy dispute was settled, and the Gloucester court in 1085.[8] Assemblies were also an instrument of conquest, an opportunity to display his new power, such as the Whitsun assembly in 1068 at the coronation of his wife, Queen Matilda, which was attended by Edwin, Morcar and leading English abbots.[9] During the brutal winter campaign in Yorkshire, William sent for the crown and insignia to be brought from Winchester – a round trip of 500 miles.

The rebellions across England 1068-75 changed this initial policy of 'reaching out' to the English dramatically and irrevocably. Those years saw revolts crushed one by one across the West Country, the Welsh borders, East Anglia and most brutally, in Yorkshire, where tens of thousands died in a devastating and brutal campaign not seen since the Viking Great Army penetrated central England in the 860s. The *Chronicle* says that he 'wholly ravaged and laid waste the shire', much elaborated upon by eleventh-century writers, but the resulting famine and depopulation is illustrated in Domesday Book in 1086, where the value of Yorkshire had fallen by two-thirds from 1066.[10] This was no longer a repeat of Cnut's rule after 1016: this was a military occupation in a foreign land with little or no pretence to legitimate authority. Norman troops ate and slept together in operational units, patrolling the hostile land, garrisoned in hastily built castles (by the conquered people) of the type we see in the Bayeux Tapestry, constructed at Hastings soon after William's landing in 1066.[11] In the words of Tacitus: 'Robbery, slaughter and plunder they falsely name empire; they make a desolation, and they call it peace.'[12]

The rebellions were not co-ordinated English revolts intending to place Edgar on the throne but a multi-ethnic series of uprisings, ending in the first 'Norman' rebellion in 1075. The entity of 'England' itself was not guaranteed. Edgar Ætheling made his way to the court of King Malcolm for protection, his sister Margaret married Malcolm and it was their daughter Eadgyth who married Henry I in 1100; their descendants formed the ruling house of England into the fifteenth century so perhaps the house of Wessex had the last laugh.[13] The greatest threat was the arrival of King Swegn's sons in 240 ships, who joined forces with Edgar and the Northumbrians, destroying the new castle at York and launching William's nuclear response.

The Danish alliances during these revolts could have kept the Normans in the south, yet again dividing the kingdom as it had been in 1016 between Edmund and Cnut and in 890 between Guthrum and Alfred, but William took no chances. The destruction in the North was this time decisive and Lanfranc ensured the primacy of Canterbury over York in 1070. Even though the English earl Waltheof made his peace with William, he was executed on a trumped-up charge after the (Norman/Breton) rebellion of 1075, the last of the Northumbrian earls. Edwin and Morcar, the last of the Mercians, broke cover in 1071, Edwin was killed by his own men, Morcar joined the East Anglian rebellion and vanishes from the record.[14] This was the end of the longest established comital house in England through four generations, under nine kings and four different royal dynasties since their great-grandfather Ealdorman Leofwine was appointed earl in 994.[15]

East Anglia and the Fens were populated by Anglo-Danish sympathisers receptive to foreign claims and remained politically one of the most insecure parts of the kingdom. The region's many monasteries were rallying points for England and Anglo-Danish loyalists; Abbot Ælfwold of St Benet of Holme in Norfolk was tasked by Harold with guarding the coast in 1066 and had fled to Denmark; the monastery at Ely had provided a base for Hereward's rebellion in 1070-71 and it was from

Norwich that the rebellion of the earls had come in 1075, sending for aid from Denmark; and it was to Denmark that Ralph de Gael, Breton earl of Norfolk, had fled after the failure of the rising.[16]

The ruling houses of Wessex, Mercia and Northumbria were extinct by 1076, but Edgar Ætheling curiously survived (the influence of Papal reforms perhaps tempered William's otherwise brutal behaviour, in contrast to the earlier purges of Cnut), his outlawry revoked in 1074. In 1085 he seems to have left England with a troop of knights for Apulia in southern Italy, appearing in 1091 during reconciliation between William II and Malcolm and again in 1097 during a campaign in Scotland; he last appears in the *Chronicle* in 1106 as a captive after Tinchebrai, forty years after Hastings.[17] In between, he seems to have made a pilgrimage to Jerusalem. One can speculate how England's history would have differed under 'Edgar II', particularly since he had such a long, active life.

If the English elites, leaderless and disunited though they were, still believed the exiled prince would return one day as both Æthelred and Edward the Confessor did, then they thought wrong. The rebellions provoked what we might call a 'shock doctrine' that was far more than a military campaign of violence, it was nothing short of a cultural conquest. This was to be an entirely new England, the old buildings pulled down and replaced with new castles, churches and personnel and the language of government was also replaced (Old English would disappear from the written record for three hundred years).

Finally, the land itself was re-allocated to a tiny group of foreigners in what was the most comprehensive takeover in English history (just 8% of the land in 1086 was held by English people, and a handful of English churchmen remained in office) a legacy that is very much with us in twenty-first-century England.[18] The mailed and spurred boot of the Norman lord remained firmly on the neck of the conquered English people. Reigns were dated in charters, letters, and statutes high and low as 'after the conquest' for five hundred years, a permanent reminder of the Norman Conquest in the national consciousness and at every level, even the most local (for example, in the Stratford-on-Avon Guild accounts concerning the endowment of the grammar school in 1482, dated 'the 22nd year of King Edward IV after the conquest'). The Early English kings were relegated to rather antiquarian sobriquets which may or may not have been contemporary, such as 'Edward the Elder,' Æthelred Unræd', 'Edmund Ironsides', or 'Edward the Confessor,' whereas after 1066, the new style of 'Edward I after the Conquest' is used. (And are used in this book since this post-Conquest convention means it is the only way we can distinguish between the various Edwards pre-1066.)[19]

Such was the contempt for anything 'English', it was all rebuilt in Continental style. For Norman-French prelates and monks, a 'complete replacement of the fabric of Anglo-Saxon churches had an ideological charge as a purging of the physical locations in which the old regime's now despised senior clergy had operated.'[20] Very few Early English churches survived in their entirety (for example at Deerhurst, Gloucestershire, Bradford on Avon, Wiltshire, Brixworth in Northamptonshire, Escomb, Co Durham). Bishops' sees were moved, from Dorchester to Lincoln, Elmham to Norwich, Lichfield to Chester, Selsey to Chichester, Sherborne to Salisbury and Wells to Bath.

The major Norman churches were conceived on a much bigger scale; every Early English cathedral and large monastic church was rebuilt, thoroughly and more quickly than any other time in the Middle Ages, eradicating the English ecclesiastical past.[21] Cnut's great royal monument in the Old Minster at Winchester was smashed to pieces and thrown out and the site of William's victory at Battle commemorated permanently. Westminster Hall was more extensive than most of the new cathedral naves, 240ft long by 68ft wide, with a roof requiring 1,760 trees; it was twice the size of the contemporary hall at Caen in Normandy, and when William II saw it, he declared it only half as big as it should be.[22]

The castle was an instrument of domination and the great churches an equally blatant assertion of power. The biggest castles were built by King William I (Oxford, 64ft high, 1,500 cubic ft) and members of his innermost circle, such as Clare (100ft high, 1,730 cubic ft), and Roger de Montgomery, William's cousin, at Arundel.[23] Ninety castles are recorded by 1100, twenty-five of them royal, mostly motte and baileys but some were of stone. The early stone castles in England exceeded those in Normandy, Norwich keep (111ft by 93ft) the White Tower in London (118ft by 107ft) and Colchester (151ft by 110ft) being notable examples. Colchester used the Roman temple footprint, Winchester, Chichester, and Pevensey also used Roman walls and foundations; indeed, the major Norman castles in 1086 covered the same area of the midlands and south-east England of the first decades of Roman occupation.[24] At Lincoln, one-third of the upper city was demolished to make way for the castle and a new cathedral. It is easy to get carried away by the efficiency of the Norman 'achievement' and the later romance of medieval castles, but this building programme caused deep misery and resentment in the newly conquered English.[25]

The twenty or so major churches, a clutch of stone keeps, and Westminster Hall amounted to the most extensive group of very large buildings erected in one go anywhere in the west since Roman times, which overall represented a vast capital investment, 'probably a greater capital investment *per capita* than this country as ever seen, at least prior to the industrial revolution of the nineteenth century.'[26] These castles and great churches were planned to be part of new urban developments for economic as well as military and spiritual expressions of power. Stone bridges were built at Durham and Oxford and by 1100 there were major stone bridges at London, Rochester, Chester, Nottingham, Stamford, and

Bristol.[27] Large water milling complexes were built after the Conquest at Chester, York, Cambridge, Ely and Arundel.[28]

All the new cathedrals but Worcester were built by bishops of Continental origin and five were on new sites, at the centre of reorganised dioceses. New senior clergy replaced the natives, the traditional liturgy was rejected, and English saints repurposed, though not completely rejected; early twelfth-century writers depicted the last years of the English church as a time of decline and corruption.[29]

New buildings and reforms went hand in hand with the growth of literacy, stricter impositions of chastity in the priesthood and increased respect for the law of the church, something which the Early English church had been attempting to achieve since Bede's time. From Early England about 2000 charters and writs (including forgeries, copies, and originals) survive, but from the thirteenth century tens of thousands survive.[30] It is possible that it was the Norman Conquest that made England 'exceptionally conscious' of written records, since making records is initially a product of distrust rather than social progress and England after 1066 was not a place of trust, to be sure.[31]

The transformation from memory to written record was not celebrated in English, since the Norman Conquest 'murdered' the written Early English language as surely as it demolished the Old Minster at Winchester.'[32] Old English poetry was abandoned, surviving by chance in obscure codices, and monastic books destroyed. William I had tried and failed to learn English according to Orderic Vitalis.[33] It did not happen overnight of course, and the Northamptonshire geld roll of 1066x83 was written in Old English and suggests that many such documents were written during this time and were available when Domesday Book was compiled in 1086, although Latin was used for routine government business towards the end of the reign.[34] The Domesday survey itself was the most remarkable multilingual event in the history of the English state.[35] Only one Old English diploma and two writs survive from William II, seven from Henry I, one from Stephen and five from Henry II; almost all are bilingual with Latin; Old English was used locally for manumissions, attested by priests and reeves or the hundred court and occasionally for administration in the north.[36] By the end of the eleventh century, the Romance languages were dominant everywhere from the lowlands of Scotland to Sicily, except in Ireland, Wales and the highlands of Scotland, so the Norman Conquest brought England into this French-speaking community.[37]

English was the predominant language of government under Edward the Confessor but very rapidly in the 1070s it was swamped by Latin, which became the main language of record for the rest of the Middle Ages. Since Latin was a clerical language it was supplemented with a vernacular, initially and briefly English under William I, French and English in the baronial reform documents of 1258-9, but it was French that was more widely used in business transactions, English not re-emerging until the mid-fourteenth century. The dismissal of English is revealed by a 1362 statute (in French!) which stated that the

> ...laws, customs and statutes of this realm are not commonly known in the realm, because they are pleaded, shown and judged in the French language, which is too unknown in the realm; so that the people who plead or are impleaded in the king's court and in the courts of others, have no knowledge or understanding of what is said to them or against them by their serjeants and other pleaders.[38]

A handful of early documents illustrate the new style of landholding by a foreign military elite, based on Early English custom combined with Norman-style ceremonies of homage. A writ from King William to the English abbot of Bury St Edmunds (in English) commands that the land of the men who died fighting the king at Hastings and who held that land from the abbot is handed over to him.[39] The writ of *c.* 1072 (in Latin) from King William orders the (English) abbot of Evesham to 'bring with you fully equipped those five knights which you owe me in respect of your abbacy,' which assumes an existing arrangement.[40] Early English abbots were no strangers to military service (Abbot Wulfsige of Ramsey died at Ashingdon) and the English warriors certainly had landed status of their own. According to an early eleventh-century manuscript, a certain thegn possessed five hides of land of his own, 'a bell and a castle-gate, church and kitchen, a seat and special office in the king's hall'.[41] A writ of Edward the Confessor (1045-58) confirms the land in Dorset of his housecarl, Urk.[42] The 'Rights and ranks of people' (1040s) gives us a very detailed description of the social ranks of mid-eleventh century English society, from thegns to bee-keepers (who are female), from sowers to slaves.[43] The thegn is entitled to his book-right (land protected by charter) and should contribute three things in respect of his land: armed service, repairing fortresses and bridge-work (ie. the *trinoda necessitas* which we have seen existed since the late eighth century) plus other duties such as equipping and guarding the coastal ships, guarding the lord, military watch, almsgiving and church dues.

The language changes within a generation as we move into a new culture from 'public' to 'private' lordship based around personal loyalty to the lord, who in turned owed that service to the king. Only very few agreements survive, probably because it was unusual to make such an individual written record in the first generation following the Conquest (although Domesday Book can be said to record the thousands of new agreements *en masse*).[44] An enfeoffment of a knight by the abbot of Westminster in *c.* 1083 shows that William Baynard was to have a farm in the township of Westminster for life by the service of one knight in place of the thegn Wulfric Bordewayte.[45] Another enfeoffment on the land of Bury St Edmunds describes how Peter, a knight of the king, will become the 'feudal man' of the abbot by performing the ceremony of homage.[46] A grant of land to be held by military service was made by Bishop Robert of Hereford, 1085, with Roger de Lacy, for the life-tenancy of Holme Lacy, Herefordshire, to seal the deal with his inheritance from Walter de Lacy.[47] The barony of the archbishop of Canterbury (1093) included over sixty holders of knight's fees, and as we would expect most are Norman-French names. There are some English names, too – Wulfsige, Wulfnoth, Æthelwine – but only a tiny minority.[48] The status of these knights was relatively lowly, with an annual income of around £2,which in Domesday society placed them in the ranks of the 'parish gentry'.[49]That this system was neither a system or indeed even effective is shown in a writ of Henry I (*c.* 1100-1117) which demands that the 'barons' of Abingdon abbey perform castle guard at Windsor as Abbot Faritius commands, since it appeared that 'you do not obey his order as you ought to.'[50]

All land was now in lordship, and there was no tenure without service.[51] Tenancies now descended unfragmented to a single male heir, which meant that the material bonding of the old kin-group was dissolved. New practices of inheritance and a new law governing tenure, devolution and descent of landed property were established, a break with the English past, which we might call a revolution, though 'transformation' might be a better way of looking at it.[52] All land was held, directly or indirectly, of the king, and all fealties ascended to him, principles sealed in Domesday and the Salisbury Oath of 1086; William combined the authority of an Early English monarchy with a feudal lordship clear cut because it had been imposed amidst conquest.

And so, to Domesday Book. Is this remarkable document a wondrous achievement of medieval England (nothing of its scale survives in medieval Europe or was done again until the nineteenth century in England) or is it a document that set a shameful mark on a humiliated people since it records the totality of the Norman Conquest?[53] The name *Domesdei* was given by the English to a book written in Latin for the French-speaking colonial elite. It does present something of a conundrum since it could not have been made without the Early English administration – the shire, sheriffs and hundred courts and so on – that was in place in the centuries before 1086, but equally it would not have been made without the Norman Conquest. It is an exceptional document, but does that make England exceptional? It was the biggest book ever produced in England, designed to be as large as the most revered bibles, using 200 of the very largest parchment sheets.[54] It is an intimidating and awesome record of the Conquest, but it was compiled because of yet another threat of invasion and it is a reminder that the conquest of 1066 was by no means secured or complete. The survey was launched at a meeting of the King's assembly in Gloucester at Christmas, 1085, where the king had 'much thought and very deep discussion' (*deope spæce*) with his advisors: this description from the *Chronicle* was written in Old English probably by a monk or cleric based in London or Westminster serving at the royal court:[55]

> Then he sent his men all over England into every shire and had them ascertain how many hundreds of hides there were in the shire, or what land and livestock the king himself had in the land or what dues he ought to have in 12 months from the shire. Also he had it recorded how much land his archbishops had, and his diocesan bishops and his abbots and his earls and – though I tell it at too great length or what or how much each man had who was occupying land here in England, in land or in livestock, and how much money it was worth. He had it investigated so very narrowly that there was not one single hide, not one yard of land, not even (it is shameful to tell – but it seemed no shame to him to do it) one ox, not one cow, not one pig was left out that was not set down on record. And all the records were brought to him afterwards.

Small wonder that it came to be known as Domesday Book (first mentioned as such in the *Dialogue of the Exchequer c.* 1176). There is no doubt in the mind of this Englishman that it was a record of conquest. The hides, shires and dues were all units and measurements of the late English state: the difference was that it was now all owned by a foreign elite, which the survey confirmed in writing. Landholders were required to attend the Domesday survey on pain of forfeiture, jurors did so on pain of fine and that most of the Englishmen who attended the survey would have been compelled to witness and confirm on oath the loss of their patrimony and social status. Of the thousands of English landholders who lost their lands, one voice alone cries out for all dispossessed Englishmen: Æthelric of Marsh Gibbon (Buckinghamshire) told the commissioners that he held four hides freely in 1066 but now held them 'at farm' from William fitzAnsculf, 'in heaviness and misery'.[56]

Robert Losinga, the French bishop of Hereford at the time, concurs with the level of intrusion; he calls it a *descriptio* and specifically notes how 'the land was vexed with much violence arising from the collection of the royal taxes.'[57] We should remember England's vast wealth and administrative ability to raise such finances since the days of Alfred through to Æthelred. On the manor of Æschere (the name of King Hrothgar's beloved follower in *Beowulf*) in Chancton, Sussex, a hoard of 3,000 pennies was found, packed into an earthenware pot in 1066/7; Chancton was worth £4 a year in 1066 so the hoard represents three times the annual value, one of the largest Early English hoards ever found, and suggestive of thegnly disposable income at this time.[58] Two successive great gelds of 72 pence on each hide of land were taken in 1084-5 and 1085-6, involving the transportation to Winchester of over 2 million pennies.[59] The councils held in Gloucester in late 1085 would have been a sort of 'tax parliament' since both meetings consented to the levying of resources for military spending.[60]

Behind Bishop Losinga's note lie the reasons why the survey was launched, namely the age-old threat of Danish invasion and money needed to deal with such a threat. In the autumn of 1085, William returned to England from Normandy to prepare for a Danish invasion, headed by an alliance between King Cnut of Denmark and Count Robert of Flanders. William brought with him an immense mercenary army, laid waste to the coastal regions to deny supplies to the enemy (and to avoid a repeat of his own success in 1066), fortified castles, repaired town walls, and deployed troops to guard the towns and beaches. When the news came that the Danes were not invading, the mercenary army was billeted in English houses in readiness for a spring invasion.[61] The king assembled his magnates to discuss what should be done. 'The king was very scared,' according to William of Malmesbury, writing in the early twelfth century. Unnamed Englishmen were seeking help from Cnut. The danger from Denmark lasted until the assassination of Cnut in July 1086, and the mercenary army was still in quarters all winter, spring and into the summer and during the time of the Domesday survey; troops have been identified in Domesday Book stationed in Southampton and Bury St Edmunds.

William's personal involvement in the Domesday survey was clear; from the Gloucester councils of late 1085, the time he spent in southern England in the spring of 1086 and to the stage-managing the oaths at Salisbury and presentation of draft writings and deciding the huge size of the final text.[62] There are around 6,500 vills in Domesday and over 60,000 witnesses participating in the survey as priests, reeves, *villani*, and jurors and this extensive public participation was intentional, to draw a line under 20 years of upheaval and to validate the radically transformed landholding structure of England.[63]

Much debate has ensued over when the final survey was completed but Professor Stephen Baxter argues convincingly that Domesday Book was 'made, checked and rearranged in seven months flat' and finished about twelve months later.[64] It took an estimated 330 days to write, and the single scribe (one assistant and five others have been identified) was either English or someone who had lived in England from an early age.[65]

Domesday Book could not have been made without the landholders' co-operation and in return they gained recognition of their titles. The decision to launch the survey was communicated through 'writ-charters' writs addressed by the king to the officers and suitors of the shire court, the chief means of making the king's will known in the localities. At the shire court meetings, the testimony of the tenants-in-chief was submitted on oath, scrutinised by the barons of the shire, a jury from each hundred or wapentake and a deputation from each vill. This process is vividly highlighted at a dispute in Hampshire (South Charford) between William de Chernet and Picot, sheriff of Cambridgeshire. De Chernet brought his testimony to the 'better men and the old men of the whole shire and hundred', while Picot brought against it the testimony of the 'villeins and common people and reeves'.[66]

The collection and assimilation of jurisdictional dues, urban assets, geld, and all the landholding details was a multilingual process. Agents of royal government were of mixed origins and many Norman sheriffs worked closely with Englishmen who had experience of royal government. Numerous Englishmen were employed at the lower levels of estate administration, linking the foreign landholding elite with the indigenous peasantry and Englishmen still formed a substantial element, if not a majority, within the religious communities in England in 1086. Bishops issued seigneurial returns and would have been assisted by their monks at Worcester, Bath, Ely, and St Augustine's Canterbury.[67] Domesday Book names eleven interpreters, four with English names and two the sons of Englishmen. Bishop Remigius was accompanied on his western circuit by two Frenchmen and two Englishmen (Nigel, Ranulf, Wulfsige and Ulf).[68]

All land was now held from the king. The most powerful man in England in 1086 was William I. William I held land in every shire except Cheshire and Shropshire; he was the wealthiest in 23 shires. In 1086 the royal demesne was worth £17,800, 23% of the total. Fourteen landholders held 26%, thus almost half of the kingdom's wealth was in the hands of 15 individuals.[69] Overall, 90% of the landed wealth of England belonged to 150 people and within that group there was a clear hierarchy: the king and the five wealthiest tenants-in-chief (including his two half-brothers) controlled 38% of the kingdom's landed wealth and the other 52% by around 140 lords.[70]

Conquest and colonisation destroyed the upper ranks of the English landed society so that by 1086 about 8% of the landed wealth remained in native hands; and that landed wealth became sharply concentrated from 37,000 landholders into the hands of 1,150 new tenants-in-chief holding newly cast estates. The great majority were Norman, but some were from Flanders, Brittany, Picardy and other parts of northern France; just thirteen were English.

In 1066, Edward the Confessor was the wealthiest man in England, just as his ancestor Alfred the Great had been the wealthiest individual; King Edward's estates were worth £8,230. Furthermore, the concentration of wealth in later Early England was intense: the top 63 landholders in 1066 account for 50%, a small enough group to fit inside a hall or large church; the witness list of Earl Harold's foundation, dedication and endowment of Waltham minster in 1062 includes 58 people, all but three identified in Domesday, and their holdings amount to 40% of the kingdom's landed wealth.[71]

What was different in 1086 then? Despite King Edward's singular wealth, King William was the ultimate source of all tenure and profit. The net value of the royal demesne doubled from 1066 (£8,230) to 1086 (£16,273). The whole structure of Domesday Book created an elaborate legal fiction of the Norman Conquest, that of William as the legitimate successor to Edward the Confessor.[72] In doing so it established a new, post-Conquest landed society not seen before, with immense power centred around the king. This was no import from Normandy and it did not arise from pre-Conquest England either; it was a unique consequence of 1066. The 'manor' illustrates this new type of hybrid socio-economic reality. The word *manerium* does not occur in a single genuine pre-Conquest English charter or any other pre-Conquest source, or indeed in pre-Conquest Norman charters; it was a post-Conquest neologism, first used in connection with the specific circumstances of conquered England and thus part of the new claim of William I to be the source of all tenure in England, a claim he could not make in Normandy.[73]

One of the main purposes of Domesday was to maximise the political and financial gains from this uniquely comprehensive right of lordship, which is why Domesday was structured by shire and then by tenant-in-chief so that sheriffs and treasury officials could administer these income streams efficiently.[74] Not only did the English landholders reduce to 1,612 individuals but the 30,000 or so free peasant farmers in 1066 were reduced to 3,000 in 1086, a widespread displacement of the peasants downwards as the ranks of the landed society extracted a greater share of the kingdom's wealth.[75] In 1086, all land was either the king's own land or held by tenants-in-chief, their estates called 'honours' or 'fiefs'. Lordship over land in 1086 was far more extensive than it had been in 1066, held either immediately or mediately from the king and it was comprehensive. Domesday Book was designed and made on the presumption that every honour could at any time fall under royal control.[76] Any idea that there was continuity from pre-Conquest landholding patterns to post-Conquest can be put aside, too. Only a small minority of honours were constituted through antecessorial grants so that the tenurial fabric was effectively 'shredded' between 1066 and 1086.[77]

Domesday Book didn't fully settle the question of *Anglia* though. The men 'sent all over England' did not cover the area north of the Tees, only patchily west to Ribble, although the modern Welsh border corresponds to the Domesday survey. Therefore, the North remained outside Domesday *Anglia* until the later eleventh century when a charter of William II confirms the possessions of the church of Tynemouth as in *Anglia*.[78] That said, the Humber, that iconic border from Bede and Alfred's day, had gone. Southern England was the focus of wealth and power (as it is today): the area under cultivation in the 29 Domesday shires in 1086 was 7.2 million acres; the official Agricultural Statistics for June 1914 give a total of 7.7. million acres of total arable acreage.[79]

Domesday Book arose from the contingency planning for a Danish invasion and evolved into a record of tax and legitimising the great land grab that followed 1066; it reveals the astonishing concentration of power into the hands of the new king and his inner circle. It is also the final 'air-brushing' of Harold's reign, too, who was subsequently eradicated from the record, a campaign of words begun by William of Poitiers soon after 1066 and completed in Domesday Book where he is referred to as *comes Haroldus* (earl Harold), a policy change from 'King Harold' in an early writ, with the time of King Edward (1066) and the time of King William as the framework of the survey, so that William's reign is linked to Edward, his kinsman. The English scribe who wrote up the final version made one slip that escaped the attention of the proof-reader: deep in the heartland of Wessex the village of Soberton, held by King William in 1086 but Harold, *when he was reigning*, took it from Leofmann who held it from Earl Godwin.[80]

The Norman military juggernaut rolled on. A great meeting was convened at Salisbury at Lammas in 1086, to include the king's councillors, and 'all the people occupying land who were of any account over all England ... all submitted to him and were his men and swore him loyal oaths that they would be loyal to him against all other men.'[81] The Oath of Salisbury performed on 1 August 1086 was part of the Domesday survey and the emergency planning arising from the threat of invasion, which had only just receded.[82] It was at Old Sarum that the ancient earthwork ramparts were filled with a citadel complex of castle and cathedral in a classic re-purposing of space for the purpose of commemoration and symbolism. In some ways, the oath at Salisbury was essentially part of the ancient Early English custom of oath-taking and allegiance.[83] The people present at the oath were not Early English though, and the relationship with the new monarchy was very different; it may only have been the 150 greatest tenants-in-chief who held 90% of England's wealth and who would fit into the newly built nave to swear the oath.

William departed for Normandy immediately after the Salisbury Oath and we are reminded that this was an Anglo-Norman kingship. Most of the wealthiest lords in England also had lands in Normandy, occasionally Brittany, Flanders, and Picardy. Charter evidence shows that William I spent three-quarters of his time in Normandy between 1072 and 1087;

Above right: Those who came before: Neolithic long barrow at Belas Knap, Gloucestershire. '… until one began to dominate the dark, a dragon on the prowl from the steep vaults of a stone-roofed barrow where he guarded a hoard…' (Courtesy of Ethan Doyle White under Creative Commons)

Below right: Going round in circles: the largest stone circle in the world, Avebury, Wiltshire. The Neolithic site sits in a region rich in ancient monuments, ridgeways and burial grounds and was settled by a medieval priory and village; today, the A361 to Devizes passes right through its centre. (Author's collection)

The far side of the world: Birdoswald, Hadrian's Wall, Northumberland. Keeping people in, or keeping them out? (Author's collection)

Above left: 'There was a dream that was Rome': the amphitheatre at Cirencester (Corinium) could seat 8,000 people, the stone tiered seating hidden in plain sight by the grass patterns. (Author's collection)

Below left: Luxurious living: hypocaust and baths at Chedworth, off the Fosse Way near Cirencester, where a mosaic was recently revealed to date from the early fifth century, suggesting continuity well beyond the military withdrawal.

Bottom: Great Witcombe Roman Villa, just off Ermine Street, south of Cirencester.

Top: Eastern approaches, Richborough, Kent: first-century supply depot, late third-century 'Saxon shore fort', possible landing spot for fifth-century pagan immigrants and St Augustine in 597. (Courtesy of Luke Purser)

Above: Into the West: Tintagel, Cornwall, thriving fifth-to-seventh-century trade hub from the Atlantic into the western Mediterranean and later medieval power-base of the earl of Cornwall and Arthurian fantasy. (Courtesy of Luke Purser)

Below: The 'misty moors' and 'desolate fens' of the migrant journeys to the new land; River Alde, Snape, Suffolk. (Courtesy of Bill Jones)

The beginnings of England? Mound 1, Sutton Hoo, Suffolk, the site of the kingly ship burial uncovered by Basil Browne in 1939, with the 27-metre ship marked out. (Author's collection)

Footprints in the sand: the remains of the ship, summer 1939 (BM). The Sutton Hoo Ship Company is now building a life-size replica. (British Library)

Sutton Hoo helmet replica: 'cheek-hinged', 'burnished' with 'an embossed ridge, a band lapped with wire' and 'hasped with gold' as per *Beowulf*. (Private collection)

Rich pickings? Lindisfarne, the view from the original Anglo-Saxon church and the Viking approaches. (Author's collection)

Keeping the wealhs in Wales: Offa's Dyke, late eighth century, near Presteigne, Powys. (Courtesy of Andrew/ARG_Flickr under Creative Commons)

Left: Dropped in the ditch: a nineteenth-century sketch of the 'Alfred jewel', a late ninth century æstel made by Alfred's command and found by a seventeenth-century ploughman.

Below: Æthelstan, first 'king of all England,' Malmesbury Abbey, Wiltshire. (Author's collection)

Odda's Chapel, Deerhurst, Gloucestershire. A mid-eleventh-century chapel, it was uncovered in the later nineteenth century after years as a cowshed. Near here in 1016, by the River Severn, King Edmund and King Cnut partitioned England into two, back to how it was under Alfred and Guthrum in 886. (Author's collection)

Pre-Conquest church, Brixworth, Northamptonshire: another rare example of the world lost after 1066. (Author's collection)

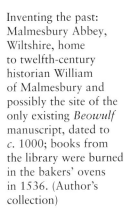

Inventing the past: Malmesbury Abbey, Wiltshire, home to twelfth-century historian William of Malmesbury and possibly the site of the only existing *Beowulf* manuscript, dated to *c*. 1000; books from the library were burned in the bakers' ovens in 1536. (Author's collection)

Top: Lionheart's folly? Richard I's nuclear deterrent, Château Gaillard, Normandy, lost by John in 1204. (Courtesy of Patrick Morio60 under Creative Commons)

Above: Home and away: Chinon castle, deep in the Angevin territories in France, base of Henry II in the 1180s and the French royal court in 1429 prior to the expulsion of the English in 1453. (Courtesy of Daniel Jolivet under Creative Commons)

Below: Military supremacy: Twelfth-century Goodrich Castle in Herefordshire. (Courtesy of Ken Dixon under Creative Commons)

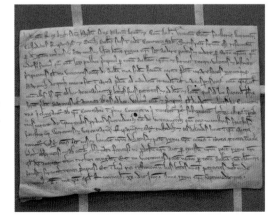

Above: Rejecting tyranny: Magna Carta, 1215; much watered down in 1217 and 1225, the final version. (British Library)

Right: Dissembling and deceit: the only surviving writ issued by King John to all the sheriffs, dated 20 June 1215, ordering them to 'hear, see and obey' the charter (but not to actually proclaim it); within a few weeks, John would repudiate the charter entirely. (Hereford Cathedral, © Hawkwood International)

Above: Bamburgh Castle, Northumberland, capital of a tenth-century kingdom. (Courtesy of Matthew Hartley under Creative Commons)

Left: Hotspur's hangout: Warkworth Castle, Northumberland, owned by the Percy family from the thirteenth century: the 12th Duke of Northumberland, Ralph Percy, resides at Alnwick today. (Author's collection)

Below left: Dunstanburgh castle, Northumberland, northern base of Thomas, Earl of Lancaster, early fourteenth century. (Author's collection)

Above: York Minster. (Author's collection)

Below left: Less is more: deep in the Welsh borders, the tiny church of St Mary and St David at Kilpeck, Herefordshire, is a world-famous example of the Herefordshire School of sculpture with its twelfth-century Romanesque carvings. (Author's collection)

Below right: 'A knight ther was, and that a worthy man…': possible tomb of Sir William de Harley, late thirteenth century, at Pershore Abbey, Worcestershire, showing unique details of mail coat, straps and buckles on the effigy of the harness. (Author's collection)

Above: 'Pigges bones'? The Becket Reliquary, Hereford Cathedral, made around 1200 in Limoges, south-west France, spirited away during the Reformation and kept by a local Catholic family until it passed back to the cathedral in 1831. The front panel shows the murder of Becket, an image which in today's terminology would be one of the most 'liked' memes in the medieval world. (© Hawkwood International)

Left: Fifteenth-century guild hall, Warwick. Reformed after the Dissolution as The Lord Leycester Hospital, which it still is today. (Author's collection)

'In praise of the laws of England': Sir John Fortescue, Chief Justice of the King's Bench and Lord Chancellor. The current Lord Fortescue still owns the manor house yards away from the church. (Author's collection; by kind permission of St Eadburgha's Church, Ebrington, Gloucestershire)

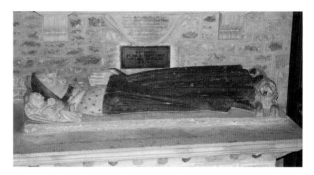

Above right and right: Economic powerhouse: The twelfth-century tithe barn at Middle Littleton, Worcestershire. If this stored one-tenth of the harvest, it suggests healthy crops in good times and certainly a bounty for the church. (Author's collection)

Above left: 'The sheep ate the men.' Late medieval ridge and furrow at Hidcote Bartrim, Gloucestershire, now a sheep farm, the famous Cotswold 'Lion' that transformed the fortunes of later medieval England. (Author's collection)

Below left: Vanishing communities: the deserted medieval village at Billesley Trussell, Warwickshire. Sir Richard Trussell died fighting at the battle of Evesham, 1265. This thriving village was close to the Roman road from Stratford on Avon to Alcester and declined from eighteen resident families in 1332 to only four people in 1428 due to a combination of Black Death, climate change and sheep farming. (Author's collection)

Dissolving the medieval millennium: what was the great abbey at Evesham, Worcestershire. The surviving Bell Tower, *c.* 1520s, reminds us how the late medieval Catholic establishment maintained its grip to the very end. (Author's collection)

Above: A glimpse of what remains: the Almonry, Evesham Abbey, now a Heritage centre. (Author's collection)

Above right: To kill a king: Richard III loses Bosworth all over again, only this time on foot since in 2019 health and safety regulations were rather different to 1485 – it was too wet to re-enact the cavalry charge. (Author's collection)

Below right: The champion of parliament meets a sticky end at the hands of royalty: Simon de Montfort loses the battle of Evesham again. (Author's collection)

Late medieval house under construction, Mary Arden's Farm, Wilmcote, Warwickshire. (Author's collection)

The deconsecrated church of All Saints at Billesley Trussell, Warwickshire, where the young William Shakespeare may have married Anne Hathaway; their grand-daughter Elizabeth married here, too. He left Anne in Stratford to raise the family while he made his fortune in London reinventing the histories of England for the stage. (Author's collection)

cross-Channel ties of lordship were crucial in holding kingdom and duchy together. The great example is William fitzOsbern, one of the king's most trusted childhood companions who took command of a swathe of property straddling the Seine valley and after 1066 took blocks of land in Herefordshire and the Isle of Wight, with manors in between, to form a great corridor of lordship.[84]

The events of 1066 can be seen as another phase in the migration and integration of the multitude of different peoples who have made up British society.[85] The Norman Conquest should no longer be regarded as an English construct – it is British and European, a part of the diaspora of peoples which constituted the first great expansion of western Europe, including the early Crusades, the wars against Islam in Spain and the start of the drive to the East, taking Flemings to Lithuania, Poland, Strathclyde and Pembrokeshire and bringing Jews into England; it was also a cultural movement which spread widely a particular brand of Christianity.[86] The Normans were adept at taking over existing systems of government and making them work more efficiently, which they had done in Normandy in the tenth century and were doing so in southern Italy and Sicily at the time of the Norman Conquest.[87]

William the Conqueror's reputation and that of his band of warriors went before him across Europe. The *Chronicle* claimed that William had Wales in his power, Scotland subdued and would have conquered Ireland if he had lived two more years. In 1074 the German emperor apparently sought William's military aid and the bishop of Santiago de Compostella plotted to hand over the kingdom of Galicia to him. William fitzOsbern planned to acquire Flanders (where he was killed on a campaign). Bishop Odo desired the papacy (he would do), and it was prophesied that William would become emperor. William of Poitiers boasted that William would have taken Troy in a day.[88] Indeed, William of Poitiers created in King William a classical hero for a Christian age; he was a modern Caesar, a true son of Rome in an age of Norman imperialism stretching from the knights in Apulia, Sicily, Constantinople and Babylon to the downlands of Sussex, an epoch that William and his men deliberately associated with the classical past.[89]

William's kingship, cloaked as it was in old English customs of crown-wearings and counsel, was deeply personal; his inner circle was composed of his younger half-brothers Odo and Robert with three childhood friends, William fitzOsbern, Roger de Montgomery and Roger de Beaumont. The closer to the king the barons were, the more property they received; there was also a strong correlation between the king's charter witnesses and wealthy landholders.

The Norman Conquest itself was a personal decision made by William alone. He only trusted a few prelates, chiefly Odo, Bishop Geoffrey of Coutances and Archbishop Lanfranc. Odo's plotting and fitzOsbern's death in 1071 hit him hard; the betrayal of fizOsbern's son, Roger, in the 1075 rebellion was a terrible insult. Earl Waltheof, collateral damage, was executed, prisoners blinded, maimed, and exiled, but Roger remained in prison for life, his sons still unpardoned in Henry I's reign.[90]

William's life and reign ended where it began, amidst violence on the Norman borders, where William burnt to death many men on a raid into Mantes and returned afflicted with an illness, to die in Rouen on 9 September 1087. His beloved wife Matilda had died in 1083, his oldest comrade William fitzOsbern was long gone, his half-brother Odo was in confinement and his son Robert estranged. The *Chronicle* noted in the obituary of 1087 how he 'had castles built and wretched men oppressed', twenty-six lines lamenting the cruelty and severity of his reign, though adding he was a 'very wise man' among other phrases of ambiguous praise.[91] From the viewpoint of the victors, it was not a conquest at all; William spent twenty years legitimising his rights against the usurper (Harold Godwinsson) in charters and in Domesday Book. William secured papal support, made generous gifts to churches, required his troops to do penance and agreed at his coronation to rule the English in the manner of kings before and indeed to lead the English in atonement for the collective sins which had precipitated their defeat.[92]

There was no Beowulf to save the English now: Grendel and all the orcs had destroyed *Heorot*. If one individual could be said to have changed the course of English history – and not necessarily for the good as it used to be assumed - between 400 and 1500, then that man is William the Conqueror. In Professor David Bates' words, 'William was the destroyer of lives, the bringer of a disaster of unnecessary proportions to the English ... the scale of human tragedy is beyond our knowing.'[93] The *Chronicle* must have the last word, before it gives way to the new histories. In 1100, a generation after the battle of Hastings, we are told that Henry I married Edgar Ætheling's sister, Eadgyth, 'daughter of King Malcolm of Scotland and the good Queen Margaret, King Edward's relative, *of the rightful royal family of England*.'[94]

ELEVEN

Continental Cousins

The Norman Conquest created an entirely new political landscape in north-west Europe. The identity of England was now linked to the Continent for the following five centuries. Far from disintegrating in later generations, the Anglo-Norman kingdom exploded out of Normandy and into central and southern France in 1154 under the rule of one man, Henry II, whose word stretched from Hadrian's Wall to the foothills of the Pyrenees. This was not planned or in any way inevitable. The development of government in England during the twelfth century included the Exchequer, King's Bench, and common law, managed by a succession of very able bureaucrats in the absence of the king abroad. A new generation of historians with English and Norman parentage began to rationalise rather than justify the horrors of 1066-75. Universities, colleges and new towns flourished in a renaissance of learning and international trade. Slavery disappeared, but the English remained subservient in their newly minted realm, their language oppressed and offices of state, high and low, firmly closed to them.

William of Malmesbury probably thought that William the Conqueror had gone to hell. Two mid-twelfth-century writers, William of Malmesbury and Henry of Huntingdon, created the post-Conquest histories of England. Both agreed that it was a disaster for the English people – an apocalypse where God had chosen the Normans to wipe out the English in a tale of extensive human ruin. William of Malmesbury echoed Gildas, in talking of decay in pre-Conquest England: there were clergy who could 'scarcely stammer out the words of the sacraments, and a person who understood grammar was an object of wonder and astonishment.'[1] The English nobility were casual in their religious observance, eating and drinking to excess and covered in tattoos; they doomed themselves to slavery by giving William an 'easy victory' rashly in a single battle.

The Normans, in contrast, were sober, polite, faithful, and pious. Dress, hairstyle, houses, personal naming patterns, intermarriage and hunting preferences are all features of the new life after 1066. William of Malmesbury's *Deeds of the Kings of the English* created the narrative of political unification of England under one king and one people and the cultural and social improvement of those peoples.[2] The Norman Conquest was deliberately presented as a new start, with kingship based on right of conquest, trial by battle, Old English laws muddled and discredited to make sense of the present and justify the past.[3]

The mirror might have cracked but this does not mean we have to accept the new version of the past as seen by these twelfth-century commentators, just as we have been wary of the Chronicles and Bede in earlier times. William of Malmesbury (d.1143) lived at Malmesbury Abbey, burial place of Æthelstan, and he travelled widely. He was one of the best-read scholars of the age, but he also had an imperialist view that the Welsh, Scots, and Irish were 'barbarian' – although Christian – and central to his vision of English history was the progress from barbarism to civilization, so that the world after 1066 was significantly superior to the one before (even though he was a native-born Englishman, and he bemoaned the loss of English). He saw himself as the first man to set in order a continuous history of England since Bede, effectively writing a sequel to the *Ecclesiastical History*. He was part of a generation of writers including Orderic Vitalis (who copied Bede), Henry of Huntingdon (who saw the Scots as 'heathen') and Geoffrey of Monmouth (who, typically, does not refer to Bede or the chosen peoples since he was in search of King Arthur – disparaged as 'nonsense' by William of Malmesbury), all born in England in the last quarter of the eleventh century to English mothers and foreign fathers, all living in the shadow of the Conquest, which made them re-imagine English history entirely.[4] Henry of Huntingdon (d.1157), a secular clerk and archdeacon of Lincoln, wrote the *History of the English People*, a very popular work since 25 manuscripts survive. He used 132 of 140 chapters from Bede's *Ecclesiastical History*.[5] Like Bede, these men drew upon oral tradition to form their new written histories. The earliest post-Conquest historian, Eadmer, claimed to have based his *Historia novorum* on 'things which I have seen with my own eyes and myself heard,' William of Malmesbury reported what he had heard things 'from credible authority' and Orderic Vitalis passed on things he had 'learned from the oldest monks'. Later, Gerald of Wales referred to 'vulgar tradition'.[6]

Perhaps one good thing that came of the Conquest was the ending of slavery. William of Malmesbury's distaste reveals the shift in attitudes to this repugnant trade: according to him, the English even sold off their female servants when pregnant into prostitution or slavery 'after they had satisfied their lust'. They would buy up men from all over England

and sell them off to Ireland, files of the wretches roped together, young persons of both sexes being put up for sale every day, a scene not that different to Bede's day. Slaves account for around 10% of the Domesday population, with the higher proportion in the west and south-west, where of course the British had migrated in the fifth century and where they had been assimilated into Wessex by Alfred in the ninth century. Picking up the thread of what happened to the British, we might propose that a great number of those who did not migrate west into modern Wales or the north or overseas to Brittany were enslaved by the English until the later eleventh century. The earliest manumission of a slave was by King Æthelstan in 925, who freed Eadhelm along with his sons. Many of the names on the manumissions are British, such as Wenerieth and Moruiw and the high-status witnesses mainly English, such as Ælfsige the Ealdorman and Wulfsige the Deacon. Other Early English wills include references to freeing slaves.[7] There is a drop in manumissions after 1066, probably because of terminology since they became serfs and by the late twelfth century, they disappear from the record.

The unfree peasantry in Domesday Book were predominantly the former 'British' people, though not necessarily former slaves. The 'English' probably constituted the bulk of the free peasants (only around 12%) and urban dwellers, and the entirely new elite were Norman-French who left few traces of their DNA with very little intermarriage among the upper echelons for well over a century.[8] 'Freedom' is a relative concept of course; slave owners had to feed and house their slaves whereas a free man was free to starve. The 1102 Council of Westminster issued a general ban on all trade in slaves in England, but it continued in Ireland, as Gerald of Wales noted in the 1170s (he also portrayed the Irish as uncivilised barbarians.) Welsh and Scottish kings took captives from England in the eleventh and early twelfth centuries who could well have been sold on.[9]

The 'English' were therefore the new slaves in a broader sense. Much of the Conqueror's legislation discriminates between the *Franci*, the Frenchmen who came to England after 1066, and the *Angli*, those who were in England before 1066 (regardless of their ethnicity). It was ethnically discriminatory justice – apartheid justice – just as the first laws of Early England had been, since the *Franci* would clear themselves by swearing oaths whereas the *Angli* had to undergo the ordeal; the new *murdrum* fine prescribed heavy penalties for lords and hundredal communities if any *Franci* were murdered, specifically to protect the Frenchmen in hostile territory.[10] After 1066, the ancient Old English laws and customs were turned upon the defeated people to imprison, maim and execute them. After the rebellions of 1068-75 that there were no further rebellions from the English until 1381 and that was local to the south-east and eastern region. Absent kings – Henry I and Henry II – in Normandy and further afield in the French possessions of Anjou and Aquitaine – and

Richard I on crusade and in captivity, led to rapid bureaucratisation of government to maximise profits from a wealthy country and to keep the peace.[11] This was not for the benefit of the English but for the benefit of the foreign rulers and landowners.

The *Dialogue of the Exchequer* provides some interesting insights into the post-Conquest society a century later. This was compiled in the form of a dialogue between master and disciple in 1177-79 by Richard fitz Nigel, bishop of London and treasurer of the Exchequer from *c.* 1150-1198.[12] The *Dialogue* believed that 'with the English and Normans dwelling together and alternately marrying and giving in marriage, the races have become so fused that it can scarcely be discerned at the present day – *I speak of freemen alone* [ie. a small proportion of society] – who is English and who is Norman by race.'[13] The villeins, were not permitted to change their status if their lords objected and made up almost half of the population, so any ethnic mixing was limited to the upper strata of society, quite possibly the 'English' rather than the 'British' who were now perhaps the bulk of the unfree classes. The *Dialogue* tells us how the native Englishmen lay in wait and killed Normans in secret (hence *murdrum*) which the Normans responded to with 'violent measures' and 'various refinements of torture'. Eventually a scheme was devised to make the Hundred pay if the killer was not brought to justice, a large sum of between £36 and £44.[14] (The same did not apply if an Englishman was killed.) This aspect of post-Conquest racial apartheid was not finally abolished until 1340, in the guise of 'presentment of Englishry', declared void forever by statute.[15]

The legal treatise of *Glanvill* was written *c.* 1190, possibly by justiciar of England Rannulf de Glanville, and tells us a great deal about the legal reforms of Henry II, especially the sworn inquest, as well as traditional forms of proof witness and ordeals.[16] Social status was still very much based upon blood lineage and confirmed or denied by the local community. *Glanvill* tells us about villein status and free status; a free person must prove this by bringing several near blood relatives to court and if they are denied or doubted, the 'men of the neighbourhood' will give their verdict.[17] In proving villein status, the opposite must be done. In gaining freedom, his lord could 'quit-claim' him from himself and his heirs, or 'give or sell him' to another to free him (although his prior status as a villein could exclude him from acting as a champion, 'even if he has been made a knight since he was freed'). No villein could buy his own freedom with his own money since his chattels were the property of his lord; a third party could provide him with money to buy his freedom, though. Another way out was living peaceably for a year and a day in a town and if admitted as a citizen into the commune (ie gild) he could be freed from villeinage. One became a villein by birth, even if one parent was free.

Following William the Conqueror was always going to be tough. William II is notable chiefly for his bizarre death while hunting in the New Forest in August 1100. William of Malmesbury is on hand to give us the details:

> When the king received the wound, he said not a word, but breaking off the shaft of the arrow where it stuck out of his body, he fell upon the ground and thus made more speedily his own death.[18]

The youngest of the Conqueror's sons, Henry, moved (suspiciously) fast to secure the throne before the eldest brother, Robert. He went immediately to Winchester where the treasury was situated at that time and thence to Westminster where he was crowned on 5 August 1100, four days after his brother's death. William of Malmesbury points out that his right to the crown was all the better for his being the only son of the Conqueror born when his father was king.[19] To gain support Henry issued a 'Coronation Charter' and agreed terms with Robert to pay him £2000 a year.[20] This proved unworkable and the armies of the two brothers met in battle at Tinchebrai, 1106, in a reversal of Hastings, where an English army defeated the Norman one, and on foot, in the space of an hour.[21] Robert was captured and kept in captivity in England until his death in 1134.

England after 1066 should be seen as entering another phase of multi-culturalism and multi-ethnicity, central features of these islands' history.[22] The Anglo-Norman axis tilted towards Normandy, which remained a decisive factor in the governance of England to 1204 and beyond. This has been called an 'empire' and after 1066 William I explicitly associated his power with an imperial hegemony, although he and his successors never took the title *imperium*.[23] After 1106, Henry I spent half of the remainder of his reign in Normandy defending it against King Louis VI of France and Count Fulk of Anjou, marrying eight of his illegitimate daughters to neighbouring princes, including King Alexander of Scotland.

England paid heavily for these wars, which, along with regnal absence, were to influence innovations in English government for the next two centuries. While Henry was absent, England was governed by a vice-regal committee that met twice-yearly at the exchequer to audit the sheriff's returns. This was supervised by Roger of Salisbury, founder of a dynasty of bureaucrats at the heart of government for most of the twelfth century. The first reference to the exchequer is in 1110; the name derived from the chequered cloth on which the annual audits of the debts owed to the king took place. These audits were recorded on a great document later called the pipe roll, because it looked like a pipe (the first surviving pipe roll was for the financial year 1129-1130.)[24]

The *Dialogue of the Exchequer* tells us that the 'exchequer' itself was a quadrangular board about ten feet in length and five feet in breadth, covered in a black cloth marked with stripes (later coloured black and white like a chess board and the *Dialogue* specifically refers to the game of chess and the chessboard.) The clerks, tellers, ushers, watchmen, silverers and melters counted the monies from the sheriffs' accounts. The head of the exchequer was the chief justiciar and in day-to-day charge was the treasurer of the exchequer. The first pipe roll of 1129-30 reveals that royal income was generated from four sources: income from royal demesne (37%); the geld (14%); profits of government, justice (17%) and royal lordship, vacancies in religious houses, escheats, wardships, marriages and reliefs (33%). None of these exactions suggest that he fulfilled his promises in the 1100 charter.[25]

The 'Establishment of the King's Household', (*Constitutio domus regis*), dated 1136, the earliest surviving account of the royal household, sets out detailed salaries and positions of royal administration, including the chancellor, the marshal, chamberlains and treasurers, stewards, dispensers, down to the fruiterers, cooks, huntsmen, hornblowers, even the man who carried the king's bow and the waferer.[26] We should not be too dazzled by the written record though, since we know from Asser how Alfred arranged his finances into portions and Alfred's charter for Ealdorman Æthelhelm include a *cellerarius* (steward) *thesaurius* (keeper of the wardrobe) and *pincerna* (butler).[27] Officials are mentioned in charters and records from Alfred's time onwards so there is no revolution in government under Henry I, educated in the 'sweets of learning' though he may have been (according to William of Malmesbury.)[28] There was a decline in crown-wearing occasions from 1110 on, perhaps because it was too expensive or because the monarchy was secure enough not to have to put on the grand shows that William I and William II had done. With the advent of the pipe rolls and judicial eyres, bureaucracy was perhaps overtaking charisma as the prime ingredient of kingship.[29]

The management of the royal finances was in the hands not of the kings, but of a remarkable family of bureaucrats. Richard Fitz Nigel was the third generation of royal administrators, the great-nephew of Roger, bishop of Salisbury, the manager of the Exchequer under Henry I, and son of Nigel, bishop of Ely, also prominent in the royal court and exchequer. This family dominated royal bureaucracy from c1120-1198, on Fitz Nigel's death. Nigel of Ely had restored the exchequer at the repeated instance of Henry II. His involvement in the royal financial administration began in the 1120s as a receiver in the Norman treasury and then court treasurer after becoming bishop of Ely, promoted by his uncle Roger, bishop of Salisbury. Roger was dismissed from office by Stephen in 1139, which cast out Nigel from favour, too, but the 1155-6 pipe roll specifically referenced his authority, the year the exchequer was fully restored following the serious disruption of Stephen's reign.

Roger was never as powerful as his uncle (Robert earl of Leicester was the presiding member of the exchequer in the first years of Henry II's reign) but probably remained actively involved with the exchequer until 1164 when he was struck by some form of paralysis.[30] Roger did manage to get his son Richard appointed to court treasurer as early as 1156 – the first in Henry II's reign – probably buying him the office for £400, according to the Ely chronicler.[31] This allowed the family of Roger of Salisbury to entrench themselves again in the royal administration for decades, undoing the expulsion of Stephen, their influence on the treasury lasting well into the thirteenth century.

Richard fitz Nigel's role as treasurer to the exchequer, the king and the justiciar was a professional, administrative position that illustrated the growing division between household and exchequer since he was rarely at court itself, and it tells us more about how individual bureaucrats were implementing the detailed policies of the broad framework established by Henry II.

The king's absence, sibling rivalry and the Anglo-Norman polity forced the pace of reform. To win support in his dash for the throne in 1100 Henry I granted a 'Coronation Charter' that explicitly restored the 'law of King Edward' and refers three times to the 'counsel' and 'common counsel' of the barons.[32] On the one hand this was a sweetener to the barons to gain support, but on the other hand it is a highly significant document, part of the 'constitutional tradition' in line with the concessions of Æthelred on his return in 1014 and his son Edward on arriving in England in 1041, and would be echoed in charters by Stephen and Henry II, becoming of great importance to the barons in 1215.[33]

If the concept of ancient counsel and consent is a theme of these charters, then legal precedent from before 1066 peculiar to England is also a feature. Charters of Stephen in 1135 confirm all the 'liberties and good laws' which Henry I (his uncle) had granted, and the good laws and good customs enjoyed 'in the time of King Edward', and promise to observe 'good laws and the ancient and lawful customs'.[34] (The so-called 'Laws of Henry I' was a treatise written in the early twelfth century and is vague and lacking authority).[35] Stephen too, came to the throne under a disputed succession but Henry II did not, although he quickly issued a general charter confirming the customs, gifts, liberties and concessions which his grandfather King Henry had granted.[36] The charter of 1100 is addressed to all the barons and vassals, 'both French and English', and it specifically refers to the 'time of King Edward' and the 'laws' of Edward (which did not exist) attempting to create a bond with the past and perhaps the 'good old days' in restoring peace and order. The 1100 charter refers to the 'kingdom' of England twice and to the 'regnum' (realm) six times in only fourteen clauses.

Henry I's best-laid plans came crashing down with the death of his only legitimate son and heir, Prince William, with the infamous sinking of the White Ship in 1121 (the crew were drunk and were racing in the dark, William of Malmesbury helpfully informs us).[37] Again, it is a tragic reminder of the fragility of Anglo-Norman geopolitics. Channel-crossing was not safe at the best of times and Walter Map recalls one such journey with Henry II when all but one – the king's ship – of the fleet of 25 were scattered and destroyed.[38] The drowning of Prince William was one of those rare moments of fate that had profound implications for the English polity, since it led to the wars between Henry's nominated heir, his daughter Matilda, and her cousin, Stephen and ultimately to Matilda's son, Henry, becoming king of England in 1154. Henry was from central France, Anjou, and his succession was to bring England further into France and all that was French culturally, spiritually, and politically for centuries.

Matilda was set to be the first woman to rule England in her own right after her father made the barons swear an oath to support her succession in 1128, but when Henry I died in 1135, Stephen emulated his uncle's move and seized power. But Stephen failed to grasp that security in Normandy was also security in England (he went only once, in 1137) and Matilda's husband, Geoffrey of Anjou, conquered the duchy in the years 1141-44 and was invested as duke; his death in 1151 left his son Henry as duke. There was much more to come, since Henry successfully courted the recently divorced Eleanor of Aquitaine, and eloped with her in 1152, a marriage that stunned western Europe since she gave him her inheritance, Aquitaine, which compromised most of south-western France.

The eighteen-year-old was duke of Normandy, count of Anjou and now in his wife's name, duke of Aquitaine, commanding territory from the shores of the English Channel to the Pyrenees. Even so, Stephen was secure in England and it looked as if the Anglo-Norman empire would finally dissolve when the young king's campaign in England failed. But it was the death of Stephen's son, Eustace, that transformed Henry's – and England's – fortunes. The Treaty of Westminster (December 1153) recognised Henry as Stephen's heir, something that with hindsight could be taken as inevitable but not in reality, since his mother Matilda had failed as much in England as Stephen had in Normandy. The momentum of the Continental possessions was a major factor in Henry's position.[39]

The strength of these Continental connections resulted in the first undisputed English succession since Edward the Confessor in 1042. Again, it was absence abroad – Henry II spent 21 of his 34-year reign on the Continent – in these (now much wider) possessions that created reform in England and again, we should ask how much the king was personally responsible for these changes. Henry II was 'polished in letters', according to Gerald of Wales, well read and multi-lingual, according to Walter Map, a man of non-stop action who wore out his court but who was accessible to the point being mobbed by the crowd on his progress.[40] He is referred to on occasion as 'the son of the Empress Maud', which gave him a sense of imperial authority.

Relations between the English crown and Rome after 1066 were certainly not on the scale of the Early English 'special relationship', despite the papal blessing of the 1066 invasion. Letters between Archbishop Lanfranc, William I and Pope Gregory VII grew increasingly fraught and threatening as the papal reform movement attempted to assert more political power over William's crown, and in 1080 William I refused to do fealty to Pope Gregory VII: 'I have not consented to pay fealty, nor will I now, because I never promised it, nor do I find that my predecessors ever paid it to your predecessors.'[41] William I did decree in 1072 that pleas relating to the episcopal laws should not be held in the hundred courts but in in a place of the bishop's choosing; no sheriff or reeve or king's official or layman was to interfere with the laws pertaining to the bishop and anyone who failed to attend the bishop's summons would be excommunicated after the third summons.[42]

The sacral nature of early medieval kingship changed after 1066. Lanfranc's successor, Anselm, insisted that a king was a layman, rather than a sacred deputy of God and therefore the bishops and abbots should not receive their ring and staff from the king anymore. This was not quite settled after years of dispute and Anselm's exile in France, but matters came to a dramatic head under Henry II, after the appointment of his worldly friend and chancellor, Thomas Becket, as Archbishop of Canterbury. The issue of 'criminous clerks' in 1163-4 was the spark for this dispute, whereby clergy could escape capital punishment in the ecclesiastical courts, supposedly resolved in the Constitutions of Clarendon.[43] Becket relented, then backtracked and fled to exile like Anselm before him. On his return in the winter of 1170, he punished all those who had been involved in the Young King's coronation and following a famous fit of rage from the king, four knights crossed the Channel to remonstrate with or possibly arrest the implacable archbishop, they put their armour on and killed in him in his own cathedral.[44] Shocking though Becket's murder was – and he was canonised in record time by Pope Alexander III in February 1173 – it did little to shake Henry II's political power.[45]

The administration of law in England after 1066 suggests a significant increase in royal intervention in the shires but this perhaps was in reaction to the disputes over land-holding and rights created by the redistribution following the invasion.[46] English sheriffs were replaced with Norman personnel from the 1070s but continuing concerns over loyalty and corruption are demonstrated by writs during William I's reign and, a new departure in the reign of Henry I, a charter of 1110 that specifically orders the shire courts and hundred courts to meet in the same places and on the same terms as the 'time of King Edward' (except if the king himself summons them); sheriffs had clearly been doing otherwise since 'I do not wish that my sheriff should make them assemble in different fashion because of his own needs or interests.'[47] This issue didn't go away since Henry II removed over twenty in 1155 (following the civil wars between Stephen and Matilda) and again in 1170, at the Inquest of the Sheriffs, replacing them with officers of the Exchequer reporting directly to the king.[48]

The Assize of Clarendon (1166), reinforced by the Assize of Northampton (1176), fundamentally changed law, which had in effect survived since the Early English era but this was nevertheless an acceleration, not an unprecedented leap forward, and it was unlikely that Henry II himself had any precise views on what he wanted substantive law to be.[49] The visitations of the itinerant justices became regular, and the sworn inquest was applied extensively for settling criminal cases. The jury was now a normal part of the administration of justice. The justices and the sheriffs were to liaise and bring the culprits to trial speedily, the sheriffs especially given powers of arrest reaching across castles, boroughs, and cities. Justice had become public, not private, and compensation was replaced with retribution; penalties in the Assize of Northampton of 1176 were more severe, and the justices had their powers increased at the expense of the sheriffs.[50] The Clarendon assize stipulated that if a man failed the ordeal of water, he would lose a foot, but after Northampton he would lose his right hand with his foot. In 1215 Pope Innocent III forbade priests involvement in the trial by ordeal. This had been coming for several decades since in 1179 Henry II ordered that trial by jury could replace trial by battle; both were aspects of the rationalisation of the law.

It was the eyre and the court at Westminster that placed the reforms under Henry II apart from earlier legal systems.[51] Eyres were regular, county-wide visitations by royal judges operating in groups and circuits covering the whole country (except Chester and Durham); they had a wide remit, from wardship and marriage-rights to criminal cases, Jewish loans, and the sale of wine. Meanwhile, the Court of the Common Pleas – the Bench – heard civil cases of all kinds, sitting for four regular law terms from the 1190s with increasingly professional judges serving for long periods. Judge-made law and state punishment finally supplanted the culture of 'feud'. The death penalty for homicide (first mentioned by *Glanvill* in the 1180s) would have made the legal reforms under Henry II that much more revolutionary if it was instigated at this time.[52] Death for thieves was in the laws of Ine (680s) but killing someone was an offence against the victim and the family; this did not mean it was not seen as a serious offence – it was – but it was not the job of the state to deal with it until the later twelfth century, stimulated by the ethnic apartheid of the Conquest, as well as developing mechanisms of the bureaucratic state. Finally, it should be remembered that these innovations had nothing to do with the absent Richard I or his brother John and everything to do with the bureaucrats who ran government, chiefly Hubert Walter, Archbishop of Canterbury and chief justiciar (1193-8) and chancellor (1199-1205), schooled in the Exchequer and co-author of the law text *Glanvill*.[53]

If we are to accept this period as the beginning of the 'common law', it is worth recalling Edgar's codes (*c*.960) where the secular section states clearly that 'every man, whether rich or poor, is to be entitled to the benefit of the common law and just judgements are to be judged for him.' This may be an expression of intent but if we are to talk of the 'birth' of the common law, then there was a very long gestation since the earliest law codes from Æthelberht of Kent in *c*.602 to Cnut in 1020 demonstrate the intent to regulate crime and punishment administered through the already ancient shires and hundreds. This becomes a much more of an incremental process than an Angevin innovation. But while this was a law common to much of Early England rather than a *common law* – and ultimately what emerged in Angevin England was notably different – it did form part of the processes that would produce common law.[54] An example is the origin of the jury, attributed to the Clarendon Assize, which can be found in Æthelred's Wantage law code of 997, where the twelve leading thegns shall 'go out and swear on the relics … they will not accuse any innocent man nor conceal any guilty one,' although there is a lack of evidence of a continuous history between the juries of the Early English and the Anglo-Normans.[55]

The assertion in the 1215 Magna Carta of the principle of the rule of law (chapter 40: the king is not to sell, deny or delay justice; chapter 39: no free man was to be imprisoned or dispossessed save by the 'lawful judgement of his peers' or by the 'law of the land') may well suggest that Henry II's reforms were not yet securely embedded (or that John's abuses were too great).[56] Furthermore, since this applied only to freemen, we should ask, whose common law? As half the population was still unfree, it was hardly 'common'. It was not until the demise of serfdom, occurring gradually throughout the fifteenth century, that the principle of law was available to most of the population, when former villeins had access to the royal courts.

The Assize of Arms (1181) was an attempt to recreate the ancient *fyrd*, or national army, to supplement the feudal levies (which even by 1100 were not a reliable force); holders of a knight's fee and free laymen holding rent or property worth 16 marks (£20) were expected to have a mail coat (hauberk), helmet, shield and a lance, those with property worth £15 had to have body armour, a headpiece and a lance and all burgesses and all other freemen quilted doublets and a headpiece of iron and a lance.[57]

All freemen were to swear allegiance to the king. No Jew was permitted to bear arms, no weapons were to be taken out of the kingdom or sold abroad without permission. This legislation reinforces the concept of the 'kingdom' but of course the oaths of allegiance to the king and burdens of military service can be found in Alfred's reign and earlier, as we have seen.

Following Becket's killing, and in the midst of the 'Great Rebellion' of 1173, William the Lion, king of Scotland, was captured at Alnwick and brought to Normandy, where he was forced to become the liegeman of Henry and do fealty to him. The clergy and church of the Scots submitted to the English Church and the earls and barons also did homage in complete and utter surrender; border castles of Roxburgh, Berwick, Edinburgh, Stirling and Jedburgh were all handed to Henry and over twenty Scottish nobles given up as hostages.[58] The Treaty of Falaise may look like an abject surrender of the Scots, but it belongs in the long line of Anglo-Scottish wars and treaties extending back to Æthelstan's summit at Eamontbridge in 927.

The author of the *Dialogue of the Exchequer* felt satisfied enough to write in the late 1170s:

> Our island content with its own, has no need of the goods of strangers.
> Therefore, with very good right, our ancestors have called it
> Truly the lap of riches, the home, too, of every delight.[59]

However, within a generation, England was crippled by heavy taxation, its king excommunicated, the realm placed under Interdict, its barons at war with the king and half the country occupied by 'strangers', namely, the French. There were two reasons for this: the loss of most of the Continental possessions, including Normandy, in 1204, and the king of England at the time, John. The result was the most significant document since Domesday Book and one that remade England with consequences that far outlasted medieval England – Magna Carta.

TWELVE

Tyranny or Law?

Up to 1272 and the accession of Edward I, every succession to the English crown was disputed or vulnerable to a rival claim, except Richard I in 1189. The journey from an illegitimate succession – duke William in Normandy – to primogeniture over the 130-odd years from 1066 to 1199 was in part acquired, in part invented and applied ad hoc.[1] This contrasted with the remarkable father-to-son succession in Capetian France from 996-1316 and it led to successive English kings granting or promising concessions to their prelates and magnates, unlike France. In 1215 the confluence of these concessions with a monarch determined to exercise his personal authority and recover lost French territories set England upon a different path to the European kingdoms.

In 1199 King John faced a succession dispute. His brother Richard I had died in April, the only king of England to die of wounds between Harold at Hastings and Richard III at Bosworth (if we discount William II's bizarre death in the New Forest).[2] John had a nephew (Arthur) by his elder brother Geoffrey and since the succession was still not established there was room for confusion. John's cruel and weak character was already known ('Lackland' and 'Softsword' pre-date his accession) but Arthur was young, and most problematically, a Breton, likely to be manipulated by King Philip of France. Reluctantly, John was backed by the leading nobles, described in the *History of William Marshal*.[3]

Ralph of Coggeshall, a monk and abbot of Coggeshall from 1207, was writing between 1201 and 1204, and was almost certainly an eyewitness.[4] He describes John's rages and threats but also the climb-downs, humble apologies, and penitential behaviour. The *Life of Hugh of Avalon, bishop of Lincoln 1186-1200* was written by Adam of Eynsham before 1213, who was extremely well informed and describes John as kind, devoted, boastful, and disrespectful. The classic 'bad king John' view comes from

The Anonymous of Béthune written soon after 1220, in the entourage of Robert de Béthune, a Flemish nobleman who had land in five English counties; this was an eyewitness of the events 1213-16 and he took notes at the time, given the level of detail.⁵ Robert de Béthune switched sides in 1216 and entered the service of Prince Louis, which explains the portrayal of John as 'bad':

> He was a very bad man, more cruel than all others; he lusted after beautiful women ... he told lies rather than the truth ... he set his barons against one another whenever he could ... he was brim-full of evil qualities.⁶

Actions speak louder than words and John's actions tell us all we need to know. He was accepted as king by Philip of France at the treaty of Le Goulet in 1200, but when conflict broke out in 1203 and Arthur, son of Geoffrey II, duke of Brittany, was captured, John had him killed by his direct command, a shocking act by the laws and conventions of the governing classes.⁷ He also hanged/starved 22 prisoners at Corfe castle, an act that was also shocking by the standards of the time. John pursued a vendetta with the leading baron William de Briouze to the death – but not William's death – instead his wife Matilda and her adult son were locked up in Corfe castle dungeon and starved to death over the course of eleven days in 1208. When the dungeon was opened, they found marks where Matilda had gnawed her son's face in desperation. John abused his power in other ways, 'seducing' the wives of barons and officials, taunting and mocking them, since they could not protest without fear of losing their lands or titles. Sources after his death fostered the view of John as a cruel, godless tyrant; Roger of Wendover (1225) tells the infamous story of Geoffrey the archdeacon of Norwich being pressed to death in a leaden cope on John's orders (variants of this appear in annals from Dunstable, Reading and Bury). Matthew Paris (*c.* 1235) dissolves into fantasy on occasion and leaves us with the image of John fatally overdosing on peaches and new cider.⁸

Distrust, fear, and loathing may have stalked the corridors of John's household but his famous brother Richard 'the Lionheart' had broken all the laws of war when he massacred hundreds, if not thousands, of Muslim prisoners in the Holy Land; Henry II had ordered – albeit indirectly – Becket's murder, and Henry I kept his brother confined for life. John's intellect and personal involvement with government got him nowhere. Instead, he ended up losing the Crown jewels and regalia and dying alone, half the kingdom occupied by French troops. The reason why was because he lost Normandy in 1204. On becoming king, he abandoned his first wife (Isabella of Gloucester) but kept her extensive lands, then stole another man's betrothed (Isabella of Angoulême, who was nine years old). Hugh of Lusignan appealed to his overlord Philip, which triggered the war with France.

On his return from the Holy Land and unexpected confinement at Durnstein castle on the Danube, Richard easily retook the gains made by Philip of France, building a vast fortress overlooking the Seine, his Chateau Gaillard, at great cost. Richard did not live long enough to reap the whirlwind of his military excesses, leaving it to John to pick up the pieces. John had none of Richard's military skill, and the combination of his own weak reputation and the death of the redoubtable Eleanor of Aquitaine in 1204 left Philip sweeping all before him as the Angevin territories collapsed like a house of cards; John's brother-in-law Alfonso VIII of Castile invaded Gascony, claiming it as her dowry now that Eleanor was dead and Guy of Thouars, Arthur's stepfather, understandably defected to Philip. The tenurial grip was not as strong in England as elsewhere post-1066, but one cannot imagine Richard going down to such catastrophe. The loss of Normandy in 1204 was not only to resonate through John's reign but through his son's reign, too, significantly impacting upon English kingship.

Like his father and brother before him, John spent most of his time on the Continent up to 1203. After the loss of Normandy, he became an English king but only by force of circumstance. Indeed, he was the most 'English' king of England since Edward the Confessor (quite apart from being born and dying in England – Richard and Henry II were buried at Fontrevrault in the Angevin heartland). He travelled an average of 12.5 miles a day, 79,612 miles in his 16-year reign, most of his stays lasting 2-3 days.[9] The bulk of his time was in the south but he visited north of the Trent every year of his reign and went on long tours of the northern counties (Nottingham his sixth most favoured residence). To be sure, Henry II had always been on the move, but John was continuously in England apart from four campaigns overseas, from 1203 to 1216. In any case, itinerant kingship was no longer needed to govern England. The exchequer had moved from Winchester to Westminster and with the Tower, the great hall at Westminster and the Abbey, London was by 1200 the chief seat of England's monarchy.

All this travelling wasn't because he loved England but because he wanted the thing all kings had wanted from England: money. John's overriding aim – his obsession – was to increase his English revenues and build up treasure to recover his Continental possessions. John's English income averaged £24,000 a year 1199-1202, but from 1207 to 1212 it averaged £49,000, plus the £40,000 tallage on the Jews in 1210 and the £100,000 church revenues during the Interdict, so by 1214 he had saved up a treasure of at least £130,000.[10] This represented the greatest level of exploitation seen in England since the Conquest. The great tax of 1207 raised £57,000, the heaviest national burden since the so-called Saladin

Tithe of 1188 and would have affected all levels of society. In 1206 he retook Gascony, but Philip was left with Normandy, Anjou and Maine.

In 1214, the climax of John's plans was reached: a grand alliance with Flanders and his nephew Otto IV, Holy Roman Emperor, was shattered at the battle of Bouvines. John had retaken Angers, his ancestral capital, but the counts of Flanders and Boulogne and John's half-brother the earl of Salisbury were captured (Otto escaped) on the field and it was Philip 'Augustus,' not John 'Softsword,' who dominated north-west Europe.

John's personal reputation and his relentless quest to recover his ancestral lands using English money from a people and, more importantly, ruling elite, who were not interested in such territories, led to assassination plots, rebellion, and the granting of yet another charter of rights to buy time and support. As in so many watershed moments in English history, events on the Continent would prove decisive and Bouvines was the last straw. The rebellion of 1215 would be more than a rebellion of the king's debtors though.[11] Richard's financial exactions after his return from his Danube sojourn were seen by Ralph of Coggeshall as the heaviest anyone could remember in history (Richard's ransom was £90,000 and between 1194 and 1198 he averaged £25,000 per year revenue from England).[12] The tax levied in 1193-4 was the highest rate of taxation in medieval England, at a quarter value of everyone's rents and moveable property.[13] Furthermore, Richard had sold off so much land and so many rights that John inherited a royal demesne worth £2,000 less a year than in 1189.

It was perhaps more than bedding his barons' wives (where castration for the adulterer was accepted in law), more even than murdering Arthur (who can't have meant a great deal to the people of England) that ultimately brought John down. It was about John's personal monarchy, his hostage taking as a system of governing, his hated foreign advisors having direct access to the king and above all, his arbitrary style of government. John of Salisbury, in his *Policraticus* (1160) wrote that the state is a kind of organism, whereby the prince occupies the head; it is lawful to slay the tyrant and indeed it is 'just and equitable to do so', since the law is justly armed against the man who would disarm the laws. 'The tyrant is one who oppresses the people by violent and despotic rule, even as the prince governs by the laws.'[14] However, the concept of the 'will' remained powerful in 1200, based on Roman law and the Bible. *Glanvill* cites Justinian's *Institutes*: 'The will of the prince has the force of law.'[15] The *Dialogue of the Exchequer* states that '...their actions ought not to be discussed or condemned by their subjects."[16] There was no consistent message in Roman law or from the Bible. Roman law asserted that the ruler was both above and bound by the law; the Bible has the anointed Saul removed (1 Samuel 15). *Glanvill* elevates the king's position to 'your highness', the *Dialogue* to 'your excellency'. Indeed, Professor David

Carpenter suggests that John was attempting to create a new kind of kingship, one of physical power but without ideological support from the political community, who instead judged him a tyrant.[17]

Maybe John thought he was a King Arthur (he was more of a Mordred since he had murdered an Arthur). In an age of sweeping administrative reforms and 'serious' historical writing, there leaps out from the page Geoffrey of Monmouth's extraordinarily successful *History of the Kings of Britain*, finished in 1139, hugely influential and immensely popular (217 manuscripts survive), which sparked centuries of debate over whether he was writing pseudo-history, romance literature or simply holding a mirror up to his own times.[18] After all, he was writing in an age which saw nothing wrong in forging charters, something indulged in by scholars, abbots and royal administrators.[19] Geoffrey was the first to link Arthur to the magician Merlin and place Arthur as a real British king in sub-Roman Britain.

Geoffrey of Monmouth confounded contemporaries and modern Arthurians alike with his reference to a 'very old book' – which can be taken to mean the pre-existing Welsh material – but his reinvention of Arthur as a great conqueror with an international court at Caerleon (which later becomes Camelot) where he wore his crown and presided over feasting and tournaments became an instant hit with the new Anglo-Norman elite of the mid-twelfth century. It didn't matter that Arthur was 'British'; by 1140 the French poet Gaimar had translated it and by 1155 the Norman poet Wace included Arthur in his Romance of Brutus – yet another history of Britain – adding the Round Table for good measure; a copy of this was given to Eleanor of Aquitaine and her son Richard I possessed Excalibur (Caliburn), Arthur's sword, and flew the dragon banner in the tradition of Arthur of Britain in the Holy Land.[20]

The heady intersection of fiction, fact and the founding myths of Christianity in Britain collided at Glastonbury when the monks 'found' the tombs of Arthur and Guinevere in 1191 following a disastrous fire in 1184 that burnt down the abbey.[21] Gerald of Wales seems to have attended the exhumation, which revealed the skeleton of a very tall man with a huge skull bearing ten wounds and the skeleton of a woman with a lock of golden hair; there was also a lead cross bearing the (Latin) inscription 'Here lies buried the renowned king Arthur on the Isle of Avalon.' The monks of Glastonbury had already faked the discovery of St Dunstan's relics and after the 1184 fire they needed money: luckily for them, Avalon was mentioned by Geoffrey of Monmouth as the resting place of Arthur following the battle of Camlann.

Henry II himself had encouraged the monks to 'excavate', since he was not only concerned about the abbey's finances but more importantly, the legends of Arthur claimed that he only slept and would one day awaken and bring the Britons to victory. Henry II needed to prove that Arthur was dead to enforce his authority over Wales and perhaps Brittany, too, that other place of the 'British,' for in 1187 his Breton-born grandson was named Arthur. This was the boy who threatened John in 1199 and perhaps this is why John resorted to the extreme and hugely risky act of nepoticide in 1204, for fear of an ancient prophecy overturning his kingship. The deep-seated fear of the ancient 'British' – the *wīlisc* of Wales, Cornwall, and their expatriate home of Brittany – driven off and enslaved by the English was perhaps never far below the surface.

John possessed an Arthurian sword named Tristan. Perhaps he was consciously using this well-known literary fantasy as part of his deeply personal method of ruling, an attempt to assert a charismatic kingship over the people. In 1209 John arranged a great assembly of 'all the men in England, rich and poor and the middling sort' to meet in the king's presence at Marlborough (his Caerleon perhaps) to swear fealty and do homage to him and his infant son, Henry, an event recorded by eleven contemporary chroniclers and annalists.[22] The sources, ranging from south Wales, Canterbury, Winchester, and the Lincolnshire fens, agree on the scale of what they saw as a momentous national episode. The immediate background were the demands by the Pope to install Stephen Langton, reinstate the monks of Canterbury and restore the church's losses, or face excommunication; John was in Scotland imposing crushing terms on William the Lion, returning early in September 1209.[23]

The oath of 1209 was different because John brought in large number of freemen to one place where normally just the magnates assembled; they then swore fealty to the king and his young heir Henry. Finally, homage as well as fealty was demanded of the freemen, something usually confined to the magnates. This was imposing on the whole free population what was normally applied to the great men only. It would mean assembling around 200,000-300,000 men, but not all in one place, since the sources make it clear it was 'throughout all England' meaning parallel assemblies probably in the shire and hundred courts.[24] Entries in the pipe rolls for 1209 and 1210 refer explicitly to the demand for homage, amercing the burgesses of Norwich 500 marks 'because they did not come at the king's summons to do their homage' and the men of Ipswich, Dunwich and Orford were all amerced for not attending his summons.

John was seeking the homage of 'all the men of England' and this demand for a general performance of homage in his presence in a particular place was without precedent. There was no other time in medieval England that witnessed such a comparable mass assembly at one location, or when a king in person appeared before so many ordinary subjects; and Marlborough castle was an intimidating place for the king to be seen in all his majesty. It was restored, upgraded, a prison, a treasury, residence of the queen and a base for the hated chief forester, Hugh de

Neville. By 1213 John had the lever of homage at his disposal, due to the 1209 oath-taking and he issued the punishment threat of 'culvertage', ie debasement to the status of a serf.[25] These were coercive measures of a draconian kind.

The 'force and will' of Angevin kingship was tempered by council, both public and private. Government in the twelfth century, as it had been since the ninth century, was conciliar: twenty-three in the eighteen years Henry I was in England (and maybe more) and five councils in the first 13 months of Henry IIs reign.[26] Richard I's absence led to the prominence of the great council. Under King John the differences between public and private counsel became more marked and he was blamed for his 'evil' (familiar) counsel, many of whom were foreigners (such as Peter des Roches and Gerard d'Athée). John's need for money and his distrust and fear of magnates took the focus away from public council to private vendettas.

Between 1209 and 1214 John virtually shut down the bench at Westminster and the eyres in the counties; Chapter 17 of Magna Carta laid down that the pleas should not follow the king but be heard in a fixed place (the *coram rege*). It was also clear in chapter 40 that justice was being delayed, denied, and sold. Both Henry II and Richard I had sold justice, but John's constant presence in the realm and personal control of the courts put all the emphasis on his behaviour, and he made many enemies. It also went against the rising tide of intellectual discourse on the back of the explosion of literacy and learning in the later twelfth century, with systematic study of canon and Roman law in schools in Northampton, Oxford, and Lincoln by 1200.

Even after the Battle of Bouvines there was no high road to Magna Carta. John had already granted concessions on debts owed to the Jews, widows, and the forests; he won a naval victory at Damme, controlled the key castles, had access to great wealth and the backing of the most powerful earls. John's quarrel with the Church was a 'major influence on the content of Magna Carta' but it was not necessarily one that caused Magna Carta.[27] In March 1208, the pope imposed an Interdict on England, excommunicating John in November 1209. What began as a lockdown turned into the winter of discontent as the bodies of the dead were left unburied and rotting. Nearly all the English bishops went into exile, a reflection of papal authority, and John seized the revenues of the church, making £100,000 from them. As with Philip of France, John was unlucky in encountering Pope Innocent III but in a typically mercurial move, John had surrendered the kingdoms of England and Ireland to the pope, in May and October 1213.[28] Another diplomatic masterstroke was taking the Cross on Ash Wednesday in 1215.

In April, the pope's letters denounced all 'conjurations and conspiracies' on pain of excommunication, but this did not prevent the rebellious barons sending John a schedule of demands that included Henry I's 1100 coronation charter and the laws of King Edward. John offered to abolish the 'evil customs' but this did no good and on 5 May the barons formally renounced their homage to John, which now meant they could take up arms free from the taint of treason and on 17 May they seized London and the exchequer at Westminster was closed. Open revolt followed, from the south-west, the Welsh border counties and the northern counties, including the knights and free tenant class; this was more than just a baronial rebellion. A large part of Northampton was burnt, and Lincoln was occupied by a northern army.

The 1100 charter was still the key document. Four versions were circulating in John's reign; one was translated into French, making it accessible to the barons and knights; a Bury St Edmunds chronicler thought that the whole 1215 affair had come about because John was trying to annul the 1100 charter, which Henry II had confirmed.[29] Stephen Langton had a copy of the 1100 charter in the Canterbury archives and there were other copies in circulation since Roger of Wendover had a copy, too, and the demands that King John should confirm the 1100 Coronation Charter were a quantum leap in the opposition programme of 1215.[30] The 1100 charter was probably pressed upon John after his return to England in late 1214 after Bouvines. However, John would be judged by far harder standards than Henry I.

The fall of London was critical and between April and May the Articles of the Barons were drawn up.[31] This was a negotiated process but nevertheless a huge leap away from the past; John agreed to the Articles as the basis of the final settlement on 10 June, winning victories on afforestation, tallage, taxation of the Jews, wardships, and overseas service, but he conceded to the revolutionary clause on security where twenty-five barons were to sit in judgement on the king's unjust disseisins, fines and amercements and 'with the commune of the land' could distrain and distress the king, they could take his castles, lands and possessions; they were also to hear complaints if the king or his ministers offended anyone about anything. This was without precedent in England or anywhere else.[32]

At this point, the role of Stephen Langton, Archbishop of Canterbury (finally) and former professor at the university of Paris becomes important: he had already refused to excommunicate the barons and, Professor David Carpenter argues, had nothing to do with the making of the Articles, although the only known copy of the Articles which was sealed by John ended up in the Canterbury archives, taken by Langton to hold as evidence of John's good faith in negotiating.[33] This suggests a breakdown before the final agreement and that Langton may have doubted the validity of the entire process, which is why he introduced the first chapter of Magna Carta, a clause absent from the Articles, confirming that the

English church 'shall be free, and shall have its rights undiminished and its liberties unimpaired'. The church clause differentiates between the free will of the king 'before the outbreak of the present dispute between us and our barons', suggesting that what follows is *not* made of the king's free will. That said, Professor Nicholas Vincent in contrast believes Langton 'acted as midwife to Magna Carta in 1215.'[34]

Negotiations began on 10 June at Runnymede, the meadow between Windsor and Staines, a site of assemblies since ancient times ('runieg' is Old English for counsel island, 'mede' being meadow). The site was bounded by the Thames and Cooper's Hill and is direct succession to the negotiated island-sites of Edward the Confessor's return to England in 1041, Edmund Ironside and Cnut's settlement of England in 1016 and King Edgar's regatta on the River Dee in 973. But according to Ralph of Coggeshall, the barons 'gathered with a multitude of most famous knights, armed well at all points, and they remained there, having fixed tents.' This was an armed camp designed to put pressure on the king.

John saw the Charter primarily as a peace treaty. His advisors are listed at the start, different to the usual where they appear listed as witnesses at the end, making it look like John and his loyal counsellors were solely responsible for the reform of the kingdom.[35] The chancellor in 1215 was Richard Marsh and most of the charters ended with 'given by the hand of Richard Marsh our chancellor', but Magna Carta ended with 'given by our hand'. On 19 June, John made peace; the barons did homage to the king, renewed their oaths of fealty, and received the kiss of peace; there followed a great feast and the next day some of the former key rebels witnessed a royal charter alongside the loyal barons.

There is no such thing as *the* Magna Carta. There are at least 23 originals, four each from 1215, 1217, 1225 and 1297, one from 1216 and six from 1300, scattered across libraries in England, mainly London and Oxford, with two originals sold to archives in Australia and the USA.[36] Four original engrossments survive of the 1215 charter. There could have been as many as 40 if each county, London and the Cinque Ports got one, or if it were just the bishops, upwards of thirteen. King John never referred to it as 'magna carta' just his 'carta'; clergy and nobles called it a 'charter of liberties'. It only came to be Magna Carta when a scribe inserted the words in 1217 to distinguish it from the smaller Forest Charter, but they never appear in the charter itself.[37]

As originally conceived, Magna Carta certainly did not offer equal protection to all the king's subjects.[38] It was a document that protected the interests of the baronial elite; it discriminated against unfree peasants and against women and it revealed the tensions and conflict between sections of society. Magna Carta did nothing at all to challenge the basic restrictions on freedom.[39] It reinforced them. The Charter reveals deep divisions in England, between men and women, free and unfree, lords and towns, lords and tenants, Christians and Jews, church and state.[40] The unfree gained no protection from the greed of their lords in the Charter.[41] It was written in Latin and quickly translated into French but not proclaimed in English until *c*. 1300 or translated into English until the sixteenth century.

The Charter was above all about money, demonstrating the grievances felt over John's years of harsh taxations and exactions (perhaps no heavier than under Richard, but John was the king at the time).[42] Specific chapters in the Charter refer to 'evil customs': increments above the farm (chapter 25), forcing of widows into remarriage (chapter 8) and inheritance payments way above the £100 relief (chapter 2). Chapter 50 removed the foreigners who had harmed the kingdom. It was attempting to 'drain the swamp', reforming royal officials in the shires and the rule of law – but the last issue wasn't clear: 'Sometimes Magna Carta stated law. Sometimes it stated what supporters hoped would become law. Sometimes it stated what its supporters hoped would become law.'[43] It did assert the *principle* of the rule of law that henceforth bound the king to that law, Chapter 39:

> No free man is to be arrested, or imprisoned, or disseised [dispossessed of property], or outlawed, or exiled, or in any way destroyed [ruined], nor will we go against him, nor will we send against him, save by the lawful judgement of his peers or by the law of the land.

And in Chapter 40: 'To no one will we sell, to no one will we deny or delay, right or justice.' As with the earliest law codes in English history from *c*.600 through to Alfred and Cnut, this was drawn from biblical texts (Deuteronomy). In 1215 'free men' were in the minority – perhaps 40% of the population – but the Charter became more socially inclusive over time; in 1354 this was defined as a 'man of whatever estate and condition he may be' and legislation made it clear that the law of the land and lawful judgement by peers meant due legal process and trial by jury.[44] Both of these chapters are still on the statute book of the UK.

Magna Carta is clear on the identity of England, though: the word 'regnum' appears twenty-one times in the 1215 charter. The kingdom gave protection to the freemen within it and of it; if the king left the kingdom, the chief justiciar took over its government. The kingdom possessed its own law (*lex regni*) and could give its common consent to taxation. There was standardisation of measurement for cloth, food and drink. In chapter 60, John declares that the concessions were to be held 'in our kingdom'. The 'law of the kingdom', 'law of the land' and 'law of England' appear six times. That land was England. There are fourteen references to

England, three to the English church. The Englishness of the charter was 'one of its chief characteristics'.[45]

The writs of 19 June (one survives) enjoined sheriffs and royal officials in the counties to have the Charter read in public, to ensure that the oath was taken to the Twenty-Five and to provide for the election of a jury of twelve knights in each county to enquire into 'evil customs'; the draft of this writ was enrolled on the dorse of the patent roll, but the only surviving example is held at Hereford Cathedral.[46] This was delivered to Engelard, sheriff of Gloucestershire, who accounted for Herefordshire at Michaelmas 1214, which is probably why the writ found its way to Hereford Cathedral.

Dissemination was done quickly. Thirteen copies of the charter were made available by 27 July. It may be that copies went to the diocese initially and then to the sheriff.[47] A fourteenth-century copy of a letter addressed to the sheriff of Kent and other royal ministers informed the sheriff that he was being sent four knights who were to receive the oaths due to be sworn according to the king's letters (of 19 June).[48]

No John, no Magna Carta? There is little doubt that John's personality and his arbitrary rule created fear and distrust on a monumental scale. Murdering his nephew, starving high-born prisoners to death, hostage-taking and coercing oaths under threats of servitude, all these things happened in a climate of intellectual and legal expertise very different to Henry I's time – but none of it would have mattered so much without the loss of the Continental possessions and repeated attempts to regain them. This led to severe financial exaction (but no more than under Richard) and intervention in government never seen since 1066 coalescing into grievances stoked by John's untrustworthy and malicious character. It would, perhaps, be better to ask: no Normandy, no Magna Carta?

Stephen Langton's suspicions were well-founded. During July, John decided to abandon the Charter even while it was being copied and despatched across the country, believing it would bring neither peace nor independence from the Twenty-Five: he asked the pope to quash the Charter. A papal bull of 24 August declared the Charter (described as 'leagues and conspiracies') 'null, and void of all validity for ever', explicitly referring to John's surrender of his kingdoms to the pope in 1213.[49] The Charter of Runnymede was dead in the water. The king's will – in John's case, tyranny – had prevailed over the rule of law.

THIRTEEN

The Community of the Realm

Magna Carta survived John and was re-issued several times in the minority of his son Henry III, becoming an essential part of the narrative of 'good governance'. Once again, the personal rule of the monarch and European affairs shaped the internal politics of England. A new departure was the emerging concept of 'parliament', which was already established before the rebellions of 1258-65. Edward I's military conquest of Wales and incursions into Scotland completed the farthest expansion of the English over the British but came at a price. By 1300 the rule of law and the consent of the 'community of the realm' were integral to the governance of England.

John had a stash of silver and jewels called in from Corfe and religious houses around the country and by August 1215 he had secured the ports and Stephen Langton was forced, on pain of suspension, to excommunicate the rebels (he left John's court soon afterwards, not to return in his lifetime). Rochester Castle was captured and retaken by John in a seven-week siege. There was no reason to think that the charter at Runnymede would ever resurface. But in the spring of 1216, the stakes changed dramatically and once again it was Continental intervention that forced the issue. Not content with regaining most of the Angevin possessions, Philip Augustus sent his son Prince Louis to invade England in May 1216. Louis landed at Thanet – that location associated with Early English settlers, Augustine's mission and the first Viking raids – and when he reached London, many of John's supporters melted away. The British kingdoms pounced, too; Alexander of Scotland, humiliated in 1209, met Louis at Dover to do homage for the northern counties and in Wales, Prince Llewellyn conquered Cardigan and Carmarthen.

John's death, as much as his life, broke the mould. He was in Lincoln and on 12 October he lost his baggage train with the royal regalia in the

Wash; sick with dynasty, he died at Newark Castle during a great storm on the night of 18 October. He left a young son, Henry, and the elderly William Marshal as regent, loyal to the last. The boy was crowned at Gloucester – no English bishop would crown Prince Louis at Westminster. William Marshal and Cardinal Guala Bicchieri, who had arrived in the spring, reissued Magna Carta in November with the security clause gone to tempt back the rebels; but it was the battle of Lincoln and a sea battle off Sandwich that mattered, French troops were crushed and leading rebels captured. In September 1217 Louis withdrew his claim to the throne.

John's death had indeed removed a major stumbling block, but the continued support for Louis was not insignificant and indicates that it was not entirely about John. In November 1217, the charter was issued once again, sealed by Guala and the Marshal and the new Forest Charter was drawn up and therefore for the first time 'Magna Carta' was so called to distinguish it from the lesser charter of the forest (the engrossments of February 1218 included the first reference to 'Magna Carta'). The 1217 Magna Charter reflects the fragility of Henry III's support: there is no list of counsellors at the start of the 1217 version, just Guala, the archbishop of York, the bishop of London and William Marshal. The 1217 Magna Carta ended up with no reference to the law of Wales (the minority government made peace with Llewellyn in March 2018) and nothing on Scotland, since at Christmas 1217 King Alexander came to Northampton and did homage for his English lands, but not homage for Scotland as his father William had done in 1174. The Forest Charter of 1217 declared that all the areas afforested by Henry II, John and Richard were to go (although many of these afforestations were not removed). The Assize of the Forest in 1184 had confirmed the enormous reach of the forests, its officials and jurisdiction, which was to cause such resentment expressed under John.[1]

Henry III was the youngest king in the history of England in 1216, aged nine, and would not reach his majority until 1227. So the transformation of Magna Carta from a peace treaty given reluctantly and not entirely in good faith by his father John into the constitutional document that it would become after 1225 owes much to senior advisors, as we have seen with Æthelwold (Edgar and Æthelstan), Wulfstan (Æthelstan and Cnut), the fitz Nigel dynasty who ran the royal finances for much of the twelfth century, and Hubert Walter, co-author of *Glanvill* and chief justice. The legendary Marshal died in 1219 but Langton was back and with Hubert de Burgh dismissed the foreign officials still at large in 1223; that year was also significant since it was overseas affairs which again impacted on English domestic politics. King Philip of France died in 1223 and his son, now King Louis, conquered Poitou and threatened Gascony (one of John's successes). To finance the defences of these overseas possessions, a tax was necessary, and a tax meant a re-issue of Magna Carta, this time the definitive version, in February 1225, along with a new charter of the Forest.[2]

The difference in 1225 was the fact that the king himself set his seal to this charter but no others; Henry had already declared that he would observe all the liberties to which he had sworn at a council meeting in January 1223, since the 1216 and 1217 charters were not issued in his name there was some doubt over their validity. This time it would be a freely struck bargain between king and kingdom – 'By our spontaneous and good will' and granted to 'everyone' rather than the freemen as in 1215. It restored the original promise not to seek anything to invalidate the Charter and had a great list of witnesses at the end, unlike all earlier versions, headed by Langton, eleven bishops and twenty abbots; Hubert de Burgh headed the laymen, followed by nine earls and twenty-three magnates, the rebels and loyalists of the 1215-1217 period alongside one another. Langton and his bishops pronounced a sentence against all those who contravened the Charter, so the church was fully behind Magna Carta now.

Stephen Langton was certainly behind the drafting of the 1225 version, which was almost identical to that of 1217. There were many differences from the 1215 version, chiefly the absence of the security clause, but the threat of excommunication had been put in its place. There were no longer the 12 knights elected in each county to abolish malpractice of the king's officials and there were unfavourable changes concerning free tenants and villeins, including amercements, disseisin, customs and services, although the Forest Charter protected the unfree from death or mutilation for offences against the beasts of the forest (imprisonment instead, since there wouldn't be any money for fines), but mostly the 1225 charter did not go below the free tenants or free men, so in that sense, the more radical 1215 charter given by John at Runnymede was never revived. Contemporaries were aware that the 1215 and 1225 versions were different.

Legal cases soon after 1215 indicate knowledge and citation of the Charter, the first successful appeal in the courts coming in 1221 in Essex.[3] The texts of the 1225 Charters became definitive (though sometimes confused then as now with the 1215 version). No new versions were issued thereafter, simply confirmations of 1225. In 1237 Henry III confirmed the liberties of the Charters and this included Peter des Roches, earl William of Warenne and Hubert de Burgh as witnesses, all of whom were John's advisors in 1215, as well as the sons of William the Marshal, reflecting continuity amongst the key personnel in the realm.

John's death in 1216 and the succession of his young son created Magna Carta anew, based on consent, recognition of royal status and concessions in return for a grant of taxation. The notorious security clause of 1215 was not needed since Henry III was not John, and he was a minor. Twenty-five great councils were summoned during Henry's minority, becoming an indispensable part of government. Had John lived, none of this was likely. By 1228, the end of Henry's regency, a major shift had occurred in the relationship between king and barons; the tyranny of John, overseas campaigns and foreign invasion had converted the charters offering vague promises into a totally different social and legal contract.

That said, would Henry III hold to these promises when his regency was over? The short answer was no. The same old problems arose: foreign favourites, the need for money and overseas territories, all interlinked. Henry III was no tyrant – he was generous and pious but 'simplex' (naïve) – and he was empowered to appoint his own counsellors and give patronage. This led to factions between his Poitevin half-brothers (his mother Isabella married Hugh of Lusignan as planned following John's death) and his wife's Savoyard uncles, which Magna Carta did not restrict or resolve. After 1224, only Gascony remained of the Continental possessions Henry III's father and grandfather had ruled. England was now the centre of the Angevin possessions, rather than the satellite it had been 1154-1204. None of the English aristocracy had estates in Poitou or Gascony.

Another failed foreign expedition in 1230 and arbitrary rule by des Roches and his nephew Peter de Rivallis led to magnate rebellion, including Richard Marshal, son of the famous William Marshal. The councils of 1233 put down Henry's rule and Magna Carta was proclaimed by the king in 1234. The Queen, Eleanor of Provence, had relatives to provide for and his half-brothers from Lusignan were deeply resented when they sought preference at court after 1247. Henry III was determined to regain overseas lands, spending £80,000 to retake Poitou in 1242 and £36,000 on a mission to Gascony in 1253-4; lavish patronage of his Lusignan half-brothers was aimed at reclaiming Poitou. From 1237 to 1258 Henry was refused every time when he asked for a direct tax – on ten occasions – mostly to raise money for foreign campaigns or meet the debts already accrued from them.[4]

This brings us to parliament, inextricably linked to Magna Carta's rebirth after 1217. It is one of the myths of English history – along with the freedoms granted in the 1215 version of the charter that didn't survive – that 'parliament' was created during the baronial rebellions of 1264 led by Simon de Montfort, earl of Leicester and the king's brother-in-law (whose father, also Simon de Montfort, had been touted as a possible replacement for John in 1212). It was not. From the mid-1230s 'parliament' moves into common use as a term for large assemblies, the first official appearance in a legal case in 1236 (*parliamentum*). Matthew Paris referred to the *parliamentum* of April 1239 and other chroniclers followed suit.[5] From the 1230s parliaments met regularly in January/February, April/May, July and October, aligned to the law terms of Michaelmas, Hilary and Easter when the courts would be in session, and from the 1250s aligned to exchequer sessions, too. This was not a matter of terminology either, since by 1258 John Maddicott argues that parliament had emerged as a 'genuinely representative body'.[6] Those attending covered a wide social range, from peers to elected knights and burgesses from the towns; if not a microcosm of the populace it was more than just the elites. The 'common good' was no longer the duty of the ruler but of the members of parliament. If Magna Carta held the king to account, then it was parliamentary consent for taxation that was the central influence on the evolution of parliament and parliament was now a platform from which the king's actions could be scrutinised and opposed in ways it could never have been before 1215.

Unlike Domesday Book, Magna Carta's transformative elements – including 'politicised debate' – are paralleled elsewhere in Europe in the charter of Peter I in Catalonia, 1205, Frederick II's *Privilegium in Favorem Principum Ecclesiasticum* of 1220, and Andrew II's Golden Bull of 1220 in Hungary.[7] However, European states did not possess a Magna Carta document that was addressed so comprehensively to 'everyone in our kingdom' (apart from the Golden Bull in Hungary) and no other country had the intense and consistent pressure put upon government or so vigorous a conciliar tradition.[8] Town representatives first appear in Leon in 1188, 1202 and 1208, in Castile in 1214, 1217, Catalonia and Aragon in 1214 and Portugal in 1253. The word 'parliament' was first used for an official assembly in England in 1236 and in France in the 1220s, but in Sweden the 1250s, Denmark 1282, Germany 1294, and Scotland 1290s. However, nobles in England were subjected to taxation like any other subject; Continental nobles were exempt to some degree. The obligation to pay tax gave the English nobility an interest in the institutions and processes. The shire and its gentry, thegns and then knights had no counterpart in France or Spain, and the English gentry had an administrative role in the shire, as sheriffs, jurors, assessors, and collectors of taxes, more so than in Europe. By European standards, John Maddicott argues, 'English society had always been exceptionally participatory.'[9]

In 1245 Henry III began rebuilding the abbey at Westminster and converting the palace into a great residence (spending £45,000). Westminster would be the new Winchester: a dynastic shrine, palatial residence and seat of government. Seven of the twelve monarchs from Henry III to Henry VIII were buried at Westminster Abbey.[10] Westminster under Henry II was the seat of the exchequer and under John the location of the treasury and the law court. With the Tower, the great hall at Westminster and the Abbey, London was by 1300 the chief seat of England's monarchy. Westminster Hall would be the setting for the Provisions of Westminster in 1259, the terms for Lord Edward's release from Montfort's captivity in 1264 and the Statute of Westminster in 1285.

The loss of Continental possessions and subsequent decrease in peripatetic kingship and the dominance of Westminster made this change possible. Whereas Henry II spent 60% of his reign abroad in almost 35 years on the throne (21 years abroad) his grandson Henry III spent 8% of his 57-year reign abroad (4 years 5 months); this was an essential pre-condition for the emergence of parliament.[11]

The crisis of 1258 was triggered by financial demands and overseas territory just as in the 1220s. Henry III's expensive failures in Poitou partially triggered the baronial rebellion of 1258. Another reason was Sicily, one of the major grievances of 1258: Henry's brother Richard became 'king of the Romans' in 1256 and his son Edmund was offered the throne of Sicily by the pope in 1252, which Henry accepted. The only object to be explicitly mentioned in the jewel accounts which survives today is one of the golden bullae (of the original thirty-five) made for the king's second son, Edmund, as titular king of Sicily.[12]

The Provisions of Oxford (1258) appointed a justiciar, a new baronial council of fifteen for the day-to-day workings of government and parliament was to meet three times a year (Michaelmas, Candlemas, and June) formally, not by custom. The Provisions of Westminster drew upon the 1236 Provisions of Merton and the definitive text of the 1225 Magna Carta. The reform movement of 1258-9 gave parliament a formal place in the country's government for the first time.[13]

The Treaty of Paris in 1259 put an end to the overseas dream since it formally renounced the claim to Normandy, Anjou and Poitou in return for Gascony, to be held as a fief from the king of France.[14] It was the end of one particular narrative arc from 1204 that contributed to the rebellions of 1215-16, bringing about Magna Carta in all its various versions, and the development of parliamentary government from the 1220s whereby the king could only get financial support by consent from the assembly. It was by no means the end of Continental relations since interaction between French and English shores was a crucial issue for English fiscal policy in the thirteenth and fourteenth centuries as well as war into the fifteenth century.[15]

The reformers of 1258 demanded that the king's castles be entrusted to men born of the kingdom of England. Suspicion of 'foreigners' was rife. The contemporary chronicler Matthew Paris believed that people feared that civil war would break out 'and that the king and his Poitevin brothers would call in aliens to aid them against his native-born subjects.' Orders were given for the gates of London to be carefully fastened at night with better bars 'for fear the deceit of Frenchmen should break into the city.'[16] There was a belief, unsubstantiated, that the Poitevins had poisoned the English nobles.[17]

The dislike and resentment of foreign counsellors was a feature of the rebellion against John, and stems from the fundamental break with

Normandy and the overseas possessions in 1204. Here was something of a contradiction since John had died in England and was buried in England (his brothers and parents were buried in the Angevin heartlands at Fontrevault Abbey) and Henry III was born in Winchester, but every monarch from Stephen (1140s) to Edward IV (1470s) married a woman of European royalty.[18] The pejorative use of 'foreigner' was a useful political tool used against specific ethnic groups – Poitevins, Gascons, and Flemings, as we shall see – not necessarily an emerging nationalism; and it was a French-born nobleman, Simon de Montfort, who brought the English realm to the brink of revolution in 1264-5.

Simon de Montfort's parliament in 1264 did give the knights an essential place denied to them in 1258 – four knights per county – but the summoning of the knights, and possibly the burgesses, was no innovation since two per county had been summoned in 1254.[19] There was perhaps a greater concern for the oppressed and the poor in the years 1258-65; the justiciar set up by the reforms swore to give justice to 'rich and poor, serf and free'.[20] The legislation benefited peasants, free and unfree, and key reforms were proclaimed in English, French, and Latin. The grant of a tax made by the council to the young Henry III in 1225 if he would reissue Magna Carta was referred to in 1264 as a grant made by 'the community of the realm' to the 'community of the land'.[21] Contemporaries had complained for decades that the Charters (Magna Carta and the Charter of the Forest) were not being enforced. Henry III had apparently breached the Charter by denying justice, common law, wardships, amercements and reversing the deforestations. And as part of his personal rule Henry III used gifts to enhance his political authority, distributing a large majority of rings and belts from the royal wardrobe to secure support during his personal rule and again following the crises of 1258-65; but the accounts also show that the counties loyal to Simon de Montfort bankrolled this political recovery.[22]

The 1265 reissue of Magna Carta formed part of a wider drive by Simon de Montfort to demonstrate his regime's popularity as well as a significant moment in the acceptance of Magna Carta within political society.[23] After de Montfort's defeat and death Henry III initially repudiated the Provisions, supported by the papacy, echoing John's actions in 1215-16; the Dictum of Kenilworth in 1266 'annulled and quashed' all writings in connection with the Provisions of Oxford.[24] However, the Statute of Marlborough in 1267 at the first parliament since de Montfort's defeat ultimately confirmed the 1258 Provisions of Oxford.[25]

Edward I succeeded to the throne of England in 1272 while in Sicily, on his return from the crusade. It is a measure of the stability in England following the disputes of 1258-65 that he did not hurry home, visiting Gascony and doing homage to Philip of France in Paris. He returned to Gascony in 1286 and was the last English king to hold court in Bordeaux in 1289.[26] The first period of Edward I's kingship was hugely successful, a broad-based leadership combined with the stunning conquest of Wales in 1277 and 1282-3. Parliament was central to his mode of kingship and provided a public platform for consensus politics – the council was the more enclosed setting where most of government took place. The great statutes including Westminster I and Westminster II, Winchester, Gloucester, *Mortmain, Quia Emptores* and *Quo Warranto* all came in or before 1290, all associated with parliament.[27]

Edward I transformed the government of England through his legal reforms and development of parliament. By furthering parliament's role as a representative forum where grievances could be aired, he used it to gain consent for vastly increased taxes and established a new basis for royal taxation. New laws were formally promulgated as statutes, generally at parliaments rather than as writs; the new statutory basis gave them authority and publicity. Edward was personally involved in these reforms, initiating, directing and seeing them through.[28] However prolific these legislative acts were in the period 1275-90, there was no attempt to codify English law and the statutes were as much concerned with the right of the king as with the liberties of the subject.[29] At his first parliament in 1275 he issued a statute, Westminster I, addressing misgovernment, and enforcing free elections and this followed the Hundred Roll inquiries into bribery and corruption among the sheriffs and royal officials.[30] The statute of Westminster I also declared that trial by jury was the common law of the land.[31]

A song against the sheriffs (*c.* 1274) reveals a popular view of the 'cruel' sheriff, who take the best of the meat and drink and whose wife must have a 'gown of rainbow hues'; but worst of all were the sheriff's clerks, who 'grow and swell' and buy up houses, lands and rents and 'pile up gold'.[32] There is, though, the usual complaint about the 'new rules' that are reckoned wisdom by the 'modern schools', perhaps the age-old feeling that times gone by were better.

The 1285 Statute of Winchester maintained the Old English custom of community responsibility; the Hundred had to answer for robberies committed and for the losses, because 'robberies, homicides and arsons are more often committed than they used to be'. Every man had to have in his house 'arms for keeping the peace' and every man between fifteen and sixty was to be sworn to arms according to his wealth. The level of equipment (mail coat, helmet, sword, knife and a horse for £15 of land or £30 of chattels, down to those with 40 shillings of land who had to have scythes, knives and other various pointed weapons) does rather suggest a society with a ready supply of sharp and dangerous weaponry at its disposal.[33]

This abundance of arms sometimes had tragic consequences. An Inquisition of 1267 records a lady by the name of Desiderata who met a male friend, William, carrying a crossbow on his shoulder on a road in Sussex; jokingly she asked whether he was chasing robbers on the king's orders and playfully wrestling him but in tripping him up she fell on top of him and stabbed herself through the heart with a poisoned arrow he happened to have under his belt, dying on the spot: 'death by misadventure' was recorded.[34] The following year, 1268, a drunken wedding party in Yorkshire assaulted local people in dispute over a ball, using 'axes and bows and arrows, and wounded very many,' killing one bystander. One wonders why they had such weapons to hand for a wedding.[35] In 1287 in Acton Scott in Shropshire, the Christmas Day gathering of a crowd of singers outside the pub was rudely interrupted by an 'immensely drunk' chaplain, Hugh de Weston, who had a hatred for a certain John, not only for his singing qualities but for his attentions shown towards some women standing nearby. Hugh 'took a naked sword' and ran at the unfortunate John, striking him three times on the head, nearly cutting off two fingers of his left hand, presumably when John defended himself, but John managed to hide under a stone wall and stabbed Hugh with his knife, killing him instantly.[36] Such incidents do not necessarily indicate a violent society; rather the point is that the availability of weapons could result in violence. Although homicide rates in thirteenth-century England have been estimated at around ten times higher than in the twenty-first century.[37]

The power of the written document went hand-in-hand with the explosion of literacy in the twelfth and thirteenth centuries. Possessing a seal was indicative of familiarity with documents, although it did not mean one could write, many more people could read than write. In February, 1267, the earl of Gloucester and Hertford dropped his seal (an impression of six small shields) crossing a bridge and had the justices proclaim this publicly, so that 'for the future no credit may be given for that device' and set up a new impression of one shield (not unlike cancelling a lost bank card and changing the PIN).[38] In 1100 only kings and some bishops possessed seals but by 1300 all freemen and probably some serfs had them; indeed, as many as 8 million charters may have been written in the thirteenth century for smallholders and serfs (Edward I's serfs were required by statute to have a seal).[39] This is reflected in the use of the sealing wax in the chancery, rising exponentially from 3.63 lbs in 1226-30 to 31.9 lbs in 1265-71; in William II's reign 15 documents a year survive on average, 41 for Henry I, 115 for Henry II.[40] It was part of a European-wide trend, including the papal court, as rulers increasingly relied on documents to assert their authority.

In 1278 Edward launched the *Quo Warranto* inquiries, to discover by what warrant various nobles held franchises; Earl Warrenne brandished an ancient sword before the royal justices, claiming this was his warrant, since his ancestors came with William the Bastard and conquered their lands with the sword and with that sword he would defend his lands. The king was forced to accept existing franchises, but he established the principle that franchises in England derived from royal authority.[41] The *Quo Warranto* proceedings were indefinitely postponed in 1294 due to war.[42]

John's defeats abroad in 1214 led to a long period of relative peace and it was not until 1294 that a king needed money to pay for a European war. The period 1294 to 1302 was a time dominated by war and its demands. The war with France began in 1294 followed by Welsh revolt and war with Scotland in 1295, which placed the crown under greater financial strain than at any time since Richard I's reign. Military expenditure from 1294 to 1298 totalled £750,000 and expenditure could only be financed by direct taxation.[43] Levies on moveables, wool exports (the *maltote*), corn and livestock, seizures of wool and demand for military service all broke up the harmonious relationship between the crown and the political nation that had existed since 1274. It created a powerful alliance between magnates and knights against oppressive royal government.

Evidence from the 1130 pipe rolls suggest that 85% of Henry I's income came from land, lordship, and jurisdiction, but this had fallen to less than 40% of Edward I's income and this in turn led to higher taxation and greater need for representation in parliament. Henry III and Edward I had to look elsewhere for money. Taxation of the clergy was one means, initially to finance crusades, then it became for good causes. In 1217 Honorius III ordered bishops to help young king Henry III and in 1254 Henry requested a clerical grant without seeking papal consent, a precedent followed in 1269 and by Edward I in 1279, 1283 and 1290. If a king had taken the Cross, they had access to further funds, as in 1250 and 1287; in 1291 Edward I raised 100,000 marks from a crusading tax.

Customs was another source of revenue; the duty of wool exports in 1275 became a permanent measure of peacetime income for the Crown, linked to the Continental credit system founded by Italian mercantile and banking houses. This was not new (Henry II used loans from Flemish businessman William Cade and Henry III owed £50,000 to the Ricciardi in the 1250s) but the scale of debt massively increased under Edward I, who owed £400,000 by 1294; half of this debt was repaid from customs receipts from a trade linked to the Italians. Customs and credit replaced the older feudal aids, levies, tallages and scutages, which fell into disuse.

Another source of income was the Jews. At the time of Magna Carta there were some 5,000 Jews in England in 1215, confined to the major towns.[44] Jews were new to England after 1066 and they played a central part in the economic life of the country because, as the Charter shows, they were moneylenders (Clauses 10-11 deal with debts owed to the Jews.). Given the Church's ban on Christian usury, the Jews were the main source of credit. All sectors of society borrowed from them – free tenants (including peasants), knights, barons, earls, bishops, monasteries. The interest rate could run at one or two pence in the pound per week, so 22% or 44% a year.[45] This was a double-jeopardy since the Jews were resented for their moneylending and persecuted for their religion (the massacre at York in 1189 resulted in hundreds killed) but there were many other attacks and killings in the 1190s; England joining the crusading movement did much to accelerate widespread anti-Semitism and violence.

Henry III's piety was conventional, and his suppression of Jews in the Statute of 1253 was in line with Continental persecution and prepared the ground for the 1275 Statute and expulsion in 1290 under Edward I (Jews were not permitted into Britain again until 1656). The level of segregation and persecution was cumulative from 1066 but accelerated across Henry III's reign. Such treatment was in line with Western European persecution though perhaps prosecuted more vehemently in England. The Statute of the Jewry, 1275, forbade usury and forced the Jews to remain in the cities and boroughs; every Jew over the age of seven had to wear a yellow badge in the form of two tables joined, and pay a tax of three pence to the king 'whose serf he is' over the age of twelve. But the statute also said that they should have the protection of the sheriffs and bailiffs of the king and live by lawful trade.[46] The Jews were not expelled until 1290 because they were a vital source of profit for the crown; the Jews were the king's own property, to be taxed at will. *The Laws of Edward the Confessor*, a twelfth-century work, has it that 'the Jews themselves and all their possessions are the king's.'[47] John put them under his special protection, writing to the major and sheriffs of London that his peace should be observed 'even if given to a dog'.[48]

When Edward I tried to levy a tax without consent in 1297, he faced open opposition from Roger Bigod, Earl of Norfolk, who refused to serve overseas in Gascony unless the king was present. The summons for a muster in July included very vague conditions of service. The destination of the campaign was uncertain, possibly Flanders. All apparent abuses were linked with the King's disregard for Magna Carta and the Forest charter. The maltote ('evil toll') of 1294-7 was six times higher than the 1275 custom charge on wool and had acquired the name 'maltote' by 1297.[49]

At the parliament in October during Edward's absence in Flanders the barons set out a manifesto of demands (the Articles of Grievance, made by 'all the community of the land'), which called for future consent from the prelates, magnates, knights, burgesses and freeman to all subsidies, the ending of the maltote and the publication of these concessions in cathedral churches.[50] In September 1297 the council issued the 'Confirmation of the Charters', proclaiming that Edward I would not in future tax 'except with the common assent of all the realm and for the common profit of the same realm'. The 'Confirmation of the Charters' refers to the 'great charter of liberties and the forest charter', which should be read twice a year and contravened on pain of excommunication; it also repeals the 'maltote on wool'.[51] The maltote was formally abolished by writs in November 1297.[52] After 1297, tax-granting representatives were present at all tax-granting parliaments – arbitrary taxation had been effectively checked.

The five years between 1297 and 1301 were marked by the most intensive and concentrated parliamentary conflicts that England had yet seen; of the eight parliaments which met during this time, six saw the king and his subjects bitterly at odds in almost all cases over the Charters: three successive sets of concessions were extracted from Edward, all of which were the product of negotiation in parliament where the king's need for money could be traded against the oppositions need for redress.[53] The more frequent attendance of knights, burgesses and lower clergy made parliament more socially comprehensive than it had been in the past.

At the parliament of 1300 the King agreed to confirm Magna Carta, ordering it to be declaimed in Westminster Hall in Latin and English. By the 1290s many of the details of the Magna Carta were unenforceable or archaic, but by 1300 it was 'not just law but totem'.[54] Edward I, in 1297 and 1300, referred to 'the Magna Carta of the lord Henry' in letters, so by this time it was fixed in the public mind.[55] The Charters were confirmed in 1253, 1265 and by Edward I in 1297 and 1300. They were proclaimed and copies sent to every cathedral, read aloud twice a year in the county; judges, sheriffs and town officials had copies. In 1300 the sheriff was to read the charters four times a year to the people in the full county court.

To be sure, the widespread opposition to the governance of King John and Henry III had much more to do with keeping a rapacious government at bay than reaching out for a more meaningful constitution.[56] But by 1300, the combined forces of Magna Carta and parliament had transformed the 'common counsel of the realm' into a 'community of the realm'.

Thomas Aquinas in his *Summa Theologia* (1260s) wrote that 'law is nought else than an ordinance of reason for the common good, made by the authority who has care of the community.'[57] The best form of government is one in which

> ...one man, as specially qualified, rules over all, and under him are others governing as having special endowments, yet all have a share inasmuch as those are elected from all, and also elected by all. This is the best form of constitution, a mixture of monarchy, in that one man a is at the head, of aristocracy, in that many rule as specifically qualified, and democracy.[58]

Tyranny could no longer be tolerated. Kings could be removed. Magna Carta ushered in a tax-based parliamentary state. If parliament failed in its duty, the people would demand restitution, and they did.

PART FOUR

Imperial England

c. 1300–*c.* 1550

Durham Cathedral, 13th century, seat of the prince-bishops of the Palatinate, final resting place of St Cuthbert and Bede. (Author's collection)

FOURTEEN

Apocalypse Now – Plague, Revolt, and Usurpation

The community of the realm was influential in deposing two monarchs in the fourteenth century. The nobles also expressed their power through parliament, in the new upper house of peers – the lords – distinct from the house of Commons. Something like half of the population was wiped out by the Black Death, and parliament was increasingly seen to be failing the people, so much so that by 1381 a revolt appealed directly to the young Richard II. Centred in the south-east and London, this was nevertheless a major uprising with specific grievances and characterised by targeted violence. It was brutally crushed by the Commons, many of whom were military veterans, equipped with legal powers of arrest. In 1399, the personal rule of the monarch sparked dispute and the century ended with the deposition of another king, this time replaced not by his own son but by his cousin, a significant departure for the English monarchy and nobility.

On 12 January 1327, the magnates and prelates decided that Edward II should be deposed, and 'articles of accusation' were drawn up to justify this radical step. The next day groups of men came to an assembly at the Guildhall, and they all swore to maintain the queen and her son Edward. There were twenty-four barons, fourteen archbishops and bishops, seven abbots and priors, thirteen members of parliament, thirty men from the Cinque ports and others from Bury St Edmunds and St Albans. On 14 January, at a crowded meeting at Westminster Hall, before lords, commoners and many Londoners, the decision to depose Edward was announced by Roger Mortimer. The crowd all acclaimed Edward's deposition and replacement by his fourteen-year-old son. Two days later the embassy was sent to Kenilworth to inform him of parliament's decision to secure his renunciation of the throne and to withdraw homage.[1]

This was the first formal deposition of a monarch in English history and parliament provided the setting and the mechanism for the transfer of power from the old to the new king. Parliament sat for 71 days from 7 January to 9 March 1327. The first session saw the deposition of Edward II and the second session was after Edward III's coronation on 1 February, when parliament presented to the new king and council the longest set of petitions (42) so far submitted by the Commons.

Edward II faced the backlash of – and the bill for – his indomitable father's incursions and invasions. An extended coronation oath in 1308 compelled him to observe English law and custom and the Ordinances of 1311 (announced by parliament) limited his powers further.[2] Favourites including Piers Gaveston (murdered in 1312) and the two Despensers became the central point of contention between the King and his great men. Their influence over Edward and his government raised broader questions concerning the proper distribution of patronage as to the right to counsel the King. Edward's victory over the earl of Lancaster at Boroughbridge in March 1322 allowed him, in partnership with the Despensers, to accumulate a fortune. Late in 1326, after Queen Isabella and Roger Mortimer had landed from the Low Countries Edward was captured and placed in custody; the Despensers were executed, and the regime swept away. Edward II was taken to Berkeley Castle in April,1327, where he died and was buried at Gloucester.

Reports of Edward II's cause of death were varied and some were bizarre, ranging from simple grief, strangulation, smothering, being flung into a deep pit of rotting carcases and, mostly outlandishly, a red-hot poker inserted in the rectum (a similar tale told in the thirteenth century of Edmund Ironside's death in 1016 and used again for Humphrey duke of Gloucester in the fifteenth). Ian Mortimer (no relation) has plausibly argued that Edward II was not murdered at all, given the confusion over the details of his death, the lack of identification of his corpse and the letter by Manuel de Fieschi discovered in the 1870s by a French archivist, which says the body at Gloucester was a porter killed by Edward II on his departure from Berkeley, suggesting that he was still alive in 1330, and indeed for some time afterwards, perhaps until 1341-2.[3] If this was the case, and if parliament knew about this, then for a time England had two living kings, something not seen since the tenth century, though it had little or no effect on the national polity.

Parliament staged-managed Edward II's deposition, a result of growing power that had little to do with taxation or Magna Carta. From *c.* 1307 both knights and burgesses were summoned regularly to parliaments. In the 1320s the author of the *Modus Tenendi Parliamentum* asserted that the knights and burgesses represented the 'whole community of the kingdom' while the magnates represent none but themselves.[4] The community, or 'communitas', as it was spoken of, was in the vernacular, the commons, and from around 1314 the term 'great council' begins to appear in the records; specifically a body of magnates sitting within parliament, often to deal with petitions and sometimes with more general matters of state, so we are beginning to see the emergence of the 'Lords' and the 'Commons'. Petitions at parliaments meant that individuals or communities could seek justice or redress directly from the king, whereas before this time, such access was restricted to those with wealth and privilege.

Parliament met on average once a year 1327-1437. The 31 parliaments between 1339 and 1371 all sat at Westminster. The exchequer never left Westminster after 1349. York, briefly a rival centre during the Scottish wars, lost its importance with the wars against France and Edward III's absence abroad concentrated power more onto Westminster.

England was perhaps the most bureaucratic government in Western Christendom, but by European standards England possessed only one large town, London, assessed in 1334 as four times larger than its nearest rival, Bristol. London was a terminus for Baltic, North Sea and Mediterranean trade, drawing people from the east Midlands and East Anglia. Analysis of fish bones from excavations in London has shown that *c.* 1250 locally caught fresh fish were replaced by salted cod from Iceland and Norway.[5] Between 1100 and 1300, 140 new towns were created across England, including Liverpool, Leeds, Portsmouth and Hull. Bristol had a vital link with Bordeaux. York and Coventry grew to become centres of international trade in the fourteenth century. The four great fairs of England were in Winchester, Northampton, St Ives, and Boston.[6]

Urban sanitation in York (and probably generally) had not improved in the 900 years since Roman Britain. Broken paving, the foul stench from the piggeries and the pigs wandering freely in the streets causing dunghills all over the place are brought to our attention in 1298 by the royal exchequer and its officials during the war with the Scots.[7] Norfolk was the richest county by some way in the taxation yields of 1334 (at £3,485) followed by Kent, Gloucestershire, Wiltshire, Lindsey and Suffolk.[8] The city of London yielded £733, more than 21 other counties; the average across 42 counties was £900. The early fourteenth-century yields had been lower, due to the famines; Gloucestershire in 1290 had returned £4,018, though it averaged around £1,300 in the taxations up to 1334.[9]

Poverty was at its peak in the period 1290-1340 due to poor weather, animal disease, warfare, and taxation.[10] Many were trapped in a poverty that persisted through the generations. The state intervened very occasionally, but it was mostly left to the parishes and communities, whose response was uneven and inadequate. The contribution of the religious houses and the Church was not on a large scale. Many poorer tenants were increasingly 'harvest-sensitive', suffering starvation, malnutrition and disease following poor harvests. Prices rose and fell in line with harvest success or failure. The gap between the very poorest and the very richest widened. Population growth led to a demand for food, real wages fell and landlords profited from the new markets (2,400 grants between 1198 and 1483 but over half before 1275); the bishop of Ely's net income rose from £920 in 1171 to £2,550 in 1298.

By 1300 England was overpopulated (up to 4 million) for a traditional economy. Prices were high, wages were low (a penny a day), but the great landowners accrued vast wealth (the earl of Gloucester who died at Bannockburn in 1314 had estates worth £6,000 a year) and merchants traded in wool and wine from the Baltic to Portugal and northern Italy. This was only a partially developed economy since there was no commercial or agricultural revolution. Compared with Italy and Flanders, it was stagnant. Half the population were under eighteen and over half the population were still serfs – unfree tenants.[11] Following flooding, some of the harvests of 1315-21 were very bad (grain yields fell by two-fifths). The Great Famine of 1315 killed millions, perhaps 20% of the European population. A bovine pestilence killed around 60% of cattle in 1319-20, which choked the milk supply, perhaps weakening the immune system of the human population prior to the Black Death.[12] The fourteenth century was also the time of a 'little ice age' and the climate did not begin to change significantly until the seventeenth.[13] Even average height decreased during the thirteenth and fourteenth centuries.[14] Evidence from the famous excavated medieval village at Wharram Percy (Yorkshire) suggests starvation and cannibalism, or attempts to batten down 'revenant' corpses by mutilating them.[15] Grim though living conditions were during this time, we should beware the historical trap of viewing it as 'medieval' in its pejorative sense; there were many ways people 'resisted' lordship and restraints placed upon them.[16]

The greatest setback in Europe's recorded history was the return of the *Yersinia Pestis* in 1348 that killed so many in the fifth-seventh centuries, otherwise known as the Black Death, which in England alone killed between one third and half of the population of five million. The population remained at 2.5 million well into the 1500s – the population levels of *c.* 1300 did not recover until the seventeenth century – no other discontinuity was on this scale.[17] There was a second, devastating outbreak in 1361-2 that was particularly virulent in Eastern England and disproportionately affected boys and young men; so much so, it was known as the 'plague of children'. The most reliable source is Henry Knighton's Chronicle, or *Knighton's Chronicon* (1380s), which tells us how the pestilence came to the coastal regions from Southampton to Bristol where almost the whole town died and it spread everywhere, 'following the course of the sun'.[18] There was also a terrible disease (murrain) of sheep everywhere, and prices collapsed, crops perished unharvested, servants and labourers were in short supply. The newly consecrated archbishop of Canterbury, renowned scholar Thomas Bradwardine, died within two days of his return from Rome, churches were left destitute by the scarcity of priests and services abandoned. Consequently, widowed men flocked to take orders, 'many of whom were illiterate'. Towns and boroughs feel into disrepair and ruin, small villages became desolate 'and it seemed likely that many such villages would never again be inhabited.' Even so, the huge mortality rate did not stop the Scots preparing an invasion, believing the plague to be an 'English disease' until it hit them, decimating their ranks, the remainder killed off by vengeful English troops (a similar belief echoed in some quarters during the pandemic of 2020/1 with the so-called 'Chinese' disease.)

The government under Edward III responded with harsh and conservative measures to the greatest crisis in England's history. The Statute of Labourers in 1351 was ordained by the king and his council

...against the malice of servants, who were idle, and not willing to serve after the pestilence, without excessive wages, that such manner of servants, as well men as women, should be bound to serve, receiving customary salary and wages in the places where they ought to serve in the 20th year of the reign of the king that now is [ie. 1347], or five or six years before, and that the same servants refusing to serve in such a manner should be punished by imprisonment of their bodies.

This was followed by detailed lists of wages for the work.[19] Knighton refers to the Statute of Labourers and tell us that it was defied, so the king levied fines on the landlords and nobles, imprisoning labourers until they promised to take only the wages allowed by 'ancient custom'. Signs of government fears of the apocalyptic death-toll were also present in the Statute of Treasons of 1352. It is act of treason if a man 'attempts or plots the death of our lord the king' or the queen and eldest son and heir, or 'levies war against the king in his realm' or adheres to the king's enemies, giving them aid or comfort, or if he counterfeits the king's seal or money, slays the chancellor, treasurer or any of the king's justices, or violates the queen, the king's eldest daughter or the wife of the eldest son and heir.[20] Other kinds of treason included the killing of a master by his servant, husband by his wife, or a cleric killing a prelate, and other potential treasons of the future which could be declared before the king and his parliament. Compulsory service too, was enforced after 1349.[21]

The Black Death and subsequent plagues marked a turning point, but in ways that were not necessarily expected. The political result of the fatalities of 1348-9 was a conservative backlash, not only of the crown and ruling elite but of the parliamentary Commons. Higher labour costs threatened the income of the gentry and changed the attitude of the Commons in parliament towards the people (the Statute of Labourers was the result of a petition). In drastically reducing the population, the plagues brought prosperity to many of the peasant survivors who migrated to towns and other lordships. The Commons had spoken up for their interests until around 1350 in the face of Edward III's wartime demands, but afterwards the Commons set its face against the rising claims of a more prosperous people, ceasing to speak for the people and instead speaking against them; the sudden opportunity to secure higher wages rallied all ranks of the landlord class to a policy of legislative suppression.[22] In 1368 they asked that labourers and artisans pay back excess prices and salaries, in 1372 they complained about employers paying excessive wages to new arrivals, in 1376 they were asking for fugitive labourers to be placed in the stocks or imprisoned and in 1377 that labourers be forced to work for designated employers with a claim.[23]

Edward III's long reign did not end well. His clerical minsters were forced from power in 1371 and in 1376 the 'Good Parliament', which lasted from 28 April to 10 July, the longest sitting to date, impeached the corrupt and incapable ministers of the crown in a new kind of trial by the lords. The process of impeachment and the office of Commons' Speaker both emerged from these proceedings, provoked by resentment at a series of poor decisions, including a truce with France that gave away fortresses in Brittany, and a papal levy. The parliament was satirised by William Langland's *Piers Plowman* in the so-called 'rat fable', which portrayed a great assembly of rats and mice unable to decide how to deal with the cruel cat.[24]

The deaths of the Black Prince in 1376 and Edward III in June 1377 resulted in the minority rule of Richard II (aged ten), the first since Henry III in 1216. War with France resumed but Parliament declared in 1379 that a Great Council could not levy a tax, in the context of the 'great perils and mischiefs threatening the realm'. Nothing had been paid into the treasury for the war.[25] The Poll Tax of 1380 was 'solely for the sustenance of the Earl of Buckingham and the other lords and men in his company in Brittany, and for the defence of the realm, and keeping of the sea'.[26] The Lords and Commons agreed that the contribution should be made by 'every lay person in the realm ... males and females alike, of whatever estate or condition, who passed the age of fifteen years, of the sum of three groats' (12 pence, one shilling, very roughly two days' wages), but to be paid according to ability to pay, the wealthiest no more than 60 groats, the minimum one groat.

The 'community of the realm' was becoming less and less of a community. There were fears of 'leagues and confederacies' among the lower orders since the poor were no longer so poor and the gentry were under threat, class tensions which exploded in the summer of 1381. That summer yet another poll tax (at 1s a head, three times higher than 1377 and 1379) sparked rebellion. The Peasants' Revolt of 1381 was the result of the deep-seated social, economic, and political concerns that parliament had failed to deal with for a decade, and many of those involved were otherwise respectable members of the parochial society with a stake in the hundred courts and county elections – it reflected the failure of parliament. Like the Good Parliament of 1376, the rebels in 1381 targeted corrupt abusers of position and power (specifically dragging Richard Lyons, impeached in the Good Parliament, out of his house and murdering him in the street), lawyers, clergymen, foreign merchants, and with especial hatred reserved for John of Gaunt ('they would accept no king who was called John' was an initial rallying cry.)[27]

The difference between 1376 and 1381 was that reform from within the system had been abandoned and the only course of action left was direct representation to the king. Court rolls in at least 56 places were burnt and the houses of JPs, MPs, tax collectors and the Duke of Lancaster were systematically attacked. They appealed to the king and attacked his 'evil advisors' acting for the 'true commons', but the rebellion was poorly planned and was over by mid-June, despite its potentially revolutionary aims and violence, dissipating into settling local scores at St Albans, Cambridge and Dunstable. In York, Bury, Scarborough and Lynn, tenants and citizens turned on each other as old restrictions clashed with more liberal charters and rights.

The Peasants' Revolt of 1381 was the first time the 'commons' – meaning people below the gentry – rebelled without the leadership of the magnates and it was the first English uprising since the rebellions against the Norman regime in 1068-72. However, it was essentially a regional event, occurring in the southeastern counties and East Anglia.[28] The *Anonimalle Chronicle* tells us that in Essex trouble started when the commissioners demanded payment that, according to the townspeople of Fobbing, had already been paid; threats were made by the armed guards of the steward, violence broke and out and the Chief Justice of the Common Pleas, Sir Robert Belknap, was sent in with indictments which only incited further killings and Belknap's swift exit. 50,000 rose up, hunting down 'all lawyers and all jurors and all the servants of the king', and the revolt spread to Kent, Suffolk and Norfolk, communicated by 'various letters'.[29] In Bury, Sir John Cavendish, a Chief Justice of the king's bench, was beheaded, along with the prior of Bury.

The rebels joined at Rochester and quickly took the castle. The mob from Maidstone, led by Wat Tyler, reached Canterbury, 4,000 entering the cathedral and demanding the head of the archbishop, which they got five days later. John Ball, self-appointed chaplain and 'prophet', urged the mob to get rid of all the lords, archbishops, bishops, abbots, prior and most of the monks. 60,000 then marched on London, burning and destroying the crops and manors of the Duke of Lancaster 'because of their hatred of the duke', demanding his head and that of Sir Thomas Orgrave, clerk of the receipt and sub-treasurer of England. All the while they maintained their loyalty to the king, seeking only to destroy the traitors to him, a kind of populist royalism, the conventional rhetoric about the 'evil councillor' being a long-standing indirect means of voicing treasonous condemnation of the king himself.

They agreed to meet at Blackheath, but the peasants demanded the heads of the Duke of Lancaster and fourteen others, including the archbishop of Canterbury and Chancellor, Simon of Sudbury, the treasurer of England and other key members of the administration, which was of course refused. At that point the 60,000 from Kent stormed into Southwark, broke open the Marshalsea, released the prisoners and destroyed the houses of any justices and jurors they could find that night; those from Essex meanwhile reached the archbishop's house at Lambeth and burnt all the chancery books.

That night John Ball delivered his famous sermon, including the famous 'When Adam delved and Eve span, who was then the gentleman?' The next day, 13 June, they burnt down houses belonging to the St John Hospital, the duke's palace at the Savoy (where they hurled gunpowder into the fire), broke into the Temple and took the rolls and books away to burn, released the prisoners in the Fleet and Westminster prisons and beheaded Roger Leggett, an assizer, along with eighteen others. The goods looted and destroyed at the duke's Savoy palace included 23 cartloads of hay and silver and gilt plate.[30] The young king was based in the Tower of London and could only watch London burning, his advisors clearly unable to counsel any sort of action. He was persuaded into releasing the traitors in the Tower.

In gaining access to the king the rebels were appealing directly to the monarch and bypassing the legitimate procedures of complaint. They also requested a royal pardon, which was written out on Friday by 30 clerks; this represented a direct link to the personal form of grace unmediated by law courts and royal officers, and much was invested in personally meeting the king (although the legal right of the king to grant manumission was questioned, the right to bestow royal mercy was not). The crown and commons were supposed to share a common understanding of pardon in an idealised relationship between monarch and subject.[31]

The next day, Friday 14 June, the mob swelled to 100,000, and the king came to Mile End with his mother and met the rebels; Wat Tyler demanded that 'no man should be a serf, nor do homage or any manner of service to any lord … no one should serve any man but at his free will, and on terms of regular covenant' (a reference to the Statute of Labourers).[32] The king granted their wish that they could seize traitors to bring them to justice, but instead the mob burst into the Tower chapel and dragged out Sudbury, the treasurer, Sir Robert Hales and Brother William Appleton, physician and surgeon to the king, and the Duke of Lancaster, and beheaded them on Tower Hill.

The rebels also called for 'any Fleming or other alien of any nation' to be caught and executed in similar fashion – and some were: 35 Flemings were dragged out of St Martin's in the Vintry and beheaded in the street, according to the *Anonimalle*. This massacre was corroborated in the City's official *Letter-Book H*, which describes a pile of decapitated bodies in the street. This and other sources, including the Westminster Chronicle and Thomas Walsingham, confirmed this was one of the bloodiest events of the Revolt.[33] Much space was devoted to the violence against the Flemings in the sources. Murders of Flemings spread outside London, to Manningtree, Bishop's Lynn, Snettisham and Yarmouth in uncoordinated attacks that indicate a general hatred of Flemings. Ten years later, Chaucer's *Canterbury Tales* indicates how well-known the killings of the Flemings were in his single reference to the Revolt, where the men of Jack Straw never shouted so shrilly as when they killed the Flemings, mad as if they were chasing the fox.[34]

Why attack the Flemings, who had nothing to do with the hated poll tax, or with the issue of villeinage? Was this premeditated or a consequence of general xenophobia? The sources, independent of one another, all point towards a specific attack. The reason is that attacking the Flemings enabled the rebels to form a community; they killed Flemings to become more English.[35] The other group targeted was the elite representatives of the English crown.

What did the rebels stand for? A vision of order and a community of free men who considered the king to be their natural leader, crucially grounded in the English language. As the (French) *Anonimalle* tells us, the (English) watchword used by the rebels was 'With whom hold you?' The correct response was 'With king Richard and with the true commons.'[36] This evoked a powerful unity, an alternative 'community of the realm' that parliament and the justices had represented – and had failed – a community based on the English language in opposition to the Latin and French languages of government. Indeed, the Flemings were mocked for their speech and pronunciation of English (a London chronicle says that 'many Flemings lost their heads at that time, since they could not say' bread and cheese' but 'kaas en brood' a Middle Dutch familiar to the chronicle's audience, especially given the inverted word order); this was a common enough test used across Europe and found in similar riots and killings.[37] In 1381, in addition, however, it was a very specific issue with Flemings, due to the immigration of the Flemings to England since the 1330s to London, the south-east and East Anglia and more recently during the 1360s and 1370s, which produced commercial tensions. Flemings were long established in England by 1381 and so the rebels were attacking familiar victims using a well-known word-test.

In this way, the Peasants' Revolt fits into the development of English identity in the fourteenth century. Attacking the Flemings, the largest and most prominent alien group in the south-east, helped legitimise the Revolt and aided the aggressive construction of English identity. That said, it might be that the Flemings were attacked because they enjoyed royal favour. Such attacks almost always took place in London and were the work of particular interest groups, and there is no evidence to conclude that much of the English population ever turned against alien workers across the country.[38]

The rebels met the king at Smithfield, where Tyler demanded that there should be no law except the law of Winchester (the 1295 statute, representing the 'good old days') expressly abolishing the hated Statute of Labourers (1351). There was to be no more serfdom, and all should be free and of 'one condition'. Tyler was perhaps appealing to the principle of community self-policing (hue and cry) without the intervention of the sheriffs and justices, an ideal age where the king exercised exclusive lordship. It was a radical programme borne out of decades of resentment and oppression, stimulated by the Black Death and the official response to that enormous event. The king granted Tyler all those demands, but when a Kentish yeoman in the king's ranks identified Tyler as a notorious thief and robber, the mood turned ugly between the mayor, William Walworth, and Tyler, who was badly wounded; the mob prepared to shoot arrows but it was the young king who rode out and commanded them to disperse to the field of St John's, Clerkenwell, during which time the word was sent out to the city wards for every man to arm himself, so that when they reconvened at Clerkenwell, the commons were enveloped 'like sheep in a pen'. The death of Tyler was the turning point: Walworth tracked him down to a hospital near St Bartholomew's, brought him back to Smithfield and beheaded him, put his head on a pole and carried it to the rebels at Clerkenwell, who collapsed at the sight of it, begging for mercy from the king, who granted it and knighted Walworth on the spot.[39]

To what extent was the Peasants' Revolt a manifestation of conflict between lords and tenants? The rebels of Kent handed in a list of fifteen noblemen they wanted beheaded, but hatred of lawyers and tax collectors is not necessarily a hatred of lords as a class. They demanded the abolition of serfdom but wanted rents fixed at 4d an acre, thereby accepting lordship. The demands for an end to serfdom at Mile End also accepted the existence of lordship and these aims were achieved gradually during the fifteenth century, not suddenly in 1381. Was the Revolt an uprising, confined to local areas and agendas, or was it an informed attempt to reframe the systems to improve the standing of the peasants and regain their status, rather than overthrow the system?[40] The chronicles were narrowly focussed and unsympathetic to the rebels, so we can only guess at the attitudes and aims of the rebels. The Norfolk rebellion was well organised and included a broad mixture of social classes, tenants, craftsmen, free and unfree, even a handful of gentry, but it remains unproven whether the rebels felt class hatred towards the gentry and aristocracy.[41]

One aspect comes across from the evidence, and that was the power of the written word. Across all regions and apparent in all the sources was the demand to adjust legal and taxation records, to destroy existing records and to replace them, witnessed and sealed as per the usual custom of English law. In early 1381 there was tax evasion on a massive scale, since people appreciated that if they avoided the records, they would avoid the tax and it was the areas where wide-scale evasion took place where the commissioners went in to enforce payment and where the rebellion raged. The people killed in the rising were targeted, put on a list, their houses searched for the hated records and destroyed; tenurial documents were rewritten in the hope that their status would also be changed.[42] Richard II's request that everyone should go home and put in writing their grievances was met with derision, the rebels proclaiming throughout London that 'all lawyers and all the officials of the chancery and exchequer and all those who could write a writ or a letter should be beheaded, wherever they could be found.'[43]

The wealthy churches and monasteries were not, by and large, attacked. Looting of the houses in London was strictly forbidden by Wat Tyler (the theft of a silver goblet from the Savoy was punished by death); but the charters, muniments and records at Westminster, Lambeth Palace, the Temple, and the Tower were systematically destroyed and the same occurred out in the local manors of Hertfordshire, Surrey and Middlesex and Suffolk.

When the king accepted Tyler's demands for charters of freedom and amnesty, the mob at Smithfield disbanded. In Norwich, Geoffrey Litser set up a mock-court and a treasury and when the news of Tyler's death spread, he sent a request to the king for a charter of manumission and amnesty and in Yarmouth a new peasant oligarchy took charge of the customs house. In Cambridge, the privileges and charters of the university were burned and quickly replaced, demanding that the university surrender all privileges given under royal donations.

Richard II authorised the grant of royal mercy at the December parliament of 1381, offering grace to all his subjects – an unprecedented act. The grant of freedom and manumission of serfs was repealed by parliament, however, and reforms made to the government generally.[44] At the parliament, the Commons' Speaker, Sir Richard Waldegrave, MP for Kent and thus well-placed to understand the rebels' grievances, cited maintenance, purveyance, the corruption of the legal system, the malpractice of royal officials and the provision of inadequate defence as the main reasons to explain the rebellion, explicitly affiliating the Commons with the rebels and warning the government of future calamity if remedies were not taken.[45] Just as rebellions of the nobility are not considered revolutionary, then neither should the peasants' in 1381. Most of the demands made in 1381 were traditional; the rebels wanted improved conditions within the legal and constitutional framework of the land.[46] The revolt of 1381 was about direct action.

The Peasants' Revolt failed as many peasants remained in bondage, but by the early sixteenth century serfs had nearly disappeared from English villages, owing to the migrations during the fourteenth and fifteenth centuries, a result of plague, demographics, and the serfs' determination to become free.[47] Labour laws were enforced and extended throughout the fifteenth century, petitions put forward privately by the social elite and Cade's revolt in 1450 repeated the grievances of 1381: abuse of purveyance, oppression by local officials.[48] From the 1380s money supply, prices and population stalled; the economy failed to recover over the fifteenth century, population remained relatively low, prices were flat and the total estimated money supply around 1460-70 was comparable with the levels around 1300 (less than £1m).[49] In the period 1375-1520, structural poverty reduced as the depleted population occupied larger holdings of land and employment opportunities expanded, with higher real wages, a diminishing tax burden between 1453 and 1521 and fewer bad harvests.[50]

In the short term, the increasing divide between the political Commons and the social commonality continued. Parliament was packed with military veterans, and after 1381, reprisals were swift and harsh, the military men commissioned to hunt down the rebels and execute them, contributing to the hardening divisions between the political Commons and the people, a trend begun by the Black Death.[51] A petition to prevent justices of assize sitting in their own county. Because of the 'great alliances and other affinities there, great evils and grievances arise in various ways,' including favouritism and injustice. This was accepted by the king in 1384.[52] There were harsher penalties against the labourers at the parliament in Cambridge, 1388: no labourer or servant, man or woman, of whatever age or condition, could leave his town at the end of his service without a letter patent under seal (delivered by the JP to the Hundred) on pain of imprisonment for 40 days; no labourer required to serve with the plough or do farm work was permitted to learn a craft; no servant or labourer was permitted to carry a dagger or sword.[53]

By 1386 Richard was relying on unpopular favourites, like Edward II, which sparked dispute, violence and the 'Merciless Parliament' of 1388 that imposed further restrictions on the crown. In 1394 Richard II's visit to Ireland revitalised English rule there with what might have been the final conquest of the island. A treaty with France in 1396 and marriage to Isabella of Valois halted the costly and damaging war. But Richard's last years as king were indisputably tyrannous; he executed Arundel, murdered Gloucester, and exiled the earls of Warwick, Derby

(Bolingbroke) and Nottingham in a massive over-reach of the royal prerogative. In the two years between 1397 and 1379 Richard seized the lands belonging to three duchies and four earldoms, dispossessing five of the great magnate families, finally seizing the Lancastrian lands on the death of John of Gaunt early in 1399, worth £12,000 a year. He packed parliament, used papal support to threaten excommunication of anyone attempting anything prejudicial to the crown; and the treaty with France promised French aid against his own people.

Mum and the Sothsegger, an anonymous alliterative English poem from the late fourteenth century, satirically describes how Richard II had a 'privy parliament to get profit for himself'; the MPs summoned argued back and forth, some had been bribed, some denounced enemies of the king, others slept and mumbled, some were 'hired men', others dull-witted, some interested only in the 'main chance' or the money the king owed them rather than the interests of the commons, and some were afraid of great men; altogether not an inspiring parliament.[54]

The treason laws were extended in 1398, since the 1352 statutes were repealed, to include 'everyone who encompasses or purposes the death of the king, or plots to depose him, or render up his liege homage, or who raises the people...'[55]

Richard II had insisted people approach him on bended knee:

On solemn days, in the evenings, the king would sit on his throne saying nothing and whenever he glanced at anyone, of whatever rank, that person had to bend the knee in obeisance; he was so hated in London and the country that he could not ride safely without an armed guard, removing the jewels from the Tower.

The duke of Hereford (Bolingbroke) was banished for ten years, Norfolk for life and the duke of York, Edmund of Langley, fourth son of Edward III, made guardian of the kingdom when he set off for Ireland.[56]

Regime change was imposed by the political and social elites, not the peasantry. Richard's absence on a second trip to Ireland in 1399 was a fatal error; Bolingbroke, now duke of Hereford and Lancaster, returned from exile and took everyone by surprise. Richard was dethroned in September. He gave up the crown in the Tower in front of a deputation of magnates and prelates, reading from the schedule which he signed with his own hand, adding that he wished the Duke of Lancaster to succeed him (Henry Bolingbroke).[57] All the sources were written after Richard's deposition and so the depth of Richard's unpopularity in the country is hard to measure since the years 1395-99 are all from a Lancastrian perspective and written with hindsight.[58] It was the king's absence, rather than his unpopularity, that led men to desert him. Only after he was captured did London support Henry and a rebellion of 1400 included the earls of Gloucester and Salisbury. It was this rebellion that led to Richard's murder later that year.

'My God, this is a strange and fickle land, which has exiled, slain, destroyed and ruined so many kings, so many rulers, so many great men, and which never ceases to be riven and worn down by dissensions and strife and internecine hatreds,' said Richard II, awaiting his fate in the Tower in 1399, according to Adam of Usk.[59] To Richard, it must have seemed a country of strife given his own personal downfall, but he was the only monarch to be deposed without a son and heir and his worldview did not chime with the country's history.

The deposition of Richard II was momentous. The only previous deposition, Edward II, had been in favour of his son, and as we have seen, Edward II may not have been murdered. Richard certainly was and crucially, he left no son, the first monarch not to do so since Richard I in 1199. Then, as in 1399, there were two possibilities, but this time they were both cousins of the late king. The earl of March, Edmund Mortimer, was seven years of age but Henry Bolingbroke was 33, a tried and tested adult but descended from a younger son of Edward III (John of Gaunt), Mortimer was descended from the older brother (Lionel, duke of Clarence). There was still no acknowledged rule of succession should the senior male line fail. Bolingbroke had the backing of the powerful Percies in the north, but it was nothing short of a *coup d'état* which landed the newly minted Henry IV with years of strife and endowed English kingship and politics decades of domestic turmoil.

Henry IV, the first usurper and founder of the Lancastrian dynasty, survived an assassination plot and faced rebellion from his erstwhile supporters, the Percies, in 1403. Northumberland's son, Hotspur, was killed at Shrewsbury and the earl himself at Bramham Moor in 1408 (Shrewsbury was the first time since 1264 that an English king had faced rebels in the field of battle); another Percy rising involved Archbishop Scrope, who was executed in 1405.

The Mortimer family, too, were involved in the 1403 rebellion and allied with Glyndŵr, led by Edmund, brother-in-law- to Hotspur, son-in-law to Glyndŵr and uncle to the young Edmund, earl of March, equal claimant to the throne with Bolingbroke; they were descendants of the Roger Mortimer who had led the palace coup against Edward II in 1327 and crucially, descendants of Lionel, Edward III's second son and therefore senior to the Lancastrian usurpers. In 1409, the Mortimer threat ceased with the death of Edmund senior and his family were taken to London; the young earl of March remained in custody until the death of Henry IV, released by Henry V to whom he stayed loyal, even to the point of revealing the Southampton Plot of 1415 (although possibly to deflect any suspicion away from himself).[60] The Mortimer line failed with Edmund, but his nephew was Richard of York, who inherited lands, titles and claim to the throne which were to eventually unseat the Lancastrian dynasty in 1461.

The fourteenth century ended where it began, with the removal of the monarch. This was not enabled by a charter or a security council or even the masses, despite the violence of 1381, but by the nobility and parliament. The depositions were not triggered by war or financial burdens or unrest but by the personal favourites and the failings of Edward II and Richard II. English society was traumatised for two generations following the Black Death and rebelled when it felt shut out from the established mechanisms of government, but it was not seeking to replace those mechanisms. Without its king, the English government could not be. Parliament was the representative assembly of the realm, but the king was the head of the community.

Edward I rarely gave his nobility the opportunity to contemplate a kingless parliament, Edward II avoided parliament in the hope of frustrating the barons; Edward III initially encouraged kingless parliaments to stimulate the finances for his foreign wars but attended more regularly after 1341 since the taxes he needed would not be granted freely without the reciprocal justice, petitions, and complaints any king needed to respond to; Richard II was relatively assiduous in attending parliament.[61] However vital the king's presence was in parliament, records suggest that kings addressed parliament in person on only eight occasions between 1324 and 1398, since most of the king's word were spoken on his behalf by the chancellor, chief justice, treasurer, or other royal minister (Henry IV addressed parliament in person eight times between 1401 and 1406, even engaging in a point-by-point argument with Speaker Savage in 1404, perhaps reflecting his origins as a nobleman who usurped the throne and who still saw himself as *primus inter pares*.)[62]

English kings, hemmed in as they were by bureaucrats and powerful nobles, returned to an age-old arena to further their wealth and power and by doing so, marked a new stage in the making of England: war.

FIFTEEN

Unfinished Business – Wales, Scotland, and France

The familial relations between England and Normandy metamorphosed into state-sponsored war between England and France that lasted intermittently from 1294 to 1485. The wars with France began with feudal legalities in Gascony, but under Edward III this widened into a claim to the French throne itself, gaining territories well beyond Gascony by 1360. Henry V almost made this claim a reality in 1420 but died before becoming king of France. Whilst these wars did not make the state, they did create a sharper identity of 'England' and 'foreigners' that played out at home. The invasions of Wales and Scotland were not part of an imperial grand design. The conquest of Wales by 1287 was a cultural conquest, but the wars with Scotland had different aims of overlordship. Ireland was entirely neglected until a brutal campaign in 1394. The conquest of Normandy under Henry V was not a 're-unification' and resulted in an unsustainable colonial rule. The defeat and withdrawal from France in 1453 significantly affected domestic politics well into the 1480s. Efforts to assert overlordship in Scotland were abandoned in the fifteenth century and by c. 1500 English territories in France had all but vanished.

Up until 1204 (and formalised in the treaty of 1259) it was impossible to consider the ruling elites as 'English', but thereafter, landholding across borders was limited or forbidden, and allegiances had to be decided one way or another. War gave the English a clearer sense of national identity. The Treaty of Paris in 1259 laid the foundations for the conquest of Wales and the wars in Scotland, as the king of England was able to concentrate solely on his British neighbours. From Edward I's reign onwards, there was no decade when England was not at war overseas or in the British Isles. The wars of the fourteenth and fifteenth centuries against the Scots, Welsh and the French were a 'forcing-house' of nationhood and self-conscious Englishness.[1]

From the late thirteenth century onwards, anti-French xenophobia increasingly identified the Norman Conquest with the destruction of English liberties.[2] In 1373 an observer said that 'the English are so filled with their own greatness and have won so many big victories that they have come to believe they cannot lose. In battle they are the most confident nation in the world.'[3] Attitudes towards the 'barbicans of the realm' varied from time and from place, with intermarriage in Ireland officially proscribed but not in Wales or on the Continent. Regional chauvinism undermined collective consciousness – the 'filthy rump-eating Irishman' was identified by a Welsh bard, and the common Anglophobic image of the tailed Englishman. The mentality was not a new one: Michael de la Pole, chancellor of England, declared at the opening of parliament in November 1384 that England was 'entirely surrounded by deadly enemies all in league with one another', including the French, the Spanish, the Flemish and the Scots.[4] Overwhelmingly, the kingdom of England must be protected by the 'buttresses' of Ireland and Wales and kept free from subjection to France when the kingship of France was added to the royal style in 1340 and 1420.

The first parliament of Richard II successfully petitioned for the expulsion of all subjects of the French king, Charles V, from English soil; any French residents seeking to remain in the kingdom would have to show that they were 'good and loyal to our lord the king and his kingdom' and recipients of royal protection now had to swear fealty to the crown of England in the chancery, marking a change from accepting an individual's general trustworthiness to nationality becoming the primary consideration for protection by the English state.[5] Memory of the Anglo-Norman past was used as part of Lancastrian propaganda to justify rule over the duchy of Normandy after Agincourt.[6] By the later fifteenth century, Sir John Fortescue was making the distinction between England, a land where kings governed by consent, and France, which was a despotism.[7] The Council at Constance in 1417 referred to the renowned 'nation of England or Britain...'[8] In the 1430s, a pamphleteer echoed the words in the *Dialogue of the Exchequer* in the 1180s when he wrote:

Keep then the seas about in special;
Which of England is the round wall
As though England were likened to a city
And the wall environ were a sea...[9]

In 1442, the Benedictines of Dunfermline did not agree:

The tyranny, cruelty and usurpation of the English are notorious to all the world as manifestly appears in their usurpation against France, Scotland, Wales, Ireland and neighbouring lands.[10]

Many traits associated with 'imperialism', such as a civilising ideology and notions of racial superiority, can be traced back to the twelfth century in the writings of William of Malmesbury and from then on into the mid-fourteenth century and what has been called England's first 'empire'.[11] This so-called 'empire' endured into the fifteenth century given the aspirations of Richard II in Ireland, the draconian response to the anti-colonial rebellion of Glyndwr and the colonisation of Normandy after 1417, which had an impact well into the 1450s.[12] Both spheres of 'British' history and 'Anglo-French' history were embraced by English kings. With two brief exceptions in 1328 (repudiated in 1333) and 1502 (the 'Treaty of Perpetual Peace' lapsed in 1512), the king of England never relinquished his claim to the 'submission, homage and other peculiar rights due of old to the crown of England from the kings of the Scots and their people'.[13]

From the outbreak of war with France in 1294 until Edward I's death in July 1307, the English fought thirteen campaigns in Wales, Scotland, Gascony and Flanders. The first twenty-two years of his reign included only three campaigns, all in Wales (1277, 1282-3 and 1287). This was no grand plan, rather his personal ambition and drive.[14] His unrelenting insistence in asserting his sovereignty on all corners of the British Isles led to perpetual war. Edward's wars in Wales, France and Scotland were driven by issues of overlordship and sovereignty. In 1276 he went to war against Llewellyn ap Gruffudd, Prince of Wales, because he refused to do homage as agreed in the 1267 Treaty of Montgomery and in 1296 he invaded Scotland to enforce his rights as King John's overlord. When Edward refused to attend the French *parlement* as Duke of Aquitaine and Philip IV's vassal, the confiscation of Gascony sparked war between England and France. Overlordship entailed the supervision of justice, but in Wales after 1278 Edward extended the royal courts and introduced English criminal law, which caused rebellion and war in 1282 and 1294 since the Welsh saw it as a matter of common right to have their own laws and customs.

There were the same issues in Scotland. The Treaty of Birgham (1290) had laid out the concerns of the community of the realm of Scotland that the rights, laws, liberties, and customs of the realm should be preserved in every respect; but in 1296 Edward abolished Scottish kingship and ruled Scotland as a land administered by Englishmen.[15] In 1304 he allowed the Scots a greater role in their own government, but this also deepened the Comyn/Bruce divide. Edward's pursuit of his claim to the overlordship of Scotland launched Anglo-Scottish conflict which lasted until the 1603 Union of Crowns; his permanent subjugation of Wales was the longest-lasting change to the power structure of Britain since 1066. In overriding Welsh native law and Scottish custom, Edward was echoing a cultural momentum increasingly intolerant of anything different to mainstream Francophile Western Christendom; this was seen in the 1290 expulsion of the Jews from England.

Edward's wars arguably accelerated the notion of the first English 'empire'. The conquest of Wales – Roman *Britannia Prima* – in 1283 was the final subjugation since the Early English settlements of the fifth/ sixth centuries (when the word 'Welsh' came to mean 'foreigner') and the renewed invasions and colonisations under Harold Godwinsson, William I and William II in the later eleventh century. English contempt for Wales and Ireland was the norm by the late twelfth century.[16] Three campaigns of conquest finally subdued Wales by 1295, with vastly expensive castles stamping England's authority on the conquered Welsh. (The conquest of Wales cost fortunes; £75,000 on castle building between 1277 and 1301 and the suppression of the 1274-5 revolt cost £55,000.) This was by now a cultural war against what the English elite saw as an inferior race of people; their language, literature and heritage were dismantled and demolished.[17]

Dafydd ap Gruffudd was put on trial and executed as a traitor, the first since Earl Waltheof in 1076, and the conquest of Wales was complete. The Statute of Wales in 1284 divided the northern region into English counties and abolished or amended Welsh laws, bringing them into the sphere of English common law.[18] Edward's heir, Prince Edward, was born at Caernarfon Castle in 1284 and in 1301, aged sixteen, became the first English Prince of Wales.

Edward I was vindictive and cruel; he slaughtered the inhabitants of Berwick in 1296, hanged, disembowelled, and quartered the Welsh prince Dafydd ap Gruffudd in 1283 and William Wallace in 1297 and displayed the countess of Buchan in a cage on the walls of Berwick castle. The severity of Edward's punishments was unprecedented, but ritual execution of traitors was a Europe-wide trend; hanging and quartering – and flaying alive – was meted out to traitors in France. Long-term empires depended on their rulers limiting their ambitions, and on negotiation; Edward I's expansionist era was significant but comparatively brief and unsustainable. The wars of Edward I perhaps reflect the boundaries of England rather than the ideals of a 'British' polity. The earls of Edward I filled their military retinues with family members, retainers, tenants, and neighbours, who usually served consistently with the same lord.[19]

In contrast to Wales, Scotland and England had enjoyed peace for most of the thirteenth century following the concessions made in Magna Carta. Scotland was ruled by a single king, unlike Wales, and the border with England had remained unchanged since the eleventh century. Territorial expansion occurred in the Highlands, with burghs, abbeys and cathedrals founded in the Lowlands. Silver pennies were minted, on a par with English sterling, and marriage alliances formed across Europe. The death of King Alexander III, falling from his horse in 1286, changed all of that, since he left as his heir a grand-daughter, Margaret, who died in 1290. Edward I asserted his overlordship to adjudicate in favour of John Balliol.

Balliol's claim was settled in 1292 and his deposition in 1296 by the Scottish nobility gave Edward the opportunity to invade in 1296, and with complete savagery; surrender was unconditional and direct rule imposed. The army that marched to Scotland in 1298 was perhaps the largest raised in Britain before the seventeenth century, including 25,700 foot soldiers; from the 1290s Edward had adopted the new method of indenture, a contract sealed by captains to raise a fixed number of men to serve for a fixed time for a fixed fee.[20] He won his wars with larger armies, better planning, and superior resources; indenture became the standard means of raising English armies into the sixteenth century. The Stone of Destiny was removed from Scone to Westminster Abbey, where it remained until 1996, indicating the cultural supremacy of the English. The political settlement of 1305 referred to Scotland not as a 'realm' or 'kingdom' but as a 'land'.

Edward II did not recognise Bruce as king, but the Scots took the war to the English borders with success, finally defeating a massive English army at Bannockburn in June 1314. Edward Balliol, King of Scotland, ceded much of the Scottish Lowlands to Edward III when he did homage in 1334, holding the kingdom as 'Lord Paramount'.[21]

The English never commanded the North Sea or subdued the north and west of Scotland. The Treaty of Northampton (1328) recognised King Robert (disowned in 1330 by Edward III) and at Neville's Cross (1346) King David II was captured, but Scottish resistance was united and persistent. When war with France broke out it took until 1357 to settle a lasting peace with Scotland. The hostility remained deep, Scottish soldiers serving with the French forces in the 1420s.

Not only did the Scots ally with the French but they also sought alliance with the Irish; in 1316 Robert the Bruce's brother, Edward, was made High King of Ireland and Edward I's stripping of resources to fund his wars in Wales left Ireland neglected and ripe for resistance (revenues in 1318 were a third of what they had been). No English king visited Ireland between 1210 (John) and 1394 (Richard II). Royal control contracted to the 'pale' around Dublin, resorting to racial and cultural segregation in a costly, lawless region ready for any sort of 'pan-Celtic' alliance against the English (not unlike Brunanburh in 937). Richard II's expedition of 1394 was one of brute military force, which slaughtered people and cattle and burned villages. Captive leaders of the Mic Mhurchadha dynasty were executed as rebels.

Edward III did homage to King Philip VI of France at Amiens in 1329 for the duchy of Gascony.[22] Gascony lay at the heart of what we call, anachronistically and inaccurately, the Hundred Years' War (it lasted in its longest extent from 1337 to 1487) replacing Normandy and Anjou which had dominated the twelfth century. In 1274 Gascony was the sole English possession in France, worth £17,000 a year in 1306-7, trading wine for English cloth and corn. The growing Franco-Scottish 'auld alliance' included offering refuge to King David II in 1334, but the demise of the Capetian dynasty in 1328 transformed local disputes and fractious international relations into the very succession of the French throne. Edward III was in no position then to exploit the succession of Philip VI, the first Valois (England was ruled by Roger Mortimer and Queen Isabella following Edward II's deposition) but when a French fleet was sighted off the Norman coast en route for Scotland in 1337 (so it was believed) war began.

The issue of Gascony was continual from Edward I through to Henry VI's defeat. Edward III ransomed King John of France, captured at Poitiers in 1356, and abandoned his claim at the Treaty of Brétigny in 1360. The war was a series of disjointed campaigns, firstly in northern France 1338-40, then Brittany, Gascony and Normandy 1341-7 (Crécy) then *chevauchées* into Gascony 1355-6 (Poitiers) and Rheims in 1359. The Anglo-French conflict spread across to encompass the Low Countries, Castile, Portugal, Scotland, Wales and Ireland, a truly European war. The Treaty of Brétigny in 1360 put sovereignty over Gascony above the claim to the French throne and the priority of diplomacy in the 1440s was the retention of the sovereign duchy of Aquitaine and the duchy of Normandy.[23]

Jean Froissart describes how Edward III was counselled to make war on France by the exiled count of Artois, 'for if he should sit still and not do his duty to recover his right, he should be more blamed than before.' An alliance was needed against the might of the French, with the emperor Louis of Germany, the duke of Bavaria, the duke of Brabant and the count of Hainault, among others.[24] The reasons for war given by Edward III to his magnates and sheriffs to proclaim at the local courts included the return of lands in Gascony, offers of marriage (refused by France), offers to go on crusade with the king of France (refused) and the breaking of the truce with the Scots.[25]

Edward III arrived on the Continent in 1338, at Antwerp, and Froissart tells us that he was made vicar-general of the Empire so that he could enact the powers of the emperor.[26] Edward launched a campaign into Flanders, laying waste to the towns and countryside of Cambrai and Tournai to bring the king of France to battle, but failing. Early in 1340, Edward III assumed the title and arms of the King of France, challenging Philip to settle the dispute either by single combat or by tournament, since a true king would either stand the test of 'ravenous lions' or 'perform the miracle of touching for the king's evil'.[27] It was ruled also in 1340 that the people of England were not to be subject or obedient to the king of

England or his heirs and successors as king of France.[28] The Battle of Sluys in 1340 was an English naval victory capturing 200 warships, and killing and drowning 25,000 of the enemy for the loss of 4,000 English.

The horrors of war did not take long to manifest themselves; the English surrounded a church in a Flemish town after an early battle in 1337, set it on fire and burnt the survivors to death in the church. Also apparent from the outset were the famous English archers who had 'put them to flight' in the first place.[29] This was a pattern repeated across the next century; Jean de Venette vividly recounted in 1359 the burning of his village, Venette near Compiègne, leaving the fields unploughed and unsown, rabbits and hares running freely, the vines unpruned and rotting, the houses and churches smoking ruins, the only bells tolled for warning, not summoning.[30]Scorched earth and other atrocities – the waging of war by 'fire, sword and famine', in the words of the late fourteenth-century chronicler Adam of Usk – were not incidental to the conduct of war but were actually routine strategy and something which the general populace of England never witnessed.

The costs of war were prodigious and unprecedented, funded by 20,000 sacks of wool granted by parliament in 1337. Estimated costs were £2,000 a day plus over £300,000 payments to his allies on the Continent, which caused a political crisis in 1339-40 just as Edward I's war effort had done in 1295-7.[31] The largest army fielded by the English was in 1346 at the siege of Calais (32,000) but armies well under 10,000 were the norm in the later campaigns, including Henry V's conquest of Normandy in 1417, thus constituting less than 1% of the population of England.[32] The systematic exploitation of territories in the occupied provinces also returned great profit, as well as a host of other sources of income, from ransoms to bribes and indemnities. Apart from the south coast, England never saw the horrors of war that English troops inflicted on the French.

It was also a war of chivalric propaganda. Mindful of his father's deposition following disastrous promotion of outsider-favourites, Edward III created six new earls in March 1337 from the ranks of knight banneret, all of whom were close household courtiers and would prove vital for the coming war.[33] The legend of King Arthur was brought to life again by both Edward I and Edward III, who made Windsor Castle his Arthurian shrine and created the Order of the Garter. The Round Table was founded by Edward III at Windsor in 1344 (he named his second son Lionel after an Arthurian hero), following four days of feasting and jousting, where the king took an oath to oversee the Round Table 'in the same manner and estate as the lord Arthur, formerly king of England,' before 300 knights; the work was accounted for in 1345 to the sum of £461 in the exchequer accounts.[34] In 1349, during the worst aftershocks of the Black Death, and perhaps because of it, the Order of the Garter was founded, including a chantry and hospital; the king and the knights heard mass bare-headed, clad in russet gowns with blue garters and afterwards sat at a common table in honour of St George.[35] In response to Edward III's undoubted bravery, rumours circulated home and abroad about his equally undoubted weakness for women. The rape of the Countess of Salisbury by Edward III in 1342 was recounted in graphic detail by the Hainaulter Jean de Bel ('he raped her so savagely that never was a woman so badly treated; and he left her lying there all battered about...') but Jean Froissart gave it no credence, even though other stories about Edward's infatuation for Joan, the 'Fair Maid of Kent' were in circulation and the rape story was most likely designed to present Edward III in the worst light on the Continent.[36]

The Treaty of Brétigny, 1360, confirmed Edward III's territories in Gascony and Guienne, Poitiers, Limousin, Périgord, Agenais, Cahors, Angoulême, Ponthieu, Calais and elsewhere, to be held in heredity and perpetuity, plus 3 million gold crowns. But he did not gain the crown of France itself, despite the brilliant victories at Crécy and Poitiers.[37] It was the end of 23 years of conflict driven by rivalry with Philip of France and fought by aristocratic armies with feudal retinues. The peace didn't last long, in 1369 war restarted. Edward reassumed the title of King of France, on the grounds that the French had usurped the title and planned an invasion of England.[38] This time though, Edward III was old and sick, reluctantly manoeuvred into war by Charles of France; even the dazzling victory at Nájera in 1367 turned out to be a pyrrhic victory, costing £400,000. The Black Prince was also a sick man and lost Gascony in 1370. In 1372 the English fleet was destroyed at La Rochelle with all its treasure (Edward III's first major defeat) and by 1374 the only possessions left were Bayonne, Bordeaux, and Calais: peace was agreed with the Treaty of Bruges early in 1375.[39]

Edward III had effectively opted for a dual monarchy after he assumed the title 'king of France,' in 1340. This multiple kingdom grew to become something of a constitutional hotchpotch, with Gascony considered to be an inalienable parcel of the English crown, like Calais, Ireland, and Wales, but there was little attempt at 'Anglicization' in Lancastrian Normandy. It was the royal dynasty that made of it a 'union in diversity'.

Prince Henry presided over a meeting of the king's council in the summer of 1412 concerning Calais, Ireland, the principality and March of Wales, and the castles of Roxburgh and Berwick in Scotland.[40] Parliament received petitions from Ireland, Wales, Scotland, Gascony, and the Channel Islands. Military service on the internal frontiers or abroad on the Continent gave the governing classes a stake in this 'empire'. Henry V's experience in multiple theatres of war covered much of his short life, from honourable captivity in Trim castle, county Meath, in 1399, the battle of Shrewsbury on the Welsh March in 1403, to the Welsh rebellion years, the Agincourt campaign and Normandy. The great victories of

Crécy and Poitiers using dismounted men-at-arms flanked by archers had actually been tested at Dupplin Moor and Halidon Hill in the Anglo-Scottish campaigns. Henry V learnt the art of war during the campaigning years in Wales in the years 1400-5, which included pincer movements, *chevauchées* (tactics learnt by the English under the Black Prince in the 1350s), raising troops, co-ordinating land and sea supply lines.

Wales posed a security problem closer to home. The Welsh rebellions under Owain Glyndŵr were prolonged, dangerous, and costly to the English crown. From 1400 to 1408, Glyndŵr launched guerrilla raids, and laid waste castles, capturing Harlech. In 1401 Glyndŵr began to seek external alliances and addressed letters in French to the king of Scotland and also correspondences in Latin to the Gaelic lords in Ireland. He allied with France in 1403 and held parliaments in 1404-5 with grand plans for an independent Wales, universities, and church. But in 1406 the English captured King James I and in 1407 formed a treaty with France.

At the hard-fought battle of Shrewsbury on 21 July 1403, the sixteen-year old Prince of Wales was horrifically wounded in the face by an arrow-head which entered his face to the left of his nose just beneath his eye and lodged in his skull at a depth of six inches, miraculously leaving arteries untouched.[41]It took two days to retrieve the arrow-head, using a special instrument made by surgeon John Bradmore, all without the benefits of modern anaesthetic, who later wrote up his account. The prince did not lose his sight or indeed his life from subsequent infection (something that would be attributed to God) but he must have been left with an ugly scar across one side of his face (which we don't see on any portrait) and psychologically this may have prepared him for the realities of the Agincourt campaign and perhaps prompted his cautionary tactics, which resulted in the English suffering a fraction of the French casualties. It could even have altered his personality, transforming him from a carefree youth to warrior, hunting heretics, rejecting his old friend Sir John Oldcastle, ruthlessly expediting the trial and execution of the earl of Cambridge, and ordering the massacre of the French prisoners at Agincourt. (He had been advised by Thomas Hoccleve that a king who 'spoke too easily' was worthy of less respect than one more circumspect with his speech.)[42]

The resumption of war with France under Henry V marked a transition from the aristocratic wars of Edward III to a national war. Henry V's reputation as an outsize king began in his own lifetime with works produced by his own chaplains (as with Alfred the Great), including the *History of Henry V* (a work of propaganda written by a priest) and the Agincourt Carol; the astonishing victory at Agincourt, triumph at Troyes and his premature death sealed his legendary status. Henry V was deeply conservative, conventionally pious, cruel, and ruthless. He left a nine-month-old son and heir, which resulted in the longest minority in English history.

The final demands of Henry V included the entire Treaty of Brétigny, the unpaid ransom of King John (captured 1356), the hand in marriage of Catherine, a vast dowry and 'the crown and kingdom of France', including the homage of Normandy, Touraine, Anjou, Maine, Brittany, Aquitaine, Flanders; in other words, the original Angevin 'empire' of the twelfth century plus the crown of France. The Dauphin had taunted Henry V with a gift of tennis balls at Kenilworth, 1414, as he was such a young man, to which Henry replied, 'I shall play with such balls in the Frenchman's court-yards that they will lose the game eventually and for their game win but grief.' The French replied with extensive territorial concessions but it was not enough and Henry made plans for war.[43] Henry V's aims were the same as Edward III's; to exploit divisions within the French nobility and press his dynastic claim, only this time Henry had the advantage of an insane king on the throne of France and the outcome was rather different, since he effectively conquered France.

Just before his departure for France in 1415, an unexpected plot against him was revealed at Southampton, apparently to assassinate him.[44] The Southampton Plot was the last gasp of Mortimer-inspired treason that had haunted Bolingbroke's reign and was very much a family affair. The earl of Cambridge, grandson of Edward III and close to the king, was indicted and executed, along with Scrope and Grey. However, there *wasn't* a plot to assassinate the king, since the most heinous charge was fabricated to guarantee the death penalty.[45] This may be why Cambridge was not attainted and his son, Richard, who inherited the title of York and all the territories of both earldoms since Edward, second duke of York and brother to the executed earl, was killed at Agincourt.

The earl of Cambridge appealed for mercy to the king, explaining his role in the plot to put the earl of March on the throne but not to assassinate the king (though consequently, one imagines that Henry would have been murdered or 'killed while escaping').[46] The king showed no mercy, probably engaging the justices to use the charge of regicide to speed up the trial. It set a terrible precedent for future executions ordered in the Star Chamber under the authority of the steward of England.[47] In the parliament of 1461, the triumphant Yorkists had the sentence passed on Cambridge in 1415 annulled as 'irregular and unlawful'. The Southampton Plot – believed by some to have been a trumped-up charge – could be said to have been the origin of the 'Wars of the Roses' that destroyed the royal Houses and savaged the nobility of England in the period 1460-1487.

The successful campaign of Henry V in 1415 began with the parliament of November 1414, which awarded the king a double tax grant to recover the king's inheritance outside the realm and on the back of that, loans could be raised; this war was fought 'as much by accountants as by soldiers'.[48] 80% of the 12,000 troops raised were archers; 26 peers contributed almost half the total fighting force, 87 German and Dutch gunners and 119 miners from the Forest of Dean.[49] There was a very strong sense of unity created by high standards of military discipline; rape and attacking churches was banned (Shakespeare's famous hanging of Bardolph for stealing from a church in the play *Henry V* was based on a real event) and the army wore the cross of St George on their front and back.

The eye-witness account of the battle (*History of Henry V*) tells us how the English faced 'incomparable' numbers of Frenchmen and when Sir Walter Hungerford wished for ten thousand of those archers in England, the king replied he would not have one more, putting his trust in God and the 'little band'.[50] 60,000 French had started the battle against 6,000 English and 'almost the whole nobility of French chivalry' died, according to the *History of Henry V*. The ratio of ten to one is nonsense, it was more like two to one, if that; probably 8-10,000 English troops and 12,000-15,000 French troops at the most, making the victory not quite so miraculous.[51] Late in the day, the English moved forward to entice the French before hunger and tiredness overwhelmed them, and battle was joined; the crush of bodies was such that the English climbed on the piles of dead. In the panic, the English killed all their prisoners, except one or two of the most noble. The French fell back, the battle lost. The numbers of French prisoners killed is uncertain but cannot have been more than a hundred since the king ordered a company of 200 archers to do the job, which included burning houses full of prisoners.[52] It was against all the laws of warfare, Henry's own ordinances and Christian ethics, but he did it anyway. Such was his reputation then, as now, that rather like his absent crusading ancestor Richard 'the Lionheart,' Henry V remains something of a Teflon king.

The victory at Agincourt was widely proclaimed and carefully publicised. The Agincourt Carol (1415) records how the French prisoners were led into London 'with joy and mirth and great renown' and the *History of Henry V* describes the king's progress through Canterbury, Eltham and thence to Blackheath where tens of thousands gathered to greet him with effigies, costumed choirs, and pageantry mocked up in tents, canopies, and various tableaux across the City of London from Cheapside to St Paul's, in an extraordinary display of theatre and Biblical references.[53]

This brought home to the people the glory of foreign war that only involved 1% of the population but made it seem like a national effort. The wars of Edward III had created opportunity for the aristocratic and knightly classes to live out their ideals and a new class of careerist warriors benefitted from decades of war, gaining riches and political appointments.[54] John of Gaunt, duke of Lancaster and brother of Edward III, was continually involved in campaigns from 1359 to 1395, including twelve major expeditions and fifteen diplomatic missions.[55]

To what extent was English society militarised? Armed service went back to the eighth century, but we saw how it was likely that Alfred's fighting troops were a small cadre of professionals funded by his personal wealth and the bulk of the troops at Hastings were also most likely to have been professional warriors. The Assize of Arms in 1181 and Westminster I in 1285 linked status with bearing arms, but a writ of 1363 to the sheriff of Kent revealed the importance of archery to the war effort. People practised it in their games but now it was seemingly neglected in favour of handball, football or 'stick-ball' (cricket?) so that the kingdom became 'truly destitute of archers'. The king ordered that 'everyone in the shire, on festival days when he has a holiday,' should practise archery with bows, arrows, bolts or crossbolts and he forbade games with balls, stones, hockey, and cockfighting 'under pain of imprisonment'.[56]

To be fair, this came after the Treaty of Brétigny, but the importance of the longbow marks the shift towards a more common, popular type of soldiering. Famous though the English longbow was, no archaeological evidence for the war bow survives at all from the fourteenth or fifteenth centuries, but the osteological evidence demonstrates that arrow wounds were not unlike modern-day gunshot wounds, something Henry V had himself experienced at Shrewsbury.[57] Mass-produced solely for military purposes, the bodkin-type arrowheads were of wrought iron with a steel surface, the arrows fletched to spin clockwise like a modern bullet, to maximise stability and accuracy.[58] By the mid-fifteenth century, a large proportion of the population seemingly owned and regularly trained with modern European weapons, evidenced in the muster rolls; Cade's revolt in 1450 was something of a military revolt coming as it did after the fall of Rouen and the Norman channel ports in the spring of 1450.[59]

The victory at Agincourt led to the conquest of Normandy 1417-20 but not without years of sieges, marches, sea battles and international alliances, finally culminating in the treaty of Troyes that confirmed the marriage to Catherine and passed the throne of France to Henry on the death of Charles, forbidding any treaty with the Dauphin.[60] In 1420, Henry V was 33 years of age, with every prospect of fathering a male heir (which he did) and living at least another twenty years (which he did not.) His father Henry IV lived to 46. The Treaty of Troyes transformed the balance of power in Europe and turned England into a mighty European power once again, though the English parliament was anxious to enforce Edward III's ruling that the kingdom of England should never be subject to the king of France.[61] It was also a serious error of judgement since it brought with it innumerable problems, not least the contradiction of acknowledging Charles VI as king but disinheriting his son, something that was always going to be difficult, if not insurmountable. When Charles died six weeks after Henry in 1422, the majority of Frenchmen came to see his heir, not Henry V's heir, as the king of France.[62]

The death of Henry V in 1422 was a massive shock. The treaty of Troyes two years before had been imposed on a sick king (whose very incapacity brought into question the legality of the treaty) by a victorious nation dependent upon alliances with Burgundy and Brittany. Now there was an infant king. Henry V had failed in the most basic task of medieval kingship: to stay alive long enough for an adult heir to assume the throne. The king's uncle Humphrey, duke of Gloucester, was appointed regent in the absence of his other uncle, John, duke of Bedford.[63]

Under the duke of Bedford, younger brother of Henry V, the English won further victories at Cravant and Verneuil, but after the coronation of Charles VII at Rheims (1428) the English began the long retreat from France. Bedford's death in 1435, mounting costs and the defection of Burgundy contributed to the direction of travel, which Henry VI's marriage to Charles VII's niece Margaret of Anjou in 1445 did little to alter, and crushing defeats in 1449-50 led to the collapse of English government in Normandy overnight, echoing the rout of 1204 under King John. In his 39-year reign Henry VI never visited Scotland or Ireland, spent a day in Monmouth, and never revisited France after his coronation aged nine.

Defeats in France played out at home. York blamed the Duke of Somerset in 1452 for the collapse in Gascony in a letter to the people of Shrewsbury; in the summer of 1453, the defeat at Castillon and the total loss of Gascony led to more turmoil in government, European territories yet again setting the pace for domestic affairs.[64] Bordeaux surrendered in July 1453 and all that remained of English possessions in France was Calais; all of Henry V's gains had been lost.

It was not the end of the 'Hundred Years' War' though. There was a very real possibility of an English return from the late 1450s to the 1470s. Charles VII of France wrote to James II of Scotland in 1457 that 'every person knows that it (Gascony) has been English for the space of three hundred years, and the people of the region are at heart entirely inclined to the English.'[65] In 1468 Edward IV told parliament that he proposed to go over the sea into France, in alliance with Burgundy and Brittany, and recover the possessions within the duchies of Normandy, Gascony, Guienne and others.[66] The treaty in July 1474 between Edward IV and Duke Charles was a formal alliance wherein Charles recognised Edward's title to the crown of France and in June 1475, Edward IV crossed the Channel with an invasion army. Duke Charles did not join him and at the Treaty of Piquigny in August, total withdrawal, a seven-year truce, a marriage alliance with the king's daughter Elizabeth and Prince Charles of France, and an annual pension was agreed.[67] This was politically misjudged and not popular since it abandoned the age-old claims to titles and possessions in France.

After Bosworth in 1485, the French could deal with Brittany without repercussions from England, which they did in 1488 at the battle of

St Aubin and in 1491 entered the duchy to force the hand in marriage of Duchess Anne to Charles VIII, ending Breton independence and hopes that England could exploit such tensions anymore. This ended the French annexations from 1450 to 1491 of Normandy, Burgundy and Brittany, and it also ended the web of dynastic connections, territorial ambitions and commercial interests that had bound English and French monarchies together since the twelfth century. From there on, a new cultural and political landscape was drawn.

The English crown effectively abandoned its claims to overlordship in Ireland and much of Scotland in the fifteenth century owing to the war with France and internal divisions during Henry VI's reign. The Anglo-Scottish treaty of 1475 and the 'perpetual peace' of 1502 marked a significant shift in relations. In Ireland, the primary concern was security and the Anglo-Irish magnates co-existed with the Gaelic ruling elite; effective rule from Dublin was impossible and the earls of Ormond and Kildare were the real power, not the crown.

In 1500 England and Wales had 25,000 men under arms (1% of the population) compared with Spain (20,000) and France (18,000). This was to change dramatically through the sixteenth century: Spain in 1532 had 100,000, France 32,000, but England still only 30,000 c. 1600.[68] The imperial pretensions of late medieval England would soon dissipate, though not without a last gasp effort from the revanchist Henry VIII. The French invasion of Italy in 1494 during the reign of Charles VIII marked the beginning of a transformation in European politics. By the 1520s, the Habsburgs and Valois were fighting their dynastic wars on Italian soil and in 1527 the Habsburg troops sacked Rome, a European event that was to alter English history dramatically and permanently.

SIXTEEN

Burning Books, Burning People: The End of the Medieval Millennium

The wars in Europe honed English identity and the late fourteenth century saw the resurgence of the English language after three centuries. This did not mean that England was turning away from Rome; far from it, punitive heresy laws crushed the anti-clerical movement of Lollardy, and England was still a staunchly Catholic country in the early sixteenth-century. There was very limited social mobility at the higher levels, though serfdom disappeared, and a new class of tenant farmers emerged. The personality of the king was still paramount and the collapse of central government in 1453 was in part due to the health of Henry VI, and in part to the defeats in France. Overmighty nobles plunged England into extremely violent conflict lasting intermittently for thirty years, with the houses of York and 'Tudor' both dependent on Continental alliances. Medieval England was brought to an abrupt end by the command of Henry VIII when the monasteries and libraries were destroyed and all links to Rome broken. The new histories of Protestant England invented King Alfred and King John as heroes and the 'Anglo-Saxons' emerge as authentic warriors of old England. The good, the bad and the ugly were immortalised in fiction by the greatest of all post-medieval writers, William Shakespeare.

The French wars impacted on the increasingly Anglican church. Most fourteenth-century popes were French-born and from 1308 to 1378 lived at Avignon. It was calculated with indignation in 1376 that the court of Rome attracted 'more than five times the tax of all the profits which belonged to the king each year from his whole realm', through simony, papal translations, debts and subsidies, so much so that clerks lost hope of preferment and people were neglecting to send their children to school;

it should be considered 'how law and reason and good faith' required that what was given to the Church should be spent for the honour of God and 'not spent outside the realm on enemies'.[1] The anti-papal statutes of 1351 and 1353, the *praemunire*, was extended in 1393, and addressed the issue of translations, bulls and 'instruments', which were seen as 'against the king's crown and in derogation of his regality'.[2] Alien priories were confiscated in 1414, so that their levies that had been sent overseas would remain in the possession of the crown and their services be conducted by Englishmen.[3] By the fifteenth century very few foreigners were appointed to bishoprics. The Great Schism 1378-1417 resulted in two or three popes, which provided room for delay and non-compliance from the English perspective. After the London cordwainers were prohibited from selling shoes on a Sunday by papal bull in 1468, some said that the pope's curse was 'not worth a fly'.[4] Pietro Aliprando, a Milanese envoy wrote to the duke of Milan in 1472 after he had been arrested as a messenger of the pope, describing the English: 'In the morning they are as devout as angels, but after dinner they are like devils, seeking to throw the pope's messengers into the sea.'[5] He added that 'They do not keep faith and are evil islanders, who are born with tails.'

Anti-papalism fuelled by war does not mean that England was exceptional or set on the path to Reformation. The weaknesses of Henry IV's reign and threats to the Church combined to enforce strict punishment of heresy in the acts of 1401 (including the burning of heretics) and 1414, which were not repealed until 1559.[6] Henry V was an ardent heresy hunter. The Lollard threat continued to swirl around the court and the country, Oldcastle breaking from cover at the same time as the Southampton Plot, believing the king had already departed from England. The Bishop of Winchester from 1404 was Henry Beaufort, Cardinal, Papal Legate for Germany, Hungary, and Bohemia from 1427. He was also Henry V's uncle and close advisor.

The devotional fashion of later fourteenth-century England did not mirror the academic discourse. *The Book of Margery Kempe*, the earliest surviving autobiography in English (although lost until 1934) was dictated by her in her later life to a priest in the 1430s. Her faith was orthodox, but Margery was accused of Lollardy several times, on one occasion a crowd demanding she be burnt.[7] Lollardy had similar spiritual roots but was the only significant heretical movement to occur in medieval England and it was not the dawn of the English Reformation. John Wycliffe, an Oxford don, inspired a series of English works and the translation of the Bible into English in 1396. Lollardy's anticlericalism appealed to a wide audience that included noblemen, courtiers and scholars and the devotion to the Scriptures and an English bible anticipated – but did not lead to – key ideas in later English Protestantism.[8] In 1431 there was evidence of 'certain insurrections' involving Lollards and other traitors at Coventry, regions near London, Salisbury, Oxford – William Perkins calling himself 'Jack Sharp' being a particular leader.[9] Lollardy failed ultimately though; and Wycliffe's corpse was exhumed and burnt in 1428 following the Council of Constance, which reflected how English clericalism was still very much in the mainstream. Even Robin Hood, first mentioned by Langland in 1377, was a devout Catholic, living in the forest; the ballads date from the 1450s.[10]

Where Lollardy did have a great impact was in its use of English. The Wycliffite Bible survives in over 250 manuscripts, making it the most prolific English book of the Middle Ages. The movement came at the peak of the 'quiet revolution' of the English language from 1350 to 1400. In 1381 the rebels' demands were made orally and King Richard II had to ask for the grievances to be put in writing; this contrasts with the Jack Cade 1450 revolt, where the grievances were all in writing from the outset, long and coherent documents. The first written record of speaking English in parliament is from 1362 and Henry IV spoke to parliament in English in 1399. Henry V discouraged the use of the French language in government and literate society. The London brewers wrote their ordinance in English, saying that 'our mother tongue. To wit, the English tongue, hath in modern days begun to be honourably enlarged and adorned...' The English delegation to the church Council at Constance in 1417 declared that a nation is marked off from others by 'blood relationship and habit of unity' or by peculiarities of language.

The earliest known property deed in English dates to 1376, the earliest will 1387. English was required in some rules and regulations of guilds in the reign of Edward III. Letters, business transactions, poems, recipes, and chronicles were increasingly in English, surviving in their hundreds. Wills show that owning books was a cultural habit among the better-off. The documents produced by central government, monasteries, noble households, town corporations, churches, gilds, and parishes have survived in their millions and there are archives that remain unsealed, unsorted and unread.[11] There were thousands of letters that were written daily but virtually all of them are lost, with the exception of small numbers of Paston, Stonor, Plumpton, Cely and Armburgh letters.

English was promoted by royalty, nobles and townspeople. English Miracle play cycles and poems were based on the northern European traditions (*Sir Gawain and the Green Knight*, *The Vision of Piers Plowman*) but also the French and early Italian renaissance writing of John Gower and his friend, Chaucer (*Troilus and Criseyde*, *The Canterbury Tales*). Sir John Paston's printed books in 1479 included the *Death of Arthur*, *Guy of Warwick*, *Troilus and Cressida* and other Chaucer works and romances.[12] This was the English language (which we call Middle English) that emerged triumphantly after 300 years of suppression. The English dialect was predominantly Midland English owing to the migration to

London from the midland shires and partly Lollardy, which was prevalent in the Midlands, too. Chaucer was concerned that his writings would be understood across England (some generations of schoolchildren would argue he wasn't concerned enough) but Caxton, in the 1470s, was cautiously optimistic that his books would be understood widely.

England's first national history, the *Brut* – named after Brutus, the legendary founder of the nation – emerges first as an Old French prose chronicle *c.* 1300, mostly found in Middle English translations in the mid-fifteenth century and it survives in over 200 manuscripts. The continuation of the *Brut* in the late fourteenth century was the first history composed in English prose since the 'Anglo-Saxon' Chronicles.[13] During the fifteenth century English almost entirely replaced Anglo-Norman and to a considerable extent Latin, as the normal language for the writing of history in England. Fact and fiction mingled freely in this new world. Caxton's prologue to *King Arthur* (1485) presents Arthur as historical fact, up there with Charlemagne and Godfrey of Boulogne, the crusader, although he concedes that 'various men hold the opinion that there was no such Arthur ... because some chronicles make no mention of him.' Caxton's evidence included the sepulchre at Glastonbury, Geoffrey of Monmouth's book, the print of his seal in St Edmund's shrine at Westminster, Gawain's skull at Dover castle, the round table at Winchester.[14] To be fair to Caxton, he was only drawing upon centuries of fake news, given what we have already seen about Geoffrey and Glastonbury.

Gaining entry to the aristocracy was virtually – but not entirely – impossible. Although the Black Death stimulated some upward social mobility it remained limited and successful careerists were a rarity since landed wealth was usually gained by inheritance or marriage, heiresses often the significant element of this class continuity.[15] The Commons petitioned the king in 1390 that anyone with rental income of less than 40s a year or priest or clerk with less than £10 preferment 'shall not keep any greyhound' if they were not fastened up or had not had their claws cut. The king consented, adding hounds, ferrets, and any other devices to take or destroy beasts of the forest, including hares, rabbits or 'other sport of gentlefolk'.[16] The sumptuary law of 1483 declared that only royalty could wear gold, or silk of purple colour on pain of £20 forfeiture; a duke could wear gold 'tissue', a lord plain cloth of gold, a knight velvet in their doublets and gowns, esquires damask or satin.[17] No man under the estate of lord could wear any kind of woollen cloth made 'outside this realm of England, Ireland, Wales and Calais, nor wear any furs of sables; no servants are to wear any cloth which exceeds 2 shillings price, or their wives to wear any clothing of higher price allowed to their husbands.' This petition arose because of the 'excessive apparel' and 'lack of execution of the same statutes', which clearly suggests upwardly mobile folk asserting themselves illegally.

Chaucer (writing in English) lampooned these social aspirations in his Canterbury pilgrims, most notably the Franklin, but the Knight, too, was satirised by Chaucer in a carefully coded message to a knowing audience as Terry Jones has demonstrated.[18] Chaucer himself, though, managed to achieve just that kind of social elevation since his marriage to Philippa Roet catapulted the former page and pantry girl (already established on an annuity) into the ranks of high society when Philippa's sister, Katherine Swynford, married John of Gaunt, duke of Lancaster, in 1394. Chaucer's son Thomas had a successful career as politician and courtier under Richard II and Henry IV and his daughter Alice, married the Duke of Suffolk; her grandson was John de la Pole, earl of Lincoln, Richard III's designated heir. The rise of the de la Poles (from wool merchants to Earls of Suffolk and ancestors to Yorkist claimants to the throne after 1485) was extraordinary but singular.

Chaucer's mercenary-knight appears in real life in Hampshire, where only one individual in two centuries married into the landed class from obscure origins and founded a lasting dynasty.[19] John Sandys was a classic soldier of fortune in the French wars of the later fourteenth century, making his name in the retinue of the Black Prince, even mentioned in the account of the battle of Nájera in 1367. Without landed wealth he could only go so far, so he abducted and married the wealthy Joan Bridges in 1376 (widowed twice over but still in her twenties), appearing on indictments for rape, murder, and huge debts. He was cleared of all charges (just before the Black Prince died, fortunately) and was knighted on another campaign abroad and thereafter settled into the life of landed gentleman. Joan inherited a family estate in Hampshire as well as properties from her first two husbands, which gave Sandys the qualification he needed to become MP and Sheriff for Hampshire. After the Peasants' Revolt, Sir John, as he now was, commanded the garrison at Southampton Castle and took an active role in crushing the rebellion. In 1393 he dined with the Bishop of Winchester's household only weeks before Richard II and his queen dined with the bishop and 234 others; the poacher turned gamekeeper may not have been born with a silver spoon, but he quickly learnt how to use one. If Sandys was Chaucer's 'worthy man' with his fustian tunic 'stained and dark', then Joan was almost Chaucer's wife of Bath, since she married a fourth time after Sandys' death in 1395, to Sir Thomas Skelton. It was her children with Sandys who continued the family estates into the sixteenth century when Sir William Sandys became Lord Sandys, 1st Baron of the Vyne, twice visited by Henry VIII; not a bad outcome for the ancestral adventurer from Cheshire, but again, it was not usual.

The community of knights and esquires that John Sandys elbowed his way into dominated the political offices as JPs, MPs and Sheriffs, though to what extent they operated within the artificial 'county' community has been a matter of debate.[20] It was more than likely that they saw themselves as regional, rather than 'county' based, which was after all a fiscal unit of government and more recent studies return to the horizontal parochial ties of patronage, localism and topography determining the *modus operandi* of the ruling class.[21] The disputed concept of 'bastard feudalism' meant that service was flexible in the great households of the crown, nobility and clergy, but land was still the key, since military service, trade and political and ecclesiastical office were ultimately limited.[22] 'Feudal rights' were neither extinct nor moribund but continued to operate alongside other financial, social and ideological links between man, lord and king, remaining a source of income and of personal connections.[23]

The legal profession remained, then as now, the preserve of the gentry. In 1475 William Worcester in his *Boke of Noblesse*, lamented the fact that the young nobles did not learn the art of war and schooling of arms as their ancestors had done in the time of King Edward III, instead now wasting their time at law school, in the courts.[24] Fortescue also describes the monopoly of the legal profession by the nobility and gentry, since it cost £13 a year plus servants to attend the Inns of Court, so that there 'was scarcely a man learned in the laws to be found in the realm who is not noble'. Attending the Inns of Court was essential because the laws of England are learned in three languages – English, French, and Latin – whereas the universities use only Latin.[25]

Villages collectively felt more independence and confidence as traditional lordship ebbed away in the fifteenth century. Contractions to the demesne estates and commutation of labour services may have been accelerated but not always initiated by the Black Death. On the Winchester bishopric, the 10,000 acres under demesne in 1301 had fallen to 7,000 by 1350 and to 4,500 by 1410.[26] John Rous, writing in the 1480s, describes the destruction and depopulation of villages (due to the impact of enclosure this time) and 'swarms of beggars'.[27] Changes in the tenurial structures gave rise to social advancements in the lesser gentry or yeomanry group, but these were not often welcomed. The Paston bailiff, Richard Calle, fell in love with Margery Paston, who was disowned by her mother and brothers, and Margery was left nothing in her mother's will.[28] The 'British', enslaved by the 'English' and made into serfs by the Normans, were now free, but probably constituted the bulk of the agrarian labouring classes, unable to benefit from any of these socio-economic changes that were moving at a glacial pace.

The enlargement of the franchise did little for the very lowest classes, either. County elections took place in the county court, presided over by the sheriff (acting as returning officer). They were dominated by the leading county gentry – who usually took it in turns to be MP, sheriff and JP – although the freeholders had a say but not the villeins, who may have been present. Elections by indenture (1406) came about owing to the 'grievous complaints' about the election of knights of the shire for parliament 'which are sometimes made by the partiality of the sheriffs', so in future, elections were to be held 'freely' in the full shire-court in the presence of the electors (sometimes up to 200 people in Buckinghamshire in 1429, for example), and the names sealed in indentures and tacked to the same writ of parliament; a 1410 statute fined any sheriff £100 if they infringed upon this (which suggests that they did).[29] The main reason behind the election statutes were concerns over lawless behaviour at large gatherings at the county court. With all wanting a voice and without any of the trappings of the modern ballot, force could prevail.[30]

Plague and the resultant population decline had created opportunity: low rents, long leases and greater social mobility exposed county elections to a more popular mandate. But when the parliament of 1429-30 agreed to the 40-shilling franchise, this limited rather than extended the franchise because of the large number of people attending parliamentary elections.[31] This limitation was not ended until 1918.[32] The 40-shilling restriction permitted superior peasants and middling farmers the vote (yeomen and husbandmen) but not wage labourers and villeins. The total electorate may have numbered about 15,000 (1% of the population). There was no enlargement of the electorate in the boroughs. The 40s freehold rule was never applied generally, even though town dwellers now formed 20% of the population.[33] Urban MPs were chosen by an oligarchic elite, usually leading councillors and merchants.

Later medieval England has been called the 'Age of the Household'. The royal household dominated administration and politics, imitated by the aristocracy, who managed their estates, resolved disputes by law and through violence, and in wider society, regulated moral standards, work and family life.[34] The Yorkist dynasty had the household at the centre of government, making the chamber, not the exchequer, the chief financial institution; household staff increased and the knights of the body rose from four to thirty, emulating the courtly practice of the Valois dukes of Burgundy, all in contrast to the smaller household of Henry VI, which was blamed for impoverishing the crown and losing Normandy. Sixty or so magnate families were pre-eminent in England, fewer after the civil wars of the 1460s-70s. Three dynasties seized the crown in the period 1399-1485, each from the magnate class; security lay with them rather than any civil service and created a sense of the monarch being *primus inter pares* (with Henry Tudor barely an equal at all). Henry IV came from the richest and greatest noble family; his father, John of Gaunt, was duke of Lancaster and worth £12,000 a year. These estates passed into the Lancastrian monarchy 1399-61. The Yorkist dynasty, arising from the earls of March, were not so rich, but the accession of Henry VII, earl of Richmond, combined not only York and Lancaster but Neville and Beaufort, which established the firmest control over the nobility and gentry.

Government and the political system did not change fundamentally between 1399 and 1509.[35] Government did become more sedentary; all 31 parliaments between 1339 and 1371 met at Westminster and nowhere else after 1459. English monarchy was still semi-spiritual at the beginning of the fifteenth century, when 'majesty' become a common form of address. The monarch could directly intervene in local affairs: in 1461, John Paston was summoned by privy seal to the king's presence after a fracas with the sheriff, Sir John Howard, responding at the third summons on pain of death.[36] Sir John Fortescue, in his *Governance of England* (1470s), differentiates between the *dominium regale* (where the king can make the laws and tax his people without their assent, such as France) and the *dominium politicum et regale* which includes England and Scotland, where the king may not rule his people 'by other laws such as they assent to', a direct link to Magna Carta and the development of parliament under Henry III.[37] Fortescue advised that the council should include twelve spiritual men and twelve temporal men from all parts of the country, on oath and without any pay except from the king; the chancellor shall be president and 'have supreme rule of all the council'.[38]

During the reigns of the three Lancastrian kings, the scope of the treason laws was significantly expanded, and in 1440 *imagining* the death of the king could bring the death penalty. In 1450 two men, John and William Merfield, were indicted for treasonable language, saying that the king was a 'natural fool' and 'no person able to rule the land'.[39] They had also threatened to rise again and leave no gentleman alive, following the Cade rebellion in May. The Cade rebellion originated in Kent, like the 1381 Revolt. Led by John Cade (calling himself John 'Amend-All'), as in 1381 the rebels claimed that England had been ruled by untrue counsel and written petitions were sent to parliament at Westminster. The mob murdered several nobles, including the treasurer, Lord Say and his son-in-law, former MP and Sheriff for Kent. Fighting took place in the city until Cade was captured and beheaded, although London remained in a state of fear and uproar, more due to the breaking conflict between the Dukes of York and Somerset.[40] Jack Cade's rebellion in 1450 was part of a chain of popular memory spanning the rebellions of 1381, 1469 and 1497 in that they were all concerned with the duty to restore the principle of the commonweal and provoked by economic recession in most cases, led by the middling band agriculturalists, craftsmen and retailers, and sustained by class hatred between village communities and the gentry.[41] These rebellions in turn influenced magnate activities in the constitutional crises of the middle fifteenth century.[42]

Government remained deeply personal. Without a sane and rational king, government could not function. In 1433, the abbot of St Albans declared that 'the king knows no superior to himself within the realm.'[43] But in August 1453 Henry VI suffered a catastrophic breakdown, probably a psychotic illness perhaps triggered by the English defeat at Castillon, that left him incapacitated for eighteen months; it was concealed for eight months but his inability to use the great seal of England eventually revealed the truth, since government itself was paralysed.[44] In January 1454, John Stodely, agent of the duke of Norfolk, wrote that when the new-born Prince of Wales was presented to the king by the Duke of Buckingham, the king showed no response.[45] He describes the tense atmosphere in London as the queen made a bill to take control over administration of the realm and the great nobles in London were arming their household troops in readiness for the inevitable power struggle (including the archbishop of Canterbury, Cardinal and chancellor John Kempe.) In November 1455 the duke of York was made protector and defender of the realm, the Prince of Wales being then only two years of age; the duke was also given powers to summon and dismiss parliament but his rule exacerbated the breakdown of order instigated by the king's illness.[46] Thus it was that the son of the earl of Cambridge, executed on a trumped-up charge of treason in 1415, now held the reins of government. The only crown he ever wore was a paper one with his head fixed to Micklegate Bar in York, although two of his sons would be king.

Defeats in France, the mental collapse of the monarch and dynastic rivalries in the royal house that stemmed from the 1399 Lancastrian usurpation all coalesced into what has been called, inaccurately and anachronistically, the 'Wars of the Roses'. The conflicts between 1455 and 1485 in fact only took place on a total of 428 days, still less than eighteen months if we include Stoke in 1487.[47] On the one hand this was a dynastic 'feud' (to employ an Early English concept) between several branches of the royal family that had little impact on the country; on the other hand, it involved blood-letting on a scale never been seen before in England, including nepoticide (the 'Princes in the Tower') and fratricide (George, duke of Clarence).[48] Trust and honour were trampled into the mud of Towton, Barnet, Tewkesbury, and Bosworth. Chivalry went out of the window as the battlefield became an excuse for score-settling executions. The duke of York was killed in 1460 at the battle of Wakefield, his son Edmund chased down and executed soon afterwards; Henry VI was captured at the battle of Northampton, found wandering on the battlefield at St Albans, deposed, restored, and eventually murdered in the Tower; his son was killed at or soon after the battle of Tewkesbury and Richard III died violently at Bosworth, also in a battle-execution, unhorsed and bare-headed. The jury is still out – and always will be – on the murder of Edward V and Prince Richard, but their deaths suited both Richard III and his successor, Henry VII.[49]

The Lancastrian dynasty was extinct and the Yorkist clan imploded, the last male executed in 1499 by Henry VII. England was exceptional in

Europe for its depositions and royal murders. Many dozens of magnates were slain along with their heirs. More significantly, where the wars in France had minimal impact on England, the great households and their retinues dragged tens of thousands of Englishmen to their deaths in the battles between 1460 and 1487. These battles were fought between intensely local armies from a shire or groups of shires at the expense of any sense of English nationality.[50] The battle of Towton (1461) resulted in the deaths of 28,000 soldiers in a single day, according to contemporary sources, which are likely to be exaggerated (and downplayed by the Tudor dynasty who lost that battle but won the war).[51] Towton remains the bloodiest battle fought on English soil, evidenced by the savage wounds inflicted on the soldiers found in a mass grave in 1996, some of whom had dozens of blunt force and blade wounds indicative of close-combat slaughter.[52]

The Continental possessions had a great impact on York's powerbase as Richard of York associated himself with the patriotic bitterness over the losses of Normandy in 1450 and Gascony in 1453, stoking fears that Queen Margaret was planning to betray Calais to the French and put the government of England into enemy hands. Richard of York and the Nevilles preserved good relations with Burgundy and exploited the tensions between Duke Philip and King Charles, Warwick and Salisbury specifically joining York in 1459 to seize power from Queen Margaret; a Burgundian troop fought with Edward of York at Towton, the victory that put Edward on the throne.[53]

Edward IV's fall from power in 1470 was a result of French support for Margaret and war on Burgundy. Edward naturally sought refuge in Burgundy with his brother-in-law, Charles the Bold, and it was from Flushing in the Burgundian Low Countries, with Flemish and English soldiers, that he launched his come-back in March 1471. The usurpation of Richard III brought foreign interests back into English dynastic politics. Richard supported Duke Francis of Brittany in a coalition of Habsburg, Orleans and Breton, attempting to control the young French king, Charles VIII. Henry of Richmond, the new figurehead of opposition to Richard, slipped out of Brittany only hours ahead of troops sent by Francis to arrest him, seeking refuge in the court of Charles VIII. The fear of coalition between England and Brittany made Henry Tudor an object of interest to the French crown and it made Bosworth a victory for French royal policy.

For only the second time since the creation of England in the tenth century, a reigning monarch was killed in battle. It was French troops paid in part by a grant from the French crown that fought against Richard III at Bosworth. The French troops recruited by Henry had been drilled in Swiss fashion in a tactic first used in the battle of Grandson (Switzerland) in 1476 and would be used again at Fornovo (Italy). At the moment Richard launched his ill-fated charge across the entire field of battle, Henry's troops closed around him in a square formation, presenting the eighteen-foot-long pikes in three ranks, something that took years of training and something Richard and his mounted troops had never seen before and could never break through.[54]

The Middle Ages did not end on 22 August 1485, a turning point so beloved of textbooks, school curricula and even professional historians (until relatively recently). It ended with the Reformation and the Dissolution of the monasteries in the late 1530s and 1540s, two generations later. The Battle of Bosworth had none of the impact that the Battle of Hastings had four centuries earlier. Almanacs, the most important means of spreading some sense of history among the population, do not normally include 1485 among their significant dates.[55] The 'Tudor Age' did not exist. There was no awakening as England marched from the barbarous medieval era into the sunny uplands of the 'early modern' age. The word 'Tudor' was hardly used or known in the sixteenth century. The Tudor name was considered an embarrassment in England; Henry VII's claim rested on his mother's Lancastrian lineage, his marriage to Elizabeth of York, parliamentary assent and his victory in battle, the final two taking precedence lest he be seen to only have a crown matrimonial and not in his own right. Little was made of his grandfather, Owen Tudor, who had married Henry V's widow, Queen Catherine; his tomb was lost at the Dissolution. Both Henry VIII and Elizabeth I were happier with their Yorkist ancestry rather than the dubious Lancastrian line, Henry VIII choosing to be buried at St George's Chapel, Windsor, close to his grandfather Edward IV, rather than at Westminster with his father.[56]

Henry VII claimed the throne by right of conquest, grant of parliament and marriage to Elizabeth of York, in that order (Elizabeth was not crowned until 1487, an unprecedented delay that reveals Henry VII's priorities). Henry VII's title was confirmed by parliament, and in 1490 the pope issued a bull confirming the matrimony and conjunction between Henry VII and princess Elizabeth with all their issue lawfully born.[57] The cult of Arthur and the concept of England as 'Britain' reached its apogee with the heir to the throne set to become the first real 'King Arthur', and with Henry VII himself being of Welsh origin.[58] The chamber was re-established by Henry VII as the principal financial institution in the 1490s, the knights of the body more than doubled from forty in 1483 to ninety-three and the court was magnificent in its chivalric display and ceremony.[59] Henry VII was also steeped in the European diplomacy of the 1470s-80s and had grown up amid the domestic plots of the 1460s. Politics became firmly centred on the king's court where loyalty to the person of the king overrode other ties of service and loyalty. This was part of a European shift in politics, as well as the character and circumstance of the king himself.[60] Henry VII's rule was conservative and even the punitive measures he is known for were in line with established legislation; expert management of the newly restored system was the secret to success.[61]

England was staunchly Catholic well into the sixteenth century.[62] A visitor to England in 1497, probably Italian, described the richness of the tomb of St Thomas at Canterbury, the wealth and prosperity of London (which gets very muddy), the great number of churches, and the extreme dislike of foreigners.[63] An Italian visitor to England in 1500 still reported that 'the English are great lovers of themselves and of everything belonging to them. They think that there are no other men than themselves, and no other world than England...'[64] The writer specifically refers to Bede's description of 'Britain'. Although they all attend Mass every day, there are, however, 'many who have various opinions concerning religion'. They have 'an antipathy to foreigners'. The sale of tin and wool brought great wealth, much of which was displayed in parish churches and the 'enormously rich' Benedictine, Carthusian and Cistercian monasteries, along with splendid tombs of English saints, especially the tomb of St Thomas at Canterbury, covered in plates of pure gold studded with precious stones – sapphires, diamonds, rubies, emeralds. The number of religious houses was 'prodigious'. Both visitors highlight the wealth and richness of churches, tombs, and monasteries (plus a dislike of foreigners based on a fear of a tiny minority, the population of England was 2.25 million with an alien population at 30,000 – only 1.3%).[65]

In less than a decade it was all gone. Between 1536 and 1540 every single abbey and priory in England, 800 in total, was dissolved or forcibly closed; as many as 14,000 monks, nuns and friars were turned out and 200 or so people were executed for opposing the Dissolution. Dissolving spiritual houses was not new; alien houses had been shut down in the fourteenth and fifteenth centuries and Wolsey had himself suppressed over twenty small monasteries; at Bayham Abbey, East Sussex this was met with fierce resistance by the locals. The Carthusians refused to accept Henry's supremacy in 1534 and twenty of them were executed or starved to death in prison. The Act of 1536 suppressed all the houses with less than £200 a year and fewer than 12 inmates.

The leaders of the Pilgrimage of Grace in 1536 were initially pardoned but this was overturned and more abbots and priors were executed; Furness Abbey 'surrendered' but the larger monasteries still hoped to survive, even as late as 1538.[66] It was not to be, and they all went, monks pensioned off if they were lucky, taking books and possessions with them if they could, but most of the vast wealth was sent to the king's receiver at the Tower of London. Bury St Edmunds had been relieved of 5,000 marks' worth of gold and jewels in 1538 and at the suppression in November 1539, a further 68kg of precious metal altar plate. Lead was stripped from the roofs and melted into large bars, and the cloisters and towers systematically pulled down using teams of masons, carpenters and plumbers and picked clean by locals. At Roche Abbey the lead was melted using the choir-stalls as fuel and the locals plundered what they could. There was no demurral from the Catholic and conservative gentry about what they were doing: Sir Anthony Browne destroyed the monastic church at Battle Abbey but made a Catholic will requesting the saying of masses in the parish church.

Medieval England was physically as well as spiritually destroyed, after 1536. Over 90% of medieval literature was lost in an orgy of vandalism in what was also a European-wide movement of iconoclasm.[67] Only 1,000 manuscripts from the sixth to the sixteenth century survived the Reformation; 6 out of 600 books from Worcester Priory survived, most of Oxford university library was either burned or disappeared and 3,000 books at Glastonbury vanished, accumulated over a millennium.[68] There were 400 medieval libraries in the smaller monastic houses which entirely or almost entirely perished.[69] Manuscripts at Malmesbury were thrown into the bakers' ovens. Rood-screens, stained-glass and sculptures were smashed, church plate, cups and robes stolen, frescoes scratched out or painted over, a lucky few hidden with plaster and uncovered centuries later. St Mary's Church, Kempley in Gloucestershire has the best complete set of medieval frescoes in Britain, dating from the twelfth to the fifteenth centuries; St Nicholas, Lower Oddington in Oxfordshire, has the largest Doom painting, St Peter and St Paul's, Chaldon in Surrey the best preserved and earliest Doom painting. Such surviving artwork points to the world we have lost. In churches in East Anglia, more than 550 late-medieval rood screens survive, testimony to the strong prevalence of Catholicism in the area.[70]

The great monasteries and priories were demolished wholesale, some converted into country houses, some used for local building, many left to rot in the remote valleys and hills where they eventually flourished as economic centres. Tintern, Glastonbury and Fountains Abbey are famously romantic ruins, though nothing much survives of the remote but once-powerful sites at Strata Florida (Wales) and Hailes (Gloucestershire). Titchfield (Hampshire) and Woburn (Bedfordshire) became houses, the latter the seat of the dukes of Bedford. These libraries, abbeys, artworks, and treasures were in use and flourishing right up to the Reformation; this was no decline or stagnation but a brutal and violent end to the medieval millennium.

The Henrician Reformation was a political break engineered by Cranmer and Anne Boleyn, and it was the sack of Rome in 1527 that ended Wolsey's plans for Henry's divorce from Catherine of Aragon. Henry VIII was forced to take matters into his own hands and went behind Wolsey's back, but this failed, too.[71] Only later, in Protestant mythology, does England's special purpose become apparent.[72] Catholicism became a kind of 'magic' in post-1540s England, the medieval church seen as having been endowed with 'supernatural' powers. The relics were denounced as fakes as part of the propaganda campaign against Rome from Cromwell to Elizabeth I, to shape the new post-Reformation narrative.[73] Their destruction caused outrage among Catholics, but many relics were preserved in private houses, hidden away. The dual status royal bones of earlier medieval monarchs and saints survived untouched in Westminster, Winchester and York. The destruction of the relics and tombs and executions of priests led to canonisation of the martyrs and prolonged pursuit of the relics.

The King's style was 'King of England France and Ireland, Defender of the Faith and of the Church of England and also of Ireland in Earth Supreme Head'.[74] The laws of treason changed: statutes making it treason to meddle with the succession and extended the statutes of Edward III.[75] Poisoning was ruled to be treason punishable by boiling to death (repealed in 1553); in 1534, 'diverse offences' were made treason, such as 'shameful slanders', specifically it was treason

> ...by words or in writing, or by craft imagine, invent, practice or attempt any bodily harm to be done to the King's most royal person, the Queen's, or their heirs apparent ... or slanderously and maliciously publish and pronounce, by express writing or words that the king our sovereign lord should be heretic, schismatic, tyrant, infidel or usurper of the Crown...

This was on pain of death without any benefit of sanctuary.[76] These laws explain partly why the destruction of medieval England was possible for Cromwell and his commissioners – fear of reprisal.

Henry VIII was quite possibly the best educated person ever to sit on the throne of England, but he was responsible for the destruction of art, literature, and artefacts of the previous thousand years. We could add him as our fourth king, along with Alfred, William I, and John as one of the 'makers' of England, although in this case, Henry VIII 'unmade' medieval England. As with earlier medieval England, none of this would have been possible without efficient bureaucrats in the tradition of Æthelwold, Wulfstan, the fitz Nigel dynasty, and Stephen Langton. The transformation from medieval to modern is nowhere better captured than in the persons of Thomas Wolsey, the butcher's son from Ipswich and the last Cardinal who failed to obtain Henry's divorce, and Thomas Cromwell, Putney blacksmith. Thomas Cromwell, in Hugh Trevor-Roper's words, 'overhauled the machinery of government as it had never been overhauled since the reign of Henry II. Modern history, if it begins anywhere, begins, in England, with him.'[77] That may be so, but without Henry VIII and his particular needs, there would have been no Reformation, no break from Rome and no decisive break with England's medieval past, an event that took centuries to play out.

Henry VIII's succession acts left a legacy of contradiction and the departure from common law that lay at the heart of the 1553 crisis and haunted Elizabeth's reign.[78]Treason, censorship, spies and torture became features of the Elizabethan age; threat of imminent invasion in 1588 inspired a new nationalism reflected in Shakespeare's plays, but he also illustrated political turmoil and treason and alluded to tyranny, coming close to investigation himself with the production of *Richard II* on the eve of Essex's rebellion in 1601.[79] The Armada was trumpeted as a great national victory, but the reality was that although the land forces may have been better prepared than hitherto argued, 'it is difficult to disagree that England was underprepared in ways which could have been remedied very easily.'[80]

After the loss of the last Continental possession, Calais, in 1559, and the failed Marian restoration of Catholicism, the thousand-year relationship with Rome was at an end, territorial ambitions in France had failed and imperialism in Britain was settled in Scotland and Wales, but not yet Ireland (Thomas Cromwell's collateral descendant, Oliver, would change all that). After 1559 England was thought of as an insular territory since the Channel had not been a natural border from the thirteenth to the sixteenth centuries, rather it was something of an 'Anglo-Norman inner lake'.[81]

It was never a simple 'in' or 'out' though; the Great Bible, the monument of the English Reformation, was printed in Paris.[82] In the long term, the Reformation brought England closer to Europe in other ways, into the German-Swiss Protestant sphere that included a Dutch and Hanoverian monarchy and a second 'hundred years' war' against Catholic and Revolutionary France.

Meanwhile, there was a scramble to reinvent medieval England. King John was re-cast as a proto-Protestant hero who defied Rome and France and governed the English church independently of the Pope in William Tyndale's *Obediance of a Christian Man,* 1528, Foxe's *Acts and Monuments,* and in Shakespeare's *King John,* where he emerges as a tragi-heroic figure, a reformer of the law who was betrayed by (Catholic) monks and cardinals with no reference to the Charter or to Runnymede.[83] This positive reputation of John lasted into the eighteenth century when David Hume's influential *History of England* (1754-62) returned to Matthew Paris and Roger of Wendover and the cowardice, treachery, tyranny, and cruelty of John became the established view. Sixteenth-century writers including Hall, Foxe, and Holinshed all believed the Yorkist claim was superior to the Lancastrian one; it was with Hume's *History of England* that 'Tudor England' became a cliché.[84]

Bede re-emerged in this culture war. In 1565 Roman Catholic priest and scholar Thomas Stapleton published the first modern translation of Bede's *Ecclesiastical History,* a pronounced argument for the Roman Catholic origins of the English church and its filial relationship to the bishop of Rome (dedicated to Elizabeth I from his exile in Douai).[85] The legend of the angelic slave boys become a fact in the translation and the *Ecclesiastical History* becomes a general history of England. Bede is on the list of good teachers in Foxe's *Acts and Monuments* (1570) but Matthew Parker, the first consecrated archbishop of Canterbury in 1559, needed to justify the independence of the new, national church from the papacy and Bede was marginal to this, and no further editions appeared until 1643.[86]

The Germanic and 'manly' origins of England were invented, too, which set in train the characterisation of the Saxons as 'rednecks' of the Middle Ages. Tacitus's *Germania* (discovered in 1455) became a European classic, and idealised the Germanic-speaking peoples, pure of blood and honour. Richard Verstegan's snappily titled *A Restitution of Decayed Intelligence in Antiquities concerning the Most Noble and Renowned English Nation*, first printed in 1605 and many times thereafter, emphasised the Germanic origins of the English peoples (and the Anglo-Scottish union was now an added factor of English or British identity).[87] The blood-feud was misappropriated by post-Conquest sources long before the Reformation, but the post-Reformation printing press and use of the English language popularised this 'mythistory'. It was in this context that George Puttenham used the phrase 'Anglo-Saxon' for the first time in the English language, in 1569.

The greatest of all English writers, William Shakespeare, a glover's son from Stratford-on-Avon, wrote in the midst of this swirl of political chicanery and religious turmoil and his works, like the poem *Beowulf*, tell us of a world gone but not forgotten. In some ways his world seems entirely untouched by fundamental Protestant doctrine since his plays are full of priests, friars and monks going about their business, and cardinals and bishops are treated in a matter-of-fact way.[88] There was no meaningful distinction in popular culture between Shakespeare's day and what we call 'medieval England'. Growing up in Warwickshire in the 1560s – a deeply conservative area that retained strong links to the 'old faith' – continuity, not disruption, characterised his view of English history to some extent.[89] John Shakespeare's move into Stratford exposed the family to the radical changes of the Reformation. Stratford was in the Worcester diocese and the bishop from 1535 was Hugh Latimer; but more significantly, the Gild of the Holy Cross was dissolved in the 1540s, the semi-official governing body of the town, almshouses, and school.[90] The Corporation, founded in 1553, consisted of a variety of businessmen of differing views all keen to maintain their new-found status. The first post-Reformation schoolmaster, William Smart, was a Protestant, ordained by Ridley, the reformist bishop, in post until 1565. However, the schoolmasters (Simon Hunt, Thomas Jenkins and John Cottam) employed at the time Shakespeare attended might have had Catholic sympathies, anomalous in a town of growing Protestantism (the town listed very few recusants).[91] Shakespeare had a typical second-generation post-Reformation upbringing. Visiting his mother's family at Wilmcote in the countryside brought him into contact with the recent past, redolent of rural medieval England. His grandfather Robert Arden was a prosperous farmer and left his daughter Mary 30 acres and an eight-ox plough team in his will.[92]

Shakespeare's upbringing, classical education and his father's financial ruin and disgrace all influenced his plays, but his writing was detached in other ways (even to the point of leaving behind all traces of Warwickshire and Cotswold dialect) with no history play set in his own lifetime.[93] In popular memory, Shakespeare's history *is* England's history, and where there was base-metal, Shakespeare spun gold.[94] The 'little band' of the *History of Henry V* becomes the 'band of brothers'; the island 'content with its own' in the *Dialogue of the Exchequer* becomes 'this sceptre'd isle'. Prince Hal transforms into a battle-hardened ruthless king and hangs Bardolph (but the massacre of the French prisoners is omitted) and Richard III reaches peak monstrosity.[95]

These are not entirely fantasies: Henry V is a complex, flawed person in the plays as in life and he did win an astonishing victory at Agincourt, though with rather more losses than the twenty-five in *Henry V*. Shakespeare confronts Richard II's usurpation and Henry IV's guilt head-on. Richard III's recently discovered body (if it is him) bears witness to the number of battle-wounds that must have occurred when he was unhorsed, just as near-contemporary sources depict; Shakespeare simply put the famous words into his mouth.[96] The remarkable discovery of Richard III under a carpark in Leicester also showed him to have had scoliosis of the spine, but this presents a dilemma to the Ricardians, since it is a kind of Schrödinger's hunchback; he has a hunchback so he must be Richard, but the hunchback was invented by Tudor propaganda to create a monster. Despite the many factual errors, telescoped and invented timelines and scenes, so convincing is Shakespeare's genius, where the written word aligns with spoken verse more perfectly than ever before or since, that we want to believe it is true.

For a brief period, England turned inwards, away from Catholic Europe. Henry VIII married four English women and Elizabeth I never married. For the first time since 1066 England was not a possession nor possessed of any overseas territories. But in 1600 the East India Company received its royal charter and in 1607 the Virginia Company of London founded James Fort, also known as Jamestown, the first permanent English settlement in the Americas, both these forerunners of England's global future.

Alfred's *Angelcynn* were about to make their presence felt on the world stage and Æthelstan's *Englalond* would become something else altogether: Great Britain.

The 1,000-year *ríce*: Hidcote Bartrim, Gloucestershire. Ten dwellings in 2022, Domesday Book records 11 households in 1086. The cottages in the foreground are all nineteenth-century reconstructions. (Author's collection)

AFTERWORD

Upstairs, Downton?

To recall the infamous line from the movie *Pulp Fiction* with regards to 'getting medieval' cited at the beginning, one hopes that this book has conjured such kingly wealth, learning and culture, all embedded within a landscape rich with monuments and memorials, as to lay the ghost of the 'dark ages' and the pejorative use of the word 'medieval'.

It is a world we have lost but is still very much with us in some ways. England today is headed by a monarch descended from Alfred the Great.[1] The monarch is Head of State, Supreme Governor of the Church, and the British Armed Forces. Most people (62%) still support having a monarchy.[2] The English/British paradigm persists: 80% of the residents of England identify strongly as English and 82% identify strongly as British (the same proportion across all generations aged 18-64); 76% felt strongly that England's history and heritage contributed to their identity.[3]

The landscape of Domesday England is remarkably unchanged. The Church of England owns 175,000 acres, making it the 4th largest landowner in England in 2020; the Crown Estates (including the Duchies of Cornwall and Lancaster and the Sandringham Estate, landward acres, foreshore and estuarial riverbeds), own 1 million acres, placing the crown second largest landowner in 2020, after the Public Sector (which includes local authorities, Forestry Commission and MOD, 2.7 million).[4]

There are around 16,000 churches in the care of the Church of England plus 350 deconsecrated churches in the care of the Churches Conservation Trust; 6,000 churches have a weekly attendance of below 16 in the congregation but 85% of the population visit a church each year.[5] A quarter of primary schools, over 200 secondary schools and 500 independent schools are Church of England (4,644 out of a total of 24,000); one million children attend Church of England schools.[6] The continuing presence of 26 bishops in the House of Lords – the only legislative assembly in the twenty-first century to include ecclesiasts except in Iran – is a legacy of the Middle Ages.

So, too, are the 92 hereditary peers who sit in the Lords, who include the 22nd Earl of Shrewsbury (Talbot, created 1442). 30% of England is owned by the aristocracy and gentry, some of whom have later medieval Norman-French ancestors. England's richest young man in 2018 was the 7th Duke of Westminster (Hugh Grosvenor) worth an estimated £10 billion, a descendant of a follower of William the Conqueror; Ralph Percy, current duke of Northumberland, is the second largest private landowner in England, his ancestor William of Percy listed in Domesday Book with over hundred manors. The 19th Earl of Derby (Edward Stanley) is descended from the 1st Earl of Derby (Thomas) who sided with Henry VII at Bosworth.

Not only do the aristocracy still control the private estates in 2022 but they remain guardians of the heritage, too. Aristocrats of ancient lineage have opened their houses to the public commercially: Arundel Castle (Duke of Norfolk); Woburn Abbey (Duke of Bedford); Blenheim Palace (Duke of Marlborough); Longleat (Marquis of Bath); Burghley House (Lord Cecil); Alnwick Castle (Earls of Northumberland); Chatsworth House (Duke of Devonshire); Stonor Park (Lord Camoys). Many others continue to live in their ancestral homes which are maintained by the National Trust (for example Apsley House, Duke of Wellington, Petworth House, Lord Egremont, Plas Newydd, Marquis of Anglesey). *Brideshead Revisited,* the novel of aristocratic decline published in 1944 but set soon after the First World War, was, in Evelyn Waugh's own words in 1962, a 'panegyric preached over an empty coffin', since it was impossible to foresee the present 'cult' of the English country house which had seemed then 'doomed to decay and spoliation like the monasteries in the sixteenth century'.[7]

History has become heritage. The heritage industry provides fact and fantasy, from historical sites and artefacts to the 'experience' of the Middle Ages, theme parks and re-enactments. Evocative names such as 'Wessex' and 'Northumbria' entice one to visit mighty fortresses and, romantic ruins. 'Living history' offers jousting, falconry, archery, knights and minstrels as a form of 'edutainment'.[8] The heritage sector in England produces a total GVA of £31 billion and provides over 464,000 jobs; there are 213.4 million visits pa with a spend of £17 billion.[9] Compare this with the car industry of £16 billion, employing 166,000 people.[10] It was anticipated that £1.2 billion would be invested into the UK's heritage between 2019 and 2024.[11] All this was of course jeopardised by the pandemic and lockdowns of 2020/2021.

The most visited places are the official heritage sites beloved of 'Ladybird' histories: The Tower of London, 2.8 million visitors in 2018, Westminster Abbey 1.5m, Roman Baths 1.3m, Hampton Court Palace 900,000.[12] The Historic Royal Palaces (Tower of London, Hampton Court Palace, Kensington Palace, the Banqueting House, Whitehall, Kew Palace and Hillsborough Castle) had 5 million visitors 2018/19.[13]

The National Trust portfolio includes 200 houses, 41 castles and chapels and 25 medieval barns.[14] Top spots included Fountains Abbey with 403,591 visitors; 246,957 to Corfe Castle; 156,769 to Bodiam Castle; 74,421 to Sutton Hoo; 73,167 to Lindisfarne Castle.

English Heritage, with over 400 sites and monuments, including 66 castles, 84 ecclesiastical sites, one battlefield, 27 forts and defences, and 47 halls and houses, had more than 6 million visitors 2018/19 (over 300,000 of them school children.)[15] The most visited places 2019 included Stonehenge (1.5 million), second place Dover Castle (350,000), Tintagel 4th place (170,000); other medieval sites visited include Clifford's Tower (150,000), Battle Abbey (126,000), Kenilworth (112,000) and Framlingham (90,000) with other famous castles and abbeys such as Lindisfarne, Old Sarum, Warkworth, Goodrich, Dunstanburgh all around 50,000 visitors.

The past is a foreign country; they do things differently there.'[16] This may be a truism but in packaging and cleansing the past into signposted, guided 'visitor experiences' we are simply remaking the pageants of the earlier twentieth century and paying homage to lords and ladies. We have been beguiled into accepting the feudal past as retold to us by the current feudal lords. Tea and scones gloss the servitude of our ancestors and forestall us asking questions, something the heritage industry is having to confront.[17] Country houses are not the heritage of us all; it is not an authentic common heritage. They are a narrow slice of elite history, artefacts that have survived now presented as everyone's heritage; the country house is an aristocratic heritage, purporting to include us all by 'sleight of hand', in Professor David Cannadine's words.[18]

In 2018 only 3% said England was a contented country at ease with itself.[19] No book on the making of England, even though it finishes in the 1500s, can omit the 'B' word. All writers are shaped by their own time and this book has of course been written in the long shadow of Brexit (as well as under the more immediate cloud of a global pandemic). Just as the middle twentieth-century historians looked for reassurance in medieval administration, strong government, and efficiency to explain their own times of imperial decline, the influence of Europe on the formation of England, the assumed exceptionalism of England, and concepts of the famed 'English' freedoms have influenced this book. The 2016 European Referendum was divisive, and the consequences will be felt for generations. It was very much an *English* Brexit; more people in the south-east and east of England (the heaviest areas of settlement of the fifth-sixth century Early English) voted to leave than Wales, Scotland and Northern Ireland combined.[20] Recent elections, general and local, are pushing those divisions further. In 2022 the United Kingdom is looking fragile. Now that it has left Brussels, it may dissolve back to the smaller kingdoms and states that emerged in the early medieval period after Rome left.

Acknowledgements

While the 2016 referendum was the initial spur to write about how England came to be, events have overtaken even that seismic shift. This book was written during the pandemic of 2020-2021. It was completed during the Russian invasion of Ukraine in 2022 where people are fighting for the idea of freedom in a way that has not been seen in England for centuries. The headlines readily use the pejorative 'medieval' to describe the nature of the invasion. There is nothing medieval about razing a city to the ground with thermobaric missiles, killing and displacing hundreds of thousands of civilians; that is a thoroughly modern mode of warfare.

I was fortunate to write in Hidcote Bartrim, Gloucestershire, a settlement of some ten homes, just as it was in Domesday Book. Walking the silent trackways above Hidcote during lockdown months of 2020 with views across to the Malvern Hills and the Welsh hills beyond – Tolkien's Shires – concentrated the mind. The limits of our world had become in that time the same as the medieval world, with no cars or planes overhead, just the footfall of the occasional walker, horse-rider and of course, Cotswold sheep. On one such walk, whilst discussing compass points, my youngest son, Laurie, came up with the mnemonic 'Normans Eliminated Saxon Warriors' – something that certainly captures part of this book.

I am grateful for the resources provided by the University of Northampton (as well as some wonderful colleagues over the years), which has provided access to journals and books online in addition to documents now digitalised and freely available. My wife, Cerys, supported the many hours devoted to the medieval past and my mother, Chrissie, and Martin provided a safe haven in which to write. Dr Guy Stimpson's sentiments on the Welsh language sparked many fruitful ideas. My parents-in-law, Bill and Gill, sadly did not live to see this book completed but unfailingly supported my writing over the years. Dr John Maddicott

Acknowledgements

kindly commented (in great detail and with characteristic speed) on the early draft, Dr David Preece and David Whitehead also read the ms but what is printed here is my responsibility. I thank Shaun Barrington and the team at Amberley for their efforts. Involvement in a Magna Carta exhibition in Washington DC with Luke at Hawkwood International was a stimulating diversion and I thank him for helpful exchanges as well as photos of several historic sites. My father believes that real history only began in 1789 but nevertheless encouraged me from a young age to ask 'why?' – a founding principle upon which this book is written. Finally, this book is dedicated to my three sons, Elgan, Ralph and Laurie. Born and bred in England and with Welsh heritage, they are also citizens of the world; the future is theirs.

Hidcote Bartrim,
Gloucestershire, 2022

Notes

For abbreviations see p.289.

Introduction: In Search of Medieval England
1. Matthews, *Medievalism: A Critical History* p.25.
2. Nelson, 'The Dark Ages', pp.191-201.
3. Nixey, *The Darkening Age* pp.xxxi-xxxiii.
4. Clanchy, *From Memory to Written Record* pp.7-14.
5. Sims-Williams, 'The Settlement of England in Bede and the Chronicle', pp.1-41.
6. Niles, 'The Myth of the Feud in Anglo-Saxon England', pp.163-200.
7. Freeman, E. A. *The Growth of the English Constitution from the earliest times*, Macmillan 1890, pp.73-74.
8. Evans, *In Defence of History* pp.16-19.
9. Bartie, 'Historical Pageants', p.866.
10. Bartie 'Historical Pageants', p. 876.
11. Bartie, 'Historical Pageants', p.869; see Roberts' *Eminent Churchillians* where he eviscerates Bryant's reputation (pp.287-322).
12. Cantor, *Inventing the Middle Ages* pp.205-244.
13. Ortenberg West-Harling,' 'Medievalism as Fun and Games', pp.1-2.
14. Old English word glossing Latin *Orcus* (Hell, Death), see Tolkien, *Beowulf*, p.163; on the witness list of a knightly enfeoffment 1066x87 there is a Frodo, probably the brother of Abbot Baldwin, listed as a tenant in chief in Domesday Book; *EHD*, ii, p.897; DB (Suffolk) 354v. See Garth, *The Worlds of J. R. R. Tolkien* for a study of the landscapes, art and architecture that inspired Tolkien, and Bates, *The Real Middle Earth: Magic and Mystery in the Dark Ages*.
15. Lawrence, *Seven Pillars of Wisdom* p.495.
16. Rosebank, 'G. N. Clark and the Oxford School of Modern History', pp.127-156.

17. Stenton, *Anglo-Saxon England*, p.554; Roach *Kingship and Consent* p.3.
18. Douglas, *William the Conqueror* p184 (my italics.)
19. Brown, *The Normans and the Norman Conquest* pp.87-88; Davis, *From Alfred the Great to Stephen* p.ix, recalls how his experiences in the War affected his research into medieval England.
20. Bates, *William the Conqueror*, where William was a 'destroyer of lives', p.526.
21. Coss, 'Presentism and the "Myth" of Magna Carta', p.229.
22. Vincent, 'The Making of a Monster', p.66.
23. Vincent, 'The Making of a Monster', p.61.
24. Church, *King John: England, Magna Carta and the Making of a Tyrant*; Morris, *King John: Treachery, Tyranny and the Road to Magna Carta*; Coss, 'Presentism', pp.230-21.
25. Licence, *Edward the Confessor* pp.264, 272, 280, 289.
26. Yeandle, *Citizenship, Nation, Empire* p.78; Cannadine, *et al*, *The Right Kind of History* p.53. Alfred was not called 'the Great', until the thirteenth century (Matthew Paris) and the Victorians loved the myth of the creation of the royal navy by Alfred.
27. Jaillant, 'A Fine Old Tale of Adventure', pp.399-400.
28. Jaillant, 'A Fine Old Tale of Adventure', p.402.
29. Kaeuper, 'William Marshal, Lancelot, and the Issue of Chivalric Identity', p.1.
30. Jaillant, 'A Fine Old Tale of Adventure', p.407, citing Marshall, *English Literature for Boys & Girls* p.58.
31. Carter, 'The Quenells', p.113.
32. Marshall, *Our Island Story* pp.51-57.
33. Marshall, *Our Island Story* pp.60-61; aboriginals in the case of Marshall's Australia.
34. Waller, *Heredity* pp.68-71.
35. *Daily Telegraph* (October 2010); Desert Island Discs BBC (February 2014).
36. Given-Wilson, *Chronicles: the writing of history in medieval England* p.118; www.gov.uk/government/publications/national-curriculum-in-england-history-programmes-of-study
37. Davies, 'Tudor: What's in a Name?' pp.37-40.
38. Davies, 'Tudor: What's in a Name?' p.33, p.42.
39. Scott, *Anne of Geierstein* (1829).
40. Goodman, *The Wars of the Roses* p.3; Dockray, *William Shakespeare, the Wars of the Roses and the Historians*.
41. Bates, '1066: does the date still matter?' p.458.
42. Molyneaux, *The Formation of the Kingdom of England* p.38.
43. Nelson, 'A Place for Medieval History in the National Curriculum?' p.103.

44. Morris, *The Anglo-Saxons: A History of the Beginnings of England*, p.6.
45. Wilton, 'What do we mean by *Anglo-Saxon*?' p.436.
46. S356 dated 871-899; S347 (891); S346.
47. S431.
48. Wilton, 'What do we mean by *Anglo-Saxon*?' p. 438.
49. Rambaran-Olm, *et al*, 'Medieval Studies: the stakes of the field', pp.356-370.
50. Wilton, 'What do we mean by *Anglo-Saxon*?' p.451.
51. Naismith, *Early Medieval Britain* pp.111-117.
52. Wickham, *Medieval Europe* p. 3.
53. Coss, 'Presentism,' p.227.
54. Given-Wilson, 'Chronicles: authorship, evidence and objectivity', p.17.
55. Dumville, 'Origins of the Kingdom of the English', p.108.
56. Nelson, 'A Place for Medieval History in the National Curriculum?' pp.103-106.
57. Wormald, 'Times of Bede', p. 61-2; Pryor, *Britain AD* p.13.
58. Church, 'Paganism in Conversion-Age Anglo-Saxon England', p.169.
59. Whitelock, 'Anglo-Saxon Poetry and the Historian', p.75.
60. Clanchy, *From Memory to Written Record* p.32.
61. Wild, 'Secrecy, splendour and statecraft', p.412.
62. Prescott, '"Their Present Miserable State of Cremation": the Restoration of the Cotton Library', pp.391-454.
63. Clanchy, *From Memory to Written Record* p.31.
64. Given-Wilson, p.15.
65. Timofeeva, 'Ælfred mec heht gewyrcan', p.122.
66. Clanchy, *From Memory to Written Record* pp.7-8.
67. Dumville, 'Origins of the Kingdom of the English', pp.71-121.
68. Wickham, *Framing the Early Middle Ages*; Blair, *Building Anglo-Saxon England* p.416.
69. Nelson, 'A Place for Medieval History in the National Curriculum?' p.104.
70. Mortimer, *The Perfect King: The Life of Edward III* pp.439-440.

One: Continuity and Collapse

1. 'Building the Future, Transforming our Past', p.8, www.HistoricEngland.org.uk
2. Pryor, *Britain AD* p.xxi.
3. Pryor, *Britain AD* pp.1-2.
4. Moreland, 'Land and Power', p.180.
5. White, 'Managing Transition', p.586.
6. Schiffels, *et al*. 'Iron Age and Anglo-Saxon genomes', p.7.
7. Halsall, *The Worlds of Arthur* p.283.

8. Halsall, *The Worlds of Arthur* p.35.
9. Higham, 'From Sub-Roman Britain', p.9.
10. Oosthuizen, 'Recognizing and Moving on from a Failed Paradigm', pp.185-186.
11. Higham, 'From Sub-Roman Britain', p.10.
12. Higham, 'From Sub-Roman Britain', p.2; Halsall, *The Worlds of Arthur* p.174.
13. Fleming, 'Recycling in Britain', pp.9-11.
14. Fleming, 'Recycling in Britain', p.13.
15. Fleming, 'Recycling in Britain', p.35.
16. Fleming, 'Recycling in Britain', p.15
17. *EHD*, v, pp.216-217.
18. www.cotswoldarchaeology.co.uk *Excavations and Observations in Roman Cirencester.*
19. Thompson, 'Zosimos', p. 453.
20. Riley, *The Roman Government of Britain* p.463.
21. Riley, *The Roman Government* p. 464.
22. Thompson, 'Zosimos', p. 455.
23. Dark, 'Stones of the Saints?' pp.239-258.
24. *Current Archaeology*, issue 371.
25. Halsall, *The Worlds of Arthur* p. 253.

Two: Natives and Migrants: what Happened to the British?
1. Hurst, & Scull, *The Anglo-Saxon princely burial at Prittlewell, Southend-on-Sea.*
2. Higham, 'From Sub-Roman Britain', p.17.
3. Fleming, 'Recycling in Britain', pp.3-4.
4. Higham, 'From Sub-Roman Britain', pp.6-7.
5. Fleming, 'Recycling in Britain', p.20.
6. Fleming, 'Recycling in Britain', p.21.
7. Fleming, 'Recycling in Britain', p.22.
8. Laing, 'Romano-British Metalworking', p.43.
9. Laing, 'Romano-British Metalworking', p.55.
10. *EH* i, 15, p.27; v, 9, p.247.
11. Ashcroft & Bevir, 'Multiculturalism in contemporary Britain', pp.1-21.
12. Yorke, 'The Anglo-Saxon kingdoms 600-900', p.75.
13. Woolf, 'The Britons: from Romans to Barbarians', p.353.
14. Halsall, *The Worlds of Arthur* p.139.
15. Higham: *The English Conquest: Gildas and Britain in the Fifth Century.*
16. *ASC* D, p.199.
17. Halsall, *The Worlds of Arthur* pp.81-2.
18. White, 'Managing Transition', p.592.

19. Pryor, *Britain AD* p.180.
20. Howe 'Rome: Capital of Anglo-Saxon England', p.151.
21. Blair, *The World of Bede* pp.25-6.
22. *EH*, i, 15, p.27.
23. *EH*, i, 15, p.26: Bede's Continental sources include Orosius's *Seven Books of History against the Pagans*, *c*.417; *Chronicles* of Prosper of Aquitaine (fifth century), *Chronicles* of Marcellinus (sixth century) *Life of St Germanus* (470s) by Constantius of Lyon, a work of hagiography but not invalid as an historical source. Everything else Bede used is 'unknown and unknowable' (Halsall, *The Worlds of Arthur* p.60.)
24. Sims-Williams, 'The Settlement of England in Bede and the Chronicle', pp.27-41.
25. *ASC*, A, E, pp.18-19.
26. Halsall, *Worlds of Arthur* p.193.
27. *ASC*, A, E, pp.12-13; Wilmott, 'Roman Richborough'; Cunliffe, *Fifth Report on the Excavations of the Roman Fort at Richborough, Kent*; I am grateful to Luke Purser to drawing my attention to this.
28. *ASC*, A, p.110.
29. Chaucer., *The Canterbury Tales* p.155.
30. Higham, 'From Sub-Roman Britain', p.16.
31. www.britishmuseum.org.
32. White, 'Managing Transition', p.590.
33. Härke, 'Anglo-Saxon Immigration and Ethnogenesis', p.9.
34. Settlers: Genetics, Geography and the Peopling of Britain http://www.oum.ox.ac.uk/settlers/; Pattison, 'Is it necessary to assume an apartheid-like social structure?' pp.2427-2428; Olalde *et al*, 'The Beaker People and the genomic transformation', pp.190-196; Härke, 'Anglo-Saxon Immigration', pp.8-9.
35. Härke, 'Anglo-Saxon Immigration', p.9
36. Leslie, *et al*, 'The fine-scale genetic structure of the British population', p.313: https://doi.org/10.1038/nature14230.
37. Schiffels, *et al*. 'Iron Age and Anglo-Saxon genomes', p.1-3.
38. Härke, 'Anglo-Saxon Immigration', p.10.
39. Higham, 'From Sub-Roman Britain', p.9.
40. Härke, 'Anglo-Saxon Immigration', p.12.
41. Fleming, Recycling in Britain', p.22.
42. Härke, 'Anglo-Saxon Immigration', p.13; and below, Chapter three.
43. White, 'Managing Transition', p.593.
44. Härke, 'Anglo-Saxon Immigration', p.14.
45. Yorke, 'The Anglo-Saxon kingdoms 600-900', p.77.
46. Higham, *Rome, Britons and the Anglo-Saxons*.
47. *EH*, i, 22, p.36; *EH* ii, I, p.61.
48. *EH*, ii, I, p.10.

49. Halsall, *Worlds of Arthur* p.240.
50. Dumville, 'Origins of the Kingdom of the English', p.75.
51. Coates,' Invisible Britons', p.189.
52. Dumville, 'Origins of the Kingdom of the English', p.74.
53. Coates, 'Invisible Britons', p.185.
54. Coates,' Invisible Britons', p. 189.
55. Pelteret, 'Slave raiding and slave trading in early England', p.100.
56. Pelteret, 'Slavery in Anglo-Saxon England', p. 119.
57. Halsall, *Worlds of Arthur* p.283.
58. Lutz, 'Celtic influence', p.241-242. The noun *wīln* and the adjective *wīlisc*, meaning 'foreign, British, Celtic, of slave status' and from late Old English onwards, also 'Welsh'.
59. Lutz, 'Celtic influence', p. 244.
60. Thomas, *et. al.*, 'Evidence for an apartheid-like social structure', pp.2651-2657.
61. Härke, 'Anglo-Saxon Immigration', p.16.
62. Ward-Perkins, 'Why did the Anglo-Saxons not become more British?' pp.514-5. Breeze, 'Seven types of Celtic loan words', pp.175-181.
63. Coates, 'Invisible Britons', p. 187.
64. Lutz, 'Celtic influence', p.227n; four words are generally accepted from Celtic to OE: *binn* 'manger', *brocc* 'badger', *cumb* 'valley' (descendant Welsh *cwm* was re-borrowed late in the second millennium) and *luh* 'sea, pool'; Coates, 'Invisible Britons', p.177.
65. Coates,' Invisible Britons', p.189.
66. Pattison, 'Is it necessary to assume an apartheid-like social structure?' pp.2423-2429
67. Leslie, S., *et al*, 'The fine-scale genetic structure of the British population', p.314: https://doi.org/10.1038/nature14230
68. Lutz, 'Celtic influence', pp.229-230.
69. Schrijver, 'Celtic influence on Old English', pp.193-211.
70. Woolf, 'The Britons: from Romans to Barbarians', p.362.
71. Schrijver, 'What Britons Spoke', p.165.
72. Halsall, *Worlds of Arthur* p.241.
73. Coates, 'Invisible Britons: 'The View from Linguistics', pp.172-3.
74. Schrijver, 'What Britons Spoke', p. 170.
75. Schrijver, 'What Britons Spoke', p.171.
76. Harland, 'Memories of migration?' pp.954-969.
77. Swift, 'Re-evaluating the Quoit Brooch Style', pp.1-55.
78. Swift, 'Re-evaluating the Quoit Brooch Style', pp.44-45.
79. Fleming, 'Recycling in Britain', p.28.
80. Behr, *et al*, 'The Bracteate Hoard from Binham', pp.44-77.
81. Härke, 'Anglo-Saxon Immigration and Ethnogenesis', p.4.
82. Harland, 'Memories of migration?' p.966.
83. *ASC* A, E, pp.14-15.

84. Halsall, *Worlds of Arthur* p.271.
85. *EH*, ii, 4-5, pp.77-78.
86. Keller *et al*, 'Ancient *Yersinia pestis* genomes', pp. 12368-9.
87. Maddicott, 'Plague in Seventh-Century England', p.11.
88. Mordechai *et al*, 'The Justinianic Plague; An inconsequential pandemic?' pp.25546-25554; Mordechai & Eisenberg, 'Rejecting Catastrophe: The Case of the Justinianic Plague', pp.3-50; Sarris, 'New approaches to the 'Plague of Justinian', pp.315-346.
89. Dumville, 'Origins of the Kingdom of the English', p.94.
90. Campbell, *The Anglo-Saxons* p.20.

Three: Rome Returns – Conversion and Coercion
1. *EH*, ii, 1, p.70.
2. Pelteret, 'Slave raiding and slave trading', pp.104-5.
3. Pelteret, 'Slavery in Anglo-Saxon England', p.131.
4. *EH*, ii, 1, p.70.
5. Dark, 'Stones of the Saints?', p.255.
6. *EH*, i, 34, p.61; *EH*, ii, 2, p.74.
7. *EH*, p.3.
8. *EH*, ii, 1, p.71.
9. *EH*, ii, 8, p.84.
10. Frankis, 'King Ælle and the conversion of the English', p.81.
11. *EH*, i, 26, p.41; *EH*, i, 32, p.59; Dumville, 'Origins of the Kingdom of the English', p.81.
12. *EH*, i, 32, p.59.
13. Stapleton, 'Pope Gregory and the *Gens Anglorum*', p.26; *EH*, ii, 9, p.87.
14. Brooks, 'English Identity from Bede to the Millennium', p.36.
15. Wormald, '*Engla Lond*: the Making of an Allegiance', p.14.
16. Frantzen, 'The Englishness of Bede, from then to now', pp.229-241.
17. Molyneaux, 'Did the English Really Think They were God's Elect?' pp.721-737.
18. O'Brien, 'Kings and Kingship in the writings of Bede', p.1497.
19. *EH*, I, 25, p.39; *ASC* A, E, pp.12-13.
20. Halsall, *Worlds of Arthur* p.284; *EH*, i, 25, p.39.
21. Wormald, '*Engla Lond*' p.13.
22. *EH*, ii, 5, pp.77-8.
23. *EH*, ii, 5, p.79.
24. *EH*, iii, 8, p.122.
25. *EH*, ii, 15, p.98.
26. *EH*, iii, 7, pp.119-120; *EH*, ii, 5, p.79; *EH*, iv, 12 p.191.
27. *EH*, ii, 5, p.79; *EH*, iii, 1, pp.110-111.
28. *EH*, iii, 18, p.138.
29. *EH*, iii, 7, p.120.

30. *EH*, iii, 2, p.111. This account of the battle 'cannot' be an historically accurate description of the Northumbrian king's actions, since a more recent liturgical cult of the cross shaped Bede's account.
31. O'Brien, 'Kings and Kingship', pp.1473-1476.
32. Cool, 'The Staffordshire Hoard', www.staffordshirehoard.org.uk
33. Rogerson, NMS-E95041: An Early Medieval Assemblage: https://finds.org.uk/database/artefacts/record/id/659168
34. Carver, *Sutton Hoo: Burial Ground of Kings?* pp. 180-181.
35. *EH*, ii, 15, p.98.
36. *EH*, ii, 12, pp.91-96.
37. *EH*, ii, 13, p.95.
38. Barrow, 'How Coifi Pierced Christ's Side', pp.693-706.
39. *EH*, i, 30, p.57.
40. Niles, 'Pagan Survivals and Popular Beliefs', p.124.
41. *EH*, ii, 9, p.84.
42. *EH*, ii, 15, p.99; ii, 20, pp.105-6.
43. *EH*, iii, 9, p124.
44. Kendall, 'Bede and Education', p.99.
45. *EH*, iii, 18, p.38.
46. Webb & Farmer, *The Age of Bede* p.188.
47. *EH*, iv, 1, p.170.
48. Cambridge University Library (MS Kk.5.16) cudl.lib.cam.ac.uk
49. *EH*, iv, 23, pp.210-211.
50. Leggett, 'The Power of Place', pp.76-94.
51. Yorke, 'The Anglo-Saxon kingdoms 600-900', p.82.
52. Cubbitt, 'The clergy in early Anglo-Saxon England', pp.284-6.
53. Forbes, p.145.
54. Forbes,' Searching for Conversion in the Early English Laws', p.152.
55. EH ii, 5, p.78.
56. Forbes,' Searching for Conversion in the Early English Laws', p.147.
57. Clanchy, *From Memory to Written Record* p.33.
58. Potter, *Law, Liberty and the Constitution* pp.10-11.
59. Halsall, *Worlds of Arthur* p.274.
60. *EH*, iii, 6, p.118.
61. *EHD*, i, pp.391-394.
62. Potter, *Law, Liberty and the Constitution* pp.13-14.
63. *EH* i, 27, pp.41-54. The issue of marrying one's brother's wife is something Henry VIII encountered in the 1520s with seismic consequences for English history.
64. Gannon, *The Iconography of Early Anglo-Saxon Coinage* p.10.
65. Gannon, *The Iconography of Early Anglo-Saxon Coinage* pp.1-11.
66. Forbes,' Searching for Conversion in the Early English Laws', p.160.
67. Forbes,' Searching for Conversion in the Early English Laws', p.163.
68. Forbes,' Searching for Conversion in the Early English Laws', p.156.

69. *EHD*, i, pp.398-407.
70. Forbes,' Searching for Conversion in the Early English Laws', p.156.
71. www.gov.uk/age-of-criminal-responsibility
72. Härke, 'Anglo-Saxon Immigration', p.12.
73. *EH*, iv, 22, pp.208-09.
74. *EHD*, i, p.392 (Æthelberht); pp.407-416 (Alfred's laws).
75. Ward-Perkins 'Why did the Anglo-Saxons not become more British?' pp.523-524; *EHD*, i, pp.401-2.
76. Härke, 'Anglo-Saxon Immigration', p.17.
77. Lutz, 'Celtic influence', p.240.
78. Wright, 'Early Medieval Settlement and Social Power', pp.24-46.
79. Wright, 'Early Medieval Settlement', p.27.
80. Wright, 'Early Medieval Settlement', p.28.
81. Blair, *Building Anglo-Saxon England* pp.113-4.
82. Hyams, 'Feud and the State in Late Anglo-Saxon England', p.21.
83. Wright, 'Early Medieval Settlement', p.29.
84. Wright, 'Early Medieval Settlement', p.30; www.esawyer.org.uk S227, S228, although the Glastonbury charter is fabricated with seventh-century elements.
85. Wright, 'Early Medieval Settlement,' pp.34-35.
86. Wright, 'Early Medieval Settlement', pp.41-42.
87. Maddicott, 'Plague in Seventh-Century England', pp.28-29.
88. *EH*, iii, 27, p.161.
89. Maddicott, 'Plague in Seventh-Century England', p.48; Mordechai & Eisenberg, 'Rejecting Catastrophe', pp.3-50.
90. Wright, 'Early Medieval Settlement', pp.24-46.
91. *EH*, iv, 24, pp.215-216.
92. EHD, i, p.455.
93. Bede, *EH*, p.5 (my italics.)
94. Luizza, 'The Tower of Babel', p.22.

Four: Heroes and Monsters

1. The dating of *Beowulf* remains unresolved. Tolkien suggested no more than a century after Sutton Hoo, i.e. up to *c*.730: Tolkien J. R. R., ed., *Beowulf: a translation and commentary* (2014), p.152, though S. Foot (2012) *Athelstan: The First King of England* attributes it to the reign of Athelstan, 924-927 (pp.115-117). I favour the earlier date.
2. BL Cotton MS Vitellius A XV; it is available online at www.ebeowulf.uky.edu, a collaboration between the British Library and Kentucky University.
3. Whitelock, 'Anglo-Saxon Poetry and the Historian', p.75. Professor Whitelock concluded that Old English poems 'will not let us into the secrets of contemporary politics' but affirms that they are worthy of investigation nevertheless (p.94).

4. Wormald, 'Times of Bede', p. 58.
5. Wormald, 'Times of Bede', p. 67.
6. Orchard, 'The Word Made Flesh', pp.293-318; although see Niles, for whom leaning on *Beowulf* as historical evidence is akin to using *Alice in Wonderland* as a basis for observations of Victorian England: 'The Myth of the Feud in Anglo-Saxon England', p182.
7. Clanchy, *From Memory to Written Record* p.9.
8. Battles, '*Genesis A* and the Anglo-Saxon 'migration myth'', p.44.
9. Neidorf, '*Beowulf* as Pre-National Epic', pp.847-875.
10. *EH*, i, 15, p.27.
11. *ASC*, A, p.66.
12. Keynes & Lapidge, *Alfred the Great* p.67.
13. Heaney, p.3, Tolkien, p.13.
14. Sayers, 'The Names *Beow, Scef, Scyld* and *Beowulf*: Shares into Swords', pp. 815-820.
15. Earl, 'The Swedish Wars in *Beowulf*', pp.32-60.
16. Alfsdotter, *et al*, 'A moment frozen in time: evidence of a late fifth-century massacre at Sandby borg', pp.421-436.
17. Tolkien, p.14; Heaney, p.4.
18. Tolkien, pp.104-5; Heaney pp.98-99.
19. Hill, 'Beowulf's Roman Rites', pp.325-335; Whitelock, 'Anglo-Saxon Poetry and the Historian'; Wells, *Barbarians to Angels* pp.41-42.
20. Niles, 'Pagan Survival and Popular Belief', p.128.
21. *EH*, ii, 9, pp.85-6.
22. *EH* (from the Moore Continuation), p.297; *ASC* E, p.49, p.51.
23. *Beowulf*, Heaney, p.5.
24. *Beowulf*, Heaney, pp.39-41.
25. *Beowulf*, Heaney, p.4.
26. *Beowulf*, Heaney, p.43, p.48.
27. http://collections.museums-sheffield.org.uk
28. *Geoffrey of Monmouth* p.217; Carpenter, *Magna Carta* p.267.
29. Hyams, 'Feud and the State', p.5; although Niles thinks *Beowulf* is 'quite obviously a fantasy in many regards': 'The Myth of the Feud', p.182.
30. Niles, 'The Myth of the Feud' does not see the feuds in *Beowulf* as 'feuds' at all, rather as acts of violence, p.194.
31. Whitelock, *The Audience of Beowul*, p.13.
32. *EHD*, i, p.863.
33. Biggs, 'The Politics of Succession in *Beowulf* and Anglo-Saxon England', p.709; Foot, 'Bede's Kings', pp.34-40.
34. *EHD*, i, pp.837.
35. *Beowulf*, Heaney, p.70.
36. Campbell, *The Anglo-Saxons* pp.59-61.
37. *Beowulf*, Heaney, p.9, Tolkien p.16.

38. S 255.
39. Brookes & Reynolds, 'The Origins of Political Order and the Anglo-Saxon State', p.92.
40. *Beowulf*, Heaney, p.77; Tolkien, *Beowulf* p.98.
41. Carver, *Sutton Hoo: Burial Ground of Kings?* pp.137-144.
42. Wickham, *Framing the Early Middle Ages* p.341; Wright, 'Early Medieval Settlement', p.27.
43. Moreland, 'Land and Power', p.183.
44. Luizza, 'The Tower of Babel', p.5.
45. *Beowulf*, Heaney, p.85, *EHD*, i, pp.869-71.
46. Blair, *Building Anglo-Saxon England* pp.124-125.
47. Härke, 'Anglo-Saxon Immigration', p.19.
48. *EHD*, i, pp.869-71.
49. *EHD*, i, pp.871-3; Luizza, 'The Tower of Babel', pp.1-35.

Five: Saints and Kingdoms
1. *EH*, pp.300-303.
2. Kendall, 'Bede and Education,' p.110.
3. Rowley, 'Bede in Later Anglo-Saxon England', pp.217-219.
4. Thacker, 'Bede and History', p.170.
5. Wormald, '*Engla Lond*', p.13.
6. Rollason, 'Lists of saints' resting places in Anglo-Saxon England', pp.61-67.
7. Hyams, 'Feud and the State', p.9.
8. *EH*, iii, 6, p.119, pp.126-9.
9. Brooks, 'English Identity', pp.42-44; Molyneaux, *The Formation of the English Kingdom* p.204.
10. S89; *EHD*, i, pp.492-4.
11. Yorke *Kings and Kingdoms and Early Anglo-Saxon England* pp.114-115; although these texts were written/rewritten in the tenth century; Brooks, 'English Identity', p.43.
12. Hyams, 'Feud and the State in Late Anglo-Saxon England', p.8.
13. Dumville, 'Origins of the Kingdom of the English', p.99.
14. Wormald, '*Engla Lond*', p.4.
15. Wormald, '*Engla Lond*', p.5.
16. Dumville, 'Origins of the Kingdom of the English', p.102.
17. Dumville, 'Origins of the Kingdom of the English', pp.106-7.
18. Dumville, 'Origins of the Kingdom of the English', p.104.
19. Fleming, 'Recycling in Britain', p.32.
20. Woolf, 'Apartheid and Economics in Anglo-Saxon England', p.120.
21. Yorke, 'The Anglo-Saxon kingdoms 600-900', p.75, citing Wickham, *Framing the Early Middle Ages*.
22. Halsall, *Worlds of Arthur* p.271.
23. Yorke, 'The Anglo-Saxon kingdoms 600-900', pp.78-80.

24. Yorke, 'The Anglo-Saxon kingdoms 600-900', pp.80-81.
25. Naismith, 'The Social Significance of Monetization in the Early Middle Ages', pp.3-39.
26. Maddicott, 'Industry and the Wealth of King Alfred', p.7.
27. Yorke, 'The Anglo-Saxon kingdoms 600-900', p.82.
28. Yorke, 'The Anglo-Saxon kingdoms 600-900', p.84.
29. Yorke, 'The Anglo-Saxon kingdoms 600-900', p.85.
30. Dumville, 'Origins of the Kingdom of the English', p.89.
31. *EH*, iii, 24, p.152.
32. S1165; *EHD*, i, pp.479-80.
33. Dumville, 'Origins of the Kingdom of the English', p.91.
34. S59; *EHD*, i, pp.502-3.
35. S58.
36. Maddicott, 'London and Droitwich', pp.56-7; Coates, 'The name of the Hwicce: a discussion', pp.51-61.
37. S773; *EHD*, i, pp.563-64.
38. Yorke, 'The Anglo-Saxon kingdoms 600-900', p.83.
39. Yorke, 'The Anglo-Saxon kingdoms 600-900', p.85.
40. Yorke, 'The Anglo-Saxon kingdoms 600-900', p.78; Campbell, 'The Late Anglo-Saxon State', p.45.
41. *EHD*, i, pp.398-407.
42. *EH*, ii, 8, p.84.
43. *EH*, iii, 25, p.152.
44. Yorke, 'The Anglo-Saxon kingdoms 600-900', p.79.
45. *EH*, v.23, p.289; S89; *EHD*, i, pp.492-4.
46. Maddicott, 'London and Droitwich', p.24.
47. Maddicott, 'London and Droitwich', pp.7-58.
48. *EH*, ii, 3, p.74.
49. *EH*, iv, 22, pp.208-209.
50. S98.
51. For Æthelbald's title, see the charter of 757 (S96).
52. Wells, *Barbarians to Angels* p.9; Tyler, 'Offa's Dyke: a historiographical appraisal', pp. 145-161.
53. *EHD*, i, p.855.
54. Insley, 'Collapse, Reconfiguration or Renegotiation?' p.236.
55. Blair, *Building Anglo-Saxon England* p.231.
56. *Life of Alfred* p.96; Molyneaux, *The Formation of the English Kingdom* p.15.
57. *ASC* A, E, pp.62-3.
58. Halsall, *Worlds of Arthur* pp.3-4.

Six: Alfred or Guthrum?

1. *ASC* E and F, pp.56-57.
2. *EHD*, i, pp.842-844.

3. S134.
4. Griffiths, 'Rethinking the early Viking Age in the West', pp.469-472.
5. www.nms.ac.uk (National Museum of Scotland).
6. *ASC*, A, E, pp.64-5.
7. Maddicott, 'Trade Industry and the Wealth of King Alfred', p.9.
8. Brooks, 'English Identity', p.46.
9. Jarman, *et al*, 'The Viking great Army in England', pp.183-199.
10. *ASC* A, E pp.75-6.
11. *Life of Alfred* p.67. Keynes & Lapidge use 'Viking' for *pagani*.
12. *Life of Alfred* pp.84-5.
13. Davis, *From Alfred the Great to Stephen* p.33.
14. Nelson, 'Alfred of Wessex at a crossroads in the history of education', p.705.
15. Reynolds, 'Official history: how Churchill and the cabinet office wrote *The Second World War*', p.402.
16. The significance of the 'people's war' and fighting 'alone' on historiography is discussed recently by Edgerton, 'The Nationalisation of British History: Historians, Nationalism and the Myths of 1940', pp.950-985.
17. *ASC* A, E, F, pp.54-7.
18. Downham, 'The Earliest Viking activity in England?' p.2.
19. *ASC*, pp.xxi-xxviii. The significance of the eleventh-century versions becomes apparent during the succession crisis of Edward the Confessor's reign.
20. Williams, *Viking Britain* pp.13-14.
21. *Alfred the Great* p.101; Gallagher, 'Asser and the Writing of West Saxon Charters', p.774.
22. *Life of Alfred* pp.197-202; p.223.
23. S215; *ASC* 'A' and 'E' pp.72-73 for 873.
24. www.ashmolean.org
25. *EHD*, i, pp.532-3.
26. *Life of Alfred* p.84; *ASC* A, p.76.
27. *Life of Alfred* pp.171-2.
28. Vegetius, *Epitoma Rei Militari* (book 3, prologue). Since Bede cited Vegetius in the *Life of Cuthbert*, it is possible Alfred knew Vegetius's work; Jones, 'Bede and Vegetius', pp.248-249.
29. One manuscript dates to the eleventh century but was largely destroyed in the 1731 fire, the other version is 13/14th century: Haslam places it in the reign of Alfred; 'The Burghal Hidage and the West Saxon burhs: A reappraisal', pp.141-182.
30. *Life of Alfred* pp.193-194.
31. Maddicott, 'Industry and the Wealth of King Alfred', p.6.
32. Molyneaux, *The Formation of the English Kingdom* pp.87-91.
33. *ASC* A p.84.

34. *Life of Alfred* p.106.
35. *Life of Alfred* p.188.
36. *Life of Alfred* p.106.
37. *Life of Alfred* pp.72-3; pp.173-178.
38. *Life of Alfred* p.178.
39. Maddicott, 'Trade Industry and the Wealth of King Alfred', p.42.
40. *Life of Alfred* pp.174-8.
41. Maddicott, 'Trade Industry and the Wealth of King Alfred', pp.44-45; Nelson, 'Debate: Trade, Industry and the Wealth of King Alfred', pp.142-163.
42. Brooks, 'English Identity', pp. 33-52.
43. S 207 (Burgred of Mercia).
44. Listed in the *Dictionary of Old English*; Timofeeva, 'Ælfred mec heht gewyrcan', p.135.
45. *ASC* A, E, pp.80-81.
46. Timofeeva, 'Ælfred mec heht gewyrcan', pp.139-141.
47. Timofeeva, 'Ælfred Mec Heht Gewyrcan', p.131; Brooks, 'Why is the Anglo-Saxon Chronicle about kings?' pp.43-70.
48. Gallagher, 'Asser and the Writing of West Saxon Charters', pp.773-808.
49. Timofeeva, 'Ælfred mec heht gewyrcan', p.144.
50. Nelson, 'Alfred of Wessex at a cross-roads in the history of education', pp.697-712.
51. Molyneaux, 'The Old English Bede: English Ideology or Christian Instruction?' pp.1290-1323; Molyneaux, 'Did the English Really Think They were God's Elect?' pp.734-5.
52. Howe, 'Rome: Capital of Anglo-Saxon England,' pp.142-172.
53. Nelson 'Alfred of Wessex at a cross-roads', pp.705-706.
54. Nelson, 'Alfred of Wessex at a cross-roads', p.705.
55. Molyneaux, *The Formation of English Kingdom* p.6.
56. Molyneaux, 'Why were some tenth-century English kings presented as Rulers of Britain?' p.78; Molyneaux, *The Formation of the English Kingdom* p.204.
57. Rowley, 'Bede in Later Anglo-Saxon England', pp.221-5; Discenza, 'The Old English Bede and the construction of Anglo-Saxon authority', p.77.
58. Molyneaux, 'The Old English Bede: English Ideology or Christian Instruction?' p.1316.
59. Waite, 'The Preface to the Old English Bede', pp.33-4; 73.
60. *Life of Alfred* pp.124-126.
61. Nelson, 'Alfred of Wessex at a cross-roads', p.705.
62. Clanchy, *From Memory to Written Record* p.34.
63. Godden 'King Alfred's Preface and the teaching of Latin in Anglo-Saxon England', p.598.
64. *Life of Alfred* p.126.

65. Nelson, 'Alfred of Wessex at a cross-roads', p.707.
66. www.ashmolean.org.uk
67. Nelson, 'Alfred of Wessex at a cross-roads,' p.709.
68. Yorke, 'The Anglo-Saxon kingdoms 600-900,' p.85.
69. Pratt, *The Political Thought of King Alfred the Great* pp.214-218; Hyams 'Feud and the State,' p.12.
70. Lambert, 'Theft, Homicide and Crime in late Anglo-Saxon Law,' p.3.
71. Whitelock, *Beginnings of English Society* pp.39-42.
72. *Life of Alfred*, p.163; Wormald, '*Engla Lond*', p.15.
73. Roach, 'Penance, submission and *deditio*', p.346.
74. Hyams,'Feud and the State', p.35.
75. Hyams, 'Feud and the State', pp.36-7.
76. Pelteret, *Slavery in early medieval England* p.84.
77. S1445.
78. *Life of Alfred* p.109.
79. Roach, 'Penance, submission and *deditio*', pp.347-8.
80. ASC, A, p.66.
81. Yorke, 'King Alfred and Weland,' pp.47-70.
82. S564; S255.
83. ASC A, pp.82-83.
84. ASC A pp.91-2.
85. Effros, 'The Enduring Attraction of the Pirenne Thesis,' pp.184-208 for a recent reappraisal.
86. Williams, *Viking Britain* p.191.
87. Barraclough, *The Origins of Modern Germany* pp.37-44.
88. Molyneaux, *The Formation of the English Kingdom* p.212.
89. Yorke, 'The Anglo-Saxon kingdoms 600-900', p.76.
90. Pratt, 'The Illnesses of King Alfred the Great', pp.39-90; *Life of Alfred* pp.88-90.

Seven: Unification?

1. Dumville, 'Origins of the Kingdom of the English,' p.72.
2. ASC D, p.107.
3. Lapidge, 'Some Latin poems as evidence for the reign of Athelstan,' p.98.
4. S401, S402, S408; S416 (931) and S425 (934). Also on coins and in poetry; Molyneaux, 'Why were some tenth-century English kings presented as Rulers of Britain? p.60.
5. ASC, A, E, pp.60-61; Dumville, 'Origins of the Kingdom of the English', p.83.
6. Insley, 'Collapse, Reconfiguration or Renegotiation?' p.7; ASC A p.94.
7. Wood, 'Æthelflæd, Lady of the Mercians, 918-2018', pp.30-32.
8. *Life of Alfred* pp.71-2.
9. *Life of Alfred* p.235, p.281; it is in the British Museum.

10. *EHD*, i, pp.546-7; S396, S397 for lands at Tebworth, Bedfordshire, Hope and Ashford, Derbyshire.
11. Insley, 'Collapse, Reconfiguration or Renegotiation?' pp.231-247.
12. Molyneaux, *The Formation of the English Kingdom* p.21, n.23.
13. Leslie, S., *et al*, 'The fine-scale genetic structure of the British population', p.313.
14. S395, 396; *ASC* C, D, p.105.
15. Maddicott, *The Origins of the English Parliament* p.20.
16. There were rumours in the twelfth century that Æthelstan murdered his other half-brother Edwin, in 933; Molyneaux, *The Formation of the English Kingdom* p.29.
17. Molyneaux, *The Formation of the English Kingdom* p.30.
18. Wood, 'Searching for Brunanburh: the Yorkshire Context of the "Great War" of 937', p.142.
19. *ASC* A pp.106-110.
20. Wood, 'Searching for Brunanburh', pp.157-8. Wood draws upon the *Historia Regum*, possibly the earliest source for the battle (940s).
21. Wood, 'The Making of King Æthelstan's Empire: An English Charlemagne?' pp.250–72.
22. Smith 'Rulers and Relics c.750-c.950', pp.73-96.
23. Dumville, 'Origins of the Kingdom of the English', pp.116-7.
24. Yorke, 'The Anglo-Saxon kingdoms 600-900', p.75.
25. Smith, 'Rulers and Relics', p86-88.
26. *EHD*, i, pp.417-427.
27. *EHD* i, p.428-9.
28. Molyneaux, *The Formation of the English Kingdom* pp.112-3.
29. The later twelfth-century sources William of Malmesbury and John of Worcester echo the contemporary *ASC*; Wood, 'Searching for Brunanburh', p.153.
30. www.yorkarchaeology.co.uk
31. *ASC* D, E, pp.112-113.
32. Dumville, 'Origins of the Kingdom of the English', p.82.
33. *ASC* B, C, D, E, p.113
34. Molyneaux, *The Formation of the English Kingdom* pp. 116-194.
35. *ASC* A, p.118
36. *ASC* A, E pp.118-121
37. Molyneaux 'Why were some tenth-century English kings presented as Rulers of Britain?' p.68.
38. Matthews, 'King Edgar and the Dee', pp.61-74.
39. Molyneaux 'Why were some tenth-century English kings presented as Rulers of Britain?' p.64; Molyneaux, '*Angli* and *Saxones* in Æthelweard's Chronicle', p.212.
40. Molyneaux 'Why were some tenth-century English kings presented as Rulers of Britain?' pp.74-75.

41. *EHD*, i, pp.434-437.
42. Brookes & Reynolds, 'The Origins of Political Order and the Anglo-Saxon State', pp.84-93.
43. *EHD*, i, pp.423-427.
44. Molyneaux, *The Formation of the English Kingdom* p.151.
45. Molyneaux, *The Formation of the English Kingdom* p.164.
46. *EHD*, i, p.432.
47. Roach, 'Law codes and legal norms in later Anglo-Saxon England', pp.465-486.
48. Molyneaux, *The Formation of the English Kingdom* pp.116-141.
49. Naismith & Tinti, 'The Origins of Peter's Pence', p.533; *EHD*, i, p.431.
50. Molyneaux, *The Formation of the English Kingdom* pp.189-191.
51. Roach, *Kingship and Consent* p.212.
52. Roach, *Kingship and Consent* p.243.
53. Maddicott, *The Origins of Parliament* pp.4-6.
54. Maddicott, *The Origins of Parliament* p.12.
55. Maddicott, *The Origins of Parliament* p.18 (The *Life of St Dunstan*).
56. *ASC* A p.112.

Eight: Nemesis
1. *ASC* D, E, pp.154-5.
2. *ASC,* D, p.200.
3. Molyneaux, *The Formation of the English Kingdom* p.37.
4. Fairburn, 'Was There a Money Economy in Late Anglo-Saxon and Norman England?' p.1083.
5. Naismith, 'Payments for land and privilege in Anglo-Saxon England', pp.277-342.
6. Fairburn, 'Was There a Money Economy?' p.1116.
7. *EHD*, i, p.439; *ASC*, D, E, pp.154-5.
8. Horne, A, *To Lose a Battle: France 1940* (1969); Bloch, M, *Strange Defeat* (1949). Bloch was a medieval historian and founding member of the *Annales* school of history, murdered in 1944 as a résistant.
9. Baxter, 'The limits of the Anglo-Saxon State', p.503.
10. Molyneaux, '*Angli* and *Saxones* in Æthelweard's *Chronicle*', pp.208-223.
11. Roach, *Kingship and Consent* p.17.
12. *Ælfric's Lives of the Saints* translated by Moilanen, 'The Concept of the Three Orders of Society', p.1338.
13. *EHD*, i, p.933-4.
14. Wormald, *Engla Lond* pp.16-17.
15. Molyneaux, *The Formation of the English Kingdom* p.226
16. *EHD*, i, pp.319-324.
17. *ASC* F, E, pp.126-7.

18. *ASC* E, p.135.
19. www.historicengland.org.uk 'Building the Future, Transforming our Past', p.22.
20. S909; *EHD*, i, pp.590-3.
21. Pollard *et al*, 'Sprouting Like Cockle amongst the wheat', pp.83-102.
22. *Life of Alfred* p.165.
23. Molyneaux, *The Formation of the English Kingdom* p.224.
24. *ASC*, E p.145.
25. Maddicott, *The Origins of Parliament* p.37.
26. Lawson, *Cnut*, p.82.
27. *ASC* E, D, F, pp.152-3
28. Eadric fled the field with the Magonsæte, people of the Herefordshire and south Shropshire Welsh borders, a reminder of the old local groups pre-dating the kingdoms and earldoms.
29. *ASC* D, E, F pp.152-3; John of Worcester, in Williams, 'Regional Communities and Royal Authority', n.4.
30. *ASC* D, E pp.154-55.
31. *EHD*, i, pp.454-467.
32. Maddicott, 'Edward the Confessor's Return', p.652.
33. *ASC* D, E, pp.192-3.
34. Maddicott, *The Origins of Parliament* p.52; *Life of Alfred* p.164.
35. Wormald, '*Engla Lond*', p.10.
36. Campbell, 'The Late Anglo-Saxon State', p.58; *EHD* i, pp.452-455.
37. Lawson, *Cnut* pp.159-160.
38. Settlers: Genetics, Geography and the Peopling of Britain (Oxford University Museum of Natural History) http://www.oum.ox.ac.uk/settlers/
39. *ASC* D, E pp157-9.
40. Parker, 'Siward the Dragon-Slayer', pp.481-493; Lawson, *Cnut* p.171.
41. Pelteret, 'The Image of the Slave', p.79.
42. Pelteret. 'The Image of the Slave', p.84.
43. *EHD*, i, pp.439-451 (Æthelred); pp.454-465 (Cnut).
44. *ASC* C, D pp.158-60.
45. *ASC* E p.161.
46. *ASC*, C, p.162.
47. *ASC* C p.162.
48. *ASC* C p.162.
49. *ASC* C pp.164-5.
50. Lawson, *Cnut* p.172.
51. Maddicott, 'Edward the Confessor's Return', pp.650-666.
52. Maddicott, 'Edward the Confessor's Return', p.662.
53. Maddicott, 'Edward the Confessor's Return', p.665.
54. Lawson, *Cnut*, pp.57-8; *ASC* C p.162, n.3.
55. *ASC*, C, D, E, pp.162-3; S1076.

56. Maddicott, *The Origins of Parliament* p.44.
57. Licence, *Edward the Confessor* pp.134-135.
58. Barlow, *Edward the Confessor* p.137.
59. S1022.
60. Campbell, 'The Late Anglo-Saxon State', p.47.
61. Baxter & Lewis, 'Domesday Book and the transformation of English landed society', p.397; Baxter, '1066 and Government', pp.136-138.
62. Campbell, 'Observations on English Government', pp.39-54; Molyneaux, *The Formation of the English Kingdom* pp.239-44.
63. Molyneaux, *The Formation of English Kingdom* p.214.
64. Williams, 'Regional Communities and Royal Authority', p.40.
65. Dumville, 'Origins of the Kingdom of the English', p.118.

Nine: William or Harold?

1. Dumville, 'The Ætheling', p.33.
2. Baxter, 'Edward the Confessor and the Succession Question', p.82, n19.
3. Baxter, 'Edward the Confessor and the Succession Question', p.78-81; Bates *William the Conqueror* pp.108-120; pp.191-200.
4. Baxter, 'MS C of the Anglo-Saxon Chronicle', pp.1189-1190.
5. Baxter, 'MS C of the Anglo-Saxon Chronicle', p.1191-2.
6. Baxter & Blair, 'Land tenure and royal patronage', pp.45-46; Williams, 'Regional Communities and Royal Authority', p.38; Wormald, '*Engla Lond*', p6.
7. Baxter, 'Edward the Confessor and the Succession Question', p.84; Bates, *William the Conqueror* p.111.
8. *ASC* C, D, E, pp.170-171.
9. Baxter & Lewis, 'Domesday Book and the transformation of English landed society', p.350; Bates, *William the Conqueror* p.112.
10. Barlow, *Edward the Confessor* p.191.
11. *ASC* C, D, E pp. 172-173.
12. *ASC* E, pp.172-3; this source is pro-Godwin but since it was based in Canterbury and ten miles from Dover, would have better detail of the events.
13. Williams, 'Regional Communities and Royal Authority', p.27.
14. *ASC* D, E, pp.174-175.
15. Williams, 'Regional Communities and Royal Authority', p.23.
16. *ASC* D p.175.
17. Williams, 'Regional Communities and Royal Authority', pp.30-31.
18. Leyser, *Communications and Power in Medieval Europe* p.109.
19. Campbell, 'The Late Anglo-Saxon State', p.57; and in Stenton's words, this had the character of a 'constitutional monarchy' (*Anglo-Saxon England* p.554.)
20. Williams, 'Regional Communities and Royal Authority', pp.32-33.
21. *ASC* C, D, E pp.172-176.

22. *ASC* D, p.176 (my italic).
23. Baxter, 'Edward the Confessor and the Succession Question', pp.89-90; Bates, *William the Conqueror* pp.118-119.
24. Holt, *Colonial England* p. xvi.
25. *The Gesta Guillelmi of William of Poitiers*, eds Davis & Chibnall; for a recent reappraisal, see Winkler, 'The Norman Conquest of the classical past: William of Poitiers, language and history', pp. 456-478.
26. Bates, *William the Conqueror* p.110.
27. *ASC* D p.176.
28. Baxter, 'Edward the Confessor and the Succession Question', p.95.
29. Bates, *William the Conqueror* p.111; p.113.
30. Barlow, *Edward the Confessor* p.117.
31. *ASC* C, D, E pp.178-182.
32. *ASC* C p.182.
33. Dumville, 'The Ætheling', p.12.
34. *ASC* D, p.185.
35. Bates, *William the Conqueror* pp.147-8.
36. *ASC* C p.162.
37. *ASC* E p123; D, p154; C, pp.158-60; Lawson, *Cnut* p.84, n8, p.85; *ASC* C, D, pp.158-159; Hooper, 'Edgar the Ætheling: Anglo-Saxon prince, rebel and crusader', pp.201-202.
38. Licence, *Edward the Confessor* pp.321-325.
39. Baxter, 'Edward the Confessor and the Succession Question', p.102. But see Licence, 'Edward the Confessor and the Succession Question: A Fresh look at the Sources', pp.113-127.
40. *ASC* D p.188-189 and it was perhaps 'tedious' because this was written after the Scandinavian invasion of 1066; various twelfth-century sources tell us more; Barlow *Edward the Confessor* p.209.
41. Baxter, 'MS C of the Anglo-Saxon Chronicle and the Politics of Mid-Eleventh-Century England', p.1197.
42. *ASC* D, E, pp.190-191.
43. Barlow, *Edward the Confessor* p.126, p.211.
44. Bates, *William the Conqueror* p.193.
45. Wilson, *The Bayeux Tapestry* plates 4-26.
46. Baxter, 'Edward the Confessor and the Succession Question', pp.107-8.
47. Bates, *William the Conqueror* pp.116-117.
48. Kempen, 'A mission he bore – to Duke William he came', p.593.
49. Bates, *William the Conqueror* p.119.
50. Kempen, 'A mission he bore – to Duke William he came', pp.591-612.
51. Bates, *William the Conqueror* pp.115-6.
52. Wilson, *The Bayeux Tapestry*, plates 4-26; Kempen, 'A mission he bore – to Duke William he came', p.593.
53. Kempen, 'A mission he bore – to Duke William he came', p.608.

54. *EHD*, ii, p.215.
55. *EHD*, ii, p.217.
56. *ASC* C, D, E pp.190-193
57. *ASC* C, D, E pp.190-193; version C does not mention Edwin and Morcar's role in the rebellion and emphasises Tostig's oppressive rule.
58. *ASC* C, D pp.190-191; Kempen, 'A mission he bore', p.606.
59. *ASC* C p.192; Licence, *Edward the Confessor* p.332.
60. Barlow, *Edward the Confessor* p.235.
61. Kempen, 'A mission he bore', p.605; Barlow was more cautious, *Edward the Confessor* p.235.
62. *ASC* C, D, E pp.192-197; Wilson, *The Bayeux Tapestry* plate 31.
63. *ASC* E p.197.
64. *ASC* C, D pp.194-5.
65. Baxter, 'MS C of the Anglo-Saxon Chronicle,' p.1213; Kempen 'A mission he bore', p.606.
66. Wilson, *The Bayeux Tapestry* plate 30.
67. John of Worcester (a twelfth century source); Licence, *Edward the Confessor* p.331.
68. The *Miracles of St Edmund* (Bates, *William the Conqueror* p.214); The *Life of Wulfstan* was uncertain as to Harold's popularity: Baxter, 'Edward the Confessor and the Succession Question', p.114; for the battle of Hastings, *ASC* D. p199.
69. *EHD*, ii, p218.
70. Baxter, S., 'Edward the Confessor and the Succession Question', p.117; Bates, *William the Conqueror* pp.118-119.
71. Dunbabin, *France in the Making* p.37; Hallam, *Capetian France* p.23.
72. Wormald, '*Engla Lond*', p.9.
73. Bates, *William the Conqueror* pp.219-222; William of Poitiers, *EHD*, ii, p.219.
74. *EHD*, ii. p.220; Wilson, *The Bayeux Tapestry* plates 35-36.
75. Lewis, 'Audacity and Ambition in Early Norman England', p.41; Wilson, *The Bayeux Tapestry* plates 35-38.
76. *ASC* D, p.175.
77. Bates *William the Conqueror* pp.234-5.
78. *ASC* D, E, pp.198-9.
79. *EHD*, ii, p.216.
80. *EHD*, ii, p.225.
81. Bachrach 'The Norman Conquest, Countess Adela and Abbot Baudri,' pp. 65-78; Lawson, *The Battle of Hastings* pp.131-1511.
82. *EHD*, ii, p.225.
83. *EHD*, ii, 225; Wilson, *The Bayeux Tapestry* plates 59-69.
84. *Life of Alfred* p.84.
85. Wilson, *The Bayeux Tapestry* plate 68; *EHD*, ii, p.226.

86. On the death of Harold and the *Bayeux Tapestry*, see Lawson, *The Battle of Hastings* pp.203-213.
87. *EHD*, ii, p216.
88. *EHD*, ii, pp.606-7.
89. *EHD*, ii, p.230.
90. *EHD*, ii, p.231.
91. https://www.archaeology.co.uk/articles/news/a-great-discovery-remains-of-king-alfred-or-his-son-found-in-winchester.htm
92. *ASC* D p.199; Baxter, 'The limits of the Anglo-Saxon State,' p.512.

Ten: Domesday
1. *EHD*, ii, p.430.
2. *EHD*, ii, pp.430-431.
3. Baxter, '1066 and Government', pp.146-7.
4. Baxter, '1066 and Government', p.142.
5. *EHD*, ii, pp.449-451.
6. *EHD*, ii, pp.399-400.
7. *ASC* E, p.219.
8. Maddicott, 'Responses to the Threat of Invasion, 1085', p.990.
9. Maddicott, *The Origins of Parliament* pp.58-60; *ASC* D p.202.
10. *ASC* D, p.204; Baxter & Lewis, 'Domesday Book and the transformation of English landed society', p.386.
11. *ASC* D, p.199; *Bayeux Tapestry* pl.49-50. If William landed on 28 September and the battle was fought on 14 October, this castle was constructed in a week or so.
12. Tacitus, *Agricola* 30; It is possible that William knew of *Agricola*, but it is not until the fifteenth century that it became widely known: Martin, 'From manuscript to print', p.245.
13. *ASC* D, pp.201-2; E, p.236. Henry I and Matilda's grandson was Henry II by their daughter Matilda, from whom the monarchy descended father to son to Richard II (1399), from his cousin Henry IV, Henry V and Henry VI (d.1471).
14. *ASC* D, E, pp.206-8.
15. Baxter, *The Earls of Mercia* p.17.
16. Maddicott, 'Responses to the Threat of Invasion, 1085', p.992.
17. *ASC* E, p.210; p.217; pp.226-7; p.234; p.241.
18. Baxter & Lewis, 'Domesday Book and the transformation of English landed society', p.371.
19. *EHD*, iv, pp.916-917.
20. Lewis, 'Audacity and Ambition', pp. 25-52.
21. Lewis, 'Audacity and Ambition', p.29.
22. Lewis, 'Audacity and Ambition', p.31.
23. Lewis, 'Audacity and Ambition', p.47; Liddiard, 'The landscape of Anglo-Norman England', pp.106-114.

24. Prior, *A Few Positioned Castles: The Norman Art of War* pp.235-239.
25. Bates, *William the Conqueror* pp.297-300.
26. Holt, *Colonial England 1066-1215* p.6.
27. Lewis, 'Audacity and Ambition', p.35.
28. Lewis, 'Audacity and Ambition', p.36.
29. Lewis, 'Audacity and Ambition', p.29.
30. Clanchy, *From Memory to Written Record* p.1.
31. Clanchy, *From Memory to Written Record* p.6.
32. Holt, *Colonial England* p.13.
33. *The Ecclesiastical History of Orderic Vitalis* p.256.
34. Baxter, 'The Making of Domesday Book and the Languages of Lordship', p.280.
35. Baxter, 'The Making of Domesday Book and the Languages of Lordship', pp.271-308.
36. Holt, *Colonial England* p.13, n63.
37. Southern, *The Making of the Middle Ages* p.19.
38. *EHD*, iv, pp.483-484.
39. *EHD*, ii, p.940
40. *EHD*, ii, p.895.
41. *EHD*, i, p.468.
42. *EHD*, ii, p.839.
43. *EHD*, ii, pp.813-816.
44. Holt, 'Politics and Property in early medieval England', p.38; Hudson, 'Life-grants of land and the development of inheritance in Anglo-Norman England', p.72.
45. *EHD*, ii, p.895.
46. *EHD*, ii, pp.896-897.
47. *EHD*, ii, pp.897-898; Purser, 'The Origins of English feudalism? An Episcopal Land-Grant Revisited', pp.80-92.
48. *EHD*, ii, pp.898-899.
49. Harvey, 'The knight and the knight's fee in England', p.21; Baxter & Lewis, 'Domesday Book and the transformation of English landed society', pp.356-7.
50. *EHD*, ii, p.921.
51. Hudson, *Land, Law and Lordship* pp.16-62.
52. Holt, *Colonial England* p.xiii; Baxter & Lewis, 'Domesday Book and the transformation of English landed society', p.403.
53. Clanchy, *From Memory to Written Record* p.6.
54. Lewis, 'Audacity and Ambition', p.38; Domesday Book is available online www.opendomesday.org and visit www.nationalarchives.gov.uk for more information and images.
55. *ASC* E p.216; Baxter, 'The Making of Domesday Book and the Languages of Lordship', p.275.
56. *DB* Buckinghamshire, folio 148v.

57. *EHD*, ii, no.198.
58. *DB* Sussex, folio 28.
59. Lewis, 'Audacity and Ambition', p.42.
60. Maddicott, 'Responses to the Threat of Invasion, 1085', p.997.
61. Maddicott, 'Responses to the Threat of Invasion, 1085', p.986.
62. Lewis, 'Audacity and Ambition', p.42.
63. Baxter, 'The Making of Domesday Book and the Languages of Lordship', p.287.
64. Baxter, 'How and Why was Domesday Made?' p.1129.
65. Baxter, 'The Making of Domesday Book and the Languages of Lordship', p.292.
66. Baxter, 'The Making of Domesday Book and the Languages of Lordship', p.286; *DB* (Hampshire, folio 44).
67. Baxter, 'The Making of Domesday Book and the Languages of Lordship', p.283.
68. Baxter, 'The Making of Domesday Book and the Languages of Lordship', p289.
69. Baxter & Lewis, 'Domesday Book and the transformation of English landed society', p.378.
70. Baxter & Lewis, 'Domesday Book and the transformation of English landed society', p.380.
71. Baxter & Lewis, 'Domesday Book and the transformation of English landed society', p.370.
72. Baxter, 'The Making of Domesday Book and the Languages of Lordship', p.292.
73. Baxter, 'The Making of Domesday Book and the Languages of Lordship', p.302.
74. Baxter & Lewis, 'Domesday Book and the transformation of English landed society', p.375.
75. Baxter & Lewis, 'Domesday Book and the transformation of English landed society', p.371.
76. Baxter & Lewis, 'Domesday Book and the transformation of English landed society', p.367.
77. Baxter & Lewis, 'Domesday Book and the transformation of English landed society', p.381, p.384.
78. Molyneaux, *The Formation of the English Kingdom* p.5.
79. Titow, *English Rural Society* p.70.
80. *DB*, Hampshire, folio 38.
81. *ASC* E, p.217.
82. Maddicott, 'Responses to the Threat of Invasion, 1085', p.996.
83. Wormald, '*Engla Lond*', p.7.
84. Purser, 'William FitzOsbern, Earl of Hereford: Personality and Power on the Welsh Frontier, 1066-1071', pp.133-146.
85. Bates: '1066: does the date still matter?' p.463.

86. Bates, '1066: does the date still matter?' p.458.
87. Abulafia *et al, The Western Mediterranean Kingdoms*, Chapter One, 'The origins of the Sicilian Kingdom', pp.3-13.
88. Lewis, 'Audacity and Ambition', pp.38-39; *ASC*, E, p.220.
89. Winkler, 'The Norman Conquest of the classical past', pp. 476-7.
90. Bates, *William the Conqueror* p.383.
91. *ASC* E, pp.220-221.
92. Bates, '1066: does the date still matter?' p.458.
93. Bates, *William the Conqueror* p.526.
94. *ASC*, E, p.236 (my italics).

Eleven: Continental Cousins
1. *EHD*, ii, pp.290-291; .
2. Gillingham, 'Civilizing the English?' p.18.
3. Clanchy, *From Memory to Written Record* p.30.
4. Lewis, 'Audacity and Ambition', pp.39-40; Garnett, *The Norman Conquest in English History* offers the latest, most detailed reassessment.
5. Frantzen, 'The Englishness of Bede', p.232; Plassmann, 'Bede's Legacy in William of Malmesbury and Henry of Huntingdon', pp.171-191.
6. Woolf, 'Oral Tradition in Early Modern England', p.28.
7. *EHD*, i, pp.607-11; *EHD*, ii, pp.836-837.
8. http://www.oum.ox.ac.uk/settlers/Settlers: Genetics, Geography and the Peopling of Britain, Oxford University Museum of Natural History.
9. Gillingham, 'Cultures of Conquest', pp.165-182.
10. Baxter, '1066 and Government', p.145.
11. The culture of feud, the violent vengeance that was an integral element of culture in the pre-Viking period, eas largely supplanted by state punishment by the thirteenth century; Lambert, 'Theft, Homicide and Crime in late Anglo-Saxon Law', p.6.
12. *EHD*, ii, pp.490-569.
13. *EHD*, ii, p.523 (my italics).
14. *EHD*, ii, p.523.
15. *EHD*, iv, p.70.
16. *EHD*, ii, pp.462-479.
17. *EHD*, iii, pp.829-831.
18. *EHD*, ii, pp.292-293.
19. *EHD*, ii, p.294.
20. *EHD*, ii, pp.400-402.
21. The battle was described in a letter by a priest of Fécamp, shortly afterwards; *EHD*, ii, p.304.
22. Bates, '1066: does the date still matter?' p.454.
23. Madeline, 'The Idea of "Empire" as Hegemonic Power', p.182, p.196; Bates, *Normans and Empire*.
24. *EHD*, ii, pp.572-3.

25. Baxter, '1066 and Government', pp.152-3; Carpenter, *Magna Carta* p.189.
26. *EHD*, ii, pp.422-427.
27. *Life of Alfred*, p.106, p.181.
28. *EHD*, ii, p.294.
29. Maddicott, *The Origins of Parliament* pp.68-69.
30. Karn, 'Nigel, bishop of Ely, and the restoration of the exchequer after the "anarchy" of King Stephen's reign', pp.303-4.
31. Karn, 'Nigel, bishop of Ely', p.311.
32. *EHD*, ii, pp.399-400.
33. Maddicott, *The Origins of Parliament* pp.99-100.
34. *EHD*, ii, pp.402-404.
35. *EHD*, ii, pp.459-462.
36. *EHD*, ii, p.407.
37. *EHD*, ii, p.297.
38. *EHD*, ii, p.390.
39. *EHD*, ii, pp.404-7.
40. *EHD*, ii, pp.386-390.
41. *EHD*, ii, p.647.
42. *EHD*, ii, pp.604-5.
43. *EHD*, ii, p.718-722.
44. Edward Grim is a detached and impartial eyewitness; *EHD*, ii, pp.761-768.
45. *EHD*, ii, pp.774-775; Barlow, *Thomas Becket* pp.237-250.
46. Bates, '1066: does the date still matter?' p.456.
47. *EHD*, ii, pp.431-434.
48. Potter, *Law, Liberty and the Constitution* p.47; *EHD*, ii, pp.438-440.
49. *EHD*, ii, pp.407-413; Hudson, *Land, Law and Lordship* pp.262, 281.
50. *EHD*, ii, pp.411-413.
51. Bartlett, *England under the Norman and Angevin Kings* pp.190-193.
52. Lambert, 'Theft, Homicide and Crime', p.6.
53. Clanchy, *From Memory to Written Record* pp.70-75.
54. Hudson, *History of the Laws of England* p.251.
55. Rambaran-Olm, 'Trial by History's Jury: Examining II Æthelred's Legislative and Literary Legacy, AD 993-1006', pp.780-1.
56. www.bl.uk/magna-carta/articles/magna-carta-english-translation
57. *EHD*, ii, pp.416-417.
58. *EHD*, ii, pp.413-416.
59. *EHD*, ii, p.524.

Twelve: Tyranny or Law?

1. Holt, *Colonial England* p.xvii.
2. Gillingham (*Richard the Lionheart*) exposed the truth of Richard's death while besieging the castle of Chalus on the borders of the Angevin

dominions; he neglected to don his mail shirt during a routine patrol and was hit by a crossbow bolt, dying days later (pp.9-23).

3. Crouch, *William Marshal* p.77.
4. Carpenter, *Magna Carta* p.97 summarises the sources regarding John's reputation; Gillingham, 'Historians without Hindsight: Coggeshall, Diceto and Howden on the Early Years of John's Reign'; Bradbury, 'Philip Augustus and King John: Personality and History', in Church ed., *King John: New Interpretations* pp.1-26; pp.347-361.
5. Carpenter, *Magna Carta* p.102.
6. Carpenter, *Magna Carta* pp.102-3.
7. The near contemporary Chronicle of Margam Abbey records the murder of Arthur (Trinity College, Cambridge University).
8. Carpenter, *Magna Carta* p.113.
9. Carpenter, *Magna Carta* p.254.
10. Barratt, 'The Revenues of John', p.88.
11. Holt, *The Northerners* p.34.
12. Barratt, 'The Revenues of John', pp.85-86.
13. Carpenter, *Magna Carta* p.242.
14. *EHD*, ii, pp.784-787.
15. *EHD*, ii, pp.462-471.
16. EHD, ii, pp.52.
17. Carpenter, *Magna Carta* p.342.
18. Farrell, 'History, Prophecy and the Arthur of the Normans', pp.99-114.
19. Eadmer and William of Malmesbury were among the forgers; Clanchy, *From Memory to Written Record* pp.320-1.
20. Bartlett, *England under the Norman and Angevin Kings* pp.249-251.
21. Grandsen, 'The Growth of the Glastonbury Traditions and Legend', pp.337-358.
22. Maddicott, 'The Oath of Marlborough', p.281.
23. Maddicott, 'The Oath of Marlborough', p.288.
24. Maddicott, 'The Oath of Marlborough', p.299.
25. Maddicott, 'The Oath of Marlborough', p.312.
26. Maddicott, *The Origins of Parliament* p.88.
27. Carpenter, *Magna Carta* p.246.
28. *EHD*, iii, pp.307-310.
29. Carpenter, *Magna Carta* p.391.
30. Carpenter, *Magna Carta* pp.311-313.
31. *EHD*, iii, p.310.
32. Carpenter, *Magna Carta* p.410.
33. Carpenter, 'Archbishop Langton and Magna Carta', pp.1053-4.
34. Vincent, 'Magna Carta: Oblivion and Revival', p.14.
35. Carpenter, *Magna Carta* p.462.
36. Vincent, 'Magna Carta: Oblivion and Revival', p.14.

37. Carpenter, *Magna Carta* p.11.
38. Carpenter, *Magna Carta* p.ix.
39. Carpenter, *Magna Carta* p.141.
40. Carpenter, *Magna Carta* p.129.
41. Carpenter, *Magna Carta* p.147.
42. Carpenter, *Magna Carta* p.34.
43. Holt, *Magna Carta* pp.300-301.
44. Carpenter, *Magna Carta* p.x.
45. Carpenter, *Magna Carta* p.309.
46. Rowlands, 'The Text and Distribution of the Writ for the Publication of Magna Carta, 1215', pp.1422-1431.
47. Rowlands, 'The Text and Distribution of the Writ for the Publication of Magna Carta, 1215', p.1428.
48. Carpenter, *Magna Carta* p.479; the copy was found by Prof. Nicholas Vincent in a cartulary of St Augustine's Abbey, Canterbury in the Lambeth Palace Library in 2014.
49. *EHD*, iii, pp.324-326.

Thirteen: The Community of the Realm

1. *EHD*, ii. pp.417-420.
2. www.bl.uk/collection-items/magna-carta-1225
3. Carpenter, *Magna Carta*, p.499.
4. Maddicott, *The Origins of Parliament* pp.170-3.
5. Maddicott, *The Origins of Parliament* pp.157-8.
6. Maddicott, *The Origins of Parliament* p.226.
7. Maddicott, *The Origins of Parliament* pp.378-380.
8. Maddicott, *The Origins of Parliament* p.439.
9. Maddicott, 'Parliament and the People', p.350; *The Origins of Parliament*, passim.
10. Steane, *The Archaeology of the Medieval English Monarchy* pp.45-71; but see Mortimer, *The Perfect King* pp.405-417 on the death of Edward II.
11. Maddicott, *The Origins of Parliament* pp.161-162.
12. Wild, 'The jewel accounts of King Henry III', p.429. The bullae is on display in the British Museum.
13. *EHD*, iii, pp.361-367, pp.370-376.
14. *EHD*, iii, pp.376-379.
15. Arnoux, 'Border, Trade Route or Market?' p.44.
16. *EHD*, iii, p.123.
17. *EHD*, iii, p.128.
18. Henry IV's first wife before he become king was the English Mary de Bohun, mother of Henry V. Edward IV's marriage to the Englishwoman Elizabeth Woodville ended his first reign.

19. Maddicott, *The Origins of Parliament* p.254.
20. Carpenter, *Magna Carta* p.509.
21. Maddicott, *The Origins of Parliament* pp.107-108.
22. Wild, 'The jewel accounts of King Henry III', p.423.
23. Vincent, 'Magna Carta: Oblivion and Revival', p.14; Ambler, 'Magna Carta: Its Confirmation at Simon de Montfort's Parliament of 1265', p.829.
24. *EHD*, iii, pp.380-384.
25. *EHD*, iii, 384-396.
26. Gillingham & Griffiths, *Medieval Britain: A Very Short Introduction* p.39.
27. Maddicott, *The Origins of Parliament* p.282.
28. King, *Edward I: A New King Arthur?* p.98.
29. Gillingham & Griffiths *Medieval Britain* p.40.
30. *EHD*, iii, pp.396-405.
31. *EHD*, iii, p.397
32. *EHD*, iii, p.917-918.
33. *EHD*, iii, pp.460-462.
34. *EHD*, iii, p.827.
35. *EHD*, iii, p.828.
36. *EHD*, iii, p.828.
37. Sharpe, *A Fiery and Furious People*, p.46; www.ons.gov.uk
38. *EHD*, iii, p.826.
39. Clanchy, *From Memory to Written Record* p.2; p.235.
40. Clanchy, *From Memory to Written Record* pp.60-63.
41. *EHD*, iii, pp.464-466.
42. *EHD*, iii, p.469.
43. Maddicott, *The Origins of Parliament* p.299.
44. Bartlett, *England under the Norman and Angevin Kings* pp.346-360.
45. Carpenter, *Magna Carta* p.148.
46. *EHD*, iii, pp.411-412.
47. Carpenter, *Magna Carta* p.148.
48. Carpenter, *Magna Carta* p.148.
49. *EHD*, iii, p.469.
50. *EHD*, iii, pp.469-72.
51. *EHD*, iii, pp.485-486.
52. *EHD*, iii, pp.488-489.
53. Maddicott, *The Origins of Parliament* pp.304-307.
54. Vincent, 'Magna Carta: Oblivion and Revival', p.14.
55. Carpenter, *Magna Carta* p.12.
56. Coss, 'Presentism', p.234.
57. *EHD*, iii, p.893.
58. *EHD*, iii, p.898.

Notes

Fourteen: Apocalypse Now – Plague, Revolt, and Usurpation

1. Maddicott, *The Origins of Parliament*, pp.360-1.
2. *EHD*, iii, p.525; p.527.
3. Mortimer, The Death of Edward II in Berkeley Castle', pp.1176-1214; Mortimer, *The Perfect King* p.210; pp.405-418.
4. Maddicott, 'Parliament and the People', p.338.
5. 'Building the Future, Transforming our Past', *Historic England*, www. HistoricEngland.org.uk p.10.
6. *EHD*, iii, p.855.
7. *EHD*, iii, p.854.
8. *EHD*, iv, pp.984-5; the total raised by the 10th and 15th levies from the lay Subsidy, ie one tenth and one fifteenth of all moveable property, was £38,170.
9. Franklin, *The Taxpayers of Medieval Gloucestershire* pp.2-3.
10. Dyer, 'Poverty and Its Relief in Late Medieval England', p.42.
11. Campbell, 'The Agrarian Problem in the Early Fourteenth Century', pp.24–44.
12. Slavin, 'The Great Bovine Pestilence', pp.1239-1266.
13. Brown, *History and Climate Change: A Eurocentric Perspective*
14. Galofré-Vilà, *et al*, 'Heights across the last 2000 years in England', pp.67-98.
15. Mays, *et al*. 'A multidisciplinary study of a burnt and mutilated assemblage of human remains', pp.441-455.
16. Smith, 'Towards a social archaeology of the late medieval English peasantry', pp.291-416, where stone robbing and poaching are examples of resistance.
17. Platt, *King Death: The Black Death and its aftermath in late-medieval England*; for the impact on one locality, Willmott *et al*, 'A Black Death mass grave at Thornton Abbey', pp.179-196, a rare mass grave of 48 men, women, and children (over 50% were aged between one and seventeen) indicating the collapse of established systems of dealing with the dead.
18. *EHD*, iv, pp.89-91.
19. *EHD*, iv, pp.993-994.
20. *EHD*, iv, p.403.
21. Bennett, 'Compulsory Service in Late Medieval England', pp.7-51.
22. Maddicott, 'Parliament and the People', p.336; Harriss, *King, Parliament and Public Finance* pp.516-7.
23. Maddicott, 'Parliament and the People', p.345.
24. Dodd, 'A parliament full of rats?' pp.21-49; Jewell, *'Piers Plowman – A Poem of Crisis'*, pp.59-81.
25. *EHD*, iv, pp.422-423.
26. *EHD*, iv, pp.126-127.

27. Dodd, 'A parliament full of rats?' pp.42-43.
28. Dobson, ed, *The Peasants' Revolt of 1381*; Bennett, 'John Gower, squire of Kent,' pp.258-282, demonstrates the localism of the Revolt.
29. *EHD*, iv, pp.127-140.
30. *EHD*, iv, p.143 (John of Gaunt's Register).
31. Lacey, '"Grace for the rebels": the role of the royal pardon in the Peasants' Revolt of 1381', pp.36-63.
32. *EHD*, iv, p.135.
33. Spindler, 'Flemings in the Peasants' Revolt, 1381', pp.59-78.
34. *Chaucer, The Canterbury Tales* (The Nun's Priest's Tale) pp.247-8.
35. Spindler, 'Flemings in the Peasants' Revolt, 1381', p.75.
36. *EHD*, iv, p.131.
37. Spindler, 'Flemings in the Peasants' Revolt, 1381', pp.69-70.
38. Ormerod & Mackman, *Immigrant England* p.249.
39. *EHD*, iv, p.138.
40. Rampton, 'The Peasants' Revolt of 1381 and the Written Word', p.46.
41. Whittle, 'Peasant Politics and Class Consciousness', pp. 233-247.
42. Rampton, 'The Peasants' Revolt of 1381 and the Written Word', p.51.
43. *EHD*, iv, p.134.
44. *EHD*, iv, pp.142-3.
45. Dodd, 'A parliament of rats?' pp.46-7.
46. Rampton, 'The Peasants' Revolt of 1381 and the Written Word', p.55; Hilton, *Bond Men Made Free* is the classic Marxist interpretation of the Revolt.
47. Razi, 'Serfdom and Freedom in Medieval England', pp. 182-7.
48. Maddicott, 'Parliament and the People', p.348.
49. Mayhew, 'Prices in England, 1170-1750', pp.23-4.
50. Dyer, 'Poverty and Its Relief', p.43.
51. King, 'What Werre Amounteth', pp.418-436.
52. *EHD*, iv, pp.484.
53. *EHD*, iv, pp.1002-1003.
54. *EHD*, iv, pp.453-454.
55. *EHD*, iv, p.406.
56. *EHD*, iv, pp.172-173.
57. *EHD*, iv, p.407.
58. Barron, 'The Deposition of Richard II', p.133.
59. Given-Wilson, 'Chronicles: authorship, evidence and objectivity', p.16.
60. Pugh, *Henry V and the Southampton Plot of 1415* pp.61-2.
61. Bradford, 'A silent presence', p.197.
62. Bradford, 'A silent presence', pp.202-3.

Fifteen: Unfinished Business – Wales, Scotland, and France
1. Gillingham & Griffiths, *Medieval Britain* p.149
2. Given-Wilson, *Chronicles: The Writing of History in Medieval England* pp.181-2.
3. Gillingham & Griffiths, *Medieval Britain* p.151.
4. Crooks, 'State of the Union', p.31.
5. Lambert & Ormerod, 'A matter of trust', p.226.
6. Bates, '1066: does the date still matter?' p.448.
7. Bates, '1066: does the date still matter?' p.448; *EHD*, iv, p.419.
8. Griffiths, 'The island of England in the fifteenth century', p.182.
9. Gillingham & Griffiths, *Medieval Britain* p.150.
10. Crooks, 'State of the Union', p.40.
11. Gillingham, *The English in the Twelfth Century*; Davies, *The First English Empire: Power and Identities in the British Isles*.
12. Crooks, 'State of the Union', pp.4-5.
13. Crooks, 'State of the Union', p.7; the citation is from the *Deeds of Henry the Fifth*.
14. M. Prestwich, *The Three Edwards* thought that it was 'inadequate resources' rather than 'administrative incompetence' (p51). J. O. Prestwich argued that by the late thirteenth century, England was a bureaucratic and authoritarian state, *The Place of War in English History*.
15. *EHD*, iii, pp.467-468.
16. Gillingham, 'The Foundations of a Disunited Kingdom', pp.48–64.
17. Morris, *A Great and Terrible King* p.376.
18. *EHD*, iii, pp.422-427.
19. Spencer, 'The comital military retinue,' p.59.
20. King & Etty, 'How successful was Edward I as king?' p.45.
21. *EHD*, iv, p.59.
22. *EHD*, iv, pp.51-52.
23. Keen, 'The Angevin Legacy', pp.144-5.
24. *EHD*, iv, pp.61-62.
25. *EHD*, iv, pp.62-63.
26. *EHD*, iv, p.64.
27. *EHD*, iv, pp.67-68.
28. *EHD*, iv, p.70.
29. *EHD*, iv, p.64.
30. *EHD*, iv, p.103.
31. *EHD*, iv, pp.63-64; Harriss, *King, Parliament and Public Finance* pp.231-232.
32. McFarlane, *England in the Fifteenth Century* p.141.
33. Raven, 'The Earldom Endowments of 1337', pp.498-529.
34. *EHD*, iv, p.75.
35. *EHD*, iv, pp.91-92; Keen, *Chivalry*.

36. Gransden, *Legends, Tradition and History* p.274; Mortimer, *The Perfect King* pp.191-198.
37. *EHD*, iv, pp.103-106.
38. *EHD*, iv, pp.114-115.
39. Mortimer, *The Perfect King* p.378.
40. Crooks, 'State of the Union,' p.13.
41. Clark, *The Chronica Maiora* p.328; Lang, 'John Bradmore and His Book Philomena', pp.121–130.
42. Bradford, 'A silent presence', p.209.
43. *EHD*, iv, p.208-9.
44. *EHD*, iv, p.210 (Walsingham's *History of England*).
45. Pugh, *The Southampton Plot* pp. xii, p.130.
46. *EHD*, iv, pp.210-211.
47. Mortimer, *1415: Henry V's Year of Glory* p.319.
48. Curry, 'How well organised was the invasion of France in 1415?' p.61.
49. www.medievalsoldier.org incudes a database of English armies 1369-1453.
50. *EHD*, iv, pp.211-214.
51. Mortimer, *1415: Henry V's Year of Glory* suggests that there were between 8-10,000 English troops and 12,000 French, p.565.
52. Mortimer, *1415: Henry V's Year of Glory*, pp.447-453.
53. *EHD*, iv, pp.215-218.
54. Ayton, 'The military careerist in fourteenth-century England', pp.4-23.
55. Walker, *The Lancastrian Affinity*, p.39.
56. *EHD*, iv, p.1182.
57. Creighton *et al*, 'The Face of Battle?' p.187.
58. Creighton, 'The Face of Battle?' p.183.
59. Bohna, 'Armed Force and Civic Legitimacy', pp.563-582.
60. *EHD*, iv, pp.225-226.
61. *EHD*, iv, pp.226-227.
62. Allmand, C. *Henry V* p. 441.
63. *EHD*, iv, p.423.
64. *EHD*, iv, pp.270-271.
65. Keen, 'The Angevin Legacy', pp.146.
66. Keen, 'The Angevin Legacy', p.151.
67. *EHD*, iv, pp.324-325.
68. Tilly, *Coercion, Capital, and European States* pp.78-79.

Sixteen: Burning Books, Burning People: The End of the Medieval Millennium
1. *EHD*, iv, p.655.
2. *EHD*, iv, pp.661-662.
3. *EHD*, iv, p.670.

4. *EHD*, iv, p.693.
5. *EHD*, iv, p.693.
6. Cavill, 'Heresy, Law and the State', pp.270-295.
7. Windeatt (ed), *The Book of Margery Kempe* p.162.
8. Hudson, *The Premature Reformation*.
9. *EHD*, iv, pp.868-869.
10. Maddicott, 'The Ballads of Robin Hood', pp.276-299.
11. Cunningham, 'Why are medieval administrative records so valuable to historians?' p.22.
12. *EHD*, iv, p.1205.
13. Given-Wilson, *Chronicles: the writing of history in England* p.140.
14. *EHD*, iv, pp.1135-1137.
15. Payling, 'Social mobility, demographic change', pp. 51-73 suggested that the Black Death stimulated upward social mobility long before the Dissolution, but Maddern argues that 'successful careerists were the exception, not the norm', 'Social Mobility', pp.113-133.
16. *EHD*, iv, p.1004.
17. *EHD*, iv, p.1178.
18. Jones's *Chaucer's Knight: Portrait of a Medieval Mercenary* turned scholarly assumptions upside down; see pp.126-135 for the discussion on the 'shabby knight'.
19. Purser: 'A 'community in the county'? Sir John Sandys and social mobility in later medieval Hampshire', pp.45-69.
20. Bennett, *Community, Class and Careerism: Cheshire and Lancashire Society*; Wright, *The Derbyshire Gentry*; Payling, *Political Society in Lancastrian England*; Carpenter, *Locality and Polity: A Study of Warwickshire Landed Society*; Acheson, *A Gentry Community – Leicestershire*. Carpenter argued that great lords wielded the most influence in the localities; 'Gentry and Community in Medieval England', pp.340-380.
21. Polden, 'The social networks of the Buckinghamshire gentry', pp.371-394; Arvanigan, 'A county community or the politics of the nation?' pp.41-61; Dodd, 'County and Community in Medieval England', pp.777-820.
22. Hicks, *Bastard Feudalism*.
23. Ross, 'The English Aristocracy and Mesne Feudalism', pp.1027-1059.
24. *EHD*, iv, p.1134.
25. *EHD*, iv, pp.490-491.
26. Page (ed), *The Pipe Roll of the Bishopric of Winchester* p.xx.
27. *EHD*, iv, pp.1015-1016.
28. *EHD*, iv, pp.1202-1203.
29. *EHD*, iv, pp.459-460; Payling, 'County Parliamentary Elections', p.244.
30. Virgoe, 'Aspects of the County Community', pp.7-11.

31. *EHD*, iv, pp.465.
32. Representation of the People Act 1918, www.parliament.uk
33. Maddicott, 'Parliament and the People', p.350.
34. Grummitt, 'Household, politics and political morality', p.395.
35. Hicks, *English Political Culture*, p.109.
36. *EHD*, iv, p.507.
37. *EHD*, iv, pp.419.
38. *EHD*, iv, pp.436-437.
39. *EHD*, iv, p.264.
40. *EHD*, iv, pp.264-268.
41. Rollison, 'Class, Community and Popular Rebellion', pp.220-232.
42. Grummitt, *Henry VI* (Routledge 2015) p.161.
43. Gillingham & Griffiths, *Medieval Britain* p.140.
44. Wolfe, *Henry VI* (Methuen 1983), pp.18-19; 270-3.
45. *EHD*, iv, pp.271-273.
46. *EHD*, iv, pp.278-279; Grummitt, *Henry VI* p.175.
47. Goodman, *The Wars of the Roses* p.228.
48. For a discussion of the legality of Yorkist claim to the throne, Bennett, 'Edward III's Entail', pp.580-609.
49. Thornton, 'More on a Murder: Deaths of the 'Princes in the Tower', pp.4-25. Research is ongoing into the whereabouts of the missing princes: https://www.revealingrichardiii.com/langley.html
50. Goodman, *The Wars of the Roses* p.225.
51. Goodman, *The Wars of the Roses* p.244.
52. Fiorato, *et al*, *Blood Red Roses* pp.90-102.
53. Keen, 'The Angevin Legacy', p.148.
54. Jones, *Bosworth 1485*, pp.166-169.
55. Davies, 'Tudor: What's in a Name?'p.31 and n30.
56. Davies, 'Tudor: What's in a Name?' pp.27-28.
57. *EHD*, v, p.445.
58. Thornton,' The battle of Sandeford', pp.436-442.
59. Grummitt, 'Household, politics and political morality', p.398.
60. Gunn, 'Politic history, New Monarchy and state formation', pp.380-392.
61. Cavill, 'The enforcement of the penal statues in the 1490s', pp.482-492; Cunningham, 'Loyalty and the usurper', pp.459-481.
62. For example, see Tankard 'The Johnson Family and the Reformation', pp.469-490.
63. *EHD*, v, pp.187-192.
64. *EHD*, v, pp.192-201.
65. Ormerod *et al*, *Immigrant England* p.57.
66. Carter, '*It would have pitied any heart to see*' pp.77-110.
67. Fritze, 'Truth Hath Lacked Witnesse, Tyme Wanted Light', pp.274-291.
68. Wood, *In Search of England* pp.111-124.

69. Dickens, *The English Reformation* pp.209-210.
70. Curteis, *et al*, 'East Anglia's Medieval Rood Screens', pp.54-59, DOI: 10.1080/00393630.2020.1752970
71. Sharkey, 'Between king and pope', pp.236-248.
72. Marshall, 'The Naming of Protestant England', pp.87-128; Evenden & Freeman, 'Print, Profit and Propaganda', pp.1288-1307.
73. Walsham, 'Skeletons in the Cupboard', pp.121-143; Thomas, *Religion and the Decline of Magic* pp.25-50.
74. *EHD*, v, pp.474-475.
75. *EHD*, v, pp.475-476.
76. *EHD*, v, pp.475-477.
77. Trevor-Roper, *Historical Essays*, cited in MacCulloch, *Thomas Cromwell* p.xxiv.
78. Ives, 'Tudor dynastic problems revisited', pp.255-279.
79. Greenblatt, *Tyrant: Shakespeare on Power* pp.17-23.
80. Younger, 'If the Armada had landed', pp.328-354.
81. Arnoux, 'Border, Trade Route or Market?' p.43.
82. Blue passports, the symbol of Brexit, are made in France.
83. Vincent, 'The Making of a Monster', p.62.
84. Davies, 'Tudor: What's in a Name?' p.29; p.31.
85. Stapleton, 'Pope Gregory and the *Gens Anglorum*', p.15.
86. Frantzen, 'The Englishness of Bede', pp.236-7.
87. Niles, 'The Myth of the Feud', p.173.
88. Davies, 'Tudor: What's in a Name?' p.39.
89. The Cloptons, Ferrers (Baddesley Clinton) and Throckmortons (Coughton Court, still there today); the ringleader of the 1605 Gunpowder Plot, Robert Catesby spent childhood years at Coughton, his mother was a Throckmorton. The Lucys of Charlecote were closely allied to Latimer.
90. Bearman, 'The Early Reformation Experience in a Warwickshire Market Town', pp.68-109.
91. It is not possible to be certain: Bearman, 'The Early Reformation Experience in a Warwickshire Market Town', pp.102-104; p.106; Winstanley, 'Shakespeare, Catholicism and Lancashire', pp.172-191.
92. www.nationalarchives.gov.uk (PROB 11/44/126)
93. Barber, 'Shakespeare and Warwickshire Dialect' pp.91-118 concludes that 'not a single claim that Shakespeare used Warwickshire, Midlands or Cotswold dialect can be upheld.' (p.115).
94. Breen, 'Shakespeare and History Writing' pp.1-10 provides a useful historiographical overview.
95. Davies, 'Information, Disinformation and Political Knowledge' pp.228-53 contains a concise overview of the sources of Richard III's usurpation and reign.

96. Appleby *et al*, 'Perimortem trauma in King Richard III: a skeletal analysis', pp.253-259; King, *et al*. Identification of the remains of King Richard III; pp.1-8. Hicks, *The Family of Richard III*; chapter 9 questions the evidence that it is Richard III.

Afterword: Upstairs, Downton?

1. Queen Elizabeth II is directly descended from George I who claimed descent from James I, who in turn descended from Henry VII's daughter; Henry VII and Elizabeth of York were descended from Edward III, whose direct ancestor was Henry I, who married Eadgyth, niece of Edgar Ætheling, a descendent of Alfred.
2. 62% (YouGov 2020: https://yougov.co.uk/topics/travel/survey-results/daily/2020/02/18/8b405/1)
3. https://yougov.co.uk/topics/politics/articles-reports/2018/06/18/young-people-are-less-proud-being-english-their-el
4. Shrubsole, *Who Owns England?* pp.309-329.
5. www.churchofengland.org 'Report of the Church Buildings Review Group', p.12; p.24.
6. www.churchofengland.org
7. Waugh, preface to revised edition of *Brideshead Revisited* (1962).
8. West-Harling, 'Medievalism as Fun and Games', pp.6-7.
9. www.historicengland.org.uk; 'The Heritage sector in England and its impact on the economy: a report for Historic England', (October 2018), pp.6-7.
10. https://commonslibrary.parliament.uk/research-briefings/sn00611/ House of Commons Library Briefing Paper Number (00611,16 December 2019): 'The motor industry: statistics and policy', pp.3-4.
11. www.heritagefund.org.uk 'Strategic Funding Framework 2019-2024' (The National Lottery Heritage Fund), p.6.
12. ALVA (Association of Leading Visitor Attractions): www.alva.org.uk
13. www.hrp.org.uk
14. www.nationaltrust.org.uk Annual Reports 2018/19.
15. www.english-heritage.org.uk Annual Report 2018/19.
16. Hartley, *The Go-Between*, p.1.
17. 'National Trust Interim Report on the Connections between Colonialism and Properties now in the Care of the National Trust, Including Links with Historical Slavery', (www.nationaltrust.org.uk 2020).
18. *In Our Time: Heritage* BBC4 (18 July 2002): www.bbc.co.uk
19. https://yougov.co.uk/topics/politics/articles-reports/2018/06/18/young-people-are-less-proud-being-english-their-el
20. 53.4% voted Leave in England, 52.5% in Wales, 44% in Northern Ireland and 38% in Scotland (www.commonslibrary.parliament.uk: Briefing Paper CBP 7639.

Select Bibliography

Abbreviations
ASC   *The Anglo-Saxon Chronicles*, ed & trans. Swanton, M., Phoenix, 2000.
EH   *Bede: The Ecclesiastical History of the English People* eds. J. McClure & R. Collins (Oxford 1994)
EHD   *English Historical Documents*: volume 1: *c*.500–1042, ed. D. Whitelock (2nd ed. 1979); volume 2: 1042–1189, edited by D. C. Douglas and G. W. Greenaway (2nd ed. 1981); volume 3: 1189–1327, ed. by H. Rothwell (1975); volume 4: 1327–1485, ed. A. Myers (1969); volume 5: 1485–1558, ed. C. H. Williams (1967).

Journal Abbreviations
ANS   *Anglo-Norman Studies* (Proceedings of the Battle Conference).
ASE   *Anglo-Saxon England.*
EHR   *English Historical Review.*
HR   *Historical Research.*
HWJ   *History Workshop Journal.*
JEH   *Journal of Ecclesiastical History.*
JMH   *Journal of Medieval History.*
P&P   *Past and Present.*

Original written sources
The Anglo-Saxon Chronicles, ed. & trans. Swanton, M., Phoenix, 2000.
The Bayeux Tapestry, Wilson, D. M., London, 2004.
Bede: The Ecclesiastical History of the English People, McClure, J. and Collins, R., eds., Oxford, 1994.
Beowulf https://ebeowulf.uky.edu/ (University of Kentucky/British Library manuscript and audible version), https://www.bl.uk/collection-items/beowulf (The British Library, Beowulf, Cotton MS Vitellius A XV).
Chaucer, G., *The Canterbury Tales* trans., Coghill, N., Penguin, 1963.
Chibnall, M., ed. and trans., *The Ecclesiastical History of Orderic Vitalis,* 6 vols, Oxford 1969-80.

Clark, J., *The Chronica Maiora of Thomas Walsingham (1376–1422)* trans. Preest, D., Boydell & Brewer, 2005.

Davis, R.H.C., & Chibnall, M. eds., *The Gesta Guillelmi of William of Poitiers*, Oxford 1998.

Domesday Book, Penguin 2003; available freely online at www.opendomesday. org

English Historical Documents: vol. 1: *c*.500–1042, ed. Whitelock, D., 2nd ed. 1979; vol. 2: 1042–1189, ed. Douglas, D.C., Greenaway, G. W., 2nd ed. 1981; vol. 3: 1189–1327, ed. Rothwell, H., 1975; vol. 4: 1327–1485, ed. Myers, A., 1969; vol. 5: 1485–1558, ed. Williams, C. H., 1967.

Franklin, P. *The Taxpayers of Medieval Gloucestershire* Alan Sutton, 1993.

Geoffrey of Monmouth: The History of the Kings of Britain trans. Thorpe, L., Penguin 1983.

Heaney, S., *Beowulf,* Faber & Faber, 2000.

Keynes, S. & Lapidge, M., *Alfred the Great: Asser's* Life of King Alfred *and other contemporary sources*, Penguin, 2004.

Page, M., ed., *The Pipe Roll of the Bishopric of Winchester 1409-1410,* Hampshire County Council, 1999.

Sawyer, P., www.esawyer.org.uk: a comprehensive list of all surviving charters of the Anglo-Saxon period.

Tolkien J. R. R., *Beowulf: a translation and commentary* ed. Tolkien, C., HarperCollins, 2016.

Webb, J., Farmer, D., *The Age of Bede* Penguin, 1988.

Windeatt, B., ed. and trans., *The Book of Margery Kempe,* Penguin 2004.

Archaeological sources and archives
www.ashmolean.org (The Ashmolean Museum, Oxford, the Alfred Jewel, Crondall and Watlington Hoards).

https://www.bl.uk/collection-items/magna-carta-1215

https://www.britishmuseum.org/ (Sutton Hoo and Mildenhall treasures).

www.medievalsoldier.org (database of English armies 1369-1453.

www.nationalarchives.gov.uk (Domesday Book; Shakespeare's Will, PROB 11/44/126).

www.nms.ac.uk (The National Museum of Scotland, the Galloway Hoard).

http://norfolkmuseumscollections.org/ (Binham and Winfarthing Hoards).

https://www.nationaltrust.org.uk/sutton-hoo

https://www.museums-sheffield.org.uk/ (Benty Grange helmet)

https://www.prittlewellprincelyburial.org/ (Prittelwell princely burial)

www.staffordshirehoard.org.uk (The Staffordshire Hoard)

www.yorkarchaeology.co.uk (Jorvik Viking Centre, York).

Secondary literature
Abulafia, D., et. al, *The Western Mediterranean Kingdoms: The Struggle for Dominion 1200-1500* Routledge, 1997.

Alfsdotter, C., Papmehl-Dufay, L., & Victor, H., 'A moment frozen in time: Evidence of a late fifth-century massacre at Sandby borg', *Antiquity*, 92 (362), 2018, pp.421-436.

Select Bibliography

Allmand, C. *Henry V*, Methuen 1992.

Ambler, S.T., 'Magna Carta: Its Confirmation at Simon de Montfort's Parliament of 1265', *EHR*, 130 (545), 2015, pp.801-830.

Appleby, J., *et al*, 'Perimortem trauma in King Richard III: a skeletal analysis', *The Lancet*, 385, 2015, pp.253-259.

Arnoux, M., 'Border, Trade Route or Market? The Channel and the Medieval European Economy from the Twelfth to the Fifteenth Century', *ANS 36*, 2014, pp.39-52.

Arman, J., *The Warrior Queen: The Life and Legend of Æthelflaed, the Daughter of Alfred the Great*, Amberley 2017.

Arvanigan, M., 'A county community or the politics of the nation? Border service and baronial influence in the palatinate of Durham, 1377–1413,' *HR* 82 (215) 2007, pp.41-61.

Ashcroft, R., & Bevir, M., 'Multiculturalism in contemporary Britain: policy, law and theory', *Critical Review of International Social and Political Philosophy*, 21 (1) 2018, pp.1-21.

Ayton, A., 'The military careerist in fourteenth-century England', *JMH*, 43 (1) 2017, pp.4-23.

Bachrach, B., 'The Norman Conquest, Countess Adela and Abbot Baudri', *ANS 35*, 2012, pp. 65-78.

Barlow, F., *Edward the Confessor* London, 1989.

Barlow, F., *Thomas Becket* California, 1990.

Barber, R., 'Shakespeare and Warwickshire Dialect', *Journal of Modern Studies*, 5, 2016, pp.91-118.

Barron, C., 'The Deposition of Richard II' in in *Politics and Crisis in Fourteenth Century England,* eds. Taylor, J., & Childs, W., Sutton Publishing 1990, pp.132-149.

Barrow, J., 'How Coifi Pierced Christ's Side: A Re-examination of Bede's Ecclesiastical History, II, Chapter 13', *JEH*, 62 (4) 2011, pp.693-706.

Bartlett, R., *England under the Norman and Angevin Kings 1075-1225*, OUP, 2000.

Barraclough, G., *The Origins of Modern Germany*, Blackwell, 1988.

Barratt, N., 'The Revenues of John and Philip Augustus revisited', in *King John: New Interpretations*, Church, S. D., ed., Woodbridge, 2003. pp.75-99.

Bartie, A., *et al*, 'Historical Pageants and the Medieval Past in Twentieth-Century England', *EHR*, 133 (563) 2018, pp.866-902.

Bates, B., *The Real Middle Earth: Magic and Mystery in the Dark Ages,* London, 2002.

Bates, D., '1066: does the date still matter?' *HR*, 78 (202), 2005, pp.443-464.

Bates, D., *Normans and Empire,* Oxford 2013.

Bates, D., *William the Conqueror,* Yale, 2016.

Battles, P, '*Genesis A* and the Anglo-Saxon 'migration myth', *ASE* 29, 2000, pp.43-66.

Baxter, S., & Blair, J., 'Land tenure and royal patronage in the Early English Kingdom: a model and a case study', *ANS* 28, 2006, pp.19-46.

Baxter, S., 'MS C of the Anglo-Saxon Chronicle and the Politics of Mid-Eleventh-Century England', *EHR* 122 (499) 2007, pp.1189-1190.

Baxter, S., *The Earls of Mercia: Lordship and Power in Late Anglo-Saxon England*, Oxford, 2007.

Baxter, S., 'The limits of the Anglo-Saxon State' in *The Early Medieval State: European Perspectives* eds. Pohl W., & Wieser, V., Vienna 2009, pp.504-513.

Baxter, S., 'Edward the Confessor and the Succession Question' in *Edward the Confessor: The Man and the Legend*, ed. Mortimer, R., Boydell & Brewer, 2009, pp.77-118.

Baxter, S: 'The Making of Domesday Book and the Languages of Lordship in Conquered England' in *Conceptualizing Multilingualism in England, c.800-c. 1250* ed. Tyler, E., Brepols, Turnout, 2011, pp.271-308.

Baxter, S., & Lewis, C. P., 'Domesday Book and the transformation of English landed society, 1066-1086', *ANS* 46, 2017, pp.343-403.

Baxter, S., '1066 and Government' in *1066 in Perspective* ed. Bates, D, Leeds, 2018, pp.133-155.

Baxter, S., 'How and Why was Domesday Made?' *EHR* 135 (576) 2020, pp.1085-1131.

Bearman, R., 'The Early Reformation Experience in a Warwickshire Market Town: Stratford-upon-Avon, 1530-1580', *Midland History*, 2007, 32 (1) pp.68-109.

Behr, C., Pestell, T., & Hines, J., 'The Bracteate Hoard from Binham: An Early Anglo-Saxon Central Place?' *Medieval Archaeology*, 58, 2014, pp.44-77.

Bennett, M., *Community, Class and Careerism: Cheshire and Lancashire Society in the Age of Gawain and the Green Knight*, Cambridge, 1983.

Bennett, M., 'Edward III's Entail and the Succession to the Crown, 1376-1471', *EHR*, 113 (452) 1998, pp.580-609.

Bennett, M., 'Compulsory Service in Late Medieval England', *P&P* 209, 2010, pp.7-51.

Bennett, M., 'John Gower, squire of Kent, the Peasants' Revolt, and the *Visio Anglie*', *The Chaucer Review*, 53, 2018, pp.258-282.

Biggs, F., 'The Politics of Succession in *Beowulf* and Anglo-Saxon England', *Speculum*, 80 (3) 2005, pp.709-741.

Blair, P. H., *The World of Bede*, 2001.

Blair, J., *Building Anglo-Saxon England*, Princeton, 2018.

Bohna, M., 'Armed Force and Civic Legitimacy', *EHR* 118 (477), 2003, pp.563-582.

Bradbury, J., 'Philip Augustus and King John: Personality and History', in *King John: New Interpretations*, Church, S., ed., Woodbridge, 2003, pp.347-361.

Bradford, P., 'A silent presence: the English king in parliament in the fourteenth century', *HR*, 84 (224), 2010, pp.189-211.

Breen, D., 'Shakespeare and History Writing. ,*Literature Compass* 14, 2017, pp.1-10.

Breeze, A., 'Seven types of Celtic loan words' in *The Celtic roots of English* eds. Filppula, M., Klemola, J. & Pitkänen, H., Joensuu, 2002, pp.175—181.

Brooks, N., 'English Identity from Bede to the Millennium', *Haskins Society Journal* 14, 2003, pp.33-52.

Brooks, N., 'Why is the Anglo-Saxon Chronicle about kings?' *ASE* 39, 2010, pp.43-70.

Brookes, S., & Reynolds, A., 'The Origins of Political Order and the Anglo-Saxon State', *Archaeology International*, 13, 2011, pp.84-93.

Brown, N., *History and Climate Change: A Eurocentric Perspective*, Routledge 2001.

Brown, R. A., *The Normans and the Norman Conquest,* Woodbridge, 2000.

Campbell, B. M. S., 'The Agrarian Problem in the Early Fourteenth Century', *P&P*, 188, 2005, pp.24-44.

Campbell, J. 'Observations on English Government from the tenth to the twelfth century', *TRHS* (25), 1975, pp.39-54.

Campbell, J., ed., *The Anglo-Saxons*, Penguin, 1982.

Campbell, J., 'The Late Anglo-Saxon State: A Maximum View', *Proceedings of the British Academy*, 87, 1995, pp.39-65.

Cannadine, D., In Our Time: Heritage BBC4 (18 July 2002): www.bbc.co.uk

Cannadine, D., J. Keating, N. Sheldon, *The Right Kind of History,* Macmillan, 2011.

Cantor, N: *Inventing the Middle Ages: The Lives, Works and Ideas of the Great Medievalists of the Twentieth Century,* New York, 1991.

Carpenter, D., 'Archbishop Langton and Magna Carta: His Contribution, His Doubts and His Hypocrisy', *EHR,* 126 (522) 2011, pp.1041-1065.

Carpenter, D., *Magna Carta*, Penguin, 2015.

Carpenter, M. C., *Locality and Polity: A Study of Warwickshire Landed Society, 1401-1499,* Cambridge, 1992.

Carpenter, M. C., 'Gentry and Community in Medieval England', *Journal of British Studies*, 33, 1994, pp.340-380.

Carter, L., 'The Quenells and the 'History of Everyday Life' in England, *c.* 1918-69', *HWJ*, 81, 2016, pp.106-134.

Carter, M., '*It would have pitied any heart to see*': Destruction and Survival at Cistercian Monasteries in Northern England at the Dissolution', *Journal of the British Archaeological Association*, 168, 2015, pp.77-110.

Carver, M., *Sutton Hoo: Burial Ground of Kings?* British Museum Press, 1998.

Cavill, P. R., 'The enforcement of the penal statues in the 1490s: some new evidence', *HR*, 82 (217) 2009, pp.482-492.

Cavill, P. R., 'Heresy, Law and the State: Forfeiture in Late Medieval and Early Modern England', *EHR* 129 (537) 2014, pp.270-295.

Church, S. D. (ed.) *King John: New Interpretations*, Woodbridge, 2003.

Church, S. D., 'Paganism in Conversion-Age Anglo-Saxon England: The Evidence of Bede's *Ecclesiastical History* Reconsidered', *History*, 93 (310) 2008, pp.162-180.

Church, S. D., *King John: England, Magna Carta and the Making of a Tyrant,* Pan, 2015.

Clanchy, M. T., *From Memory to Written Record: England 1066-1307*, 3rd edition Wiley-Blackwell, 2013.

Coss, P., 'Presentism and the "Myth" of Magna Carta', *P&P,* 234 , 2017, pp.227-235.

Coates, R., 'Invisible Britons: 'The View from Linguistics' in *Britons in Anglo-Saxon England* ed. N. Higham, Boydell & Brewer, 2007, pp.172-191.

Coates, R., 'The name of the Hwicce: a discussion', *ASE*, 42, 2013, pp.51-61.

Cool, H: 'The Staffordshire Hoard', *Historic England* Research Issue 2 Winter 2015-16, pp.3-7.

Creighton, O. H., *et al*, 'The Face of Battle? Debating Arrow Trauma on Medieval Human Remains from Princesshay', *The Antiquaries Journal*, 100 (2020), pp.165-189.

Crooks, P., 'State of the Union: Perspectives on English Imperialism in the Late Middle Ages', *P&P*, 212, 2011, pp.3-42.

Crouch, D., *William Marshal: Court, Career and Chivalry in the Angevin Empire*, Routledge, 1990.

Cubbitt, C., 'The clergy in early Anglo-Saxon England', *HR* 78 (201) 2005, pp.273-287.

Cunliffe, B., *Fifth Report on the Excavations of the Roman Fort at Richborough, Kent*, Society of Antiquaries, 1968.

Cunningham, S., 'Loyalty and the usurper: recognizances, the council and allegiance under Henry VII', *HR*, 82 (217), 2009, pp.459-481.

Cunningham, S., 'Why are administrative records so valuable to historians?' *Exploring and Teaching Medieval History* Historical Association, 2018, pp.18-22.

Current Archaeology, 'Britain's first 5th-century mosaic identified?' Issue 371, December 2020, https://archaeology.co.uk/articles/news/britains-first-5th-century-mosaic-identified.htm

Curry, A: 'How well organised was the invasion of France in 1415?' *Exploring and Teaching Medieval History*, Historical Association 2018, pp. 60-63.

Curteis, T., Wrapson, L., & Berry, J., 'East Anglia's Medieval Rood Screens: Conserving Sensitive Painted Artworks in Uncontrolled Church Environments', *Studies in Conservation 65*, sup.1, 2020, pp.54-59.

Dark, K., 'Stones of the Saints? Inscribed Stones, Monasticism and the Evangelisation of Western and Northern Britain in the Fifth and Sixth Centuries', *Journal of Ecclesiastical History*, 72:2 (2021), pp.239-258.

Davies, C. S. L. 'Information, Disinformation and Political Knowledge under Henry VII and Early Henry VIII', *HR* 85 (228) 2012, pp.228-53.

Davies, C. S. L., 'Tudor: What's in a Name?' *History* 97 (325), 2012, pp.24-42.

Davies, R. R., *The First English Empire: Power and Identities in the British Isles, 1093-1343*, Oxford 2000.

Davis, R.H.C., *From Alfred the Great to Stephen*, Hambledon Press, 1990.

Dickens, A. G., *The English Reformation*, Fontana, 1988.

Discenza, N., 'The Old English Bede and the construction of Anglo-Saxon authority', *ASE* 31, 2002, pp.69-80.

Dobson, R. B., *The Peasants' Revolt of 1381*, 2nd ed., London 1983.

Dodd, G., 'A parliament full of rats? *Piers Plowman* and the Good Parliament of 1376', *HR*, 79 (203), 2006, pp.21-49.

Dodd, G., 'County and Community in Medieval England,' *EHR* 134 (569) 2019, pp.777-820.

Douglas, D. C., *William the Conqueror*, London 1964, repr. 1990.

Downham, C., 'The Earliest Viking activity in England?' *EHR* 132 (554), 2017, pp.1-12.

Dumville, D: 'The ætheling: a study in Anglo-Saxon constitutional history', *ASE* 8 1979, pp.1-33.

Dumville, D., 'Origins of the Kingdom of the English' in *Writing, Kingship and Power in Anglo-Saxon England*, eds. Naismith R., & Woodman, D., Cambridge, 2017, pp.71-121.

Dunbabin, J. *France in the Making*, Oxford 1985.

Dyer, C., 'Poverty and Its Relief in Late Medieval England', *P&P*, 216, 2012, pp.41-78.

Earl, J. W., 'The Swedish Wars in *Beowulf*', *Journal of English and German Philology*, 114, 2015, pp.32-60.

Edgerton, D., 'The Nationalisation of British History: Historians, Nationalism and the Myths of 1940', *EHR* 136: 581 (2021) pp.950-985.

Effros, B., 'The Enduring Attraction of the Pirenne Thesis', *Speculum* 92/1, 2017, pp.184-208.

Evans, R. J., *In Defence of History*, London, 1997.

Evenden E., & Freeman, T., 'Print, Profit and Propaganda: the Elizabethan Privy Council and the 1570 Edition of Foxe's 'Book of Martyrs', *EHR* 129 (484) 2004, pp.1288-1307.

Fairburn, H., 'Was There a Money Economy in Late Anglo-Saxon and Norman England?' *EHR*, 134 (570) 2019, pp.1081-1135.

Farrell, J., 'History, Prophecy and the Arthur of the Normans: the question of audience and motivation behind Geoffrey of Monmouth's *Historia Regum Britanniae*', *ANS* 37, 2015, pp.99-114.

Fiorato, V., Boylston, A., and Knüsel, C. (eds) *Blood Red Roses: the archaeology of a mass grave from the Battle of Towton AD 1461*, Oxbow, Oxford, 2000.

Fleming, R., *Britain after Rome: The Fall and Rise 400 to 1070*, Penguin 2011.

Fleming, R., 'Recycling in Britain after the Fall of Rome's Metal Economy', *P&P* 217, 2012, pp.3-45.

Foot, S., *Athelstan: The First King of England*, Yale, 2012.

Foot, S., 'Bede's Kings,' in *Writing, Kingship and Power in Anglo-Saxon England*, eds. Naismith R., & Woodman, D., Cambridge, 2017, pp.25-51.

Forbes, H. F., 'Searching for Conversion in the Early English Laws' in *Transforming Landscapes of Belief in the Early Medieval World and Beyond: Converting the Isles II*, eds. Edwards, N. Mhaonigh, M. & Fletcher, R., Brepols, 2017.

Frankis, J., 'King Ælle and the conversion of the English: the development of a legend from Bede to Chaucer' in Scragg, D., & Weinberg, C. eds., *Literary Appropriations of the Anglo-Saxons from the Thirteenth to the Twentieth Century*, CUP 2000., pp.74-92.

Frantzen, A.J., 'The Englishness of Bede, from then to now' in *The Cambridge Companion to Bede*, DeGregorio, S. ed., CUP 2010, p229-241.

Fritze, R. H., '"Truth Hath Lacked Witnesse, Tyme Wanted Light": The Dispersal of the English Monastic Libraries and Protestant Efforts at

Preservation, ca. 1535-1625', *The Journal of Library History*, Vol. 18, No. 3, 1983, pp. 274-291.

Gallagher, R., 'Asser and the Writing of West Saxon Charters', *EHR* 136 (581), 2021, pp.773-808.

Galofré-Vilà, G., A. Hinde, A., and Guntupalli A. M., 'Heights across the last 2000 years in England', *Research in Economic History*, 34, 2018, pp.67-98.

Gannon, A., *The Iconography of Early Anglo-Saxon Coinage: Sixth to Eighth Centuries*, OUP 2010.

Garnett, G., *The Norman Conquest in English History; Volume I: A Broken Chain?* OUP 2021.

Garth, J., *The Worlds of J. R. R. Tolkien*, Quarto, 2020.

Gillingham, J., 'The Foundations of a Disunited Kingdom' in *Uniting the Kingdom? The Making of British History*, eds. Grant, A., and Stringer, K. J., Taylor & Francis, 1995, pp.48-64.

Gillingham, J., *Richard the Lionheart*, Weidenfeld & Nicolson, 1989.

Gillingham, J., *The English in the Twelfth Century: Imperialism, National Identity and Political Values*, Woodbridge, 2000.

Gillingham, J., 'Civilizing the English? The English histories of William of Malmesbury and David Hume', *HR*, 74 (183) 2001, pp.17-43.

Gillingham, J., 'Historians without Hindsight: Coggeshall, Diceto and Howden on the Early Years of John's Reign' in *King John: New Interpretations*, Church, S., ed., Woodbridge, 2003, pp.1-26.

Gillingham, J., 'Cultures of Conquest: Warfare and Enslavement in Britain Before and After 1066' in *Conquests in Eleventh-century England, 1016, 1066*, eds. Ashe, L., Ward, E. J. (Boydell, 2020), pp.165-182.

Given-Wilson, C., *Chronicles: the writing of history in medieval England*, London, 2004.

Given-Wilson, C., 'Chronicles: authorship, evidence and objectivity', *Exploring and Teaching Medieval History*, Historical Association, 2018, pp.15-17.

Godden, M., 'King Alfred's Preface and the teaching of Latin in Anglo-Saxon England', *EHR* 117 (472) 2002, pp.596-604.

Goodman, A., *The Wars of the Roses*, Routledge 1991.

Gransden, A., 'The Growth of the Glastonbury Traditions and Legend in the Twelfth Century', *JEH*, 27 (4) 1976, pp.337-358.

Gransden, A., *Legends, Tradition and History in Medieval England*, Bloomsbury 1992.

Greenblatt, S., *Tyrant: Shakespeare on Power*, London 2019.

Griffiths, D., 'Rethinking the early Viking Age in the West', *Antiquity* 93 (368), 2019, pp.469-472.

Griffiths, R., 'The island of England in the fifteenth century: perceptions of the peoples of the British Isles', *JMH*, 29 (3), 2003, pp.177-200.

Grummitt, D., 'Household, politics and political morality in the reign of Henry VII', *HR*, 82 (217) 2009, pp.393-411.

Grummitt, D., *Henry VI*, Routledge 2015.

Gunn, S., 'Politic history, New Monarchy and state formation: Henry VII in European perspective', *HR* 82 (217) 2009, pp.380-392.

Hallam, E. M. *Capetian France 987-1328*, London 1980.

Halsall, G., *The Worlds of Arthur: Facts and Fictions of the Dark Ages*, OUP 2013.

Härke, H., 'Anglo-Saxon Immigration and Ethnogenesis', *Medieval Archaeology 55*, 2011, pp.1-28.

Harland, J., 'Memories of migration? The "Anglo-Saxon" burial costume of the fifth century AD', *Antiquity* 93 (370), 2019, pp.954-969.

Harriss, G., *King, Parliament and Public Finance in Medieval England to 1369*, OUP 2005.

Hartley, L. P., *The Go-Between*, Penguin, 2004.

Harvey, S., 'The knight and the knight's fee in England', *P&P* 49, 1970, pp.3-43.

Haslam, J., 'The Burghal Hidage and the West Saxon burhs: A reappraisal', *ASE*, 45, 2016, pp.141-182.

Hicks, M. A. *Bastard Feudalism*, Longman, 1995.

Hicks, M. A., *English Political Culture in the Fifteenth Century*, Routledge 2002.

Hicks, M. A., *The Family of Richard III*, Amberley, 2015.

Higham, N. J., *Rome, Britons and the Anglo-Saxons*, London, 1992.

Higham, N. J., *The English Conquest: Gildas and Britain in the Fifth Century*, Manchester 1994.

Higham, N. J., 'From Sub-Roman Britain to Anglo-Saxon England: Debating the Insular Dark Ages', *History Compass* 2, 2004, pp.1-29.

Hill, T. D., 'Beowulf's Roman Rites: Roman Ritual and Germanic Tradition', *Journal of English and Germanic Philology*, 106 (3) 2007, pp.325-335.

Hilton, R. H., *Bond Men Made Free: Medieval Peasant Movements and the English Rising of 1381*, London 1973.

Hurst, S. & Scull, C., *The Anglo-Saxon princely burial at Prittlewell, Southend-on-Sea*, MOLA Monograph series 73, 2019.

Holbrook, N., ed., *Excavations and Observations in Roman Cirencester 1998-2007*, www.cotswoldarchaeology.co.uk 2008.

Holt, J. C., 'Politics and Property in early medieval England', *P&P*, 57, 1972, pp.3-52.

Holt, J. C., *Colonial England 1066-1215*, London, 1997.

Hooper, N. 'Edgar the Ætheling: Anglo-Saxon prince, rebel and crusader', *ASE* 14, 1985, pp.197-214.

Howe, N., 'Rome: Capital of Anglo-Saxon England', *Journal of Medieval and Early Modern Studies*, 34, 2004, pp.142-172.

Hudson, A., *The Premature Reformation: Wycliffite texts and Lollard History*, Oxford 1988.

Hudson, J. 'Life-grants of land and the development of inheritance in Anglo-Norman England', *ANS*, 12, 1990, pp.67-80.

Hudson, J., *Land, Law and Lordship in Anglo-Norman England*, OUP, 1994.

Hudson, J, *History of the Laws of England* (Vol. II: 871-1216), OUP, 2012.

Hyams, P., 'Feud and the State in Late Anglo-Saxon England', *Journal of British Studies* 40 (1), 2001, pp.1-43.

Insley, C., 'Collapse, Reconfiguration or Renegotiation? The Strange End of the Mercian Kingdom', 850-924, *Reti Medievali Rivista*, 17, 2, 2016, pp.231-247.

Ives, E., 'Tudor dynastic problems revisited', *HR* 81, 2008, pp.255-279.

Jaillant, L., '"A Fine Old Tale of Adventure": Beowulf Told to the Children of the English Race, 1898-1908', *Children's Literature Association Quarterly*, 38 (4), 2013, pp.399-400.

Jarman, C. L., Biddle, M., Higham, T., Ramsey, C. B., 'The Viking great Army in England: new dates from the Repton Charnel', *Antiquity*, 92 (361) 2018, pp.183-199.

Jewell, H., '*Piers Plowman* – A Poem of Crisis: an analysis of Political Instability in Langland's England' in *Politics and Crisis in Fourteenth Century England*, eds. Taylor J., & Childs, W., Sutton Publishing 1990, pp.59-81.

Jones, C., 'Bede and Vegetius', *The Classical Review, 46*, 6 (1932), pp.248-249.

Jones, M. K., *Bosworth 1485: Psychology of a Battle*, Tempus 2002.

Jones, T., *Chaucer's Knight: Portrait of a Medieval Mercenary*, Methuen 1980.

Kaeuper, R. W., 'William Marshal, Lancelot, and the Issue of Chivalric Identity', *Essays in Medieval Studies*, 22, 2005, pp.1-19.

Karn, N., 'Nigel, bishop of Ely, and the restoration of the exchequer after the "anarchy" of King Stephen's reign', *HR*, 80 (209), 2007, pp.299-314.

Keen, M., *Chivalry*, Yale 1984.

Keen, M. 'The Angevin Legacy, Dynastic Rivalry and the Aftermath of the Hundred Years War, 1453-1491' in *Contact and Exchange in Later Medieval Europe: Essays in Honour of Malcolm Vale*, eds. Skoda, H., *et al*, Boydell & Brewer, 2012, pp.145-158.

Keller, M., *et al*, 'Ancient *Yersinia pestis* genomes from across Western Europe reveal early diversification during the First Pandemic (541-750)', *Proceedings of the National Academy of Sciences* 116 (25), 2019, pp. 12368-9.

Kempen, Ad F. J., '"A mission he bore – to Duke William he came": Harold Godwineson's *Commentum* and his covert ambitions', *HR* 89 (246) 2016, pp.591-612.

Kendall, C., 'Bede and Education', *The Cambridge Companion to Bede*, DeGregorio, S. ed., CUP 2010, pp.99-112.

King, A., '"What Werre Amounteth": The Military Experience of Knights of the Shire, 1369–1389', *History*, 2010, pp.418-436.

King, A, *Edward I: A New King Arthur?* Penguin 2016.

King, A., & Etty, C., 'How successful was Edward I as king?' *Exploring and Teaching Medieval History*, Historical Association, 2018, pp.43-46.

King, T. E. *et al.* 'Identification of the remains of King Richard III', *Nature Communications* 5 (5631), 2014, pp.1-8.

Lacey, H. '"Grace for the rebels": the role of the royal pardon in the Peasants' Revolt of 1381', *JMH* 34, 2008, pp.36-63.

Laing, L., 'Romano-British Metalworking and the Anglo-Saxons' in *Britons in Anglo-Saxon England* ed. Higham, N., Boydell & Brewer, 2007, pp.42-56.

Lambert, B., & Ormerod, W. M., 'A matter of trust: the royal regulation of England's French residents during wartime, 1294-1377,' *HR*, 89 (244), 2016, pp.208-226.

Lambert, T. B., 'Theft, Homicide and Crime in late Anglo-Saxon Law', *P&P*, 214, 2012, pp.3-43.

Lang, S. J., 'John Bradmore and His Book Philomena', *Social History of Medicine*, Volume 5 (1), 1992, pp.121–130.

Lapidge, M., 'Some Latin poems as evidence for the reign of Athelstan', *ASE* 9, 1980, pp.61-98.

Lawrence, T. E., *Seven Pillars of Wisdom*, Jonathan Cape, 1940.

Lawson, M.K., *Cnut: England's Viking King*, Tempus, 2004.

Lawson, M.K., *The Battle of Hastings* (Tempus 2002), available to download, pdf edition 2016.

Leggett, S., 'The Power of Place: Colonization of the Anglo-Saxon Landscape by Royal and Religious Ideologies', *Journal of Literary Onomastics*, 6 (1), 2017, pp.76-94.

Leslie, S., Winney, B., Hellenthal, G. *et al*, 'The fine-scale genetic structure of the British population', *Nature* 519, 2015, pp.309-314.

Lewis, C. P., 'Audacity and Ambition in Early Norman England and the Big Stuff of the Conquest', *ANS 40*, 2018, pp. 25-52.

Leyser, K, *Communications and Power in Medieval Europe*, ed. Reuter, T., London 1994.

Licence, T., 'Edward the Confessor and the Succession Question: A Fresh look at the Sources', *ANS* 39, 2017, pp.113-127.

Licence, T., *Edward the Confessor: Last of the Royal Blood*, Yale, 2020.

Liddiard, R., 'The landscape of Anglo-Norman England: Chronology and Cultural Transmission' in *People, Texts and Artefacts: Cultural Transmission in the Medieval Norman Worlds*, eds. Bates D., *et al*, University of London Press, 2017, pp.106-114.

Luizza, R. M., 'The Tower of Babel: The Wanderer and The Ruins of history', *Studies in the Literary Imagination* 36 (1) 2003, pp.1-35.

Lutz, A., 'Celtic influence on Old English and West Germanic', *English Language and Linguistics* 13 (2) 2009, pp.227-249.

MacCulloch, D., *Thomas Cromwell*, London 2018.

Madeline, F., 'The Idea of "Empire" as Hegemonic Power under the Norman and Plantagenet Kings (1066-1204)', *ANS*, 40, 2018, pp.179-196.

Maddern, P., 'Social Mobility' in *A Social History of England 1300-1500*, ed. Horrox, R., CUP, 2006, pp.113-133.

Maddicott, J. R., 'The Ballads of Robin Hood', *EHR* 93 (367), 1978, pp.276-299.

Maddicott, J. R., 'Industry and the Wealth of King Alfred', *P&P*, 123, 1989, pp.3-51.

Maddicott, J. R., 'Plague in Seventh-Century England', *P&P* 156, 1997, pp.7-54.

Maddicott, J. R., 'Edward the Confessor's Return to England in 1041', *EHR*, 119 (482), 2004, pp.650-666.

Maddicott, J. R., 'London and Droitwich, c.650-750: trade, industry and the rise of Mercia', *ASE,* 34, 2005, pp.7-58.

Maddicott, J. R., 'Responses to the Threat of Invasion, 1085', *EHR*, 122 (498), 2007, pp.986-997.

Maddicott, J. R., *The Origins of the English Parliament 924-1327*, OUP, 2010.

Maddicott, J. R., 'The Oath of Marlborough, 1209: Fear, Government and Popular Allegiance in the Reign of King John', *EHR* 126 (519), 2011, pp.281-318.

Maddicott, J. R., 'Parliament and the People in Medieval England', *Parliamentary History*, 35 (iii) 2016, pp.336-351.

Maitland, F. W., *Domesday Book and Beyond*, Fontana, 1960.

Marshall, H. E., *Our Island Story: A History of Britain for Boys and Girls*, Thomas Nelson 1905, repr. 2005.

Marshall, P., 'The Naming of Protestant England', *P&P* 214, 2012, pp.87-128.

Martin, R.H., 'From manuscript to print' in *The Cambridge Companion to Tacitus,* Woodman, A., ed., CUP 2010, pp.241-252.

Matthews, D., *Medievalism: A Critical History*, Woodbridge, 2015.

Matthews, S., 'King Edgar and the Dee: The Ceremony of 973 in Popular History Writing', *Northern History*, 46 (1) 2009, pp.61-74.

Mayhew, N. J., 'Prices in England, 1170-1750', *P&P*, 219, 2013, pp.3-39.

Mays, S., *et al.* 'A multidisciplinary study of a burnt and mutilated assemblage of human remains from a deserted Medieval village in England', *Journal of Archaeological Science: Reports* 16, 2017, pp.441-455.

McFarlane, K. B., *England in the Fifteenth Century*, London 1981.

Moilanen, I., 'The Concept of the Three Orders of Society and Social Mobility in Eleventh-Century England', *EHR* cxxxi, 553, 2016, pp.1331-1352.

Molyneaux, G., 'The Old English Bede: English Ideology or Christian Instruction?' *EHR* 124 (511), 2009, pp.1290-1323.

Molyneaux, G., 'Why were some tenth-century English kings presented as Rulers of Britain?' *Transactions of the Royal Historical Society*, 21, 2011, pp.59-91.

Molyneaux, G., 'Did the English Really Think They were God's Elect in the Anglo-Saxon Period?' *JEH* 65, 2014, pp.721-737.

Molyneaux, G., *The Formation of the Kingdom of England in the Tenth Century*, OUP, 2017.

Molyneaux, G., 'Angli and Saxones in Æthelweard's Chronicle', *Early Medieval Europe* 25, 2017, pp.208-223.

Mordechai, L., *et al*, 'The Justinianic Plague; An inconsequential pandemic?' *Proceedings of the National Academy of Sciences* 116 (51), 2019, pp.25546-25554.

Mordechai, L., & Eisenberg, M., 'Rejecting Catastrophe: The Case of the Justinianic Plague', *P&P*, 244, 2019, pp.3-50.

Moreland, J., 'Land and Power from Roman Britain to Anglo-Saxon England?' *Historical Materialism* 19 (1), 2011, pp.175-193.

Morris, M., *A Great and Terrible King: Edward I and the Forging of Britain*, Hutchinson, 2008.

Morris, M., *The Anglo-Saxons: A History of the Beginnings of England*, Penguin, 2022.

Mortimer, I., The Death of Edward II in Berkeley Castle', *EHR*, 120 (489), 2005 pp.1176-1214.

Mortimer, I., *The Perfect King: The Life of Edward III, father of the English Nation*, London, 2006.

Mortimer, I., *1415: Henry V's Year of Glory*, The Bodley Head, 2009.

Naismith, R., 'Payments for land and privilege in Anglo-Saxon England', *ASE*, 41, 2012, pp.277-342.

Naismith, R., 'The Social Significance of Monetization in the Early Middle Ages', *P&P*, 223, 2014, pp.3-39.

Naismith, R., & Tinti, F., 'The Origins of Peter's Pence', *EHR*, 134 (568), 2019, pp.521-552.

Naismith, R., *Early Medieval Britain c500-1000* (CUP), 2021.

Neidorf, L., '*Beowulf* as Pre-National Epic: Ethnocentrism in the Poem and its Criticism', *English Literary History* 85, 2018, pp.847-875.

Nelson, J. L., 'A Place for Medieval History in the National Curriculum?' *HWJ* 29, 1990, pp.103-6.

Nelson, J. L. 'Debate: Trade, Industry and the Wealth of King Alfred', *P&P*, 135, 1992, pp.142-163.

Nelson, J. L. 'The Dark Ages', *HWJ* 63, 2007, pp.191-201.

Nelson, J. L. 'Alfred of Wessex at a cross-roads in the history of education', *History of Education*, 42 (6) 2013, pp.697-712.

Niles, J., 'Pagan Survivals and Popular Beliefs' in *The Cambridge Companion to Old English Literature*, eds. M. Godden, M., & Lapidge, M., CUP 2013, pp.120-136.

Niles, J., 'The Myth of the Feud in Anglo-Saxon England', *Journal of English and Germanic Philology* 114 (2) 2015, pp.163-200.

Nixey, C., *The Darkening Age: The Christian Destruction of the Classical World*, Picador, 2017.

O'Brien, C., 'Kings and Kingship in the writings of Bede,' *EHR, 559*, 2017, pp.1473-1498.

Olalde, I., Brace, S., Allentoft, M. *et al*, 'The Beaker People and the genomic transformation of north-western Europe', *Nature*, 555, 2018, pp.190-196.

Oosthuizen, S., 'Recognizing and Moving on from a Failed Paradigm: The Case of Agricultural Landscapes in Anglo-Saxon England *c*.AD 400-800', *Journal of Archaeological Research*, 24, 2016, pp.179-227.

Orchard, A., 'The Word Made Flesh: Christianity and Oral Culture in Anglo-Saxon Verse', *Oral Tradition* 24 (2) 2009, pp.293-318.

Ormerod, W. M., Lambert, B., Mackman, J., *Immigrant England, 1300-1550*, Manchester 2019.

Parker, E., 'Siward the Dragon-Slayer: Mythmaking in Anglo-Scandinavian England', *Neophilologus* 93 (3) 2014, pp.481-493.

Pattison, J. E., 'Is it necessary to assume an apartheid-like social structure in Early Anglo-Saxon England?' *Proceedings of the Royal Society*, B 275, 2008, pp.2427-2428.

Payling, S. J., *Political Society in Lancastrian England: the Greater Gentry of Nottinghamshire*, Oxford, 1991.

Payling, S. J., 'Social mobility, demographic change, and landed society in late medieval England', *Economic History Review*, 45 (1), 1992, pp. 51-73.

Payling, S. J., 'County Parliamentary Elections in Fifteenth-century England', *Parliamentary History* 18 (3), 1999, pp.237-259.

Pelteret, D., 'Slave raiding and slave trading in early England', *ASE* 9, 1980, pp.99-114.

Pelteret, D., 'Slavery in Anglo-Saxon England' in *The Anglo-Saxons: Synthesis and Achievement*, eds. J. Woods, J., & Pelteret, D., Wilfrid Laurier University Press, 1986.

Pelteret, D., *Slavery in early medieval England from the reign of Alfred until the twelfth century*, Woodbridge, 1995.

Pelteret, D. 'The Image of the Slave in Some Anglo-Saxon and Norse Sources', *Slavery and Abolition*, 23 (2), 2002, pp.75-88.

Plassmann, A., 'Bede's Legacy in William of Malmesbury and Henry of Huntingdon' in Bates, D., *et al*, eds., *People, Texts and Artefacts: Cultural Transmission in the Medieval Norman Worlds*, University of London Press, 2017, pp.171-191.

Platt, C., *King Death: The Black Death and its aftermath in late-medieval England*, Toronto, 1997.

Polden, A., 'The social networks of the Buckinghamshire gentry in the thirteenth century', *JMH*, 32 (4) 2006, pp.371-394.

Pollard, A.M., *et al*, '"Sprouting Like Cockle amongst the wheat": The St Brice's Day Massacre and the Isotopic Analysis of Human Bones from St John's College Oxford', *Oxford Journal of Archaeology*, 31 (1) 2021, pp.83-102.

Potter, H., *Law, Liberty and the Constitution: A Brief History of the Common Law*, Boydell & Brewer, 2015.

Pratt, D., 'The Illnesses of King Alfred the Great', *ASE* 30, 2001, pp.39-90.

Pratt, D., *The Political Thought of King Alfred the Great*, CUP, 2007.

Prescott, A., '"Their Present Miserable State of Cremation": the Restoration of the Cotton Library' in *Sir Robert Cotton as Collector: Essays on an Early Stuart Courtier and His Legacy*, ed. Wright, C. J., London, 1997, pp.391-454.

Prestwich, J. O., *The Place of War in English History, 1066–1214*, ed. M. Prestwich, Boydell 2004 (the 1983 Ford Lectures.)

Prestwich, M., *The Three Edwards*, Weidenfeld & Nicolson, 1980.

Prior, S., *A Few Positioned Castles: The Norman Art of War*, Tempus 2006.

Pryor, F., *Britain AD: A Quest for Arthur, England and the Anglo-Saxons*, London 2005.

Pugh, T. B. *Henry V and the Southampton Plot of 1415*, Southampton Records Series, 30, 1988.

Purser, T., 'Constructs of Childhood in Early Medieval England *c.* 500–*c.* 1100', in *A Child in History: between dignity and enslavement*. Vol 1, eds., Elwira J. Kryńska, Łukasz Kalisz, Agnieszka Suplicka, Białystok 2021, pp. 167-175.

Purser, T. 'William FitzOsbern, Earl of Hereford: Personality and Power on the Welsh Frontier, 1066-1071' in *Armies, Chivalry and Warfare in Medieval Britain and France*, ed. Strickland, M., Woodbridge, 1998, pp.133-146.

Purser, T., 'The Origins of English feudalism? An Episcopal Land-Grant Revisited', *HR*, 73 (180), 2000, pp.80-92.

Purser, T., 'A "Community in the County"? Sir John Sandys and Social Mobility in Later Medieval Hampshire', *Southern History*, 41, 2019, pp.45-70.

Rambaran-Olm, M., 'Trial by History's Jury: Examining II Æthelred's Legislative and Literary Legacy, AD 993-1006', *English Studies*, 95 (7), 2014, pp.777-802.

Rambaran-Olm, M., *et al*, 'Medieval Studies: the stakes of the field', *Postmedieval: a journal of medieval cultural studies* 11, 2020, pp.356-370.

Rampton, M., 'The Peasants' Revolt of 1381 and the Written Word', *Comitatus: A Journal of Medieval and Renaissance Studies*, 24, 1993, pp.45-60.

Raven, M., 'The Earldom Endowments of 1337: Political Thought and the Practice of Kingship in Late Medieval England', *EHR*, 136: 580 (2021), pp.498-529.

Razi, Z., 'Serfdom and Freedom in Medieval England: A Reply to the Revisionists', *P&P*, 2007, Supplement 2, pp. 182-7.

Reynolds, D., 'Official history: how Churchill and the cabinet office wrote *The Second World War*', *HR*, 78 (201), 2005, pp.400-422.

Reynolds, S., *Fiefs and Vassals: The Medieval Evidence Reinterpreted*, Oxford, 1994.

Riley, A., *The Roman Government of Britain*, Oxford, 2013.

Roach, L., 'Penance, submission and *deditio*: religious influence on dispute settlement in later Anglo-Saxon England (871-1066)', *ASE*, 41, 2012, pp.343-371.

Roach, L., *Kingship and Consent in Anglo-Saxon England, 871-978: Assemblies and the State in the Early Middle Ages*, CUP, 2013.

Roach, L., 'Law codes and legal norms in later Anglo-Saxon England', *HR*, 86 (233) 2013, pp.465-486.

Roberts, A., *Eminent Churchillians*, Orion, 1995.

Rogerson, A., Portable Antiquities Scheme NMS-E95041: An Early Medieval Assemblage, 2015: https://finds.org.uk/database/artefacts/record/id/659168

Rollason, D., 'Lists of saints' resting places in Anglo-Saxon England', *ASE*, 7, 1978, pp.61-67.

Rollison, D., 'Class, Community and Popular Rebellion in the Making of Modern England', *HWJ*, 67, 2009, pp.220-232.

Rosebank, J., 'G. N. Clark and the Oxford School of Modern History, 1919-1922: Hidden Origins of 1066 and All That', *EHR*, 135 (572), 2020, pp.127-156.

Ross, J., 'The English Aristocracy and Mesne Feudalism in the Late Middle Ages', *EHR*, 133 (564), 2018, pp.1027-1059.

Rowlands, I, 'The Text and Distribution of the Writ for the Publication of Magna Carta, 1215', *EHR*, 124 (511), 2009, pp.1422-1431.

Rowley, S., 'Bede in Later Anglo-Saxon England', *The Cambridge Companion to Bede*, ed. DeGregorio, S., CUP 2010, pp.216-28.

Sarris, P., 'New approaches to the 'Plague of Justinian', P&P 254 (2022), pp.315-346.

Sayers, W., 'The Names *Beow, Scef, Scyld* and *Beowulf*: Shares into Swords', *English Studies* 97 (8), 2016, pp. 815-820.

Schiffels, S. *et al*, 'Iron Age and Anglo-Saxon genomes from East England reveal British migration history', *Nature Communications* 7:10408, 2016, pp.1-9.

Schrijver, P., 'What Britons Spoke around 400 AD' in *Britons in Anglo-Saxon England* ed. Higham, N., Boydell & Brewer, 2007, pp.165-171.

Schrijver, P., 'Celtic influence on Old English: phonological and phonetic evidence', *English Language and Linguistics* 13 (2) 2009, pp.193-211.

Sharpe, J., *A Fiery and Furious People: A History of Violence in England*, Penguin, 2016. Sharkey, J., 'Between king and pope: Thomas Wolsey and the Knight mission', *HR* 84 (224), 2011, pp.236-248.

Shrubsole, G., *Who Owns England? How We Lost our Green and Pleasant and How to Take it Back* William Collins 2009.

Sims-Williams, P., 'The Settlement of England in Bede and the Chronicle', *ASE* 12, 1983, pp.1-41.

Slavin, P. 'The Great Bovine Pestilence and its economic and environmental consequences in England and Wales, 1318-50', *The Economic History Review* 65, 4, 2012, pp.1239-1266.

Smith, J. M. H., 'Rulers and Relics c.750-c.950: Treasure on Earth, Treasure in Heaven', *P&P*, 206, 2010, Supplement 5, pp.73-96.

Smith, S., 'Towards a social archaeology of the late medieval English peasantry: power and resistance at Wharram Percy', *Journal of Social Archaeology*, 9, 2009, pp.291-416.

Spencer, A., 'The comital military retinue in the reign of Edward I', *HR*, 83 (219), 2010, pp.46-59.

Spindler, E, 'Flemings in the Peasants' Revolt, 1381' in *Contact and Exchange in Later Medieval Europe: Essays in Honour of Malcolm Vale*, eds. Skoda, H., *et al,* Boydell & Brewer, 2012, pp.59-78.

Southern, R. W., *The Making of the Middle Ages*, Hutchinson, 1988.

Stapleton, P., 'Pope Gregory and the *Gens Anglorum*: Thomas Stapleton's Translation of Bede' in Cobb, C. (ed.), *Renaissance Papers*, Boydell & Brewer, 2008.

Steane, J., *The Archaeology of the Medieval English Monarchy*, Routledge 1999.

Stenton, F.M. *Anglo-Saxon England*, Oxford 1943, reissued 2001.

Swift, E., 'Re-evaluating the Quoit Brooch Style: Economic and Cultural Transformations in the 5th Century AD, with an Updated Catalogue of Known Quit Brooch Style Artefacts', *Medieval Archaeology* 63 (1), 2019, pp.1-55.

Tankard, D., 'The Johnson family and the Reformation, 1542–52', *HR,* 80 (210) 2007, pp.469-490.

Thacker, A., 'Bede and History', *The Cambridge Companion to Bede*, ed. DeGregorio, S., CUP, 2010, pp.170-190.

Thomas, K., *Religion and the Decline of Magic*, London 1997.

Thomas, M., Stumpf, M., Härke, M., 'Evidence for an apartheid-like social structure in early Anglo-Saxon England', *Proc. R. Soc. B* 273, 2006, pp.2651-2657.

Thompson, E. A., 'Zosimos 6.10.2 and the Letters of Honorius', *Classical Quarterly* 32, ii, 1982, pp.445-462.

Thornton, T., 'The battle of Sandeford: Henry Tudor's understanding of the meaning of Bosworth Field', *HR* 78, 201, 2005, pp.436-442.

Thornton, T., 'More on a Murder: Deaths of the "Princes in the Tower", and Historiographical Implications for the Regimes of Henry VII and Henry VIII', *History* 106 (369) 2021, pp.4-25.

Timofeeva, O. 'Ælfred mec heht gewyrcan: Sociolinguistic concepts in the study of Alfredian English', *English Language and Linguistics* 22 (1), 2018, pp.123-148.

Tilly, C. *Coercion, Capital and European States, AD 990-1990*, Blackwell, 1993.

Titow, J. Z., *English Rural Society, 1200-1350*, London, 1969.

Tyler, D. J., 'Offa's Dyke: a historiographical appraisal', *JMH,* 37 (2), 2011, pp.145-161.

Vincent, N, 'Magna Carta: Oblivion and Revival', *The Historian* (spring 2015) pp.12-14.

Vincent, N., 'The Making of a Monster: King John in fiction from Bale to the Victorians', *International Review of Law and Economics,* 47, 2016, pp.60-66.

Virgoe, R., 'Aspects of the County Community in the Fifteenth Century' in Hicks, M., ed. *Profit, Piety and the Professions in Later Medieval England,* Sutton Publishing 1990, pp.7-11.

Waite, G., 'The Preface to the Old English Bede', *ASE,* 44, 2016, pp.31-93.

Walker, S. J., *The Lancastrian Affinity: 1361-1399,* OUP 1996.

Ward-Perkins, B., 'Why did the Anglo-Saxons not become more British?' *EHR* 115 (462), 2000, pp.513-533.

Walsham, A., 'Skeletons in the Cupboard: Relics after the English Reformation', *P&P* 206 (Supplement 5), 2010, pp.121-143.

Waugh, E., *Brideshead Revisited,* 1962.

Wells, P., *Barbarians to Angels: The Dark Ages Reconsidered,* Norton 2009.

West-Harling, V., 'Medievalism as Fun and Games', *Studies in Medievalism,* xviii, 2010, pp.1-16.

White, R., 'Managing Transition: Western Britain from the end of Empire to the Rise of Penda', *History Compass* 11 (8), 2013, pp.584-596.

Whitelock, D, 'Anglo-Saxon Poetry and the Historian', *Transactions of the Royal Historical Society,* 31, 1949, pp.75-94.

Whitelock, D., *The Audience of Beowulf,* OUP 1951.

Whitelock, D., *The Beginnings of English Society,* Penguin, 1952 repr. 1987.

Whittle, J. 'Peasant Politics and Class Consciousness: the Norfolk Rebellions of 1382 and 1549 Compared', *P&P,* 195 (Supplement 2) 2007, pp. 233-247.

Wickham, C., *Framing the Early Middle Ages: Europe and the Mediterranean 400-800,* OUP 2005.

Wickham, C., *Medieval Europe,* Oxford 2016.

Wild, B. L., 'Secrecy, splendour and statecraft: the jewel accounts of King Henry III of England, 1216-72', *HR,* 83 (221) 2010, pp.409-430.

Wilmott, T., 'Roman Richborough', *Historic England* Research Issue 16, 2020, pp.5-14.

Williams, A: 'Regional Communities and Royal Authority in the Late Old English Kingdom: The Crisis of 1051-1052 Revisited', *History,* 98 (329), 2013, pp.23-40.

Williams, T, *Viking Britain*, William Collins, 2018.

Willmott H., *et al*, 'A Black Death mass grave at Thornton Abbey: the discovery and examination of a fourteenth-century rural catastrophe', *Antiquity* 94 (373), 2020, pp.179-196.

Wilton, D., 'What do we mean by *Anglo-Saxon*? Pre-Conquest to the Present', *Journal of English and Germanic Philology*, 119, 4 (2020), pp. 425-456.

Winkler, E. A. 'The Norman Conquest of the classical past: William of Poitiers, language and history', *JMH*, 42 (4) 2016, pp. 456-478.

Winstanley, M., 'Shakespeare, Catholicism and Lancashire: A Reappraisal of John Cottom, Stratford Schoolmaster', *Shakespeare Quarterly* 68 (2), 2017, pp.172-191.

Wolfe, B., *Henry VI*, Methuen, 1983.

Wood, M., 'The Making of King Æthelstan's Empire: An English Charlemagne?' in Wormald, P., Bullough, D., and Collins, R., eds., *Ideal and Reality in Frankish and Anglo-Saxon Society: Studies presented to J. M. Wallace-Hadrill*, Oxford, 1983, pp.250-72.

Wood, M., *In Search of England: Journeys into the English Past*, Penguin, 2000.

Wood, M., 'Searching for Brunanburh: the Yorkshire Context of the 'Great War' of 937', *Yorkshire Archaeological Journal* 85 (1), 2013, pp.138-159.

Wood, M., 'Æthelfæd, Lady of the Mercians, 918-2018', *The Historian*, autumn, 2018, pp.30-32.

Woolf, A., 'The Britons: from Romans to Barbarians' in *Regna and Gentes: the relationship between Late Antique and Early Medieval Peoples and Kingdoms in the Transformation of the Roman World*, eds. Goetz, H-W., Jarnut, J., & Pohl, W., Brill 2003, pp.345-380.

Woolf, A., 'Apartheid and Economics in Anglo-Saxon England', in *Britons in Anglo-Saxon England*, ed. Higham, N., Boydell & Brewer, 2007, pp.115-129.

Woolf, D. R., 'The "Common Voice": History, Folklore and Oral Tradition in Early Modern England', *P&P*, 120, 1988, pp.26-52.

Wormald, P., '*Engla Lond*: the Making of an Allegiance', *Journal of Historical Sociology* 7 (1), 1994, pp.1-24

Wormald, P., *The Making of English Law: King Alfred to the Twelfth Century*, vol. i: *Legislation and its Limits*, Blackwell, 1999.

Wormald, P., *The Times of Bede: Studies in Early English Christian Society and its Historian*, ed. Baxter, S., Blackwell, 2006.

Wright, D. 'Early Medieval Settlement and Social Power: The Middle Anglo-Saxon "Home Farm"', *Medieval Archaeology* 59 (1), 2015, pp.24-46.

Wright, S. M., *The Derbyshire Gentry in the Fifteenth Century*, Derbyshire Record Society, 8, 1983.

Yeandle, P., *Citizenship, Nation, Empire: The Politics of History Teaching in England, 1870-1930*, Manchester, 2015.

Younger, N., 'If the Armada had landed: A Reappraisal of England's Defences in 1588', *History*, 2008, pp.328-354.

Yorke, B., *Kings and Kingdoms and Early Anglo-Saxon England*, London, 1990.

Yorke, B., 'The Anglo-Saxon kingdoms 600-900' in *The Early Medieval State: European Perspectives*, eds. Pohl, W., & Wieser, V., Vienna 2009, pp.381-407.

Yorke, B., 'King Alfred and Weland: Tradition and Transformation at the Court of King Alfred' in *Transformation in Anglo-Saxon Culture: Toller lectures on Art, Archaeology and Text*, Oxbow, 2017, pp.47-70.

Websites and linked articles

www.alva.org.uk Association of Leading Visitor Attractions.

https://www.archaeology.co.uk/articles/news/a-great-discovery-remains-of-king-alfred-or-his-son-found-in-winchester.htm

www.britishmuseum.org

cudl.lib.cam.ac.uk

https://commonslibrary.parliament.uk/research-briefings/sn00611/ House of Commons Library Briefing Paper Number (00611,16[th] December 2019): 'The motor industry: statistics and policy,' pp.3-4.

www.churchofengland.org 'Report of the Church Buildings Review Group.'

http://collections.museums-sheffield.org.uk

www.commonslibrary.parliament.uk: Briefing Paper CBP 7639.

www.english-heritage.org.uk Annual Report 2018/19

www.historicengland.org.uk; 'The Heritage sector in England and its impact on the economy: a report for Historic England', October 2018.

www.HistoricEngland.org.uk 'Building the Future, Transforming our Past: Celebrating development-led archaeology in England 1990-2015', *Historic England* (2015).

www.heritagefund.org.uk 'Strategic Funding Framework 2019-2024' (The National Lottery Heritage Fund), p.6.

www.hrp.org.uk (Historic Royal Palaces)

www.gov.uk/age-of-criminal-responsibility

www.gov.uk/government/publications/national-curriculum-in-england-history-programmes-of-study

www.nationaltrust.org.uk Annual Reports 2018/19.

www.nationaltrust.org.uk 'National Trust Interim Report on the Connections between Colonialism and Properties now in the Care of the National Trust, Including Links with Historical Slavery', 2020.

http://www.oum.ox.ac.uk/settlers/ Settlers: Genetics, Geography and the Peopling of Britain, Oxford University Museum of Natural History.

https://yougov.co.uk/topics/travel/survey-results/daily/2020/02/18/8b405/1)

https://yougov.co.uk/topics/politics/articles-reports/2018/06/18/ young-people-are-less-proud-being-english-their-el

https://www.revealingrichardiii.com/langley.html

Index

Note: kings are in **bold**, pre-927 kingdoms attached; contemporary writers are listed in first-name order, e.g. John of Salisbury and Geoffrey of Monmouth; emperor, archbishop, bishop and abbot are abbreviated to emp, archbp., bp. and abb.

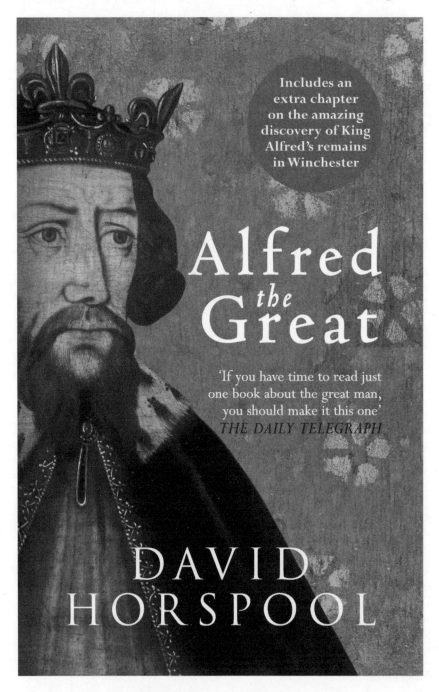